I0029506

Race and Rurality
in the Global Economy

FERNAND BRAUDEL CENTER
STUDIES IN HISTORICAL SOCIAL SCIENCE

Series Editor: Richard E. Lee

The Fernand Braudel Center Studies in Historical Social Science will publish works that address theoretical and empirical questions produced by scholars in or through the Fernand Braudel Center or who share its approach and concerns. It specifically seeks to promote works that contribute to the development of the world-systems perspective engaging a holistic and relational vision of the world—the modern world-system—implicit in historical social science, which at once takes into consideration structures (long-term regularities) and change (history). With the intellectual boundaries within the sciences/ social sciences/humanities structure collapsing in the work scholars actually do, this series will offer a venue for a wide range of research that confronts the dilemmas of producing relevant accounts of historical processes in the context of the rapidly changing structures of both the social and academic world. The series will include monographs, colloquia, and collections of essays organized around specific themes.

VOLUMES IN THIS SERIES:

Questioning Nineteenth-Century Assumptions about Knowledge, I: Determinism
Richard E. Lee, editor

Questioning Nineteenth-Century Assumptions about Knowledge, II: Reductionism
Richard E. Lee, editor

Questioning Nineteenth-Century Assumptions about Knowledge, III: Dualism
Richard E. Lee, editor

The *Longue Durée* and World-Systems Analysis
Richard E. Lee, editor

New Frontiers of Slavery
Dale W. Tomich, editor

Slavery in the Circuit of Sugar: Martinique and the World-Economy, 1830–1848
Dale W. Tomich

The Politics of the Second Slavery
Dale W. Tomich, editor

The Trade in the Living
Luiz Felipe de Alencastro

Race and Rurality in the Global Economy
Michaeline A. Crichlow, Patricia Northover, and Juan Giusti-Cordero, editors

Race and Rurality
in the Global Economy

Edited by

Michaeline A. Crichlow,
Patricia Northover, and Juan Giusti-Cordero

FERNAND BRAUDEL CENTER
STUDIES IN HISTORICAL SOCIAL SCIENCE

SUNY
PRESS

On the cover: Traditional round mud and thatch houses forming a family compound in Northern Ghana, near Tamale. Photo by ZMS. Wikimedia Commons.

Published by State University of New York Press, Albany

© 2018 State University of New York

All rights reserved

No part of this book may be used or reproduced in any manner whatsoever without written permission. No part of this book may be stored in a retrieval system or transmitted in any form or by any means including electronic, electrostatic, magnetic tape, mechanical, photocopying, recording, or otherwise without the prior permission in writing of the publisher.

For information, contact State University of New York Press, Albany, NY
www.sunypress.edu

Library of Congress Cataloging-in-Publication Data

Names: Crichlow, Michaeline A., editor. | Northover, Patricia, editor. | Giusti-Cordero, Juan A., editor.
Title: Race and rurality in the global economy / edited by Michaeline A. Crichlow, Patricia Northover, and Juan Giusti-Cordero.
Description: Albany : State University of New York Press, [2018] | Series: SUNY series, Fernand Braudel Center studies in historical social science | Includes bibliographical references and index.
Identifiers: LCCN 2017053070 | ISBN 9781438471310 (hardcover : alk. paper) | ISBN 9781438471303 (pbk. : alk. paper) | ISBN 9781438471327 (ebook)
Subjects: LCSH: Rural development. | Rural population—Economic conditions. | Race—Economic aspects. | Globalization.
Classification: LCC HN49.C6 R325 2018 | DDC 330.9173/4—dc23
LC record available at https://lccn.loc.gov/2017053070

10   9   8   7   6   5   4   3   2   1

CONTENTS

TABLES AND ILLUSTRATIONS

FOREWORD

In organizing the Race and Rurality in the Global Economy Conference at Duke University in spring 2015, the organizers, Michaeline Crichlow, Anne-Maria Makhulu, Patricia Northover, and Caela O'Connell, sought to link historic agrarian transformations to a reformulation of "development" as a process with substantive rural and racial foundations. This is a prescient intervention that refocuses attention on the racial implications of the rural-urban divide in development outcomes and intentions. By advocating a *longue durée* methodological approach, the organizers encourage a scholarly taking stock of the racialized history of the modern world. Such an approach is quite undeveloped in the chronicling of the rise of capitalist modernity, and what is outstanding about this set of essays is the way in which historic divisions of labor, enclosures, and displacements construct and/or implicate rural spaces in unique ways as havens and/or hells for racially marginalized peoples.

Each of the chapters answers this proposal in distinctive ways, providing an overall kaleidoscopic glimpse of the multiple experiences of disadvantaged communities across racialized time/space relations.

The overall theme here is entirely apposite in an era of coordinated assault on so-called "people of the land" in the contemporary "land grab" (Liberti 2013). The organizers' insistence on the *longue durée* perspective enables recognition of the historical legacy of enclosure—which has etched the devaluation of rural communities into the process of "emptying of the countryside" as an instrument of racial domination. Interestingly, classical Marxism's approach to the "agrarian question" treats the fate of the peasantry as an economic question, ignoring its racial/ethnic dimensions and to all intents and purposes naturalizing a process of "de-peasantization" (Araghi 1996; McMichael 2013). The intent of the organizers is to reopen this question to historical and cultural analysis that both transcends economism and pays attention to specific historical experiences faced (and acted upon) by racialized rural inhabitants.

Karl Marx's observation that slavery was the "pedestal" of wage labor was not simply a theoretical statement regarding the stimulus of the slave trade to the rise of industrial capitalism (1965). It also signaled the centrality of slavery to capitalism (Tomich 2004; Eric Williams 1944)—a relationship that has not only endured with countless forms of forced labor still in existence, but importantly for this project underscoring the racialized foundations of capitalist modernity. Given present political circumstances across the world, and especially in the United States, it is not difficult to view racism as the more significant and durable legacy of modernity than democracy (cf. Winant 2001). There is an irony in conventional historiography of modernity—perhaps best expressed in the disjuncture between Barrington Moore's methodological nationalist account of the history of English democracy depending on the elimination of the English peasantry (1966), paired with Mike Davis's world-historical account of how the Indian peasantry was supplying 20 percent of England's bread by the turn of the twentieth century (2001).

Historic rural diasporas associated with colonial labor-force formation, and colonization itself, set precedents for contemporary processes of eviction and renewal of diaspora. One palpable instance is the "great turnaround" in southern Europe today—from this region supplying labor to northern Europe in the post–World War II capitalist expansion, to southern Europe now receiving waves of African migrant labor, living precariously in material, legal and racial terms (cf. Corrado 2011). Such movements express a long-standing world division of labor, where racial geographies map onto an unequal state system, and its generation of transnational circuits of labor. Such migrant labor circuits evidence the effects of neoliberal policy, including resource-based accumulation and militarization, and environmental stress. In a sense, the current crisis of global (financial) capitalism is revealing the deep structure of world history originating in colonialism. Thus, rather than view racism as an outcome of the uneven development of capitalism, the chapters here flip that commonsense view by insisting on rethinking the racial presuppositions of capitalist development.

—Philip McMichael

References

Araghi, Farshad. 1996. "Global Depeasantisation, 1945–1990." *The Sociological Quarterly* 36 (2): 337–368.

Corrado, Alessandra. 2011. "Clandestini in the Orange Towns: Migrations and Racisms in Calabria's Agriculture." *Race/Ethnicity* 4 (2): 191–201.

Davis, Mike. 2001. *Late Victorian Holocausts: El Niño Famines and the Making of the Third World*. London: Verso.

Liberti, Stefano. 2013. *Land Grabbing. Journeys in the New Colonialism*. London and New York: Verso.

Marx, Karl. 1965. *Capital*, vol. 1. Moscow: Progress Publishers.

McMichael, Philip. 2013. *Food Regimes and Agrarian Questions*. Halifax, NS: Fernwood Press.

Moore, Barrington, Jr. 1966. *Social Origins of Dictatorship and Democracy: Lord and Peasant in the Making of the Modern World*. Boston: Beacon Press.

Tomich, Dale. 2004. *Through the Prism of Slavery: Labor, Capital, and the World Economy*. Lanham, MD: Rowman & Littlefield.

Williams, Eric. [1944] 1994. *Capitalism and Slavery*. Chapel Hill: University of North Carolina Press.

Winant, Howard. 2001. *The World Is a Ghetto: Race and Democracy since World War II*. New York: Basic Books.

Introduction

Michaeline A. Crichlow, Patricia Northover,
and Juan Giusti-Cordero

. . . topographies of the rural—have obscured and concealed that which sustains
them—the topographies of power.

—Jonathan Murdoch and Andy Pratt, *Contested Countryside Cultures*

Materiality, representation and imagination are not separate worlds.

—David Harvey, *Justice, Nature and the Geography of Difference*

These chapters emerged from a symposium held at Duke University in March
2015.[1] They seek to bring to the forefront questions of rurality concerning
indigenous peoples, blacks, and other people of color—centering them in a dialogue that investigates the outcomes of globalization and development in its various
effects, namely cultural, social, economical, ecological, and political.

From multiple viewpoints, these studies propose ways of understanding how processes of making space and place configure rurality in a globalizing world economy,
and how these processes are articulated through optics of raciality that are shaped
by and performed through, its intersections with class, gender, identity, land, and
environment (Cloke and Little 1996; Cloke 2006a, 2006b; Dupuis 2006; Sibley
2006; Dupuis and Vandergeest 1996; Duncan et al. 2004). In a sense, the chapters in this volume seek to understand rurality through raciality, and its converse.
Underlying the "topographics of the rural," as Murdoch and Pratt (1997) argue, are
of course, the "topographies of power" that operate to map, obscure, and manage

rurality and raciality through projects of citizenship and statecraft, governance and development (Pratt 1996; Murdoch and Pratt 1997; Cloke 2006a; Halfacre 2006; Goldberg 2002). Accordingly, these processes, working through overlapping spatial zones and temporalities of globalization, will differentially incorporate and mark *places* (as well as bodies and states) in racialized relations of power, governmentality, and conflict, as well as creolizing ambivalences tracing both tactics of resistance and accommodation (see Amin 2011; Crichlow and Northover 2009a, 2009b; Trouillot 2002; Perry and Mauer 2003; Cohen 1999). In examining these processes, the geographies covered in this collection include, Asia, notably Thailand, as well as Africa and the Americas, including the United States and the Caribbean. However, as Massey (1995) reminds us:

> The description, definition and identification of a place is . . . always inevitably an intervention not only into geography, but also, at least implicitly, into the (re)telling of the historical constitution of the present. It is another move into the continuing struggle over the delineation and characterization of space time . . . it may be useful to think of places, not as areas on maps, but as constantly shifting articulations of social relations through time . . . the identity of places, indeed the very identification of places *as* particular places, is always in a sense temporary, uncertain, and in process. (Massey 1995: 188–190)

Through provocative readings and analyses of these areas, emphasis is therefore placed on the different spatial, scalar, and temporal registers of relational historical formation, as highlighted in the methodological approach of key analysts of processes of globalization and development, such as Michel-Rolph Trouillot (1988, 2002, 2003),[2] Doreen Massey[3] (2005), Philip McMichael (1990), and Tania Murray Li (2001). Perspectives gathered in this volume range from the complex historical conjunctures punctuating Braudel's *longue durée* amidst contesting global formations, to the strategy and tactics of more recent vintages of neoliberal capitalist development impacting on nation-states, local communities, and regions; and from postcolonial governmentality projects for producing new identities of place and citizenry, to the micro-politics of dynamic space-making through fluid subjectivities and the complex relations between places, people, and things. In tackling the dynamics of place, the chapters also consider the heightened risks and multiple states of insecurity in the global economy;[4] the logics of expulsion and primitive accumulation dynamics shaping a new "savage sorting" (Sassen 2010); resistance and transformation in the face of globalization and political and environmental change; plus the steady decline in the livelihoods of people of color globally, their deepened vulnerabilities, and the complex reconstitution of systemic and lived racialization within these processes.

Interrogating Race and Rurality in the Time-Spaces of Globalization and Development

While these essays are concerned with the themes of race and rurality, it would be wrong to suggest that any unified concept of race or rurality animates our discourse.[5] Taking a cue from Du Bois in *Dusk of Dawn*, these terms tend to operate as signifiers of a complex set of "contradictory forces, facts and tendencies."[6] Race and rurality moreover seem to overlap as heirs of a history of analysis that has both privileged (and indeed fetishized) them as explanatory categories and then denied their very relevance to understanding (social) spaces and the lived experiences within them. This tendency is reflected in the many calls to do away with the "rural," most notably Hoggart (1990), and of course, to eschew notions of race, most notably by Paul Gilroy (2002), and other pronouncements on its death, as John Jackson (2005) remarks. However, as the *Handbook of Rural Studies* (Cloke et al. 2006), *Critical Rural Theory* (Thomas et al. 2011), and the continued discourse on race attest, the complex terrains of the social, body-political, and temporal, as mapped through constructs of race and rurality, and their hegemonic politics of othering, continue to animate and demand our attention, investigation, and indeed our theoretical efforts to make sense of the globalizing spaces of modern capitalism and development.[7]

The chapters in this volume therefore view race and rurality as signifiers anchored to complex material, symbolic-political, bodily, and socio-spatial realities. For example, as the epigraph quoted from David Harvey (1996) intimates, and as Paul Cloke (2006c: 24) notes, "rather than understanding material, imaginative and practiced ruralities as somehow separate, it is possible—indeed strongly advisable—to see them as intrinsically and dynamically intertwined and embodied with 'flesh and blood' culture and with real life relationships." Similarly, Murdoch and Pratt dispute the existence of an essential rural or urban condition distinct from power relations:

[T]here is no essential rural condition, no point of reference against which rurality can be measured. Each practice of dividing and distinguishing the rural is saturated with assumptions and presuppositions. It is, of course, impossible to step outside of these; the only alternative, we believe is to adopt a reflexive approach . . . one that takes account of the ways in which we do the dividing and distinguishing, and that considers the ways in which our categories and concepts, the very accounts we write, perform power relations, so that these might become more visible and contestable. (Murdoch and Pratt 1997: 56)

Accordingly, Murdoch and Pratt consider that the rural is an inherently relational, unstable category that is

contingent, fluid, detached from any necessary, stable socio-spatial reference point. Its meanings are asserted relationally (most notably in contradistinction to the urban) and are situationally specific; that is, we can know the rural only from and through particular socio-spatial positions. (Murdoch and Pratt 1997: 58)

In line with this analytical positioning, the chapters herein by and large have sought to identify and explore "the topological suppositions which frame the performance of difference" (ibid: 58) with the intention of revealing or questioning the sets of power relations that inhere in the topographies *producing* the rural, or rather, as Cloke (2006a) emphasizes, the "hybridities of rural spaces," as well as the racial. In other words, this text addresses rurality as a politics of (social) space and offers to examine the imbricated relations between the production of space, race, and rurality. Or perhaps, in keeping with an emphasis on *processes of formation*—material, representational and imaginary—it is more revealing to flag the *racialization*[8] of (social and political) spaces, as well as bodies, as Didier Fassin (2011) emphasizes, that leads to fractured and fractious states of be/longing and un-be/longing. Indeed, as Hortense Spillers (1987) also reminds us, such bodies inhabiting processes of racialization have been problematically rendered (un)gendered and differentially abjected as "flesh," in the grotesque violence and most peculiar temporalities of the modern world, as interrogated most notably by W. E. B. Du Bois (1903), Frantz Fanon (1967), Stuart Hall (1980), Étienne Balibar and Immanuel Wallerstein (1991), Ann Laura Stoler (1995), Sylvia Wynter (1995),

Paul Gilroy (1987, 2002), Robert Miles (1989), Michael Omi and Howard Winant (1994), Eduardo Bonilla-Silva (1997), and Charles Mills (1997).

Anchored by a sensitivity to historical experiences, the chapters promote a critical-studies approach to the social history of development—one that shifts the focus from historicist modernization (or proletarianization) mantras that assume linear rapid change from agrarian to urban/industrial status; and from peasant or rural frameworks that tend to underestimate the extent of temporal and relational complexity in historical transformations. Of course, linear perspectives have also been rendered deeply problematic by the positivistic and dichotomous methodologies that underlie them. In contrast then, the chapters gathered here probe the various relational fields generating contested mappings, and the competing imaginaries of urban-rural spatialization processes that unsettle typical narratives of development or modern transformational forces. This means that they set out to critically examine the constitution and dynamic formation of historically contingent yet structurally constrained *productions* of rural and urban spaces through the optics of race, land, and rurality; question the nature of the development experience within hegemonic processes of capitalist formations and its rhetorical promises of progress; and finally, try to better understand the comparative racialization of hi/stories (human identity stories)[9] and spaces, as well as the fissures, or fault lines, they provoke within projects of development, or rather, the *haunted* quest for sustainability in the management of global spaces. This intervention we felt would thus enable a better engagement with the vital issues related to the well-being and political futures of diverse populations of color facing existential threats from globalization, development, and climate change, as Naomi Klein (2014) forcefully reminds us in *This Changes Everything: Capitalism vs. The Climate.*

We posit that such an approach to the dual dilemmas of displacement and dispossession, and the sorts of reactions and resistances that tend to be associated with the experiences of racialized subjects being increasingly divested of land and livelihood, requires exploring the continuity between the spaces of the rural and the urban and their mutual, historical constitution. From Africa to Asia, and the rest of the world, the rise of emergent middle classes alongside widening racialized dispossession and informalization processes driven by neoliberal governmentality have generated new rural-urban relationships as well as deeper and more complex socioeconomic pressures.[10] This present rural-urban conjuncture is further complicated by the fact that climate change has added its own pivotal weight upon the growing pressure on the global food supply, and has breathed new life into large-scale agrarian production models through the phenomena of "land grabbing," or large-scale land acquisitions for food and non-food uses (White et al. 2012). Moreover, as we discussed at the symposium, cities have become home not only to the recently urbanized—displaced rural communities—but cities, in turn, reflect changing patterns in the rural-urban continuum in which the countryside is increasingly given over to industrialization while many urban areas are "ruralized," with significant back-and-forth movement that further complicates past distinctions. To the degree this is the case then, "land" and "the countryside"—perceived as spaces of belonging as well as sites for resource conflicts and struggles for place as well as development projects—are being increasingly reshaped as a *central problem field signaling* not just the changing fates of former agrarians, minorities, and marginals (generally), but also *a new spatial politics* rooted, as Michael Levien (2013) argues, less in a "politics of exploitation," and more deeply in a "politics of dispossession." In particular, informed by his own analytical and research effort on India to go beyond Harvey's (2003) recent discussion rethinking Marx's concept of "primitive accumulation" through the lens of "Accumulation by Dispossession," Levien is asking us *to further probe the nature of the political* inhabiting capitalist processes of accumulation.

Contextualized more generally then by the aforementioned critical lens, the discourses assembled here approached our entangled global spaces, through which world economic processes of development are articulated, as being formed through both relational histories and geographies. This method when applied to specific geographies and sociocultural phenomena promises to highlight more clearly the coevality of disparate development patterns constituting rural and urban spaces and their blurring. Thus, it offers a more nuanced mapping of world-making, whereby the intersectionality of seemingly far-flung geographies, cultural practices, and economic and political processes can be more clearly apprehended.

Overall, the essays included in this volume shed light on the complex production of fluid rural spaces through analyses of particular transformations and racializations. For example, Ray Kea in "Global Economies and Historical Change: Rethinking Social Struggles and Transformations in Africa's Zones of Rurality (1500–1800)" offers a *longue durée* frame for this volume through his broad historical sweep analyzing the regional social processes and contested zones of rurality within African historicity that became complexly imbricated in modes of Western economic globalization and its own racialized mode of modern world-making. Drawing upon a Marxist-inflected materialist perspective, Kea deeply scrutinizes the social and political dynamics of West African social formations over the period between 1500 and 1800 in Western/Atlantic history and argues for a *rethinking* of the nature of these processes to highlight their intrinsic and relational logics.

Accordingly, Kea calls for examining African social formations' "own systemic logics and dynamics, rationalities, oppressions, crises, practices and capacities." This he provides through a much closer examination of the agencies, classes, institutional-organizational complexes, and contesting Islamic and non-Islamic ideologies that shaped the shifting terrain of regional economic and political ties. By interrupting the hegemonic narratives of a singular globalization event, Kea highlights the older global and regional economies at work in African historicity, which drew upon largely tributary modes of accumulation that became strategically articulated but eventually dominated by Western modes of commodity capitalist accumulation. Guided by two principal hypotheses on the forms of the social and material contradictions characterizing what he describes as the late imperial and post-imperial period, Kea highlights the important role of rural spaces in fueling a universal and revolutionary ethos that became unsettled by the pressures for securing dominant political rule through the appropriation and exploitation of slave economies.

Complementing this wide sweep of Afro-Atlantic history offered by Kea, the other chapters offer close studies of particular events, singularly or comparatively, investigating the enactment of particular development projects occurring during the hopeful postcolonial moments, when states attempted to engineer socialist technologies of rule, as James Giblin in his essay discusses, highlighting the role of the developmentalist state in the *ujamaa* villagization project in Tanzania. Here, in contrast to James Scott's treatment in his book *Seeing like a State*, which focuses on the ways that "high modernist projects" flatten and make legible local sociocultural practices in order to shape, condition, and bring into being new ways of thinking and doing (technologies of governing, as Foucault would say), Giblin offers a more nuanced reading. His approach begins from the ground up to examine actual people's responses to these homogenizing development projects, which displaced them physically and psychically.

In "Making Development through Rural Initiative 'Unthinkable': Tanzania in the Time of *Ujamaa*," Giblin focuses on the villagization project in Tanzania where the socialist government of Julius Nyerere embarked upon the resettlement of most of the country's rural population into government-created villages. While much of the literature has focused on the merits of governmental efforts toward this end, Giblin offers a people-based account of these efforts. He captures the active engagement with memories of particular traditions that these villagization projects erased, perhaps unwittingly, given the urgency and unbounded socialist enthusiasm with which they attempted to drag Tanzanians into a future unknown, but one in which state officials were formally invested. Rather than resulting in a raising of aspirations and morale, these projects served instead to distance their intended clients. Threading his argument through Michel-Rolph Trouillot's notion of "unthinkability," Giblin argues that Tanzanian officials could not think the possibility of rural development outside of state direction—a position shared by many decolonizing elites in the Global South. Yet the imagination of state officials remained firmly and contradictorily wedded to racialized Western notions of modernization and progress. To implement these ideas of centralization the villagization program silenced older histories, leading to resistance and foot-dragging against state agendas. Giblin argues that ironically this resistance was spurred by unsavory memories of colonialism's own racialized despotisms, which villagers felt resembled the edicts and demands of such state projects. Precolonial cultural practices were mobilized in opposition to undercut the new subjectivities and territorial reorganization that *ujamaa* villagization aimed to produce.

This attempt by states to remake place and populations, and to redesignate spaces through racializing practices, is the focus of Daniel B. Ahlquist and Amanda Flaim in their discussion of state/society reconfiguration of territorial space in Thailand. In their textured essay, "Racialization and the Historical Production of Contemporary Land Rights Inequalities in Upland Northern Thailand," the authors patently show the biopolitical drive to reengineer space for the privileging of ethnic Thais over uplanders. Here the projects of state building are fully invested in projects of othering associated with the division of territories. This state racialization project has fundamentally replaced earlier, more fluid ethno-spatial differences. Racialization takes on its usual trajectory of hierarchizing spaces and bodies among non-Western peoples themselves, in order to entrench unequal access to rights generally—a phenomenon witnessed in land rights. Ahlquist and Flaim argue that this racialized project underwrites the disparities between uplanders and ethnic Thais in terms not reminiscent of Western practices of racialization. Their adoption of the lens of race in a situation where no visible phenotypical difference exists between the populations under scrutiny speaks compellingly to the bio-rationales of racial constructions and reminds us that any body is open to racialization, since the underlying project really concerns power and the complex ordering of spaces of be/longing or un-be/longing. Thus, the essay demonstrates forcefully the technologies and organizational logics of such a project, and the enduring consequences of the "vulnerabilization" of the uplander population even as they share space with ethnic Thais from the "civilized" lowlands who have been relocating upland.

This ground-level scrutiny is also seen in the essay by Olivia Maria Gomes da Cunha, which focuses on Maroon women as they seek to rebuild places of comfort. Indeed, in "Making Things for Living, and Living a Life with Things," Gomes da Cunha reveals how Ndyuka women in Moengo (eastern Surinam) created gardens that transformed a former industrial landscape in ways that combine urban and rural socio-spatial logics. Moengo is a company town formed in the early twentieth century around the large Suralco bauxite operation. During civil war in the 1980s, Ndyuka who lived on the outskirts of the town, and who were largely involved in forest clearing, fled Moengo with their families to refugee camps further in the interior. Upon their return in the early 1990s, they occupied the land of the bauxite installations and transformed them into a settlement where dwellings are surrounded by gardens planted with bananas, plantains, mangos, ackee and calabash trees, medicinal bushes, and crops. Activities such as clearing the fields to selling food produce, medicinal herbs, and processed food in the cities mobilize and reinforce a set of work, kinship, and neighbourhood relations, as well as ecological and spiritual ties. In this new configuration, relations infused with social and cultural meaning linked to long-standing ties to the territory—and its gods and spirits—that increasingly involve the Cottica Ndyuka with non-Maroon interlocutors, connect life inside and outside the villages. Here one witnesses the intimacies between place and things up close as these Ndyuka families forced by circumstance adapt in innovative ways, unsettling the spatio-temporalities of the urban and rural. In Tanzania, subject/citizens resisted "ruralization," or the form that it took; here a ruralized sort of urbanization enacts a form of resistance.

In other entanglements with development, Wazir Mohamed, in his chapter, "Race and Class Marginalization in the Globalization of the Rice Industry," examines different practices of modulating the pressures of globalization (expressed in the effects of agricultural commodification on lives and landscapes) to reveal the historical depth and cultural impact of food cultures based on small-scale rural livelihoods. Yet despite the long duration of these counter-plantation-scapes, his contribution highlights the brutal reorganization of the rural and the changing dynamics of a racializing displacement, expressed in lost livelihoods and the emergence of different agents, during the onset of the neoliberal era marked by the implementation of myriad structural adjustment policies in the Global South. In particular, Mohamed discusses the recalibration of a racial-social class structure in Guyana along a seemingly intransigent Afro/Indo divide (a subject that Brackette Williams [1991] has provocatively discussed in her book, *Stains on My Name: War in My Veins*),[11] which is replicated in the politics of neoliberalism playing itself out in the rice sector. That sector seems to have experienced a series of intra-racial social-class displacements, first of Afro-Guyanese and now of the Indo-Guyanese small holders, leading to the consolidation of properties of considerable acreages.

These neoliberal shifts in globalization allowed for the unequal dismantlement of the protectionist political economy of preferential trade agreements, leaving small farmers, states, and other vulnerable constituencies economically overwhelmed by the larger hegemonic economies in the West. Left behind, also, were deeper inter- and intra-national socioeconomic asymmetries—often with devastating effects on the rural nonwhite populations of the Global South. These outcomes, captured vividly in Abderrahame Sissako's film *Bamako* and the documentary *Life and Debt* by Stephanie Black, underscore the lament and charges of Africans (Mali) and Caribbean people (Jamaicans) respectively in the face of such economic and political onslaught from neoliberal development projects. In these films, what is palpably clear is the damaging impact that these policies have inflicted on people's lives, particularly those who relied on primary agricultural products for export, by the undercutting of state authority.

Yet as Gabriela Valdivia's chapter on Ecuador's *Revolución Ciudadana* (Citizen's Revolution) discusses, even in ostensibly inclusionary political maneuvers, imaginaries of development fed by globalization processes also embolden states to engage in practices of inclusionary exclusion given spatial projects designed to effect governmentality regimes for making modern citizens and subjects. In this chapter, "At the Margins of Citizenship: Oil, Poverty, and Race in Esmeraldas, Ecuador," Valdivia shows how that country's political process unfolds in uneven ways in rural and urban milieu even though stronger "citizenship" is presumed to be its overarching goal. Esmeraldas, a mostly urban region, is strategically important to the *Revolución Ciudadana,* as it is home to Ecuador's largest oil refinery and a key thermoelectric plant (that is expected to facilitate transition to greater use of hydroelectric power) as well as to an Afro-Ecuadorean population with divergent political loyalties.

In Ecuador, a differentiated construction of citizenship simultaneously reconstructs urban/rural space via a political project ostensibly revolutionary in its claims. Through an ethnographic comparison of 15 de Marzo and Tabete—an urban and a rural community, respectively—the study pays attention to the political economy that ushers in the revolutionary project, and its effects on everyday life. Valdivia especially focuses on Ecuador Estratégico, a government program of mega public works that aims to connect isolated spaces to the larger economy and infrastructural grid, and to provide basic services in health and housing. Valdivia concludes, however, that the rhetoric of transformation of the *Revolución Ciudadana* made the unevenness of the process invisible and thus silenced the significance and role of the economic and social divide in electoral or political capital existing between rural and urban communities, especially given that government projects ran through established clientele networks. The resulting paradox of the *Revolución Ciudadana* was a deepening of social inequality. Moreover, a heavy-crude pipeline was run through the space of rural Tabete, apparently provoking a deadly landslide resulting in the community being scheduled for removal. In comparison, the urban space of 15 de Marzo, though relatively better off, hardly escaped the precarity or toxic consequences of its large oil facilities.

As Arturo Escobar ([1995] 2012) and the late Michel-Rolph Trouillot (2003) have argued, the idea of development is borne from an imaginary that produces a temporal axis which situates people and spaces along a trajectory of backward and modern, or even outside of any location in modern space-time as *problems unassimilable* to the terms of a modern political imaginary of place, society, and its rightful others. Those cast into relations of "inclusive exclusion," as Giorgio Agamben (1998, 2005) highlights, or who discover themselves outside of a "place in time," becoming "flesh" as Hortense Spillers (1987) argues, or thrust into the non-place of "abject blackness" as Patricia Northover (2012) avers, become grist for diverse practices of a racializing governmentality that marks particular bodies, spaces, and places in zones of radical difference ("shitholes," to use the widely debated racialized language attributed to the current US president).[12] Therefore, the development project mobilizes a complex ensemble of desires and antinomies, imaginaries and materialities that are sutured into topographies of power that compose, transpose, and reconfigure rural landscapes and livelihoods as witnessed again in our final set of contributions.

The last three chapters on the United States reflect on the country's inner, as well as intrinsic, colonial spaces. They underscore the ways in which questions of race and rurality encompass the imperial metropole itself and confirm the internal relationality of the global yet differentiated character of these processes. Indeed, it may be that it is within the imperial metropole where these processes of coloniality appear with greatest clarity, as shown by the persistence of the old and new Jim

Crowism,[13] the racialized allotment of Indian lands, and the hot spots of resonant cultural transformation—all possessing a specific historical quality and a revealing formal political density of their own.

These chapters emphasize questions of race and class, culture and politics, in which rurality offers the analytical space for going beyond the issues of poverty, self-government, and civil rights that typically envelop discussion of these inner colonial spaces. Relevant issues raised include the wide-ranging impact of trans-formations in ecology and labor; the importance of cultural/legal dimensions in racist practices; and the role of cultural resistance and transformation, as framed by discussions on "creolization" that largely originated in research on the Caribbean but have gained much wider coinage and some oversimplification.

In "Racing the Reservation: Rethinking Resistance and Development in the Navajo Nation," for example, Dana E. Powell examines the complex terrain of development struggles in one American Indian reservation, the Navajo (Diné) nation in the US Southwest, that is caught in the liminal space of a sovereign autonomy embedded in an imperial power structured by a history of racial rule and convoluted forms of postcolonialism. In her analysis, Powell highlights the multiple and contradictory interests at work in the "will to improve" the space of the reservation, from the US government, the Navajo state agencies, globally active extractive industrialists, environmentalists, to the elder women of the Navajo nation. She argues for understanding the struggles for space and place within the context of multiple modes of racialization that serve to displace the interests of the indigenous community members, or silence the actual "structures of feeling and imagination," to borrow a concept from Raymond Williams (1971), that members of the Navajo Diné community have invested in livelihoods and landscapes. Powell highlights the way in which US state practices, such as the census, try to depoliticize place by reducing indigenous political identities to fictive racial categories of belonging (thus silencing the history of violent appropriation and displacement through a mode of racial governmentality). She also reveals other kinds of racialization tactics as deployed by environmental activists such as the instrumental appropriation and overwriting of indigenous cultural difference for battles against the global natural resource extraction economy. Pushing against simple caricatures of the subjects of development as either victims or resistors, Powell offers a case study of elder females' activism that is critical yet accommodative of natural resource extraction activity, even as they pursue their own construal and defense of rural space, local place, and historical identity against the tide of other discourses of indigeneity.

Juan Giusti-Cordero's comparative survey also examines complex strategies of resistance/accommodation in the US internal periphery, focusing on cultural creation in the "internal colony" of the post–Civil War Mississippi Delta and in Loíza, Puerto Rico, under Spanish colonial rule (though increasingly subject to Anglo-American economic imperatives). Giusti-Cordero explores the environmental and labor history of the Delta and Loíza in order to understand why these sites became known as "hot spots," respectively, for the rise of the blues and of the Santiago Apóstol festivities (which also contributed to the *bomba* music tradition). These are major place-related icons of African American and Afro–Puerto Rican culture.

Giusti-Cordero provocatively connects two zones that on first impression appear disparate, but which share the status of cultural hot spots and occupy, with the Navajo (Diné) nation, a common position under US postcolonial colonialism today. The study draws connections (too infrequently made) between the US South and the Caribbean but inflects the exercise further by comparing the Mississippi Delta, which had far more swamp forest than plantations before the Civil War, with a similarly "atypical" Caribbean locale that was *not* dominated by plantation slavery in Spanish colonial times and where a free, colored population predominated. These prior histories of weak plantation presence were followed by significant periods of expanded freedom in both locations (1790–1830 in Puerto Rico, 1865–1875 in the Reconstruction Delta), which were then ended by intensified plantation dominance. The results were forceful, and sometimes violent, involving struggles over land occupation as well as innovative cultural expressions such as the Delta blues and the Santiago festivities, with far-reaching resonance.

In her chapter on race relations in the twentieth-century South, Jeannie Whayne traces the evolution of the Southern question in connection with the modernization of capitalist agriculture. Whether as peons caught up in the labor-intensive sharecropping system of the early twentieth century or as underemployed wage laborers in the capital-intensive portfolio plantations of a hundred years later, African Americans had little economic or political clout. As the nature of farming operations evolved in this period, African American farmers "freed" from plantation landlords were no longer necessary and were forced to migrate, or if they stayed, continued to endure staggering exploitation. Whayne's chapter focuses on those who stayed behind, and who continue to find their way—long after the civil rights movement—under persistent poverty, a toxic disease environment, renewed educational segregation, new challenges to their voting franchise, and racist attitudes expressed in subtle and sometimes violent ways.

These discussions on race and rurality serve to open up further inquiry into the way in which divisions such as urban and rural are constructed and the interplay between their overlapping sociocultural practices and the social relations reproducing certain topographies of power. The forays into these emergent particularities stress that we pay attention to the play of power, including the biopolitical movements through which place and spaces are produced and experienced. And they reinforce the idea of the enduring contestations that mark the relationship between various populations and states as each struggles to gain a foothold over the conditions and possibilities of development projects. In this general "will to improve," the ubiquity of these struggles underscores the ways in which locales are being undone and redone in the wake of the demands of capital in its continuing drive to accumulate and in the interplay of power among different kinds of authorities broadly interpreted.

The instances captured here in these essays signal Marx's observation about the political economic tendencies of global capital. But these are tendencies, always unfinished or rather always becoming, always unstable, always more or less contentious considering the diverse responses to exclusions, dispossessions, and dislocations. Indeed, the powers of capital are mediated by the modalities of power (as weaved through, notably, the dynamic fields of race and rurality), leaving the character of capital accumulation in historical flux, and more or less in a contingent process of transformation. Yet, precisely because these interwoven tendencies exist within globalization processes, they point in the direction of a method that would allow us to treat emergent socioeconomic phenomena as nodal points that, in spite of their differences, can be suitably compared within a broader world economy generative of a politics of race, space, and place.

Notes

1. In writing this introduction, we would like to thank the conference's main sponsor, the Department of African and African American Studies at Duke, especially its former chair, Tommy Defrantz; and its cosponsors, Duke Human Rights Center at the Kenan Institute for Ethics, through its director, Suzanne Shanahan; Duke's former dean of the social sciences, Linda Burton; Duke's Department of Sociology; the Duke University Center for International Studies; Office of the Provost at Duke; Duke's Franklin Humanities Institute; and the director of the Institute of African American Research at the University of North Carolina, Chapel Hill, Karla Slocum.

2. Worthy of note here is Vanessa Agard-Jones's (2013) work on the French island—the Overseas Department of Martinique—that draws inspiration from Trouillot but pushes his

methodological frame to encompass how globally articulated systems of racialized environments/spaces affect the bodies inhabiting them.

3. We lament the passing of the brilliant geographer Doreen Massey, whose work on space and place especially has been so influential to our thinking about such issues.

4. Despite what Tania Murray Li (2007) refers to as the "will to improve"—a will that is paradoxically implicated in the dynamic of the modernity/coloniality relation analyzed by Walter Mignolo (2000) and others.

5. See, however, several important efforts to guide the analytical engagement with these key and problematic concepts, notably Cloke's (2006c) essay seeking to assemble a method for "conceptualizing rurality," Da Silva's (2007) text theorizing a "Global Idea of Race," and Melissa Weiner's (2012) more tactical and pragmatic offering of a conceptual guide for research on "Critical Global Race theory."

6. As W. E. B. Dubois stated, "Perhaps it is wrong to speak of race at all as 'a concept' rather than a group of contradictory forces, facts and tendencies" ([1940] 2007: 67).

7. See especially, in this regard, the work of Tania Li Murray (2007) and the recent calls for engaging more forcefully (at a critical and analytical level) with the legacies of race in the field of development studies, Northover (2012), Kothari (2006), and McCarthy (2009).

8. For a discussion of the genealogy of the concept of racialization, see Barot and Bird (2001). David Theo Goldberg (2002) in a footnote comment on racialization also reminds us that while this multivalent concept has often been deployed to identify attributions of racial meaning to social groups, or to explore exclusionary, contradictory, or contesting standpoints that tend to rely on sociological, cultural, or biological reductions on race, Fanon in *Black Skin, White Masks* understood "to racialize" in contrast with "to humanize" (2002: 12). Thus one needs to address not just 1) the *historical situatedness* of processes/practices of racialization within specific milieus of the human/"man" as indeed stressed by Sylvia Wynter (1995); one must also be sensitive to 2) their critical inflection points as articulated by the *imaginary of forms of being-in-the-world* within racialization projects, as highlighted by the cultural studies approach within Britain, discussed by Audrey Kobayashi (2004: 242–243); and finally it is essential to recognize 3) the ineluctable *comparative and temporal horizons* invoked in racialization experiences and practices as animated by the education of a subject's desire and the social exercise of a will to power and place, see Fanon ([1967] 1986), Ann Stoler (1995), Shih Shu-Mei (2008), and Crichlow and Northover (2009, 2015).

9. "Human identity stories"—a term that we (Crichlow and Northover [2009]) have coined.

10. For a discussion of the tensions between modern "urbanites" and more "rural"-oriented mine workers given the unfulfilled dreams among copper miners in Zambia, see James Ferguson (1999), *Expectations of Modernity*. For an outline of the changing patterns of rural-urban social-economic formation in India, see Shah and Harris-White (2011); for an analysis of the effects of a politics of neoliberal racial dispossession in South Africa, see Arrighi et al. (2010). For a more general review of patterns of globalization and agrarian

change, see Akram-Lodhi and Kay (2009), and on the historical patterns of informalization involving rural spaces, see Tabak and Crichlow (2000).

11. See also the critique by Raymond T. Smith (1995), " 'Living in the Gun Mouth': Race, Class, And Political Violence in Guyana." *New West Indian Guide/Nieuwe West-Indische Gids* 69 (3 & 4): 223–252.

12. See, in this regard, Tim Bunnell and Neil Coe (2005), "Re-fragmenting the Political: Globalization, Governmentality and Malaysia's Multimedia Super Corridor." *Political Geography* 24: 831–849.

13. See in particular the recent discussion on the nature of mass incarcerations in the United States as indicative of the rise of a new Jim Crow politics of racial oppression that is offered by Michelle Alexander (2011).

References

Agamben, Giorgio. 1998. *Homer Sacer: Sovereign Power and Bare Life*. Translated by Daniel Heller-Roazen. Stanford, CA: Stanford University Press.

———. 2005. *State of Exception*. Translated by Kevin Attell. Chicago and London: University of Chicago Press.

Agard-Jones, Vanessa. 2013. "Bodies in the System." *Small Axe* 42: 182–192.

Akram-Lodhi, A. Haroon, and Cristóbal Kay. 2009. "The Agrarian Question: Peasants and Rural Change." In *Peasants and Globalization: Political Economy, Rural Transformation and the Agrarian Question*, edited by A. Haroon Akram-Lodhi and Cristóbal Kay, 3–34. London: Routledge.

Alexander, Michelle. 2011. *The New Jim Crow: Mass Incarceration in the Age of Colorblindness*. New York: The New Press.

Amin, Samir. 2011. *Global History: A View from the South*. Cape Town and Dakar: Press and CODESRIA.

Balibar, Étienne, and Immanuel Wallerstein. 1991. *Race, Nation, Class: Ambiguous Identities*. Étienne Balibar translated by Chris Turner. New York: Verso.

Barot, Rohit, and John Bird. 2001. "Racialization: The Genealogy and Critique of a Concept." *Ethnic and Racial Studies* 24 (4): 601–618.

Bonilla-Silva, Eduardo. 1997. "Rethinking Racism: Toward a Structural Interpretation." *American Sociological Review* 62 (3): 465–480.

Braudel, Fernand. 2009. "History and the Social Sciences: The *Longue Durée*." Translated by Immanuel Wallerstein. *Review* XXXII (2): 171–203.

Bunnell, Tim, and Niel Coe. 2005. "Re-fragmenting the Political: Globalization, Governmentality and Malaysia's Multimedia Super Corridor." *Political Geography* 24: 831–849.

Cloke, Paul and Little, Jo, eds. 1997. *Contested Countryside Cultures: Otherness, Marginalization and Rurality*. London and New York: Routledge.

Cloke, Paul, Terry Marsden, and Patrick Mooney, eds. 2006. *Handbook of Rural Studies*. London, Thousand Oaks, and New Delhi: Sage.

Cloke, Paul. 2006a. "Rurality and Racialized Others: Out of Place in the Countryside." In *Handbook of Rural Studies*, edited by Cloke et al., 379–387. London, Thousand Oaks, and New Delhi: Sage.

———. 2006b. "Rurality and Otherness." In *Handbook of Rural Studies*, edited by Cloke et al., 447–456. London, Thousand Oaks, and New Delhi: Sage.

———. 2006c. "Conceptualizing Rurality." In *Handbook of Rural Studies*, edited by Cloke et al., 18–28. London, Thousand Oaks, and New Delhi: Sage.

Cohen, Phil, ed. 1999. *New Ethnicities, Old Racisms*. London and New York: Zed Books.

Crichlow, Michaeline, with Patricia Northover. 2009a. *Globalization and the Post-Creole Imagination: Notes on Fleeing the Plantation*. Durham, NC: Duke University Press.

———. 2009b. "Homing Modern Freedoms: Creolization and The Politics of Making Place." *Cultural Dynamics* 21 (3): 283.

———. 2015. "Whatever Happened to Diaspora and Why (not) Global Blackness?" Unpublished manuscript.

Da Silva, Denise Ferreira. 2007. *Toward a Global Idea of Race*. Minneapolis: University of Minnesota Press.

Du Bois, W. E. B. [1903] 1996. *The Souls of Black Folks*. New York: The Modern Library.

———. [1940] 2007. *Dusk of Dawn: An Essay Toward an Autobiography of A Race Concept*. Henry Louis Gates, Jr. (series editor), 49–67. Oxford: Oxford University Press.

Duncan, James, Nuala Johnson, and Richard Shein, eds. 2004. *A Companion to Cultural Geography*. Malden: Blackwell Publishing.

DuPuis, E. Melanie. 2006. "Landscapes of Desire?" In *Handbook of Rural Studies*, edited by Cloke et al., 124–132. London, Thousand Oaks, and New Delhi: Sage.

DuPuis, E. Melanie, and Peter Vandergeest, eds. 1996. *Creating the Countryside: The Politics of Rural and Environmental Discourse*. Philadelphia: Temple University Press.

Escobar, Arturo. [1995] 2012. *Encountering Development: The Making and Unmaking of the Third World*. Princeton, NJ and Oxford: Princeton University Press.

Fanon, Frantz. [1967] 1986. *Black Skin, White Masks*. Translated by Charles Lam Markmann, London: Pluto Press.

Fassin, Diddier. 2011. "Racialization: How to do Races with Bodies." In *A Companion to the Anthropology of the Body and Embodiment*, edited by Frances E. Mascia-Lees, 419–434. Malden: Blackwell Publishing.

Ferguson, James. 1999. *Expectations of Modernity: Myths and Meanings of Urban Life on the Zambian Copperbelt*. Berkeley: University of California Press.

Gilroy, Paul. 1987. *Ain't No Black in the Union Jack: The Cultural Politics of Race and Nation*. Chicago: University of Chicago Press.

———. 2002. *Against Race: Imagining Political Culture Beyond the Color Line*. Cambridge, MA: Harvard University Press.

Goldberg, Theo. 2002. *The Racial State*. Oxford and Malden: Blackwell.

Halfacre, Keith. 2006. "Rural Space: Constructing a Three-fold Architecture." In *Handbook of Rural Studies*, edited by Cloke et al., 44–62. London, Thousand Oaks, and New Delhi: Sage.

Hall, Stuart. 1980. "Race, Articulation and Societies Structured in Dominance." In *Sociological Theories: Race and Colonialism*, edited by the United Nations Educational, Scientific and Cultural Organization (UNESCO). Paris: UNESCO: 305–346.

Harvey, David. 1996. *Justice, Nature and the Geography of Difference*. Malden and Oxford: Blackwell, 322.

———. 2003. *The New Imperialism*. Oxford: Oxford University Press.

Hoggart, Keith. 1990. "Let's Do Away with the Rural." *Journal of Rural Studies* 6: 245–257.

Hsiao, Li-Chua. 2007. "The Black Body and Representations of the (In)human." CLCWeb: *Comparative Literature and Culture* 9 (1): 1–12. http://dx.doi.org/10.7771/1481-4374.1020.

Jackson, John. 2005. "A Little Black Magic." *South Atlantic Quarterly* 104 (3): 373–402.

Klein, Naomi. 2014. *This Changes Everything: Capitalism vs. the Climate*. New York: Simon and Shuster Paperbacks.

Kobayashi, Audrey. 2004. "Critical Approaches to Cultural Geography." In *A Companion to Cultural Geography*, edited by James Duncan, Nuala Johnson, and Richard Shein, 238–249. Malden: Blackwell Publishing.

Kothari, Uma. 2006. "An Agenda for Thinking about 'Race' in Development." *Progress in Development Studies* 6: 9–23.

Levien, Michael. 2013. "The Politics of Dispossession: Theorizing India's 'Land Wars.'" *Politics and Society* 41 (3): 351–394.

Li, Murray, Tania. 2001. "Relational Histories and the Production of Difference on Sulawesi's Upland Frontier." *Journal of Asian Studies* 60 (1): 41–66.

———. 2007. *The Will to Improve: Governmentality, Development and the Practice of Politics*. Durham, NC: Duke University Press.

———. 2009. "To Make Live or Let Die? Rural Dispossession and the Protection of Surplus Populations." *Antipode* 41 (S1): 66–93.

Massey, Doreen. 1995. "Places and their Pasts." *History Workshop Journal* 39 (Spring): 182–192.

———. 2005. *For Space*. London: Sage.

McCarthy, Thomas. 2009. *Race Empire and the Idea of Human Development*. Cambridge: Cambridge University Press.

McMichael, Philip. 1990. "Incorporating Comparison within a World-Historical Perspective: An Alternative Comparative Method." *American Sociological Review* 55 (3): 385–397.

Mignolo, Walter. 2000. *Local Histories/Global Designs*. Princeton, NJ and Oxford: Princeton University Press.

Miles, Robert. 1989. *Racism*. London: Routledge.

Mills, Charles. 1997. *The Racial Contract*. Ithaca, NY: Cornell University Press.

Moore, Donald, Anand Pandian, and Jake Kosek. 2003. "The Cultural Politics of Race and Nature: Terrains of Power and Practice." In *Race, Nature and the Politics of Difference*, edited by Donald Moore, Jake Kosek and Anand Pandian, 1–70. Durham, NC: Duke University Press.

Murdoch, Jonathan, and Andy Pratt. 1997. "From the Power of Topography to the Topography of Power: A Discourse on Strange Ruralities." In *Contested Countryside Cultures*, edited by Paul Cloke and Jo Little, 51–69. London and New York: Routledge.

Northover, Patricia. 2012. "Abject Blackness, Hauntologies of Development and the Demand for Authenticity—A Critique of Sen's 'Development as Freedom.'" *Global South* 6 (1): 66.

Omi, Michael, and Howard Winant. 1994. *Racial Formation in the United States*. Minneapolis: University of Minnesota Press.

Perry, Richard, and Bill Mauer, eds. 2003. *Globalization Under Construction: Governmentality, Law and Identity*. Minneapolis and London: University of Minnesota Press.

Pratt, Andy. 1996. "Discourse of Rurality: Loose Talk or Social Struggle." *Journal of Rural Studies* 12 (1): 69–78.

Sassen, Saskia. 2010. "A Savage Sorting of Winners and Losers—Contemporary Versions of Primitive Accumulation." *Globalizations* 10 (1): 23–50.

Shah, Alpa, and Barbara Harriss-White. 2011. "Resurrecting Scholarship on Agrarian Transformations." *Economic and Political Weekly* XLVI, no. 39 (September): 13–18.

Shu-Mei, Shih. 2008. "Comparative Racialization: An introduction." *PMLA* 123 (5): 1347–1362.

Sibley, David. 2006. "Inclusions/Exclusions in Rural Space." In *Handbook of Rural Studies*, edited by Cloke et al., 401–410. London, Thousand Oaks, and New Delhi: Sage.

Smith, Raymond T. 1995. "'Living in the Gun Mouth': Race, Class, And Political Violence in Guyana." *New West Indian Guide/Nieuwe West-Indische Gids* 69 (3 & 4): 223–252.

Spillers, Hortense. 1987. "Mama's Baby, Papa's Maybe: An American Grammar Book." *Diacritics* 17 (2): 64–81.

Stoler, Laura Ann. 1995. *Race and the Education of Desire: Foucault's History of Sexuality and the Colonial Order of Things*. Durham, NC: Duke University Press.

Tabak, Faruk, and Michaeline Crichlow, eds. 2000. *Informalization: Process and Structure*. Baltimore: Johns Hopkins University Press.

Thomas, Alexander, Brian Lowe, Gregory Fulkerson, and Polly Smith, eds. 2011. *Critical Rural Theory: Structure, Space, Culture*. Lanham, MD: Lexington.

Trouillot, Michel-Rolph. 1988. *Peasants and Capital: Dominica in the World Economy*. Baltimore: Johns Hopkins University Press.

———. 1995. *Silencing the Past: Power and the Production of History*. Boston: Beacon Press.

———. 2002. "The Otherwise Modern: Caribbean Lessons from the Savage Plot." In *Critically Modern: Alternatives, Alterities, Anthropologies*, edited by Bruce Knauft, 220–237. Bloomington: Indiana University Press.

———. 2003. *Global Transformations: Anthropology and the Modern World*. New York: Palgrave.

Weiner, Melissa. 2012. "Towards a Critical Global Race Theory." *Sociology Compass* 6 (4): 332–350.

White, Ben, Saturnino M. Borras Jr., Ruth Hall, Ian Scoones, and Wendy Wolford. 2012. "The New Enclosures: Critical Perspectives on Corporate Land Deals." *Journal of Peasant Studies* 39 (3–4): 619–647.

Williams, Brackette. 1991. *Stains on My Name, War in My Veins: Guyana and the Politics of Cultural Struggle*. Durham, NC: Duke University Press.

Williams, Raymond. 1977. *Marxism and Literature*. Oxford: Oxford University Press.

Wynter, Sylvia. 1995. "1492—A New World View." In *Race Discourse and the Americas: A New World View*, edited by Vera Lawrence Hyatt and Rex Nettleford, 5–57. Washington, DC: Smithsonian Institution Press.

1

Global Economies and Historical Change

Rethinking Social Struggles and Transformations in Africa's Zones of Rurality (1500–1800)

Ray A. Kea

History is nothing but the activity of [men and women] pursuing [their] aims.

—Karl Marx, *The Holy Family*

Introduction

I would like to begin with an observation. The consolidation of a new stage of generalized monopoly capitalism (neoliberalism), the emergence of religious and market fundamentalisms, the interventions of subaltern studies, world-system analysis, poststructuralism, postcolonialism, and postmodernism are factors of the late twentieth and early twenty-first centuries that have produced a new conjuncture for theoretical work on the contradictory worlds of the African past and present (Ahluwalia 2010; Comaroff and Comaroff 2012; Kea 2012a; Idahosa and Shenton 2004). What does theoretical work on the African past mean?

The aim of the present study is to uncover dimensions of social class, rebellion, revolution, and societal antagonisms in western/Atlantic African history between 1500 and 1800. It proposes a method for assessing evidence and for understanding how cumulative socioeconomic changes, or changes in the composition and socio-cultural weight of rural communities, can erupt into mass social transformations.

On the whole, Africanist historiography excludes any notion of collective subaltern class experiences and the dynamics of social (class) conflict and revolution as part of a *longue durée*. The dialectical relationship between continuity and societal order and stability, on the one hand, and discontinuity and rupture and instability, on the other, is conceptualized in terms of noncapitalist modes of production and exchange, as well as in terms of political, social, ideological, and cultural issues. In line with this theoretical approach the following discussion pursues alternative ways of thinking about the sites and subjects of western/Atlantic African historicity.

In revisiting African historicity between 1500 and 1800, I draw upon David Wallace's insight that "differentiation of human experience stems above all from questions of scale" (Wallace 2004: 189). There are different temporal scales, such as the event, the conjuncture, and the long duration and different spatial scales, for example, global, regional, subregional, and local (Braudel 2009). The discussion pays particular but not exclusive attention to western/Atlantic African zones of rurality and their mediated relationship to local and regional political economies, different sociopolitical and sociocultural focal points or institutional complexes, and more broadly the European Atlantic mercantile-capitalist global economy and the ancient Afro-Eurasian tributary global economy (Amin 2013). Here the emphasis is placed on the fact that the demands and needs of dominant, urban-based elites of western/Atlantic Africa (in particular the Upper and Middle Niger basins and Senegambia)—those who owned and/or controlled access to the means of production/destruction and exchange and who organized regimes of surplus extraction—required, among other strategizing projects, the subjugation or at least the allegiance of a differentiated countryside with its divisions of labor and its cultural, social, and professional organizations and networks and affiliations (Monroe and Ogundiran 2012; Kea 2012b; Kea 2003; Robion-Brunner 2013; Meillassoux 1991). A pivotal fact of social life was the rural-urban division of labor, a matter that pertains to forms of social appropriation and labor's relationship to land.

The following discussion employs the category "institutional complex" as a basic unit of analysis. It carries definable features as a power structure and as a site of collective sovereignty, a site of agency, a site of mediation, a site of resistance, and a site of centrality or social appropriation. Four institutional complexes are considered: (1) the *fandugu* ("town of power, wealth, and fame") or political-administrative capital of the political-military aristocracy; (2) the *markadugu* or town of merchants (and artisans); (3) the *moridugu* (also *morikunde*; *bilad al-fuqaha*) or town of cleric-scholars or jurisconsults (s. *alim*, pl. *ulamā*; s. *faqih*, pl. *fuqaha*) and their students and clients, and (4) the *zawiya*, a rural settlement of Sufi-scholars and their students, disciples, and followers. Each complex possessed its own set of practices, its particular forms of cultural, social, and symbolic capital, and its own relations to the means of production, exchange, and consumption.

Recent studies readily acknowledge the layered complexities of the African past in their scrutiny of disease, historical demography, institutions and governance, the impact of the export slave trade, colonialism, cultural conservatism, and ethnic formations/identities without however delving into analyses that specify which factors were necessary (or structural) and which were contingent (Richard and MacDonald 2015; Akyeampong et al. 2014). The present analysis operates in terms of the structural and the contingent in its investigation of the historicity of social relations of production (social appropriation) and forces of production (appropriation of nature) and the conflictive processes they generate, for example, in the rural-urban division of labor and in the interactions of different institutional complexes. Social relations of production and institutional complexes were always the result of the praxis of historical subjects ("social selves") who were individuals as well as members of localities, classes, status groups, associations, and factions. In their praxis they embodied different degrees of agency and identity.

The period under review is divided into two temporalities—the late imperial era, which falls between the mid-thirteenth and the late sixteenth centuries, and the post-imperial era, which falls in the seventeenth and eighteenth centuries. A justification for this periodizing strategy is that each era has distinctive charac-teristics. Specifically, the late imperial period is defined by the unifying imperial suzerainty of the Mali Sultanate under the Keita Dynasty (1230–1464) and the Songhai Sultanate under the Sunni Dynasty (1420–1493) and its successors, the Askiya Dynasty (1464–1591) and Askiya Caliphate (1498–1591) or Askiyate.

The Mali and Songhai imperial regimes can be described as tributary-mercantile systems of class and power relations. Both embraced a political theology that identified each domain as a universal empire (for a discussion of the emergence of this idea across Afro-Eurasia, see Subrahmanyam 1999). In the case of the Mali Sultanate, the ruling dynasty drew upon an indigenous, non-Islamic cosmology. In 1498 the Askiya Dynasty redefined itself in the caliphal tradition of *dar al-Islam*. According to a seventeenth-century chronicle, the inceptive matrix of the Askiya Caliphate's power and wealth had three components: urbanism, commerce, and religion (Hunwick 1999). These power configurations maintained a substantial institutional, cultural, and political presence in the Askiyate, constituting a complex sociopolitical totality of dynastic rule through interacting networks and the institutional complexes and praxis of political-military, merchant/artisan, and clerical-scholarly elites.

The end of Askiyate ascendancy has a global dimension. The dynasty's collapse is to be understood against the backdrop of international geopolitics and complex and contingent local events, including internecine conflict and insurrections. The Moroccan invasion and conquest of the Askiyate heartland in 1591 is to be seen in the global, geopolitical context of competing and contending Mediterranean-Saharan political formations and the multilateral processes of interaction between an expanding modern mercantile-capitalist system and an ancient tributary-mercantile system (Dramani-Issifou 1982). In the 1580s the Askiyate core zone experienced violent factionalism among the ruling classes, which led to a divisive and bitter civil war. At the same time and extending into the early 1590s, rebellions of enslaved subalterns occurred on royal estates and other landed estates of the core zone.

The late imperial epoch is conventionally viewed in Africanist historiography as a West African Golden Age. Indeed, the period is construed in contemporary epic literature as a time of the triumphant and heroic horseman whose life—defined by chivalry, warfare, and martial skills—symbolized adventure, power, prestige, and wealth. The hero's world always included a landscape of fortifications (Iliffe 2005: chapters 1–2; Conrad 1990; Courlander 1982; Tymowski 1974; Cissiko 1969). A contrasting historiography interprets the post-imperial era as a time of catastrophes (famines and epidemics), crises, disorder, insecurity, and social regression; a time of reform, rebellions, and revolutions, as well as banditry and warlordism across rural landscapes. The agency, interplay, and rivalries of institutional complexes, which privileged coherence and control, were crucial elements in shaping the era's geopolitics. In this matrix the political theology of universal empire was no longer sustainable.

A Materialist Approach to African History

The writings of Amilcar Cabral are instructive for this historical study. In the middle of an anticolonial and liberation struggle in Portuguese Guinea (today Guinea Bissau) in the 1960s, he pronounced that history was a theoretical enterprise that could elucidate and guide this struggle. He established the intellectual status and the relevance of Marxist theory to the aims of the mass struggle and to the analysis of the historical processes and conjunctures that created the struggle's conditions of existence. His thesis is that any given trajectory of political and social development is a product of a society's own immanent dynamics. The motive force behind the dynamics is, he argues, the class struggle that develops as a "function of at least two essential and interdependent variables—the level of productive forces and the pattern of the ownership of the means of production" (Cabral 1969). A mode of production, as Cabral views it, refers to the varied material and nonmaterial ways that human beings collectively produce the means of subsistence in order to survive and enhance social being. The method of producing the necessities of life requires the unity of the productive forces (unity of the means of production and labor), the relations of production (social conditions of production), and property ownership. Cabral's materialist understanding is relevant to an understanding of the economic, ideological, and social conditions under which the struggles and resistance of the countryside were conducted. The revolution in Guinea-Bissau, a recent chapter of western/Atlantic African history, had deep roots in the trajectories of its wider region.

Revolutionary consciousness and armed struggle for social justice and the creation of alternative power structures were very much part of the socio-historical horizon in post-imperial zones of rurality in the Middle and Upper Niger basins and the Senegambia region (Kea 2012b; Robinson 2000; Barry 1992; Boulègue and Suret-Canale 1985; Rodney 1970). The socio-historical horizon was itself a result of the productivity of collective rural labor. An archaeological study considers the scale of this productivity in a survey of the extensive ruins of fortifications (*tatas*), which stretched from the Atlantic to the Lake Chad basin, were constructed by "millions of man [-woman] hours in the stoneless soils where most people farmed and . . . where most people lived" (Darling 1998: 17). From the perspective of the ruling classes, "consumers" of fortifications, the countryside was not the site of conscious social subjects but was rather an object of social appropriation. In the seventeenth and eighteenth centuries, rural initiatives carved out of the fortified landscapes, spaces for banditry and warlordism, on the one hand, and millenarianism, rebellion, Islamic proselytizing, and revolution, on the other.

Different kinds of non- (or pre-) capitalist modes of production represent abstract typologies denoting forms of social development and the possibilities of historical multilinearity (as opposed to a preconceived chronological linearity or evolutionism leading to capitalism). In western/Atlantic Africa noncapitalist tributary, slaveholding, mercantile, and domestic/household relations of social production prevailed, and use-value, not exchange-value, was a preeminent feature of the political economy. Infrastructural social organization and networks of administration, gift exchange, reciprocity, social power, and commodity exchange reveal the inter-linkages of the different social production modes, which can be read horizontally in geographical space and vertically in social-institutional space. The tributary mode of production was dominant in the sense that it subjected the dynamic and functions of other modes of production to the requirements of its own reproduction.

In *The Structure of World History*, Kojin Karatani provides a novel view of the long-term history of humanity in terms of four autonomous types of exchange (*Verkher*: "intercourse," "traffic"): reciprocity/gift-return, plunder-redistribution, commodity exchange, and associationism. Exchanges are differentiated as either reciprocal or nonreciprocal and as either free or unfree. Each had its own systemic logic or dynamic. Only the first three have predominated in particular periods of human history, according to Karatani (Karatani 2014). The fourth, free mutual exchange or association, prefigured in religion, millenarian movements and utopian imaginaries, has never been dominant in any historical society. Societies of different historical periods and geographies involve specific articulations of these modes of exchange, the fourth mode of exchange excepted. *Fandugu*s (plunder-redistribution), *markadugu*s (commodity exchange), *moridugu*s (reciprocity/gift-return), and *zawiya*s (commodity exchange; reciprocity gift-return) are to be understood in their geographical and sociopolitical contexts. In Cabral's terms the central driving force of history is the continual, ever-present dynamic of struggle between classes, status groups, and factions, which were involved in one or more institutional complex.

Institutional complexes were embedded in contradictory social processes according to boundaries established by the agenda-setting of particular interests—military, commercial, and so on—and their alliance networks. The present discussion postulates that contradictions were a driving force in western/Atlantic African tributary-mercantile formations. In the late imperial period the primary structural contradiction occurred in the form of coups and armed rebellions within the sphere of the ruling classes, that is to say, the principal form of societal conflict materialized as confrontational social struggles and violent factionalism within the ruling classes of the Askiyate. Struggles of this sort erupted into a destabilizing civil war toward the end of the sixteenth century. Rival political-military dynamics and interests set the societal agenda. A secondary contradiction was the class conflict between the ruling classes, on the one hand, and the (late-sixteenth-century) uprisings of their free and unfree subjects, on the other.

Re-Centering Africa in Globalizing Economies

Samir Amin identifies three different stages of globalization in world history. Each stage is tied to a particular global economy and specific forms of socio-spatial organization. They are the tributary-mercantile global economy (500 BCE–1500 CE), the mercantile-capitalist global economy (1500–1800), and the industrial-capitalist global economy (1800 to present) (Amin 2011). The tributary-mercantile global economy was dominant in much of Afro-Eurasia before 1500. Amin links this phase of globalization to long-distance trade and exchange routes (e.g., the Silk Roads, Indian Ocean networks, and trans-Saharan routes), the transfer of technologies (e.g., craft and military technologies), and the spread of religions and ideas (e.g., Christianity and Islam). He identifies China, India, and the Middle East as principal centers or power structures in ancient globalization. In my view western/Atlantic Africa, with the Middle Niger basin as a historic core zone, was another ancient center (Kea 2014, 2004). That is to say, the positional relationship of western/Atlantic Africa within the sphere of the tributary global economy was defined by a spatial-structural interdependence.

Amin also draws a theoretical contrast between ancient tributary globalization and the mercantile-capitalist global economy. In contrast to the tributary global economy, the mercantile-capitalist global economy was structurally polarizing, creating in the wake of colonial conquests in the Americas and Caribbean hierarchies of core, semi-periphery, and periphery zones in the European Atlantic world. The noncapitalist tributary global system created through long-distance exchange networks interacting centers or core zones at the global level but not periphery zones or monopolistic structures of global domination. The dynamics of this system did not produce a Global North and a Global South (Amin 2011). The two systems had different rationalities and systemic logics. The rationality of mercantile-capitalist trading companies was structured by a market rationality based on the primacy of private property and commodity production and exchange. The social formation of Atlantic mercantile-capitalism consisted of massive, privately owned slave labor camps ("plantations") in the Americas, which functioned as a source of absolute surplus value. Tributary-mercantile societies of western/Atlantic Africa were defined by the primacy of use-values over exchange-values and by a political rationality based on the dominance of the political over the economy: political authorities administered the organization of the economy by fixing the boundaries of economic activity according to the dictates of predation (warfare and plunder), gift-exchange, tax/tribute collection, and the strategies of surplus (re-)distribution (Amin 2011; additionally, Kea 2012c; Diagne 1992; Barry 1992; Meillassoux 1971). Atlantic mercantile-capitalism engaged western/Atlantic tributary-mercantile formations in a commercial rather than a political (and colonizing) form.

In either case of tributary-mercantile or mercantile-capitalist globalization western/Atlantic African societies remain central, if their modes of production are to be assessed at the level of the totality of their social production relations and the global interconnections of these relations (Kea 2015, 2012a; Viti 2001; Diagne 1992). Historian Catherine Coquery-Vidrovitch examines an aspect of African globality that is seldom met with in world history historiography by addressing the issue of the continent's world-historical centrality as a general feature of African historicity. She begins with geography:

> Geographically, Africa is located at the core of three worlds. Africa allowed them to be connected one with the other: the Mediterranean world, the Indian Ocean world, and (later) the Atlantic world. Therefore, from the beginning of Ancient history to the present, Africa was not marginal but played a major worldwide role. [A]ll over successive historical globalizations, Africa south of the Sahara was no more nor less than other "worlds" (Indian Ocean world, Mediterranean world, far east Asia, Europe, etc.) at the center of the other worlds. Europeans have built "their" idea of Africa, which they believed and still believe they had "discovered," while they were by and large the last ones to do so. Africa and Africans developed a long history before Europeans interfered. Moreover, they played a prominent role at different stages of world globalization before Western intervention. (Coquery-Vidrovitch 2012)

Coquery-Vidrovitch provides then a large-scale framework in which events in western/Atlantic Africa can be located. Other studies corroborate Coquery-Vidrovitch's thesis about the centrality of Africa in the global economy and world history (e.g., Barendse 2002; Keita 2002).

The concrete re-centering of Africa in global historical processes confounds the widespread and popular contention that the ascendancy of European Atlantic centers, the conquest and colonization of the Americas, and the growth of the trans-Atlantic slave trade dictated the nature of historical processes and social dynamics in western/Atlantic Africa and contributed to the general underdevelopment of contemporary Africa (Akyeampong et al. 2014; Pomeranz and Topik 1999). However, the dynamics of political sovereignty and social transformation in western/Atlantic Africa's tributary-mercantile social formations cannot be reduced to external causalities alone without reference to the formations' internal structural and functional determinations and the connections of their space of places (cities and villages) and space of flows (interacting networks) to the global commodity chains of tributary and capitalist world systems (Monroe and Ogundiran

2012; Kea 2012b, 2012c). The singularity of the historical conjuncture in which the trans-Atlantic slave trade emerged relates not only to the organized activities and interconnections of European-Atlantic mercantile-capitalist core zones whose economies were based on exchange-value. More to the point, singularity also relates to the complex, uneven, and overdetermined character of social reality—the deep structures and social processes of domestic/household, tributary, slave-holding, and mercantile relations—of western/Atlantic Africa societal formations whose economies were based on use-value, notwithstanding the prominence of internal market relations, and whose structures maintained intense and diverse connections to the ancient tributary-mercantile system (Kea 2012a, 2012c; Viti 2001; Meillassoux 1991; Meillassoux 1971; Diagne 1992). In this structural matrix primary and secondary contradictions worked themselves out through the interactions of different institutional complexes.

The Late Imperial Age: The Askiyate

Merchant, clerical, and military-administrative elites formed a single, land-owning, ruling class, which united all aspects of the life of Askiyate society—cultural, economic, political, ideological, and military. A second process was also at work, namely, the formation of a single class of hierarchically ranked bonded subjects out of different social elements, such as free peasants, war captives, and social outcasts. The material base for these social processes was the heartland of the Askiyate, a densely populated and urbanized commercial-artisanal center that extended over a thousand kilometers along the Middle Niger floodplain, from the city of Jenne in the west, through Timbuktu and Gao, to the city of Kukiya in the east. In the heartland a socially differentiated ruling class exercised power over bonded social groups and land. It represented a new level of surplus accumulation and property possession.

From the late fifteenth through the sixteenth century, Askiyate authorities promoted the cultivation of (Asian) rice as a principal cereal crop through technological development. They launched the large-scale colonization and reclamation of new land along the Niger floodplain and constructed an irrigation infrastructure (canals, dams, cisterns, levees, water tanks, and wells). This public works project included the establishment of agricultural settlements inhabited by tens of thousands of servile groups or serfs. The rising demand for rice in different sectors—the royal household and court, military garrisons, urban populations, and Saharan markets—meant that agricultural production became more labor intensive. Askiya Muhammad granted large estates with their bonded dependents, whose numbers amounted to hundreds and even thousands, to wealthy merchants and Muslim literati (*ulama*). As estate owners, the status difference between merchant and religious elites, on the one hand, and military-administrative elites, on the other, was erased. The stability of the mass-scale character of servile estates/settlements was maintained, militarily, by means of cavalry garrisons that were set up throughout the Askiyate and, ideologically, by a hierarchical system of hereditary castes and caste endogamy, which created legal and social differences and boundaries among servile, dependent groups. In addition, some estates had Koranic, or tablet, schools, indicating that serf families had access to an elementary education (Paré 2014; Tymowski 2005, 2004; Hunwick 1999, 1996; Kubbel 1969).

An argument has been made that during the reign of *al-hajj* Askiya Muhammad Turay (1493–1528), the founder of the Askiya Dynasty, there was a transition from the slave latifundia of the Mali and Sunni Dynasty periods to forms of exploitation akin to serfdom with the establishment, from Jenne and to Kukiya, of numerous agricultural settlements or landed estates (plantations), inhabited by servile groups (*zunuj*; s. *zanj*) and their overseers (*fanafi*; s. *fanfa*) (Paré 2014; Tymowski 1970; Kubbel 1969). Under the Sunni Dynasty free peasants were subject to corvée labor, but Askiya Muhammad abolished this impost, replacing it with a tax (or rent) in kind. Servile cultivators had their own plots of land and received from the state seeds and leather sacks (for harvested rice). The ruler introduced a range of laws that pertained to the landed estates' dependent cultivators and artisans. One such law forbade marriage between members of different casted servile groups; for example, cultivators were not allowed to marry blacksmiths or leather workers, and none of them could marry a free person. If a free man or woman married a person of servile status, their child became the property of the ruler. Servile cultivators were economically stratified. Thus, on the Abda plantation near Kukiya there were serfs who owned large boats, serfs who had small boats, and serfs who had no boats. The overseer of the plantation, who was also a serf, had his own house in Gao, the Askiyate political capital, his own fields worked by his slaves, and large rice granaries; he had at his disposal boats and their crews, and he was in charge of the serfs responsible for the plantation's livestock of cattle, sheep, goats, and horses. In the mid-sixteenth century a ruler set up a royal estate in the vicinity of Timbuktu to quell lower-class food riots. Thirty royal serfs produced rice for the subsistence needs of the poor of Timbuktu (Wise and Taleb 2011; Kubbel 1969).

Research to date indicates that until the 1580s bonded subjects on landed estates caused practically no trouble for the Askiyate authorities. No social unrest and uprisings were reported, although there were disputes that had to be settled by a legal authority such as a *qadi* (judge) (Haïdara 2006). In the 1510s and 1520s there was a widespread rural-based, anti-Askiyate millenarian movement in districts west of the city of Jenne, but whether any estates actively participated in it is presently unknown. However, from 1583 onward there are explicit references to revolts of the *doghorani*, or descendants of slaves/serfs settled on landed estates (Kubbel 1969). In addition, from the 1520s onwards, rebellions and attempted coups by ruling-class factions were a persistent feature of political life. These actions culminated in a disastrous civil war in the late 1580s, thus paving the way for the 1591 Moroccan invasion and conquest of the Askiyate heartland (Sangaré 2011).

The Post-Imperial Age: Agents and Structures

A post-conquest Moroccan administration known as the Pashlik of Timbuktu dominated the Middle Niger basin from 1592 to 1623; however, it emerged as just one among several competing *fandugu*s, none of which could establish an indisputable suzerainty over the former Askiyate heartland and restore the property regime based on landed estates. In the new political environment, serfs and other dependent groups from the estates joined the Moroccan army in 1591 and between 1591 and 1593 attacked and plundered urban centers from Jenne to Gao. Between 1610 and 1620 the assaults continued unabated. The rebellious social struggles of insubordinate *zunuj* and their descendants turned *fandugu*s and *markadugu* into fortified garrison communities (Wise and Taleb 2011; Hunwick 1999; Willis 1985; Abitbol 1979; Tymowski 1974). The *zunuj*, in effect, declared war on the cities. To borrow the language of Leon Trotsky, the struggles of the *zunuj* represent a history of the forcible entrance of the rural masses into the realm of rulership over their own destiny.

In the Askiyate imperial system, social groups associated with *fandugu*s, *markadugu*s, and *moridugu* enjoyed privileged statuses. In the aftermath of the downfall of the Askiya Dynasty, reestablishing the dominance of the political (predation; appropriation) meant creating the shared hegemony of different elite groups— political-military, commercial, and religious. On the other hand, the rebellions and violent assaults of the *zunuj* meant establishing the dominance of the social (millenarianism; association) and the hegemony of free and unfree subaltern groups. The *fandugu* and the *zawiya*, representing contrapositions, were particularly effective sites of radical transformation. The *fandugu* was at the epicenter of a combined political and cultural revolution, a revolution imposed from above. The *zawiya*-based social and cultural revolution mobilized subaltern classes and was a movement from below. It set forth millenarian visions of universalism, expressed with reference to geopolitical and geocultural entities like *dar al-Islam, jamaa al-sudaniyya, umma al-muhammadiyya*, and humanism (appeals to social justice, social equality, and the dissemination of knowledge).

Military Aristocracies and *Ulama*: *Fandugu* and *Moridugu*

Embracing a composite of technological and institutional changes linked to state-building projects and strategies—warfare, standing armies of mercenaries, slave warriors, and professional soldiers, fortifications (*tatas*), and new weaponry (firearms, cannon, and siege equipment)—the military elites' revolution can be summed up as the militarization of the societal order and the citadelization of *fandugu* political and settlement geography. According to historian P. Diagne, the structural transformations that occurred between 1600 and 1800 affected various aspects of economic, cultural, ideological, political, and social life are evidence of the consolidation of *fandugu* dominance with political-military groups at the helm (Jansen 2015; Kea 2015; MacDonald 2012; Monroe and Ogundiran 2012; Diagne 1992; Barry 1992; Meillsaaoux 1991; Bazin 1988; Roberts 1987; Bah 1985; Boulègue and Suret-Canale 1985; Abitbol 1979; Tymowski 1974; Cissoko 1969). Transformations were tied to ruling military dynasties' need to wage war and intensify the tributary mode of surplus extraction as booty, tribute, taxes, and rent; to expand spheres of influence against rival and competing polities through lavish gift-giving relations and liberal redistribution policies; and to enhance military capabilities for the purposes of extending and expanding predation activities against rival polities and in the countryside against rebellious villages, hamlets, and encampments. Moreover, large-scale endowments of land and labor were needed to support a standing army of several thousand horsemen and a network of *tatas*. The military sector was enhanced through the elaboration of different categories of servitude in direct service to this sector as soldiers, sappers, military engineers, artisans, cultivators, herders, and miners. New legal systems and laws organized the administration of bonded and enslaved labor. Among Muslim rulers new legal systems, based on Sunni Malikism, institutionalized fiefs or landed estates, either as state, corporate, or household property, rulers' estates allocated to officials, military commanders, wealthy merchants, and clerics, according to the ruler's pleasure. Land speculation was legalized. The changes are to be interpreted with reference to the military elites' redistributive and gift-exchange relations, which reinforced patronage and clientage relations with dependable and undependable allies, and its constant resort to warfare, raids, and confiscations as sources of distributable wealth. These practices continually created and re-created the effect of a militarized structure (Diagne 1992; Meillassoux 1991, 1975; Bazin 1988; Roberts 1987; Abitbol 1982, 1979; Barry 1992). The political dynamics of the military aristocracies set societal agendas but not without opposition from subordinated rural groups and their supporters.

The spread of a hierarchical system of higher and lower artisanal and service castes into the countryside and a corresponding decline of urban-based artisan guilds, especially in the Senegambia region, was another aspect of *fandugu* political dynamics. The result of this social development was increased occupational specialization in particular rural areas and the decline of traditional rural crafts associated with women (making pottery) or age-group associations, which worked in metal, wood, and leather and were associated with household/domestic social production. These dislocations contributed to the spread of two oppositional movements into the countryside from the towns and cities—Sufism (Islamic mysticism) and non-Islamic organizations like the Poro Society and Komo-related associations (Diagne 1992; Barry 1992; Levtzion 1987b, 1987c). It is likely that descendants of the Askiyate's plantation labor force were among those who joined Sufi organizations and/or a Komo-related association.

The genealogy of Africa's world-historical centrality is to be located in the conditions of life in a countryside dominated by militarized *fandugu*s in which the spatial and temporal division between work performed for survival or needs—reproducing a realm of necessity—and work performed for a dominating sociopolitical practice—building towns and fortifications—was a structural feature of tributary-mercantile relations. Accordingly, an aspect of militarized tributary-mercantile relations is described in one work as follows:

West Africa was the source of a slavery that was to mark extreme "otherness"—not without the collaboration of the powerful African kingdoms that were emerging. . . . The African slave trade presupposed the tyranny of the slave plantation, the concentration camp in the slave stations [i.e., Atlantic Africa's world ports], and the establishment of tightly hierarchically arranged military states in key West African countries, capable of delivering the quota of commercial goods, namely slaves. It was the slave trade that was the source of dominant wealth in West Africa as much as in Europe, North America, and the Caribbean. (O'Callaghan: 27)

The militarized states or *fandugu*s imposed discipline over intransigent subordinate groups by declaring war on the turbulent and rebellious countryside. This was a response to the *zunuj* declaration of war on the cities. Another study notes that the slave trade gave impetus to the social differentiation within *fandugu* societies: "a concentration of wealth and its means on one pole and poverty on the other" (Boulegue and Suet-Canale 1985: 529). Such polarization mirrored in patterns of urban-rural spatialization—that is, a concentration of wealth and the means of acquiring it in urban formations, and the concentration of poverty in the coun-tryside—was a structural feature of a social power that systematically determined access to resources and the means of wealth distribution. Economic disparity between town and country was an effect of a political dynamic to subdue and repress initiatives of the rural social world.

*Fandugu*s employed Muslim clerics (s. *faqih*; *fuqaha*) and cleric-scholars (s. *alim*; *ulama*) as officials, teachers, advisors, and prayer leaders, rewarding them with grants of land, livestock, servants, slaves, luxury goods, and gold and cowrie currencies. In addition, they engaged Muslim cleric-scholars of autonomous and semi-autonomous *moridugu*s in different capacities as allies or clients and also as hired envoys, diplomats, and negotiators. Clerics known as *mubashshirun*, that is, "propagators of the faith," did not seek to found independent polities; instead, they peacefully promoted Islam in villages, encampments, and hamlets where they built mosques and set up Koranic schools. In keeping with their tradition of political neutralism and pacifism *moridugu*s functioned as places of refuge for criminals, debtors, escaped slaves, the poor, social outcasts, and others who were characterized as the dregs of society (Kane 2003; Roberts 1987; Willis 1992; also Hunwick 1999). Ostensibly, their way of life was antithetical to the martial ethos of the *fandugu*s' military aristocracies. One *moridugu* clerical group, the Jakhanke, illustrates a typical client-patron relationship:

The king has asked us and given us a choice about taking up arms and joining battle, and, on the other hand, about building a fortress. We have said,
if we are asked to build a fortress we shall build it, and if we are asked to
take up arms and join battle, we shall build a fortress. We are entirely at
his beck and call. (Sanneh 1976b: 92)

The interactions of *moridugu* clerics were complex and ambiguous. Building a
fortress for a patron-king contributed to the infrastructure of a *fandugu* administrative order and the organization to surplus extraction. Converting villagers to Islam
meant the introduction of new forms of cultural, social, and symbolic capital into
the lives of peasants, pastoralists, miners, casted artisans, and others, and implied
the possibility of new commercial and political connections.

Merchants and *Ulama*: *Markadugu* and *Moridugu*

Through the history of western/Atlantic Africa military groups and merchant
groups have always been associated—sometimes merchants were in opposition,
sometimes they were tribute-paying subjects, and sometimes they were allies. The
political and economic ascendancy of *markadugu*s as autonomous city-states in the
Middle and Upper Niger basin in the first half of the seventeenth century was
supported by mercenaries who served as caravan guards and as a militia. In the
rural hinterland, the city-states were served by enslaved cultivators, artisan castes,
and tribute-paying peasants.

In the 1640s peasants and slaves successfully rebelled against the *markadugu*s,
destroying a number of large towns with their palaces and houses of the rich.
Mosques were spared. Mercenaries joined the uprising, which defeated the merchants' towns and reduced them to a tribute-paying status. The victors founded a
fandugu political organization described by some historians as a military machine
devoted to predation and the seizure of captives (Kea 2012b, 2003; Wilks 2000;
Roberts 1987; Abitbol 1979). While dependent on merchants' trade networks and
on merchants as commercial agents and creditors, the new military aristocracies'
way of life necessitated the political subordination of the merchant class and hence
the suppression of the logic of trading capital and mercantile accumulation through
periodic confiscations of merchants' property (Bazin 1988; Meillassoux 1991, 1971).
The primary contradiction of *markadugu* society was the class struggle between

the merchants and their political economy of commodity exchange and predation and free and unfree rural producers. A necessary historical struggle of *markadugu*s was to increase and control their resource-producing hinterlands through the coerced or voluntary incorporation of autonomous rural settlements. This strategy also included exercising security over vital communication and caravan routes and extending mercantile/commercial activities into agrarian, pastoralist, and mining communities (Wilks 2000; Mabogunje and Richards 1985).

*Markadugu*s supported a way of life that included markets, warehouses, schools, libraries, mosques, craft guilds, caravans, caravanserai, and trading networks (Meillassoux 1991; Boutillier 1987; Roberts 1987; Wilks 1968). Their lifestyle affirmed the logic of capital as profit and interest and commodity exchange. Characteristically, *markadugu* rural hinterlands included farms cultivated by indebted peasants and plantations worked by enslaved laborers (Mabogunje and Richards 1985; Meillassoux 1991; Barry 1992; Roberts 1987). Trading capital subsumed the surplus labor of peasant debtors for the consumption needs of urban households. Unfree cultivators and unfree artisans produced for trans-regional markets in the Sahara and North Africa as well as throughout West Africa. The enslaved were either purchased in markets or were received as gift-exchanges from rulers or elite military households. Enslaved labor was distributed over three sectors: agriculture, which supplied Saharan oases with produce; commercial activities in which slaves were porters or agents; and crafts, especially textile production. The great merchant families of nineteenth-century Sansanding, a major Middle Niger *markadugu*, owned between two hundred and a thousand slaves; and the town of Bamako had six hundred enslaved weavers producing for North African markets (Meillassoux 1991; Roberts 1987).

Sufi-Scholars and *Zawiya*

A distinctive figure, the Sufi, appeared in the Middle Niger basin in the course of the fifteenth and sixteenth centuries. By the eighteenth century the Sufi and Sufism were commonplace. Sufism is said to represent the popularization of urban Islam in the countryside. Sufis had their own institutional base in the form of "brotherhoods" or *turuq* (s. *tariq*) (e.g., Qadiriyya, Khalwatiyya, Mahmudiyya, and Shadhaliyya). Sufi cultural-educational networks, independent of local political regimes, were extensive, stretching, for example, from the Senegambia region and the Middle Niger basin to Saharan oases and North Africa centers. Sufis had their own economic resources (long-distance commerce, farming, craft industries, and pastoralism). Associated with their rural settlement organization or *zawiya* were students, disciples, and social outcasts as well as mosques, Koranic schools and *madrasa*s, libraries, and caravanserai. They were heavily involved in both local village trade and long-distance commerce across the Sahara to Mediterranean entrepôts. Their avenues of communication included wide-ranging bulk goods and prestige-goods networks and cultural-information networks. Saharan-based *zawiya*s were instrumental in the construction of oases and water management systems (wells and *foggara*s) throughout much of the desert. In spite of the importance of trade relations Sufis did not obey the logic of personal profit as a lifestyle but advocated personal austerity, spirituality, contemplation, and the social distribution of wealth (Kea 2003; Kane 2003; Robinson 2000; Levtzion 1987a, 1987c; Stewart 1976; Batran 1974).

Zawiya spiritual leaders and their students, disciples, and followers were not only trained in Sufi traditions (*gnosis*) but also in the Islamic sciences (*'ilm*) and in one or more handicrafts (sandal makers, rope makers, basket makers, weavers, and so on). Education combined theoretical and practical knowledge, hence the division between mental labor (abstract knowledge) and manual labor (concrete knowledge) was surmounted (Kane 2003; Kea 2003; McDougall 1987; Willis 1985; Stewart 1976; Batran 1974). Like *moridugu*s, *zawiya*s functioned as sanctuaries, providing security for the socially dispossessed, outcasts, debtors, escaped slaves, rebels, exiles, the impoverished, and the like. Indeed, *zawiya* social structure was open to male and female without distinction, regardless of social status and life circumstances. In contrast to *markadugu*s and *moridugu*s, *zawiya*s were not slaveholding establishments. *Zawiya* leadership (*murabitun*) relied on the labor of students, disciples, followers, and clients as well as the economic support of peasant and pastoralist communities. Similar to the *mubashshirun*s from *markadugu*s and *moridugu*s, they promoted literacy in Arabic as well as local languages (Sonhai, Malinke, Bamana, Fulfulde, Tamashaq). In fact, it was in the seventeenth and eighteenth centuries that more than a dozen western African languages were written for the first time in the Arabic alphabet, thanks to the initiatives of *moridugu* and *zawiya* clerics (Kane 2003; Gutelius 2002; McDougall 1987; Stewart 1976; Wilks 1968).

The Revolutionary Countryside

An unprecedented wave of rebellious and revolutionary movements swept across much of western/Atlantic African zones of rurality. Sufism structured the discursive field in which armed insurgency was written about (Robinson 2000; Levtzion 1987c). In the middle decades of the seventeenth century, from the Atlantic to the Lake Chad Basin, rural-based revolutionary movements called for social and political equality, the destruction of towns and cities, and the overthrow of all local dynasties that were corrupt, oppressive, and in alliance with the Ottoman Empire. These actions recall the uprisings of the late-sixteenth and early-seventeenth-century *zunuj* of the Askiyate. The movements pitted Sufi mystics of the countryside, associated with long-distance trade (merchant capital), agro-pastoralism and herding, and Islamic scholarship, against the *fuqaha* of the *fandugus* (Kea 2012b; Barry 1992; Levtzion 1987c; Rodney 1970).

The movements marked the geopolitical ascendancy of Islamic-oriented zones of rurality (Robinson 2000; Barry 1992; Levtzion 1987a, 1987c; Stewart 1976; Rodney 1970). The zones served as sites for the promulgation of new political ideologies, new expressions of sovereignty, and new sociocultural paradigms. On the offensive, *zawiya*s emerged as active sites of rural-based revolutionary and/or millenarian movements, partly in the tradition of rebellion of the *zunuj* of the Askiyate, partly in response to the destabilizing effects of Atlantic-based mercantile capitalism, and partly to the antagonisms of militarized *fandugus* exacting regimes of surplus extraction and predatory confiscations (Robinson 2000; Meillassoux 1997, 1991; Levtzion 1987c; Hodgkin 1976). The movements enabled an oppressed countryside to make sense of the massive and brutal transition from an Askiya imperial political geography to a radically different political geography of *fandugu* militarism. In these conditions the *zawiya* leadership of Sufi-scholars became *mujahidun*, or militant activists, and in league with peasants, pastoralists, craftspeople, and some *moridugu*s fought to establish their own political sovereignty.

Some zones of rurality, for example in Senegambia, materialized as sites of social emancipation in the sense that rural folk appeared as active participants and leaders in the movements. A seventeenth-century activist, Nasir ad-Din, proclaimed in villages and pastoral encampments that "God does not permit kings to plunder, kill, or enslave their subjects; on the contrary, kings are to protect their subjects: the people were not made for kings, but kings were made for the people" (Barry 1992).

The ideals of active jihadis led to the founding of a new kind of state system and a redefinition of the political realm: "imamates" (Robinson 2000; Barry 1992; Boulègue and Suret-Canale 1985; Hodgkin 1976a, 1976b; Rodney 1970). At the same time, Sufi adherents popularized the idea of trans-regionality by urging an identification with *umma al-muhammadiyya* (Community of Muslims) and *jama'at al-sudaniyya* (Community of Muslims of the Sudan) as encompassing rural zones of militant and quietist struggle. In opposition to the *markadugu*-clerics, who were supporters of alliances with *fandugu*s, and *moridugu*-clerics, who were adherents of quietism, seventeenth-century *zawiya* mystic-clerics advocated revolutionary activism against military aristocracies, especially in the Senegambia region where *fandugu*s waged war on a rebellious countryside and on dissident *markadugu*s and *moridugu*s (Barry 1992).

By the eighteenth century *zawiya* political discourse embraced two strategies of social transformation and activism: a strategy of armed struggle led by *mujahidun* ("revolutionaries") and a strategy of quietism led by a *mujaddid* ("reformer"). *Zawiya*s in the Middle Niger basin and the southern Sahara largely abandoned armed insurrection and open warfare as instruments of political and social change. Instead, emphasis was placed on diplomacy and negotiation in matters of dispute and armed conflict, and the accumulation of wealth through trade and pastoralism (MacDougall 1986; Batran 1974). Accumulated wealth was not for personal aggrandizement but was to be distributed among the urban poor and in rural communities. Sufi practitioners were urged to dedicate themselves to personal asceticism by living a simple life, learning a craft (e.g., sandal making or rope making), refusing to use political office for personal gain, and avoiding conspicuous consumption and general *embourgeoisment* (Kea 2015, 2012b; Levtzion 1987c; Willis 1985; Hodgkin 1976a, 1976b; Batran 1974).

Jihadism and quietism were built on what Thomas Hodgkin calls the radical or revolutionary tradition in Muslim West Africa, the roots of which are traceable to the writings of political activists from the mid-eleventh to the mid-nineteenth century. Hodgkin summarizes the tradition's features: (1) it emphasizes the rights of common people against the claims of their rulers; (2) it takes a leveling egalitarian attitude to differences of status, rank, wealth, sex, ethnic origin, and privileges based upon these; (3) it is concerned with changing institutions as a precondition of changing human beings, and opening up new possibilities for their development; (4) it attaches importance to the widest possible diffusion of knowledge and education; (5) it lays particular stress on the principle that men [and women] belong (in some sense) to an international community, whose claims transcend those of a particular state, religion, ethnic, or linguistic group (universalist in approach and outlook); (6) it stresses the agency of social change, or reform regarded as justifying (in some circumstances at least) the use of revolutionary methods to achieve it (Hodgkin 1980, 1976a, 1976b).

Counterrevolution: The *Zawiya* as *Fandugu*

What happens after rural movements of liberation successfully challenge *fandugu* systems of inequality, injustice, and oppression and embark on state-building projects? One study offers a positive appraisal of the movements and argues for their contemporary relevance to the Islamic world: "The point here is that this effort by African 'ulamā' to establish working theocracies is original and significant for Universal Islam; that is to say the study of this movement has shown to be of use and relevance to understanding modern Islamic history in general" (Ross 1994: 27). An interesting case study is the trajectory of the movement that founded the Futa Jalon imamate (1725–1896). Led by *moridugu* and *zawiya* clerics, the movement, consisting of wealthy merchants and rich cattle owners, who funded it, and commoners (peasants, pastoralists, and casted artisans), established a hierarchical and bureaucratic political system ruled by a clerical faction (aristocracy of the book and pen) and a military faction (aristocracy of the sword and lance) under the leadership of an imam. The internal structure of each faction formed a hierarchy of ranked statuses. Power was both centralized (the military sphere) and dispersed (the clerical sphere).

The Futa Jalon internalized the structure of a militarized *fandugu* polity. The oligarchic ruling class adopted a political culture that combined militarism with scholarship. *Moridugu*s and *zawiya*s were incorporated into the administrative structure as semiautonomous institutional complexes. At the end of the eighteenth century the state had a standing army of fifteen thousand to twenty-five thousand, consisting of free and unfree horsemen who were employed in wars of territorial expansion throughout the history of the imamate. In the eighteenth century, war captives were either sold into Atlantic slaving or were put to work on the great landed estates. The hierarchical administrative system was based on meritocracy, that is, on educational achievement and military success on the battlefield. Koranic schools and institutions of higher learning were established through the state. By the end of the century more than 80 percent of the free commoner population was literate, primarily in local languages and not classical Arabic (a preserve of the upper classes), and a smaller percentage of servile status groups were also literate. There were different free status groups that had limited access to the political arena. Members of the ruling class owned landed estates based on the labor of slaves, serfs, and hereditary, endogamous artisan castes, all of whom were hierarchically ranked and were excluded from public and political affairs of the state. Peasants, on the other hand, ceased to exist as a distinct social class and status group associated with agriculture: the revolution transformed their conditions of existence. Estate production was intended for slave ships that traded at Futa Jalon ports and for Middle Niger and Saharan markets. The unfree population represented between 50 and 75 percent of the population in the 1790s (Barry 1992; Rodney 1970). The practices of the military-clerical aristocracy constructed various bounded social and political arenas where some people were admitted and others excluded. The trajectory of the Futa Jalon radical movement indicates that in its trans-regional interactions it succumbed to a wider process of centralization and militarization instigated by the *fandugu* political revolution.

Conclusion

The historical dynamics and social processes that distinguish the 1500–1800 time frame of western/Atlantic African history turn on four institutional complexes or institutions of power—the *fandugu*, the *markadugu*, the *moridugu*, and the *zawiya*—and their societal struggles, as configured in an urban-based political revolution, initiated by *fandugu*s, and a rural-based social revolution, led by *zawiya* clerics. The genealogy of each revolution is traceable to changes in the geopolitical and imperial sphere of the sixteenth-century Askiyate that opened a space for large-scale insurgencies of the servile classes (*zunuj*) who worked in the Caliphate's rice estates. The seventeenth and eighteenth centuries of the Askiyate can thus be interpreted as a clash between an urban-based political revolution and a rural-based social revolution, where each revolution sought to prevail and to realize its own millenarian imaginary.

References

Abitbol, Michel, ed./trans. 1982. *Tombouctou au milieu du XVIIIe siècle d'après la chronique de Mawlāy al-Qāsim B. Mawlāy Sulaymān.* Paris: G.-P. Maisonneuve et Larose.
———. 1979. *Tombouctou et les Arma. De la Conquête marocaine du Sudan nigérien en 1591 à l'hégémonie de l'Empire Peuhl du Macina en 1833.* Paris: G.-P. Maisonneuve et Larose.

Ade Ajayi J. F., and Michael Crowder, eds. 1985. *History of West Africa, I*, 3rd ed. Harlow: Longman Group Ltd.

Amselle, Jean-Loup. 1990. *Logique métisse: Anthropologie de l'identité en Afrique et ailleurs*. Paris: Payot.

Bah, Thierno Mouctar. 1985. *Architecture militaire traditionnelle et poliorcétique dans le Sudan Occidental*. Yaounde: Editions Cle.

Banaji, Jairus. 2013. "Putting Theory to Work, Historical Materialism." *Research in Crucial Marxist Theory* 21 (4): 129–143.

———. 2010. *Theory as History: Essays on Modes of Production and Exploitation*. Chicago: Haymarket Books.

Barry, B. 1992. "Senegambia from the Sixteenth to the Eighteenth Century: Evolution of the Wolof, Serer, and 'Tukuloor.' " In Ogot, *General History of Africa*.

Batran, A. A. 1974. "The Qadiriyya-Mukhtariyya Brotherhood in West Africa: The Concept of Tasawwuf in the Writings of Sidi al-Mukhtar al-Kunti (1729–1811)," *Transafrican Journal of History* 4: 1–2, 41–70.

Bazin, Jean 1988. "War and Servitude in Segu." *Economy and Society* 3 (2): 107–144.

Berendse, R. J. 2002. *The Arabian Seas: The Indian Ocean World of the Seventeenth Century*. Armonk, NY: M. E. Sharpe.

Blum, Charlotte, and Humphrey Fisher. 1993. "Love for Three Oranges, or, The Askiya's Dilemma: The Askiya. al-Maghīlī, and Timbuktu, c. 1500." *Journal of African History* 34 (1): 65–91.

Boulègue, Jean, and Jean Suret-Canale. 1985. "The Western Atlantic Coast." In Ade Ajayi and Crowder, *History of West Africa*, 503–530.

Braudel, Fernand. 2009. "History and the Social Sciences: The *Longue Durée*." *Review* XXXII (2): 171–203.

Cabral, Amilcar. 1969. *Revolution in Guinea: Selected Texts of Amilcar Cabral*. New York and London: Monthly Review Press, 91, 93–94.

Callinicos, Alex. 2005. *Making History. Agency, Structure, and Change in Social Theory*. Chicago: Haymarket Books.

Clarke, P. B. 1980. "Islamic Millenarianism in West Africa: A 'Revolutionary' Ideology?" *Religious Studies* 16 (3): 317–339.

Comaroff, Jean, and John Comaroff. 2012. *Theory from the South or, How Euro-America Is Evolving toward Africa*. London and New York: Routledge.

Conrad, David. 1990. *A State of Intrigue: The Epic of Bamana Segu*. Oxford: Oxford University Press.

Coquery-Vidrovitch, Catherine. 2012. "Rethinking Africa's Transcontinental Continuities." Unpublished paper presented at the international conference "Rethinking Africa's Transcontinental in Pre- and ProtoHistory," African Studies Center, Leiden, the

Netherlands, April 12–13, 2012, http://www.shikanda.net/Rethinking_history_conference/rethinki.htm.

Courlander, Harold, with Ousmane Sako. 1982. *The Heart of the Ngoni: Heroes of the African Kingdom of Segu.* Amherst: University of Massachusetts Press.

Darling, Patrick. 1998. "Aerial Archaeology in Africa: The Challenge of a Continent." *Aerial Archaeology Research Group Newsletter* 17: 9–18.

Diagne, P. 1992. "African Political, Economic, and Social Structures during the Period." In Ogot, *General History of Africa,* 23–45.

Dramani-Issifou, Zakari. 1982. *L'Afrique noire dans les relations internationales au XIVe siècle.* Paris: Karthala.

Goody, Jack, ed. 1968. *Literacy in Traditional Societies.* Cambridge: Cambridge University Press.

Hodgkin, Thomas. 1980. "The Revolutionary Tradition in Islam." *History Workshop* 10: 138–149.

———. 1976a. "The Radical Tradition in Muslim West Africa." In *Essays on Islamic Civilization: Presented to Niyazi Berkes,* edited by Donald Presgrave Little, 103–117. Leiden: Brill.

———. 1976b, "Scholars and the Revolutionary Tradition: Vietnam and West Africa." *Oxford Review of Education* 2 (2): 111–128.

Howard, Allen M., and Richard Matthew Shain, eds. 2005. *The Spatial Factor in African History: The Relationship of the Social, Material, and Perceptual.* Leiden: Brill.

Hunwick, John O., ed./trans. 1999. *Timbuktu and the Songhai Empire. Al-Sa'di's Ta' rīkh al-sūdān down to 1613 and other Contemporary Documents.* Leiden: Brill.

———. 1985. "Songhay, Borno, and the Hausa States, 1450–1600." In Ade Ajayi and Crowder, *History of West Africa,* 323–371.

Idahosa, Pablo L. E., and Bob Shenton. 2004. "The Africanist's 'New' Clothes." *Historical Materialism: Research in Critical Marxist Theory* 12 (4): 67–113.

Iliffe, John. 2005. *Honor in African History.* Cambridge: Cambridge University Press.

Inikori, Joseph E. 2007. "Africa and the Globalization Process: Western Africa, 1450–1850." *Journal of Global History* 2: 63–86.

———. 1992. "Africa in World History: The Export Slave Trade from Africa and the Emergence of the Atlantic Economic Order." In Ogot, *General History of Africa,* 74–112.

Jansen, Jan. 2015. "In Defense of Mali's Gold: The Political and Military Organization of the Northern Upper Niger, c. 1650–c. 1850." *Journal of West African History* 1 (1): 1–36.

Kane, Ousmane. 2003. *Intellectuels Non-Europhones.* Dakar: CODESRIA.

Karatani, Kojin. 2014. *The Structure of World History. From Modes of Production to Modes of Exchange.* Translated by Michael K. Bourdaghs. Durham, NC and London: Duke University Press.

Kea, Ray A. 2015. "Africa in World History, 1400 to 1800." In *The Cambridge World History Vol. VI: The Construction of a Global World, 1400–1800 CE*, 2 Parts, edited by Jerry H. Bentley, Sanjay Subrahmanyam, and Merry Q. E. Wiesner-Hanks, 243–268. Cambridge: Cambridge University Press.

———. 2012a. "The Local and the Global: Historiographical Reflections on West Africa in the Atlantic Age." In Monroe and Ogundiran, *Power and Landscape*, 339–375.

———. 2012b. "Intellectual Life and Scholarship in the Islamic Western Sudan during the Seventeenth and Eighteenth Centuries: A Political and Social View." In *Reclaiming the Human Sciences and Humanities through African Perspectives*, 2 vols., edited by Helen Lauer and Kofi Anyidoho, 726–745. Legon, Accra: Sub-Saharan Publishers.

———. 2012c. *A Cultural and Social History of Ghana from the Seventeenth to the Nineteenth Century. The Gold Coast in the Age of Trans-Atlantic Trade*, 2 vols. Lewiston, PA: The Edwin Mellen Press.

———. 2003. "Science, Technology, and Learning: Eighteenth Century Moliyili (Dagomba) and the Timbuktu Intellectual Tradition." In *History and Philosophy of Science for African Undergraduates*, edited by Helen Lauer, 238–270. Ibadan: Hope Publishers.

Keita, Maghan. 2002. "Africa and the Constructions of a Grand Narrative in World History." In *Across Cultural Borders: Historiography in Global Perspective*, edited by Eckhardt Fuchs and Benedikt Stuchey, 285–308. Lanham, MD: Rowman & Littlefield Publishers.

Kubbel, L. E. 1969. "On the History of Social Relations in the West Sudan in the 8th to the 16th Centuries." In *Africa in Soviet Studies 1968 Annual*, 109–128. Moscow: Nauka Publishing House.

Levtzion, Nehemia. 2000. "Islam in the Bilad al-Sudan to 1800." In Levtzion and Pouwels, *The History of Islam in Africa*, 63–91.

Levtzion, Nehemia, and Randall L. Pouwels, eds. 2000. *The History of Islam in Africa*. Athens, Oxford, and Cape Town: Ohio University Press, James Curry, and David Philip.

Levtzion, Nehemia. 1987a. "Rural and Urban Islam in West Africa: An Introductory Essay." In Levtzion and Fisher, 1–20.

———. 1987b. "Merchants vs. Scholars and Clerics in West Africa: Differential and Complementary Roles." In Levtzion and Fisher, *Rural and Urban Islam in West Africa*, 21–38.

———. 1987c. "The Eighteenth Century. Background to the Islamic Revolutions in West Africa." In Levtzion and Voll, *Eighteenth-Century Renewal and Reform in Islam*, 21–38.

Levtzion, Nehemia, and Humphrey J. Fisher, eds. 1987. *Rural and Urban Islam in West Africa*. Boulder and London: Lynne Rienner Publishers.

Levtzion, Nehemia, and John O. Voll, eds. 1987. *Eighteenth-Century Renewal and Reform in Islam*. Syracuse, NY: Syracuse University Press.

Mabogunje, Akin L., and Paul Richards. 1985. "Land and People—Models of Spatial and Ecological Processes in West African History." In Ade Ajayi and Crowder, *History of West Africa*, 5–47.

MacDonald, Kevin. 2012. "The Least of Their Inhabited Villages Are Fortified." *Azania: Archaeological Research in Africa* 47 (3): 343–364.

Manji, Firoze, and Bill Fletcher, Jr., eds. 2013. *Claim No Easy Victories. The Legacy of Amilcar Cabral.* Dakar: CODESRIA and Daraja Press.

McDougall, E. Ann. 1987. "The Economics of Islam in the Southern Sahara: The Rise of the Kunta Clan." In Levtzion and Fisher, *Rural and Urban Islam in West Africa*, 39–54.

Meillassoux, Claude. 1997. "The Slave Trade and Development." *Diogenes* 45 (3): 21–29.

———. 1991. *The Anthropology of Slavery. The Womb of Iron and Gold.* Translated by Alice Dasnois. Chicago: University of Chicago Press.

———, ed. 1975. *L'esclavage en Afrique pré-coloniale.* Paris: Maspero.

———, ed. 1971. *The Development of Indigenous Trade and Markets in West Africa.* London: Oxford University Press.

Monroe, J. Cameron, and Akinwumi Ogundiran, eds. 2012. *Power and Landscape in Atlantic West Africa: Archaeological Perspectives.* Cambridge and New York: Cambridge University Press.

O'Callaghan, Marion.1995. "Continuities in Imagination." In *The Decolonization of the Imagination: Culture, Power, and Knowledge*, edited by Jan Nederveen Pieterse and Bhikhu C. Parekh, 22–42. London/New York: Zed Books.

Ogot, B. A., ed. 1992. *General History of Africa vol. 5: Africa from the Sixteenth to the Eighteenth Century.* Berkeley: University of California Press.

Paré, Moussa. 2014. "L'économie rurale dans le Bilad al-Sudan occidentale XVe-XVIe siècle." *Études Rurales* 193: 95–106.

Roberts, Richard. 1987. *Warriors, Merchants, and Slaves: The State and the Economy in the Middle Niger Valley, 1700–1914.* Stanford, CA: Stanford University Press.

Robinson, David. 2000. "Revolutions in the Western Sudan." In Levtzion and Pouwels, *The History of Islam in Africa*, 131–152.

Rodney, Walter. 1970. *A History of the Upper Guinea Coast 1545–1800.* Oxford: The Clarendon Press.

Ross, Eric. 1994. "Africa in Islam: What the Afrocentric Perspective Can Contribute to the Study of Islam." *International Journal of Islamic and Arabic Studies* 11 (2): 1–36.

Saad, Elias N. 1983. *Social History of Timbuktu. The Role of Muslim Scholars and Notables 1400–1900.* Cambridge: Cambridge University Press.

Sangaré, Souleymane. 2013. "Les Tentatives de Déstabilzation des pouvirs Politiques en Afrique: Le Cas de l'Empire Songhaï au XVIe Siècle." *Perspectives Philosophiques* 111 (5): 220–238.

Sanneh, Lamin. 1981a. "Futa Jallon and the Jakhanke Clerical Tradition. Part I: The Historical Setting." *Journal of Religion in Africa* XII (1): 38–64.

———. 1981b. "Futa Jallon and the Jakhanke Clerical Tradition. Part II: Karamokho Ba of Touba in Guinea." *Journal of Religion in Africa* XII (2): 105–126.

————. 1976a. "The Origins of Clericalism in West African Islam." *The Journal of African History* 17 (1): 49–72.

————. 1976b. "Slavery, Islam, and the Jakhanke of West Africa." *Africa: Journal of the International African Institute* 46 (1): 80–97.

Subrahmanyam, Sanjay. 1999. "Connected Histories: Notes Towards a Reconfiguration of Early Modern Eurasia." In *Beyond Binary Histories: Re-Imagining Eurasia to c. 1830*, edited by Victor Lieberman. Ann Arbor: University of Michigan Press.

Tymowski, Michal. 2005. "Le territoires et les frontières du Songhaï à la fin du XVe et au XVIe siècle. Le problème du centre et des territoires périphériques d'un grand état de l'Afrique occidentale." In *Des frontières en Afrique du XIIe au XXe siècle*, 213–237. Bamako: UNESCO.

————. 2004. "Treasury Systems, Types of Territorial Control, Reciprocity, and Exploitation Limits in an African Pre-Colonial State: The Case of Songhai in the Late 15th–16th Century." *Hemispheres: Studies on Cultures and Societies* 19: 165–180.

————. 1974. *Le développement et régression chez les peuples de la boucle du Niger à l'époque précoloniale.* Warsaw: Warsaw University.

————. 1967. "Le Niger, voie de communication des grands états du Sudan Occidentale jusqu'à la fin du XVIe siècle." *Africana Bulletin* 6: 73–95.

Vali, Abbas. 1993. *Pre-Capitalist Iran: A Theoretical History.* New York: New York University Press.

Viti, Fabio F. 2001. "Al centro della periferia. La relazione centro-periferia negli stati dell'Africa." *Recherché di storia politica* 2: 203–214.

Wallace, David. 2006. *Premodern Places: Calais to Surinam, Chaucer to Aphra Behn.* Malden and Oxford: Blackwell Publishing.

Wilks, Ivor. 2000. "The Juula and the Expansion of Islam into the Forest." In Levtzion and Pouwels, *The History of Islam in Africa*, 93–115.

Wilks, Ivor. 1968. "The Transmission of Islamic Learning in the Western Sudan." In *Technology, Tradition, and the State in Africa*, edited by Jack Goody, 161–197. Oxford: Oxford University Press, 1971.

Willis, John Ralph. 1985. "The Western Sudan from the Moroccan Invasion (1591) to the Death of Al-Mukhtar Al-Kunti (1811)." In Ade Ajayi and Crowder, *History of West Africa*, 531–576.

Wise, Christopher, and Haka Abu Taleb, ed./trans. 2011. *Ta'rīkh al-fattāsh. The Timbuktu Chronicles 1493–1599.* Trenton, NJ: Africa World Press.

Zahan, Dominique. 1950. "Pictographic Writing in the Western Sudan." *Man* 50: 136–138.

2

Making Development
through Rural Initiative "Unthinkable"

Tanzania in the Time of *Ujamaa*

James Giblin

Introduction

One of the largest and best-known development initiatives in early postcolonial Africa was *ujamaa* villagization in Tanzania. During the late 1960s and
1970s, the government of Julius Nyerere attempted to resettle nearly the entire
rural population of Tanzania, which then made up perhaps 90 percent of the
national population, in new villages. In part the concerns behind this movement
were practical: Nyerere's government believed that concentrating scattered villagers into larger settlements would facilitate provisions for schooling, medical care,
and roads. Yet the impetus behind *ujamaa* was also aspirational: Nyerere hoped
to create a socialist society where rural people would raise their productivity and
improve their living standards by participating in communal farming.

When I first went to Tanzania in the early 1980s, I read a great deal of the
scholarly writing on villagization. Tanzania's aspirations and socialist inclination
attracted many scholars during the 1960s and 1970s, and the literature, at least by
the standards of African studies, was vast. At that time I did not intend to study
ujamaa, but I did want to gain some sense of current-day rural life in preparation
for doing historical research in the countryside on earlier periods. Indeed, I lived
in one of the villages that had been founded in the 1970s and watched *ujamaa*
in its death throes. Having meanwhile done much research on rural Tanzania

during the colonial period (present-day Tanzania became a German colony in the late 1880s, and after the First World War was a League of Nations Mandate and United Nations Trust Territory under British administration before gaining national independence in 1961), a few years ago I reread the *ujamaa* literature. What shocked me was its apparent ignorance of the decade or two immediately preceding the *ujamaa* period. Rereading *ujamaa* with much greater appreciation in particular for rural Tanganyika in the 1950s, I now saw, as I had not when I first read about *ujamaa*, that contemporary writing about *ujamaa* took no notice of the immediate past. Whether they were scholars or government officers, Westerners or Tanzanians, virtually all who wrote about villagization during the *ujamaa* period ignored the rural past.

The following pages suggest that this erasure of the past was a fundamental tendency within the *ujamaa* project. I begin by discussing contemporary commentary about *ujamaa* villagization written by scholars, Tanzanian government officials, and international development experts. Its dominant concerns, categories, and criteria of development, a reading of this literature shows, reflected neither awareness of nor curiosity about the rural past. I then briefly describe the past that was ignored, emphasizing that efforts to achieve material and social improvement were widespread across rural Tanganyika during the 1950s. I close by describing the consequence of ignoring the past: the frustration that erupted when government officials encountered the villagers. Among the villagers, individual and community identity were inseparable from memory. Their memories reflected the continuities of long-established cultures and their experience of oppression and upheaval during the colonial period. Guided by the lessons of their own experience, rural communities often rejected *ujamaa* villagization and other forms of resettlement proposed by a state authority that misunderstood their priorities and aspirations. By contrast, the bureaucrats, woefully ignorant of both the recent past as well as deeper history, understood resistance to their well-intentioned policies as the products of irrationality, ignorance, and indolence.

How should this separation of Tanzania's rural population from its past be understood? Certainly it bears comparison with omissions and silences that historians find in historical narratives. One of them, Michel-Rolph Trouillot, has written powerfully about the function of silences within historical accounts, arguing that the effectiveness of narrative depends as much on its silences as its content. Indeed, the "facts" used to construct narratives, he suggests, inevitably create silences. Historical "facts," he argues, are fashioned from surviving "traces," which can never reveal the past in its full complexity. "The production of traces," he says, "is always also the creation of silences. Some occurrences are noted from the start; others are not. . . . [Surviving] traces . . . limit the range and significance of any historical narrative" (Trouillot 1995: 29).

While Trouillot's view that the complexity of the past can never be captured fully by any narrative will surprise few historians (as he puts it, "historical process" has "autonomy" from narrative (Trouillot 1995: 13), one of his examples of the production of narrative silence is particularly useful for thinking about the relationship between *ujamaa* and the deeper rural past. This is the example of the Haitian Revolution. He argues that its causes and course, including most crucially the centrality of the agency of Haiti's enslaved within the revolution, were entirely misunderstood by both contemporary observers and later historians. It was misunderstood, he believes, because it was "unthinkable." So deeply unthinkable was the Haitian Revolution, says Trouillot, that even eyewitnesses denied its sweeping and transformative nature, believing instead that they were witnessing disconnected acts of violence. But why "unthinkable"? Trouillot suggests that a matrix of "ontological and political assumptions" blinded observers to the true character of revolution (Trouillot 1995: 82). These assumptions, he elaborates, encompassed scientific racism and confidence in Western cultural superiority among other influences. Together they created a worldview—one shared, says Trouillot crucially, by observers who might otherwise be separated by quite different political viewpoints (Trouillot 1995: 99)—that left no space for the possibility that enslaved Africans might possess the ambition, the dreams, the thirst for liberty and the capacity for planning and tactical brilliance that made revolution possible. Indeed, Trouillot pushes the argument further to suggest that, at least until events had proceeded far enough to make the transformative nature of their struggle undeniable, even the enslaved of Haiti found the prospect of overthrowing slavery unthinkable.

Trouillot's conception of ontological blindness as cause of omission or silence within historical narrative offers a useful point of comparison for historians of Tanzanian *ujamaa*. If a revolution of the enslaved was "unthinkable" in Haiti, so too in Tanzania by the mid-1960s was the possibility of rural development without the state. Of course, the assumptions on which state-led development strategies were founded in the 1960s were by no means as powerful, pervasive, or deeply rooted as the ideas of racial and cultural difference that made a revolution of the Haitian enslaved unthinkable. Yet, they did shape observers' perceptions of the rural Tanzanians. Among them was the view of development that prevailed during the *ujamaa* period as a process that must be organized by a state; another was the view that rural poverty, premodern cultures, and lack of education meant that agrarian communities had no prospect of achieving development without the guidance of the state. The same assumptions about racial and cultural difference that for Trouillot are crucial in Haiti's narratives of revolution were also shared by bureaucrats and scholars whose political sympathies might otherwise extend in quite different directions.

By the mid-1960s in Tanzania, state management had become not only essential to bureaucratic imagining of what effective rural development might look like, but was also becoming a pervasive fact on the ground throughout the nation's rural regions. Indeed, this is the great insight found in the treatment of *ujamaa* villagization by sociologist James C. Scott. Although he might have overshot the mark in exaggerating the importance of a high-modernist aesthetic in the villages, his observation that the "thinly veiled subtext of villagization was . . . to reorganize human communities in order to make them better objects of political control" was on target (Scott 1998: 224). Indeed, the body of reportage from the villages discussed in the following pages was largely a product of vastly expanded state surveillance of the countryside after Independence. Any historian who has read both the archive of the colonial state and records of rural administration in the 1960s and 1970s can have no doubt the density of observation in the villages by government officials as well as scholars, with its expanded ability to count cultivated acreage, estimate the size of harvests, and know the population of villages, went far beyond the capability of the colonial state. Thus not only ontological assumptions but also the daily practices of bureaucratic state management contributed to reinforcing a dominant image of "development" that made the state appear essential while also disqualifying as an example of true "development" the informal local initiative that prevailed in the 1950s. Rural Tanzania's experience in the last colonial decade now appeared irrelevant to the challenges of the comprehensive development proposed by the *ujamaa* state. In this way, development as both ideological construct and state practice distanced the very generation of farmers who settled the *ujamaa* villages from their own prior experience of informal agrarian improvement. Thus like Trouillot's narrative "facts" they imposed silence on the past. Yet perhaps because this silence was maintained through the day-to-day interventions in rural communities of government officers who could be questioned, engaged in debate, and defied, silence about the past in *ujamaa* Tanzania was porous. Sometimes, villagers broke it and spoke back to the state. The final paragraphs later describe such an instance, when frustration developed when villages spoke from their experience to officials who denied its relevance.

Defining a Narrative of State-Led Development

Indicative of the scale of contemporary scholarship on *ujamaa* villagization was a bibliography on villagization compiled in the early 1980s. It included more than four hundred items (McHenry 1981). It is no exaggeration to say that a whole generation of Tanzanian intellectuals (including the nation's president from 2005 to 2015, Jakaya Kikwete) devoted the 1970s to this issue. Studies of villagization ranged from very broad questions about the nature of development to highly specific issues of agronomic technique. Although scholars and government officials approached *ujamaa* villages with a variety of interests, however, all shared the fundamental assumption that development could not succeed without deep state intervention into agrarian society.

Among the big issues addressed in the *ujamaa* literature were class exploitation, macroeconomic performance, and financial dependence. While some authors argued that villagization would benefit rural communities by decreasing the exploitation of farmers (for example, Cliffe 1971 and Raikes 1975), others asked whether villagization was the cause of Tanzania's declining agricultural production in the 1970s (Briggs 1979; Samoff 1981; Kjaerby 1989) and asserted that villagization had only increased Tanzania's financial dependence upon Western creditors and donors (Lofchie 1989). By contrast, a wealth of literature considered important but much narrower questions, such as planning new communities (Jayarajan 1963; Raikes 1972), irrigation (Berry and Kates 1970), mechanization of agriculture (Msambichaka 1975), the effectiveness of extension services (De Vries 1976, 1978), and the provision of credit to villages (Due 1977, 1980).

If any single phrase from this wide-ranging scholarly literature captured its outlook, it was "Socialism from Above," the title of an important 1977 publication (Boesen, Madsen, and Moody 1977). Contemporary scholarship on *ujamaa*, like some recent work, focused primarily upon the formation and implementation of this state policy. This state-centered orientation can be seen in the range of literature, which, despite considerable variations in viewpoint, has attempted to explain the motivations and circumstances that led the government of Tanzania to adopt the policy of *ujamaa* villagization. Scholars considered how *ujamaa* reflected the state's concern with achieving economic and social development (McHenry 1979), and in different ways argued that villagization was a means of controlling (or "capturing": Hyden 1980) or monitoring (Scott 1998) rural society. Another recent book on the period also studies state policy and bureaucracy (Schneider 2014).

Yet, a state-centered approach did not spare the Tanzanian government from criticism over its management of rural development. Numerous scholars understood *ujamaa* as a policy imposed by government upon an indifferent, if not hostile, rural population. Where they disagreed was over the question of whether this bitter medicine was necessary for rural people in the long term. One also finds a willingness to criticize the state in publications that examined relations between villagers and government officers. Frequently scholars portrayed such relationships as problematic and as a hindrance to the implementation of villagization (Ingle 1972; Van Velzen 1973; Fortmann 1980). One study of this kind that lent exceptional insight, was S. S. Mushi's "*Ujamaa* Planning and the Politics of Allocation: The Case of Morogoro District" (1976). Yet, even this analysis of the political relationship between government and *ujamaa* villages shared with other studies the tendency to say relatively little about the villages themselves, and to portray villagers as being rather passive in their interaction with politicians and government officers. Although some of the most trenchant studies of villagization asked searching questions about the practical impact of villagization on rural environments and modes of land tenure, they, too, were framed as critiques of state policy. One particularly important essay considered villagization in relation to local ecology, settlement patterns, and farming systems, but marshaled this information in order to criticize government failure to understand these aspects of rural life (Kjekshus 1977). Another incisive essay considered the question of land in relation to *ujamaa*, but again shaped its argument around criticism of government policy (Shao 1986). Yet, while commentators frequently found that the government mishandled rural resettlement and development, no one suggested that the development ought to be left to the initiative of the villagers.

There was nevertheless an important stream of contemporary scholarship—most of it done by younger Tanzanian scholars—that described conditions in the new villages in detail. Scholars at the University of Dar es Salaam and other Tanzanian institutions took the lead in creating an impressive body of case studies of *ujamaa* in particular regions and villages (for example, Gunza 1971; Kahurananga 1976; Kasoga 1990; Kauzeni 1979; Kauzeni, Shishira, and Mung'ong'o 1988; Lyimo 1975; Moody 1972; Tendwa 1979). These studies remain an important resource for further investigation into *ujamaa*. Nevertheless, neither these case studies nor important reports from *ujamaa* villages found in Tanzanian publications from the University of Dar es Salaam (*Taamuli*) and Kivukoni College (*Mwenge, Mbioni,* and *Ujamaa; Gazeti la Wajenga Taifa*) were successful in placing villagization in the context of the earlier historical development of rural communities.

The lack of historical perspective was reflected in the vocabulary used in *ujamaa* studies. Indeed, in an important way the descriptive terms applied to agrarian peoples during the *ujamaa* period resembled the historical "facts" described by Michel-Rolph Trouillot, for both generated silence and omission of critical aspects of the past. Naturally, in a period of intense nationalism when scholars as well as government officers understood themselves to be engaged in *kujenga taifa*, or "nation building," contemporary observers avoided the colonial tendency to refer to villagers by their ethnicity or as "tribesmen." Alternatives that referred to specificity of occupation or environment, some of which were familiar to villagers themselves, were of course available. Nevertheless, contemporary studies of *ujamaa* overwhelmingly settled on "peasant" when referring to villagers in general, while using terms such as "kulak" or, in Kiswahili, *makabaila* (feudal nobles) and *wabepari* (capitalists) when describing the village opponents of villagization. These terms betrayed a latitudinal, rather than longitudinal, bias. They were intended to situate rural Tanzania not merely in the broad context of comparative agrarian development, but to place them within a global class struggle whose universal dimension was often taken for granted in the 1970s. What they did not do, by contrast, was to place agrarian societies in deep streams of historical experience. Indeed, they often served to imply that history was much less useful than class-based comparison for understanding the rural societies of the Global South.

The terminology used in *ujamaa* studies not only lacked a historical perspective, but also generated lack of curiosity about specific conditions and vital differences within rural society. Few studies discussed varieties of environmental conditions within particular regions or the differences of gender, generation, wealth, and status that shaped rural social relationships. As the historian Michael Sheridan has pointed out, most studies of *ujamaa* described "abstract entities and homogeneous groups such as the state, market, peasantry and bureaucracy instead of examining the diverse experiences and strategies of rural Tanzanians as they coped with increasing state intervention" (Sheridan 2004: 92). Here again, the term "peasant," reflected a tendency toward abstraction and homogenization. The meaning readers were invited to draw from this term was that rural people occupied a subordinate and exploited position comparable to that, perhaps, of prerevolutionary Russian or Chinese peasants. Placing stress on the character of the rural population, which made it comparable to the rural societies of other nations, diverted scholars' attention not only from history, but also from both differentiation *within* villages as well as specific ecological, social, and economic circumstances shaping village life in Tanzania.

The tendencies toward both homogenization of rural society and emphasis upon the role of government are found in even the best studies of villagization, including Michaela Von Freyhold's *Ujamaa Villages in Tanzania: Analysis of a Social Experiment* (1979). This was a study of villagization in Handeni, a district in Tanzania's northeast. Like other scholars of the 1970s, Von Freyhold took a markedly state-centered approach. The reason why socialism did not take root in the villages, she argued, was because the government failed to support the poorer and middle-level villagers against the "kulaks" who opposed *ujamaa*. As with so much of the *ujamaa* literature, *Ujamaa Villages in Tanzania* was more a story about the Tanzanian state than about rural communities.

Among Von Freyhold's insights was the point that "petty capitalist tendencies" "dominated" among the villagers of Handeni. Like the analytical technique of opposing "kulaks" against poorer villagers, however, here again the choice of terminology sacrificed specificity and history. Her insight lay in the realization that business and cash-crop farming were extremely important to the people of Handeni. However, her use of terms that were so characteristic of the 1970s obscured the fact that, in a drought-prone district such as Handeni, these activities were rooted in historical experience. They had long represented ways of accumulating resources in anticipation of future drought and crop failure, and also of avoiding unrewarding employment during the colonial period on nearby sisal estates. Moreover, using the term "kulak" in reference to the villagers who were the most successful accumulators both overlooked their vulnerability to abrupt reversals of fortune, and also simplified their relationships with fellow villagers, who included their family members as well as neighbors. Indeed, like almost all studies of resettlement in *ujamaa* Tanzania, *Ujamaa Villages in Tanzania* failed to recognize the social and moral significance of kinship. For example, the book misunderstood the refusal of villagers to move into new settlements located on land that was recognized as the possession of particular clans. Von Freyhold understood villagers invoked such arguments as an expedient way of fending off government pressure to relocate. While such considerations were quite likely in the minds of defiant villagers, what

Ujamaa Villages did not recognize was that recognition of clan rights in land was the foundation of complex reciprocal obligations that influenced a great variety of social activities, from the choice of marital partners to the ways in which villagers organized cooperative labor parties for farming and construction of houses.

Omission of the past occurred not only in the writing of scholars, but also in accounts by villagers who participated in resettlement. One example comes from the early period of resettlement. Although the settlement of rural populations in socialist villages became government policy following President Nyerere's Arusha Declaration of early 1967, which set Tanzania on the path toward socialism, socialist villagization was preceded by earlier forms of resettlement. Indeed, even in the colonial period extensive compulsory resettlement had been undertaken by British colonial officials as a form of disease control. Immediately after Independence and before the turn to socialism, however, new forms of resettlement emerged. One of them was initiated by the Nyerere government. Called "settlement schemes," these projects were constructed around production of export crops, and relied on substantial investment and close supervision by government. I discuss one of these schemes later. In addition, spontaneous initiatives by villagers themselves appeared in many places. They were often organized by landless young people and sometimes attracted limited support from government. The best known of these spontaneous projects was the Ruvuma Development Association (RDA) in the southwestern region of Ruvuma. The RDA was established in 1960 by about a dozen young men, and by 1969 had expanded into a network of seventeen small villages. As a recent study has argued, the RDA seems to have served Nyerere as a model of how low-cost villagization might work. Nevertheless, the RDA was unpopular with some government officials, perhaps because they found its youthful leaders lacking in deference, and was disbanded by the government in 1969 (Schneider 2014).

Among the RDA organizers were Ntimanjayo Millinga, a local activist in the ruling party, and Ralph Ibbott, a British national who was running an agricultural development scheme in southern Rhodesia when he first came into contact with Millinga and the RDA in 1961. He and his family settled in the largest RDA village in 1963. Much has been written about the RDA, Millinga, and Ibbott, but here I wish only to touch upon their historical perspective on the villagers whom they were organizing. In 1964 they wrote, "[The villagers are] used to spending most of the winter [that is, the dry season] doing very little [and] had to be encouraged to work [in clearing land] . . . as a first step in trying to achieve an object which most of them hardly understood . . . people's hopes are not really very high. They have very little confidence within themselves that they can succeed. This confidence has to be supplied by the leaders and the leaders themselves have to be given the confidence. It is for these sort of reasons that development with a *peasant people* is so much more than making plans and finding the necessary finances" (Milinga and Ibbott 1964; my italics). A year later they provided a more pessimistic assessment: "People cannot live and work together without a certain basic morality and honesty which is not evident in a *broken society* as exists now." They described themselves as battling "against lethargy and lack of any feeling in most people that they themselves can do anything to change their state. . . ." (Milinga and Ibbott 1965a; my italics). In 1965 they again described the society in which they worked as one where "real villages *have broken up*, and each man with his wife, or wives, is on his own" (Milinga and Ibbott 1965b; my italics). They returned to this theme when they made a presentation about their work in Dar es Salaam: "The old customary close villages that used to exist have split up with changing conditions . . . old customs [regarding birth and marriage, for example] . . . have become largely meaningless, giving only a pretense of social life" (Ruvuma Development Association 1966a). Not all of the many government officers and development experts who visited RDA villages shared these attitudes. Indeed, one administrator remarked on the villagers' "tremendous confidence in themselves" (Kivukoni College File K\S.30\2, R.G.I. Kiambo). On one occasion, however, a consultant in agricultural development who was attending a village celebration was overheard ". . . whispering to Ralph that singing was all these chaps could do, they could not get down to hard work" (Ruvuma Development Association 1966b).

What Was Missing from the State-Centered Narrative of *Ujamaa* Development

The RDA leaders who expressed these views were highly sympathetic to the villagers, whose initiative, capacity for organization, and industry they often praised. Moreover, they were fiercely opposed to government interference and could be scathingly critical of bureaucrats and development consultants, whether Tanzanian or European. Yet, their words betrayed an attitude about the past that was shared by many of the experts. Their view of Ruvuma as a "broken society" conveyed an idea about history, but it was an imagined idea. They believed that colonialism had destroyed social cohesion and solidarity. So commonsensical did such an idea seem in the early years of national independence that they felt no need to elaborate on how this might have happened.

Ruvuma in fact suffered grievously under colonial rule. It was devastated during 1905–07 in the course of the great rebellion against German rule called Maji. When after the First World War a huge territory located immediately to the east was demarcated as a game reserve where settlement and travel were forbidden, Ruvuma was cut off from the Indian Ocean ports that had served as its precolonial trade outlets. Ruvuma then became a source of migrant labor for distant, European-owned sisal plantations in Tanzania's northeast. In speaking of the decline of social solidarity, it is likely that Millinga and Ibbott had in mind the impact of labor migration, which caused long absences from home for many men and a good many women as well.

Yet, as I learned when I studied the adjoining district of Njombe, which also became a reserve of migrant labor, the reality of labor migration was more complex. While the economy of labor migration imposed severe hardship, the mostly youthful laborers transformed it into a way of learning about the colonial economy. When they returned from terms of labor in distant Tanga, they brought with them unfamiliar consumer goods and also knowledge—knowledge of the transport infrastructure, of new crops (migrant laborers often returned with cuttings and seeds), of cities and urban life, and, most crucially, of markets and the opportunities that they offered. As a result, as men and women became tired of the itinerant life, they returned home to market farming. Others found opportunity in the migrant labor economy, opening eateries and guesthouses for traveling workers. Having experienced for themselves the difficulties created by lack of literacy while traveling and living in towns, often they became committed to educating their children. Relations among family, friends, and neighbors not only remained robust, but provided the chief means of organizing entrepreneurial activities (Giblin 2005).

This was the dynamic rural history that was effaced by the view—no matter how sympathetically it was expressed—that colonialism had "broken" village society. The results of such dynamism were impressive, and they show that Tanzania's nationalist movement was more a consequence of rising expectations than of immiseration. Colonial Tanganyika's population was overwhelmingly agrarian: more than 90 percent of its African population worked in agriculture in 1961. During the decade before Independence, its farmers increased production of market crops by 90 percent, and "subsistence" crops (food crops that could be sold as well as consumed by producers) by 20 to 25 percent. This increase occurred despite either lack of investment in food production or improvement in yields. Production increased because rural communities were flexible and adaptable in organizing farm labor, particularly by relying on networks of kinship. Thus they were able to seize market opportunities by putting more land under cultivation. One sign of growth in the agrarian economy was the expansion of cooperatives. In 1961, the World Bank commented that the "cooperative movement has been a leading factor in agricultural development, handling one-third of exports, particularly cotton and coffee. Some 330,000 Tanganyikans belong to the producer cooperatives, which are now federated in a National Union. The cooperatives have encouraged cash crop production and have sought by negotiation and by the operation of processing facilities to increase the net return to the African farmer. They have also provided community and education facilities." As farm incomes rose, so too consumer consumption increased between 1954 and 1961 by 36 percent. Similar growth occurred in education, with primary school enrollment doubling in the same period. It is true that state of education remained one of the major indictments of British administration, for schools were few and African pupils were confined overwhelmingly to the lower primary grades. Nevertheless, parents and pupils increasingly took advantage of the scarce opportunities available to them (World Bank 1962: 12).

A Past Ignored Creates Frustration

I have pointed out that the nationwide campaign of *ujamaa* villagization was preceded in the early and mid-1960s by early forms of resettlement. Some, such as the RDA in Ruvuma, were the initiative of villagers. Others—the so-called "settlement schemes"—were established by government in cooperation with private investors or multilateral lenders. One of the settlement schemes was a sisal-producing project located at Kabuku in the northeastern district of Handeni. The Kabuku scheme is well documented, and provides a vivid example of what happens when the past is ignored or forgotten.

Kabuku was the largest of about twenty-five settlement schemes established from 1963 to 1965. It was part of a novel attempt by the Nyerere government to enter into a partnership with private business to stimulate rural development while simultaneously rescuing a failing industry. Kabuku was expected to produce sisal, the fiber used in manufacturing gunnysacks, rope, and other products. The settlement benefited from extensive credit and material assistance provided by a sisal-producing firm, Amboni Estates, one of the largest operators of sisal plantations in Tanzania. Amboni's chief goal was to ensure the profitability of a nearby processing factory by increasing supplies of raw sisal leaf. About half of the funds to establish Kabuku were provided by a loan from Amboni (Tanzania, Ministry of Land, Settlement and Water Development, Survey Division 1966).

Amboni sought to maintain close supervision of the production process. By providing tractors for clearing and plowing the sisal fields, Amboni agreed to prepare one hectare of sisal land for each settler per year for the first ten years of operation. Thus each settler family would eventually control ten hectares of sisal, together with an additional plot for a house and garden (settlers were obliged to construct their own houses). Planners expected that the settlers would retire their debts to Amboni after thirteen years and to the government after twenty-five years. At that point, they were to be provided freehold title to their sisal fields and homestead plots. The price for company assistance, however, was that Amboni employees frequently inspected the sisal fields. Their inspections and ceaseless criticism of the settlers' work ethic would become a major source of discontent among settlers.

The first task of administrators was recruiting settlers. Recruiting began in late 1964, the first settlers began arriving early in 1965, and by November of that year recruiters had reached their target of 250 households (Nellis 1965b). Recruiters focused on highland areas of northern Tanzania where they expected that land shortages would inspire interest in Kabuku among young men. When they began recruiting in the nearby Usambara Mountains, they encountered a range of concerns, all of which were rooted in the historical experience of Usambara's people. The failure of scheme administrators to heed their concerns resulted in simmering discontent and finally violence.

Recruiters in Usambara learned that prospective settlers juggled three aspirations, all of which grew out of the experience of the post–Second World War colonial period that I have described earlier. Villagers in Usambara who considered joining Kabuku were interested in a government scheme that offered access to schools, clinics, and most importantly, land (Feierman 1985: 129), but also wished to form independent households (Fleuret 1980) while remaining connected to their support networks of kin. Recruiters found land shortage to be the chief factor pushing prospective settlers in Usambara toward Kabuku (Interviews at Kabuku 2007). "All the Usambara men," found John Nellis, an American doctoral student accompanying recruiters, "repeatedly mentioned one fact that overrode their initial reluctance to join the scheme—the people have no land" (Nellis 1965a). Yet, despite their desperation about land, Usambara villagers were reluctant to join Kabuku. Rather than accepting assurances that settlers would eventually gain freehold possession of homesteads and sisal fields, prospective recruits were likely to think of recruitment as a form of conscription (their colonial experience had left residents of the northeastern highlands well acquainted with labor conscription as well as the military draft). Thus prospective recruits were highly distrustful of government and tended to find the precedents set by colonial government a better guide to understanding its intentions than the pronouncements of Nyerere and his party.

Recruiters heard many other doubts and worries as well, all of which were associated with responsibilities to maintaining the health and welfare of families. One concern was the "fear of the mountain people for malaria," while another was the scarcity of rainfall and water in eastern Handeni (Nellis n.d.). A major worry concerned the likelihood that settlers would be able to maintain ties (and through them, claims to land) with family and kin in Usambara. Prospective recruits doubted that they would be allowed off the scheme to make visits home, particularly for funerals and weddings (Interviews at Kabuku 2007). Their fears were realized, for when they reached Kabuku they were told, "Forget the past [*Usahau ya nyuma*]" (Nellis n.d.). Potential recruits also intensely disliked the stipulation that they would not be permitted to bring family members, aside from one wife and her children, to the scheme.

Recruiters were barraged with questions concerning family responsibilities. Prospective recruits and their families worried that settlers at Kabuku would lose access to the healers and pharmacopeia on which the people of Usambara relied. Recruiters were asked, "When Wasambaa women get pregnant, will they be allowed to return to the house of their mother, where traditionally deliveries are made? Who will look after the *wazee* [elders] when [recruits] depart?" Potential recruits also asked, "May we return when [the *wazee*] die?" Parents of prospective settlers also put to recruiters this scenario: "I have heard that my son at Kabuku is ill? I have heard also that I cannot go and see him? Is that so?" This example, commented Nellis, "points out how the view of schemes is more closely aligned to that of the army post, rather than a settlement." Prospective recruits asked if men who had more than one wife would be admitted to the scheme. Villagers also pointed out to the recruiters that "many of the Wasambaa have ritual duties—rain-maker, etc.—[and asked] will they be allowed to continue their practices for the Wasambaa on the scheme. . . . If no, they refuse to go." When the recruiting party moved on to the Mlalo area of Usambara, they found that "the divorce matter is very much in their minds, for these *wazee* immediately raised the issue." The recruiters also heard "fear for the breakup of the extended family unit." As John Nellis noted, however, the Mlalo villagers were not voicing unalloyed traditionalism, for "they worry about lack of schools and lack of hospitals [at Kabuku] and see not one contradiction with their traditional attitudes" (Nellis n.d.).

Scheme managers wanted very young settlers, and confined selection of men to those aged eighteen to twenty-five. Both government officials as well as villagers in Usambara were critical of this preference, arguing that it excluded precisely the mature, experienced farmers who were needed at Kabuku. Disregard for conventional understandings of maturity and adulthood was only one of the ways in which scheme admissions preferences violated common conceptions of family and intergenerational relations. Just as some prospective recruits in Usambara had anticipated, the Kabuku scheme decided to admit only married men who had no more than one wife. Family members such as brothers, sisters, cousins, nephews, and nieces, were not permitted. One final—indeed, the most obvious—way in which the view of officials diverged from the settlers' own understandings of family and household concerned women. Both in planning and recruiting phases, scheme officials thought only of men. Indeed, they equated households simply with their male heads, and often expressed their counts of the scheme's population in terms of male householders. Whereas prospective recruits and their families asked many questions about the conditions of women on the scheme—including questions not only about potential crises stemming from childbirth and marital discord, but also about scarcity of water and rainfall, which in daily life were problems dealt with primarily by women—scheme management seemed to give no thought to the burdens women would face at Kabuku. Probably no other planning problem caused as much misfortune for the Kabuku scheme as the failure to consider the concerns of women.

In economic terms, Kabuku was successful. The settlement maintained its schedule of debt repayment. A government report in 1971 said of Kabuku that, "by any standard, it is prosperous" (Tanzania, Ministry of Land, Housing and Urban Development, Town Planning Division 1971). However, declining world demand for sisal from the late 1960s eventually undercut its core enterprise. Even before Amboni allowed the village to abandon sisal altogether in 1978, villagers had already turned to maize and other food crops. Thanks to its location on a major highway Kabuku had ready access to several urban markets.

Nevertheless, many tensions developed between settlers and the scheme administrators, and they were caused less by world market adversity than by administrative blindness toward the concerns and priorities of the settlers. One source of tension was diversification of production; settlers were quick to realize that they would be better off concentrating on food crops, but administrators opposed all attempts to divert labor away from sisal. Two other interrelated problems, poor health and inadequate supplies of water, became major grievances, particularly for women, who were responsible for supplying their households with water and for the care of ill children. Perhaps the fundamental grievance of settlers, however, stemmed from their past, that is, from their socialization and prior experience in a culture where everyday life and entrepreneurial striving for material development were dominated by family interaction. The Kabuku settlers continued to define family and the responsibilities of adult men and women just as they had in their home villages. Despite opposition from scheme administrators, they invested much effort in traveling home frequently. Efforts by management to prevent settlers from traveling to home regions were a constant cause of discord. A particular source of bitterness was management objection to attempts by families to take their dead home for burial. However, by sending children to healthier highland homes, and by returning home to attend funerals and weddings, the men and women of Kabuku maintained their places in large, inclusive family groups.

Conclusion

These tensions produced dissent. First, a sizeable group of discontented settlers left Kabuku, moving to a location in Morogoro where they established another community. Then tensions exploded in 1968 when the scheme manager was attacked and nearly killed, and for a long period afterward the settlement was occupied by police. Thus frustration was the outcome at Kabuku, just as it was following the disbandment of the RDA in Ruvuma, and just as it would be in many places once the large campaigns of *ujamaa* villagization got under way. Frustration was linked with ignorance of the rural past, of course, though how they were linked varied somewhat from place to place. In Ruvuma, RDA and government officials worked with an imagined narrative of decline in social cohesion that obscured the history of change and innovation that many residents of Ruvuma had experienced in the 1950s. At Kabuku, by contrast, recruiters and administrators recognized part of the history of twentieth-century Usambara—the history of increasing land scarcity that made some young people willing to consider moving to Kabuku. Yet they ignored the deeper history and culture of intimate social relationships, which, in their view, threatened to interfere with administrative management and work discipline.

The violent crisis at Kabuku occurred just as the Nyerere government was gearing up for its large-scale campaigns of resettlement in *ujamaa* villages. In at least two respects, the situation at Kabuku foreshadowed circumstances that would emerge in the *ujamaa* villages as well. The first has to do with the authorities who implemented villagization. For the most part, they sincerely intended it to improve the material and social conditions of Tanzanian rural life. From the senior ranks of ministers and chief secretaries through the mid-rank bureaucrats and technocrats, and down to the junior officers who supervised the day-to-day administration of individual villages, most of these civil servants shared the experience of having grown up in the villages. They did not deliberately seek to oppress rural communities. Thus to understand how they came to participate in a project of rural transformation that inflicted enormous hardship on rural Tanzanians, we need to understand that they worked—to return to Michel-Rolph Trouillot's phrase—within the confines of pervasive "ontological and political assumptions." These assumptions shaped their understanding of what was possible and what was "unthinkable." Chief among these assumptions was the view that meaningful rural development could occur only under the guiding hand of the state, and that change that occurred beyond the reach of the state could never be true development.

This leads directly to the second aspect of *ujamaa* villagization that was fore-shadowed in Kabuku. This aspect was also a product of the assumption that the independent agency of rural communities was "unthinkable" as a form of development. Just as did the settlers at Kabuku, so too the farming communities resettled in *ujamaa* villages wished to rely on their accumulation of historical experience. Across Tanzania, agrarian societies had for generations relied on two kinds of continuing social practice. One was the day-to-day work of constantly constructing and animating of networks of kinship. The second was an equally ceaseless process of innovation in farming. The first provided robust sources of support and cooperation, while the second produced diversified patterns of farming as hedges against drought and pestilence. During *ujamaa* resettlement, farmers could well remember how both these forms of creative action had served them well as they pursued rural improvement during the 1950s. Such social, organizational, and technological innovation required, of course, that farming communities have space for the exercise of autonomous creativity. By dispersing communities, disrupting networks of kinship, and encouraging simplification of farming practices, however, the *ujamaa* state methodically reduced such spaces. Consequently, across Tanzania during *ujamaa* villagization—and not merely in the RDA villages or Kabuku—the result was frustration and resentment of a developmentalist state that remained obdurately blind to the precedents and lessons of the agrarian past.

References

Berry, L., and R. W. Kates. 1970. "Planned Irrigated Settlement: A Study of Four Villages in Dodoma and Singida Regions Tanzania." BRALUP Research Paper no. 10, Bureau of Resource Assessment and Land Use Planning, University of Dar es Salaam.

Boesen, Jannik, Birgit Storgaard Madsen, and Tony Moody. 1977. *Ujamaa—Socialism from Above.* New York: Africana Publishing.

Briggs, John. 1979. "Villagization and the 1974–6 Economic Crisis in Tanzania." *Journal of Modern African Studies* 17 (4): 695–702.

Cliffe, Lionel. 1971. "The Policy of Ujamaa Vijijini and the Class Struggle in Tanzania." *Rural Africana* 13: 5–27.

De Vries, James. 1976. "On the Effectiveness of Extension: A Case Study of Maize-Growing Practices in Iringa, Tanzania." *Eastern Africa Journal of Rural Development* 9 (1, 2): 37–56.

———. 1978. Selected Bibliography on Agricultural Extension in Tanzania. Department of Rural Economy, Faculty of Agriculture, Forestry and Veterinary Science, Technical Paper no. 3, University of Dar es Salaam, Morogoro.

Due, Jean M. 1977. "The Allocation of Credit to Ujamaa Villages and to Small Private Farmers in Tanzania." N.p.

———. 1980. *Costs, Returns, and Repayment Experience of Ujamaa Villages in Tanzania, 1973–1976.* Washington, DC: University Press of America.

Feierman, Steven. 1985. "Struggles for Control: The Social Roots of Health and Healing in Modern Africa." *African Studies Review* 28 (2–3): 73–147.

Fleuret, Patrick. 1980. "Sources of Material Inequality in Lushoto District." *African Studies Review* 23 (3): 69–87.

Fortmann, Louise. 1980. "Peasants, Officials, and Participation in Rural Tanzania: Experience with Villagization and Decentralization." Ithaca, NY: Rural Development Committee, Center for International Studies, Cornell University.

Giblin James. 2005. *A History of the Excluded: Making Family and Memory a Refuge from State in Twentieth-Century Tanzania.* Oxford: James Currey.

Gunza, J. K. F. 1971. Rwamkoma [Musoma] "Pilot Village Settlement Scheme: A Case Study." Bachelor's diss., University of Dar es Salaam.

Hyden, Goran. 1980. *Beyond Ujamaa in Tanzania: Underdevelopment and an Uncaptured Peasantry.* London: Heinemann.

Ingle, Clyde. 1972. *From Village to State in Tanzania: The Politics of Rural Development.* Ithaca, NY: Cornell University Press.

Interviews at Kabuku by James and Blandina Giblin, 2007.

Jayarajan, C. K. 1963. "Report of a Physical Planning Survey Conducted in Selected Five Villages in the Dar es Salaam Sub-Region." Dar es Salaam: Institute of Public Administration.

Kahurananga, F. M. K. S. 1976. "Ujamaa: The Tulieni Ujamaa Village Experience." Sociology Department, University of Dar es Salaam.

Kasoga, Lenin Bega. 1990. "An Evaluation of the Ujamaa Village Policy: A Case Study of Musoma Vijijini District in Tanzania, 1974–1987." PhD diss., Michigan State University.

Kauzeni, A. S. 1979. "Some Characteristics and Economic Activities of Selected Villages in Bagamoyo, Handeni, Korogwe, and Morogoro Districts." BRALUP Research Paper no. 61, Bureau of Resource Assessment and Land Use Planning, University of Dar es Salaam.

Kauzeni, A. S., E. K. Shishira, and C. G. Mung'ong'o. 1988. "People's Organization at Village Level: A Case Study of Four Villages in Rukwa Region, Tanzania." University of Dar es Salaam, Institute of Resource Assessment, Research Report no. 76 (New Series).

Kiambo, R. G. I. 1969. "Thoughts on the Implementation of Ujamaa Vijijini." Kivukoni College File K\S.30\2.

Kjaerby, Finn. 1989. *Villagization and the Crisis: Agricultural Production in Hanang District, Northern Tanzania.* Copenhagen: Centre for Development Research.

Kjekshus, Helge. 1977. "The Tanzania Villagization Policy: Implementational Lessons and Ecological Dimensions." *Canadian Journal of African Studies* 11 (2): 269–282.

Lofchie, Michael. 1989. *The Policy Factor: Agricultural Performance in Kenya and Tanzania.* Boulder, CO: Lynne Rienner.

Lyimo, Francis F. 1975. "Problems and Prospects of Ujamaa Development in Moshi District." Master's thesis, University of Dar es Salaam.

McHenry, Dean E. 1979. *Tanzania's Ujamaa Villages: The Implementation of a Rural Development Strategy.* Berkeley: Institute of International Studies, University of California.

McHenry, Dean E. 1981. *Ujamaa Villages in Tanzania: A Bibliography.* Uppsala, Sweden: Scandinavian Institute of African Studies.

Millinga, Ntimanjayo, and R. Ibbott. 1964. "Ruvuma Development Association Newsletter." Kivukoni College File K\S.30\2.

———. 1965a. "Ruvuma Development Association, Tanzania, Newsletter." Kivukoni College File K\S.30\2.

———. 1965b. "Ruvuma Development Association, Tanzania, Newsletter." Kivukoni College File K\S.30\2.

Moody, Tony. 1972. *A Comparative Study of Six Ujamaa Villages in Karagwe District, West Lake Region*. Copenhagen: Institute for Development Research.

Msambichaka, L. A. 1975. *Agricultural Mechanization in Ujamaa Villages: Prospects and Problems*. University of Dar es Salaam: Economic Research Bureau.

Mushi, S. S. 1976. "Ujamaa Planning and the Politics of Allocation: The Case of Morogoro District." *Taamuli* 6: 68–92.

Nellis, John. 1965a. Confidential: Kabuku–Report no. 1, Syracuse University Village Settlement Project, Reports nos. 1–43, East Africana Collection, University of Dar es Salaam Library.

———. 1965b. Confidential: Kabuku–Report no. 2, Syracuse University Village Settlement Project, Reports nos. 1–43, East Africana Collection, University of Dar es Salaam Library.

———. N.d. Unpublished field notes.

Raikes, Philip. 1972. "Village Planning for Ujamaa." *Taamuli* 3 (1): 3–26.

———. 1975. "Ujamaa and Rural Socialism." *Review of African Political Economy* 3: 33–52.

Ruvuma Development Association. 1966a. Details for Discussion with OXFAM on June 5, 1966 at Kivukoni College, Dar es Salaam. Kivukoni College File K\S.30\2.

———. 1966b. "The Origin and Growth of Litowa." Kivukoni College File K\S.30\2.

Samoff, Joel. 1981. "Crises and Socialism in Tanzania." *Journal of Modern African Studies* 19 (2): 279–306.

Schneider, Leander. 2014. *Government of Development: Peasants and Politicians in Postcolonial Tanzania*. Bloomington and Indianapolis: Indiana University Press.

Scott, James C. 1998. *Seeing Like a State: How Certain Schemes to Improve the Human Condition Have Failed*. New Haven and London: Yale University Press.

Shao, John. 1986. "The Villagization Program and the Disruption of the Ecological Balance in Tanzania." *Canadian Journal of African Studies* 20 (2): 219–239.

Sheridan, Michael J. 2004. "The Environmental Consequences of Independence and Socialism in North Pare, Tanzania, 1961–68." *Journal of African History* 45: 81–102.

Tanzania Ministry of Lands, Housing and Urban Development, Town Planning Division. 1971. "Study of Physical Planning Aspects of Ujamaa Villages." Tanzania National Archives, Dodoma Zonal Office PMO UV/U.4.

Tanzania Ministry of Lands, Settlement and Water Development, Survey Division. 1966. "The Rural Settlement Commission: A Report on the Village Settlement Programme from the Inception of the Rural Settlement Commission to 31st December, 1965." Tanzania National Archives 515/EE/KBK/63.

Tendwa, Michael John. 1979. "Growth and Development of an Ujamaa Village (a Case Study at Kwasemangube Village)." Undergraduate diss., University of Dar es Salaam.

Trouillot, Michel-Rolph. 1995. *Silencing the Past: Power and the Production of History.* Boston: Beacon Press.

Van Velzen, Thoden H.U.E. 1973. *Staff, Kulaks and Peasants: A Study of a Political Field.* In *Socialism in Tanzania*, 2: *Policies*, edited by Lionel Cliffe and John Saul. Nairobi: East African Publishing House.

Von Freyhold, Michaela. 1979. *Ujamaa Villages in Tanzania: Analysis of a Social Experiment.* New York: Monthly Review Press.

World Bank. 1962. *Tanganyika—The economy.* Africa Series no. AF 3 Washington, DC: World Bank. Accessed at http://documents.worldbank.org/curated/en/1962/12/1559903/tanganyika-economy.

3

Racialization and the Historical Production of Contemporary Land Rights Inequalities in Upland Northern Thailand

Daniel B. Ahlquist
Amanda Flaim

Introduction

For centuries in mainland Southeast Asia, constructions of group identity and difference have been entwined with conceptions of space. Before the European colonial project gave rise to territorially sovereign nation-states in the region in the late nineteenth and early twentieth centuries, arguably the most salient marker of difference in the eyes of lowland societies was not located in the bodies of those deemed "other," but in the spaces they inhabited (Laungaramsri 2001; Vandergeest 2003; Jonsson 2006; Scott 2009). From the vantage point of the lowland, paddy rice–farming ethnic Thais, the forested uplands and the diverse, swidden-farming peoples who have long resided there were not only geographically peripheral, they existed altogether beyond the bounds of civilization (Wolters 1982; Winichakul 2000; Sturgeon 2005; Scott 2009). Whereas most states in the region have largely adopted paternalistic agendas of inclusion of their ethnic minority populations in recent decades (to varied effects), the modern Thai state continues to employ policies and narratives of difference to justify agendas that keep upland groups—including Akha, Hmong, Mien, Lahu, Lisu, Karen, and others—at arm's length from full inclusion in the Thai nation (Laungaramsri 2001; Vandergeest 2003; Vaddhanaphuti 2005; Sturgeon 2005; Jonsson 2006).

In recent decades, increasing numbers of ethnic Thais from the lowlands have begun settling upland areas in search of land and livelihoods. As they do, the centuries-old politics of ethnicity, space, and national belonging are playing out in new ways and to new effects as inequalities between uplanders and ethnic Thais begin to manifest *within upland spaces*. In this chapter, we reveal and interrogate a striking disparity between uplanders and ethnic Thais in access to state-recognized land rights in the northern uplands. Our analysis of data from the 2010 UNESCO Highland Peoples Survey II[1] shows that ethnic Thais moving into the northern uplands are *more than five times as successful* as upland groups in securing formal land title (*chanot*), and roughly 2.5 times as successful as upland groups in accessing any land rights, including usufruct rights (see figure 3.1).

We argue that the disparity in access to state-recognized land rights between uplanders and ethnic Thais living in the northern uplands is a symptom of a historically specific and ongoing process of racializing once-fluid ethno-spatial difference. This power-laden process of racialization essentializes perceived ethnic difference and locates it within a social hierarchy, affixes ethnic identities to bodies, and simultaneously facilitates and justifies unequal access to rights and resources (Vandergeest 2003; Silverstein 2005; Jonsson 2006; Bonacich et al. 2008). We suggest that, while uplanders' political rights and livelihood prospects remain mired in deeply entrenched and exclusionary politics of space and difference, ethnic Thais moving into upland areas are able, by virtue of their ethnic privilege and their

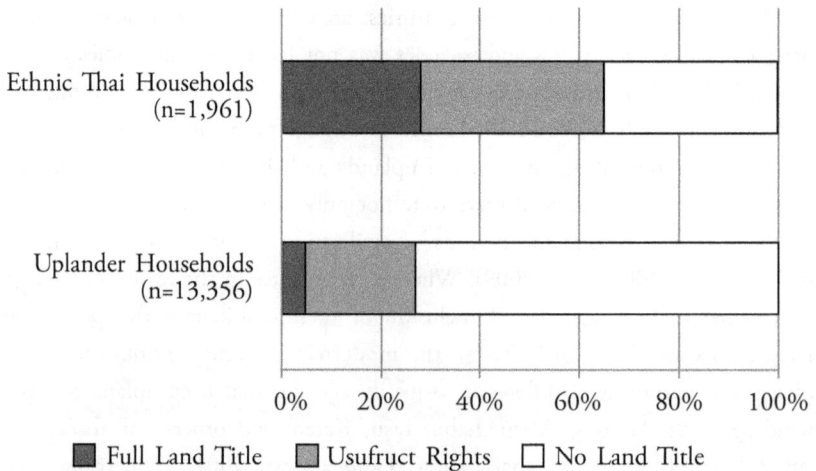

Figure 3.1. Land rights in northern uplands, by ethnicity of household, 2010.

historical association with "civilized" lowland (Thai) spaces, to secure land rights at drastically higher rates than their upland neighbors.

Land Rights Disparity in the Uplands

Upland groups have lived in what is now northern Thailand for generations, since before the creation of the modern Thai nation-state. Yet, data on household ethnicity and land rights from the 2010 UNESCO Highland Peoples Survey II (HPS) reveal that only 5 percent of upland households possess legal land title (*chanot*), and 22 percent of upland households possess usufruct rights, which are often limited and temporary in nature (see figure 3.1). One might attribute this low rate of land rights to the fact that the near entirety of the northern uplands—including the fields and villages of upland communities—is designated as state forestland, and thus off-limits to private ownership. However, this simple explanation is complicated by the finding that ethnic Thai households, which are located in these very same upland villages, and which are ostensibly subject to the same restrictions on land ownership, have proven far more successful in accessing state-recognized land rights than their uplander neighbors. According to the HPS data, 28 percent of ethnic Thai households in upland areas possess legal land title (*chanot*), and an additional 37 percent possess usufruct rights (see figure 3.1).[2]

In and of itself, the finding of an acute disparity in land ownership between ethnic Thais and uplanders is significant in that it signals a new phase in upland-lowland (uplander-Thai) inequalities. While the literature has long acknowledged inequalities between uplanders and ethnic Thais, such inequalities tend to map onto political and spatial disparities between the upland periphery and the lowland core, or between uplanders and ethnic Thais in accessing such rights as citizenship or education. In part due to the limitations of existing data sets, most of which cannot be disaggregated by ethnicity, relatively little attention has been paid to the emerging inequalities between uplanders and ethnic Thais *within upland spaces*. As we discuss later, ethnic Thais moving from the lowlands into the uplands would have once forfeited their membership in Thai society upon leaving the lowlands. Today, however, the landless farmers and other ethnic Thais moving into the uplands in search of land and livelihood opportunities not only retain their Thainess, their Thai ethnicity gives them a political advantage over their upland neighbors in the racialized upland landscape.

The Racialization of Ethno-Spatial Difference

Scholarship on group identity formation and constructions of difference in mainland Southeast Asia rightly employs the language of "ethnicity" rather than "race." Historically, the ethno-spatial categories of difference and belonging in the region have been based on such mutable and fluid identity markers as elevation, language, religion, political systems, and land use practices, rather than on any assumed innate qualities associated with perceived physical difference (Leach 1954; Laungaramsri 2003; Wyatt 2003; Tooker 2004; Sturgeon 2005; Jonsson 2006; Scott 2009). Additionally, argues Vandergeest (2003: 21), the concept of "race" is problematic in that it "slips easily into essentialist or biological assumptions about the empirical presence of racial groups." For these reasons and others, the Western concept of "race" has little explanatory or analytical value in the Thai or mainland Southeast Asian context. Drawing on Vandergeest (2003) and Jonsson (2006), however, we employ the lens of "racialization" to interrogate the power-laden processes and ethnic identity politics underwriting contemporary disparities in access to legal land rights between uplanders and ethnic Thais.

The concept of racialization "signif[ies] the extension of racial meaning to a previously racially unclassified relationship, social practice or group" (Omi and Winant 2004: 17). But the use of racialization as an analytical lens to interrogate the highly unequal processes of extending and fixing "racial meaning" need not assume the existence of "race," per se. Silverstein (2005: 364) argues that:

> Racialization . . . refers to the process through which any diacritic of social personhood—including class, ethnicity, generation, kinship/affinity, and positions within fields of power—comes to be essentialized, naturalized, and/or biologized. . . . Racialization thus indexes the historical transformation of fluid categories of difference into fixed species of otherness.

In the context of Southeast Asia, argues Vandergeest (2003: 21), the process of racialization involves essentializing "ethnic and national differences . . . with or without explicit reference to biology." The process of "[r]acialization often builds on ethnic differences," he argues, "by stereotyping [these differences] and making them the basis of discriminatory practices" (2003: 21). For example, as we discuss later, the process of essentializing ethnic difference in Thailand and across mainland Southeast Asia involves narratives that locate upland and lowland spaces and people within a civilizational hierarchy, and that treat particular land uses or cultural practices as "natural" for one group or another (e.g., swidden cultivation as natural for uplanders and wet rice cultivation as natural for lowland Thais), while simultaneously assigning value judgments to such practices (Vandergeest 2003; Sturgeon 2005; Jonsson 2006). Importantly, the lens of racialization attends to the processes through which ethnic categories are constructed, and through which ethnic identities are assigned and affixed to bodies, thus serving as portable identity markers that forever locate its bearers within or outside of a social hierarchy. We thus employ the term "racialization" to signify the political, ideological, and historically specific process of reducing complex social characteristics to stereotyped identities, and of discursively and politically affixing those identities to the bodies of those thus represented, in the context of highly unequal relations of power (see: Silverstein 2005; Vandergeest 2003; Anthias and Yuval-Davis 1992; Bonacich et al. 2008; Hall 1997).

The process of racialization produces both privileged and subordinated ascribed statuses that serve not only to facilitate or hinder access to rights and resources, but to justify such inequalities (Bonacich et al. 2008; see also Vandergeest 2003). For example, the racialization of colonized peoples by European colonial powers served to justify the violence, oppression, exploitation, and countless dispossessions that characterized the colonial project (Bonacich et al. 2008) and continue to inform the disparities between the Global South and North. Similarly, the racialization of upland people in northern Thailand—a process that has gone hand-in-hand with the extension of Thai state sovereignty into what were previously considered non-Thai spaces—has served to justify exclusionary state interventions and the subordination of uplanders' interests to those of the Thai nation-state. Later, we highlight processes through which the boundaries between ethnic Thais and upland groups have been racialized, as well as the ways in which these racializing processes have translated into highly unequal access to rights and resources.

Mapping the "Foreignness" of the Hill Tribes

Just inside the main entrance of Chiang Mai's Tribal Museum is a map bearing the rather benign English title, "The Migration of the Tribes."[3] Surrounded by mannequins in ethnic dress, dioramas depicting "traditional" practices of the so-called "hill tribes" (*chaokhao*), and photographs of the "development" of the "hill tribes" by the benevolent Thai state, the map is intended to help visitors make sense of upland ethnic minority groups in relation to the Thai nation-state. Simple in both form and function, the map consists of a free-floating outline of Thailand on a white background. Empty of history and devoid of context, the map's tidy boundaries and flat whiteness matter-of-factly broadcast to visitors that the nation-state it represents is both timeless and internally coherent. Or at least it was, visitors are led to assume, until the "hill tribes" arrived.

The map's Thai title, which translates to "The Migration of the Hill Tribes *into* Thailand" (emphasis ours), betrays the politically freighted nature of the narrative it represents. As if tracking an invasion, the map features nine colored arrows, each corresponding to the supposedly coherent and supposedly known migration pattern of the various "hill tribes" into the country. Originating in the unmapped spaces labeled as Laos and Myanmar (Burma), the arrows penetrate Thailand's clear and sovereign borders from the north and west, violating the internal coherence of the Thai geo-body.[4] Absent from the map's narrative is the history of the migration of ethnic Thais into the already inhabited lowland plains and river valleys of what is now Thailand from southern China and northern Vietnam centuries ago. Also obscured is the fact that the upland groups in question have lived in the Himalayan foothills of mainland Southeast Asia for centuries and that nearly all of the upland groups in what is now northern Thailand arrived before the country's political boundaries were drawn or even conceived, and certainly before the state developed the capacity to imbue its boundaries with any salience beyond the aspirational maps in the offices of distant state administrators. Yet, in projecting the territorial lens of the modern Thai nation-state backwards on historical space and time, the map lends spatiotemporal permanence to the Thai geo-body and legitimacy to the notion of *chaatthai*, a term that translates as "Thai nation" or "being of the Thai people." At the same time, in flattening topography and suggesting in no uncertain terms that the "hill tribes" immigrated into an already formed and ethnically pure Thai nation-state, the map reinforces their perceived foreignness and essentializes their otherness.

The narrative encapsulated in the map at the Tribal Museum saturates public discourse around upland groups and their place—historical, geographical, cultural, and political—within or outside of the Thai nation. Yet, a little over a century ago, neither the map nor the ethno-nationalist narrative it perpetuates would have made sense to Thais, officials or otherwise. Indeed, the Westphalian-inspired framework of territorially bounded and evenly operational state sovereignty that

European imperial powers imposed on the region in the late nineteenth and early twentieth centuries bears little resemblance in form or logic to the political system over which it layered (Anderson 1991; Winichakul 1994; Wyatt 2003).

Behind the Map: Historical Racialization of Spatial Difference in Thailand

Precolonial Southeast Asia

Prior to the geopolitical upheavals wrought by the British and French imperial projects in mainland Southeast Asia, the political landscape of the region was characterized by a tributary system of geographically amorphous, overlapping lowland polities defined by radiating circles of political and civilizational influence that emanated from their central cities and their respective kings (Wolters 1982). In contrast to the more rigid, territorially defined European system of nation-states, this system was characterized by a constellation of "fluid power [and] shifting relationships" (Stuart-Fox 2003: 70), where sovereignties nested and overlapped, and where state control focused more on population and labor than on territory, per se (Wolters 1982; Winichakul 1994; Wyatt 2003; Scott 2009).

Within this system, the *muang*—the lowland kingdom and its central city—was "a phenomenon of the lowlands" (Wolters 1982: 32). In contrast to the region's rugged, heavily forested, and ethno-linguistically diverse uplands, the valleys and arable plains of the lowlands were much more conducive to the projection of state military and administrative power. However, both diminished, along with the perceived moral and civilizational influence of the king, with distance from the center, and dissipated entirely upon contact with the forested mountain slopes that marked what Scott (2009) calls the "barbarian periphery" (see also Wolters 1982).

For lowland Thais, who "view[ed] the upland environment as worthless and its inhabitants as less than human" (Kirsch 1973: 6), the perceived wildness of upland forests and peoples were inseparable. The Thai term for upland people during this period and well into the twentieth century was *chaopaa*, meaning "forest people" or "wild people" (Winichakul 2000; Laungaramsri 2001; Jonsson 2006). Likely, it meant both, as the Thai word for "forest," *paa*, similarly translates as "wild" and carries connotations of unruliness and darkness. The *paa* in precolonial Thai societies (e.g., the Lanna kingdom centered on the northern city of Chiang Mai) was thus not simply out-of-bounds of civilization; it was a foreboding and perilous place populated by dangerous wild animals and peoples (Winichakul 2000; Laungaramsri 2001). In lowland Thai cosmography, the very location of upland peoples in the forested mountains served as a marker of their profound otherness and as evidence of their inferiority to lowland Thais (Winichakul 2000; Laungaramsri 2001; Sturgeon 2005; Jonsson 2006).

The inseparability of space and ethnic difference in precolonial mainland Southeast Asia is evidenced by the apparent impermanence of ethnic identity, which shifted over time as people moved from one space to another. Jonsson (2006: 9) argues that "prior to the colonial era[,] ethnic identity was analogous to rank in the pervasive tributary systems of the time"—a rank, it seems, that was more spatial in nature than it was inherent in the bodies of those who bore it. Wyatt (2003) and Scott (2009) highlight the phenomenon of upland people "becoming Thai" by leaving the mountains, learning Thai ways, speaking Thai, paying tribute, and practicing Buddhism. To be sure, this process of becoming Thai took years or even generations, as most upland people who relocated to the lowlands were brought there as slaves. Nevertheless, the barriers to becoming Thai were traversable over time in the land-rich and labor-poor context that characterized precolonial Southeast Asia. Indeed, the survival of the *muang* depended on the incorporation of subjects and their labor power (Wyatt 2003; Scott 2009).

Importantly, the impermanence and spatial character of ethnic identity operated in both directions, as lowlanders who fled to the mountains ceased to be Thai from the perspective of the *muang* (Sturgeon 2005; Scott 2009). This spatializing of ethnic difference and racializing of upland space as uncivilized was far from a coincidence. From the perspective of the *muang*, argues Scott (2009: 30),

Ethnicity and tribe began, by definition, where sovereignty and taxes ended. The ethnic zone was feared and stigmatized by state rhetoric precisely because it was beyond its grasp and therefore an example of defiance and an ever-present temptation to those who might wish to evade the state.

Indeed, as flight to the hills was perhaps the only option for lowland peasants and slaves seeking to escape their drudgery and bondage, corvée labor, taxes, and military conscription, the state had an active interest in dissuading people from doing so (Scott 1998, 2009; O'Connor 2000). Since the mid-twentieth century, state narratives about upland spaces have changed considerably, with upland forests now seen as playing an essential role in the national well-being. Nevertheless, the historical stigmatization of upland spaces and people informs the enduring legacy in state policy and the Thai national imagination of upland people as fundamentally non-Thai.

The Creation of the Modern Thai Geo-Body

While Thailand—or Siam, as it was known until 1939—was never formally colonized, the European colonial projects in the nineteenth and early twentieth centuries dramatically altered both the geopolitics of the region and the project of governance by reframing state sovereignty as spatially exclusive and evenly operational over everything and everyone that falls within a country's clearly defined borders (Anderson 1991; Winichakul 1994). Within this new geopolitical landscape, the Siamese state, once flat and geographically amorphous, was now faced with the task of extending its administrative reach across its territory, including its now-*internal* mountain periphery. This project of "internal territorialization" (Vandergeest and Peluso 1995) involves drawing territories, resources, and populations into the state's administrative and economic purview, in part by defining and regulating them according to the optics and needs of the state. But before a state can effectively monitor, regulate, tax, manage, and police the territory, populations, resources, and economic activities within its borders, argues Scott (1998), it must first be able to "see" them through its administrative lenses. To gain this vision, states employ such "visual" technologies as maps, censuses, and cadastral surveys that seek to simplify complexity and summarize the particular aspects of a territory— such as political borders, populations, land uses, or natural resources—that are of immediate interest to their statecraft. In doing so, they create a historical record that orders both space and the past to align with present state interests and that silences alternative histories, meanings, and relationships to the land (see Trouillot 1995; Braun and Wainwright 2001).

Beyond simply redefining upland spaces, the state's territorializing project in the northern uplands has involved physically and economically controlling upland forests, as well as the movements and land uses of upland people, whose very presence in and use of the forest violates the state's definition of what a forest is and how it should be used (Vandergeest and Peluso 1995; Usher 2009; Ahlquist 2015). Over the course of the twentieth century, few activities more consistently frustrated the state's territorializing efforts than upland groups' swidden-cultivation practices.[5] Characterized by mobility and diversity, swidden-farming systems did not lend themselves to mapping or other tools of imposing administrative legibility. And, because swidden systems depend on the ability of farmers to rotate fields, which requires clearing and burning forest and/or fallow lands, they represented an affront to both the productionist and conservationist optics of the Royal Forest Department (Vandergeest and Peluso 1995, 2006a, 2006b; Scott 1998, 2009; Laungaramsri 2001; Sturgeon 2005; Usher 2009). Whether in relation to timber production, conservation, or watershed protection, upland people and their land use activities were viewed by the state and lowland Thais as an unwelcome presence that threatened the country's forest resources and the national well-being (Vandergeest and Peluso 1995, 2006a, 2006b; Sturgeon 2005; Usher 2009).

Forging a Thai-Land

Beyond the problem of establishing administrative control over its territory and population, one of the formidable challenges facing the government of Siam in the early twentieth century was the forging of a unified, "national" identity among its diverse population (Anderson 1991; Winichakul 1994; Wyatt 2003). While early Siamese nationalism appears to have been confined to the urban elite, the first half of the twentieth century saw a number of political and cultural reforms that sought to encourage the formation of a Thai national identity by defining the characteristics of members of the national "we." King Vajiravudh (r. 1910–1925) famously defined "Thainess" (*khwaambpenthai*) along three pillars: loyalty to the monarchy (*phramahakasat*), the practice of Buddhism (*sassana*), and being of the Thai people or Thai nation (*chaatthai*) (Wyatt 2003)—a definition of Thainess still widely employed by Thais today. While not explicitly exclusive of non-ethnically Thai peoples living within the country, the third pillar, *chaatthai*, leaves open the question as to whether "Thai nation" and "Thai ethnicity" are or were ever distinct in this official and still influential definition of Thainess.[6] In the 1930s, the government began to enact policies that explicitly linked Thai ethnicity and Thai nationality. For example, the Thai term *chonchaat* ("nationalities," "ethnic groups")—used to signal difference among historically fluid ethnic groups, including between ethnic Thais and upland peoples—came to be understood not only in terms of space and civilizational status, but as "flesh and blood ancestry, and corresponded to the lingering racialism in Thai nationalist ideology at the time"

(Jonsson 2006: 46). "[T]he *choncha[a]t* terminology conveys the Thai as progressed and racially of Thai space," argues Jonsson (2006: 47), while also conveying that "'[r]acially' non-Thai peoples are not of Thai national space."

The 1930s marked a time of dramatic political transition and ethnocentric nation-building in Siam/Thailand, including a series of ethno-nationalist cultural mandates that sought to further codify Thainess in a way that explicitly moored Thai nationalism to a fixed Thai ethnicity. The most well-known mandates officially changed the country's name from Siam to Thailand (*prathetthai*)[7] and made Thai the country's official language. What is perhaps most striking about these mandates is their singular and unabashed focus on the country's ethnic Thai majority. While more inclusive of the regionally distinct, but still ethnically Thai (Tai) peoples of the country's lowland extremities (e.g., Issan and northern Thailand), the various official attempts to codify Thainess repeatedly and systematically neglected the country's non-ethnically Thai populations, including the numerous upland groups of the north. "[W]hen ethnicity is conceptualized as closed, exclusive, and tied to nation," argues Vandergeest (2003: 22), "it becomes racialized." Indeed, this exclusionary silence in the definition of Thainess echoes through Thai nationalist discourse to this day and continues to inform the racialization of ethnic difference and the exclusion of upland people from many of the rights and benefits of full membership in the Thai nation-state.

While the cultural mandates and other efforts to codify Thainess can be understood as both tools and manifestations of a state-led ethno-nationalist project seeking to marry Thai ethnicity and Thai nationality to Thai space, they must also be seen as a product of the collision of two world systems and part of what Winichakul (2000) calls the "quest for *siwilai*."[8] After centuries with China occupying the apex of the East and Southeast Asian tributary world system, the early twentieth century saw Europe establish itself as the locus of world economic and military power, as well as the pinnacle of world civilization in the eyes of Thai elites. Increasingly aware of this new, Europe-centered world order, "Siam had to reconceptualize itself in relation to the rest of the world, including the new supreme sources of power" (Winichakul 2000: 533). In their "quest for *siwilai*," a simultaneously outward- and inward-looking project, Thai elites sought to demonstrate that Thailand and the Thai people were as civilized as the Europeans and culturally superior to their Southeast Asian "others." These "others" from whom Thai elites sought to distinguish themselves were both external, including the Lao and Burmese, and internal. These internal others included rural peasants and ethnic Chinese living in Thai cities, as well as the *chaopaa* ("forest people") of the northern uplands. In contrast to the "real Thai" people of the lowlands, who "have progress . . . [and] are not peoples of the forest,"[9] upland peoples' cultures, land use practices, and *location* in the forested mountains marked them as non-Thai others (Jonsson 2006) and as the very antithesis of *siwilai*. "Even before the word *siwilai* became popular," argues Winichakul (2000: 535), "*pa [paa]*[10] was an antonym to explain the idea of *siwilai*."

As the state's ethnocentric policies and nationalist discourse conflated Thai ethnicity and national belonging in part by excluding the country's internal others, the historically spatial boundaries between Thainess and otherness became increasingly racialized. In addition to narratives that framed upland groups as less evolved than Thais, uplanders were defined out of the Thai nation through their classification as foreigners. For example, in his influential catalogue of the peoples of northern Thailand's Chiang Rai Province, Bunchuai Srisawat includes in his list of "foreigners" the "Mountain Peoples (*chaokhao*) such as Khamu, Lhamet, Meo [Hmong], Yao [Mien], Musoe [Lahu], I-kaw [Akha], Khe-Risaw [Lisu], Kui, etc" (1950: 16, as quoted in Jonsson 2006: 51). This framing of lowland (ethnic) Thais as "real Thais" and upland groups as immigrants remains prevalent today and is reinforced by popular media and officially sanctioned texts such as the map in Chiang Mai's Tribal Museum. Through this "nationalization of space, identity, and history that [has] accompanied the racialization of the Thai landscape," argues Jonsson (2006: 47), uplanders and other non-ethnically Thai peoples have been "deprived of agency" in the politics of national belonging.

Racialization and Contemporary Inequalities in Land Ownership

The complex history of racializing ethno-spatial difference informs contemporary inequalities between ethnic Thais and upland groups with regard to land ownership in the highlands in a number of ways. As Vandergeest (2003) and Bonacich et al. (2008) note, the processes of racialization not only affix difference to bodies, they circumscribe or facilitate access to resources and state benefits along these identity axes. In this section, we highlight the processes of racialization in the operation of state sovereignty in the northern uplands, and examine how they inform the highly divergent outcomes in land ownership among uplanders and ethnic Thais.

Repositioning Upland People and Forests vis-à-vis the Thai Nation

Neither the racialization of upland people over the course of the twentieth century nor contemporary inequalities in land rights can be understood apart from the conceptual repositioning of upland spaces in the Thai national imagination or the state's century-long effort to eradicate the practice of swidden cultivation. In the late nineteenth century, in large part due to British teak interests in the north, Thailand's vast forests came to be seen as a valuable resource for national development—a resource deemed to be threatened by the presence of the "hill tribes" and their practice of swidden cultivation (Laungaramsri 2001; Vandergeest and Peluso 2006a, 2006b; Usher 2009). Later, amidst the political tumult in the decades after World War II, swidden cultivation and its upland practitioners assumed center stage in a morally freighted political discourse around the so-called "problems of the hill tribes," a bundle of perceived threats to the Thai nation that included communist insurrection, opium production, poverty, and deforestation (Laungaramsri 2003; Vaddhanaphuti 2005; Jonsson 2006; Forsyth and Walker 2008). These narratives, which frequently framed the problems collectively as resulting from the "primitive" lifestyles and land use practices of upland peoples, served to reinforce the otherness of uplanders and to legitimate paternalistic and heavy-handed state interventions in upland communities, including forced sedentarization and resettlement, arrests and deportation (Vaddhanaphuti 2005; Jonsson 2006; Forsyth and Walker 2008; Usher 2009).

For decades, the state sought to address the "problems of the hill tribes" through interventions ranging from agricultural development projects to outright evictions of entire upland villages. Few interventions, however, had as sweeping an impact on upland lives and livelihoods as the state's forest conservation project. The gazetting of reserved forests for logging began as early as the end of the nineteenth century, and the first conservation-focused protected areas were created in the 1960s. It wasn't until disastrous floods and mudslides in southern Thailand in 1988, however, that national attention and state policy turned in earnest to preserving Thailand's dwindling forests (Usher 2009).[11] Following the disaster, forests—especially upland watershed forests—assumed a new position of importance in the Thai national consciousness as critical to the well-being of the Thai people, and as spaces requiring state protection from logging, infrastructure development, expansion of lowland settlements and agriculture, and upland peoples' land use practices. In 1989, the government enacted a nationwide logging ban that prohibited cutting any tree on state-designated forestland. The ban disproportionately affected upland communities not only because most of the country's remaining forests were in the northern and western uplands, but because virtually the entirety of the northern uplands—including the villages, fields, and fallows of upland communities—was designated by the state as forestland. This "implicit rejection of customary rights" (Usher 2009: 85) served to frame upland people living in these "forest" areas as trespassers and criminal destroyers of national resources (Usher 2009; Sturgeon 2005).

Still in effect and rigorously enforced today, the logging ban has effectively crippled the swidden-farming systems of upland communities. In fixing villages and their agricultural zones in place, the ban and other forest enclosures triggered a series of dispossessory and disempowering transformations in upland communities by severely curtailing the ability of farmers to maintain soil health and combat weeds by rotating their fields with multiyear fallows (Ahlquist 2015). As a result, agriculture in most upland communities has come to be characterized by the production of input-intensive cash crops, debt, soil erosion, water pollution, and health problems resulting from the heavy use of agricultural chemicals applied to combat declining soil fertility, pests, and worsening weed problems (Ahlquist 2015). Just as the swidden-cultivation practices of upland farmers spawned a century of degradation narratives condemning the destruction of Thai forest resources by non-Thai "hill tribes," the agricultural practices that now characterize upland agriculture have given rise to a new degradation narrative about upland farmers who, in their greed for the material trappings of modernity, disregard the well-being of the environment and the Thai people who live downstream from them (Ahlquist 2015). Once again, the location and land use practices of upland people in the northern mountains came to be seen as threatening to the well-being of lowland (ethnic) Thais and the Thai nation.

As upland forests have been repositioned in the Thai national imagination over the past half century, a number of subtle but nonetheless racializing linguistic shifts have occurred in state and popular discourse that serve to conceptually reposition upland groups vis-à-vis the forest while reinforcing their marginal position vis-à-vis the Thai nation. For example, the Thai word for forest, *paa*, with its connotations of unruliness and darkness, has given way to the word *thamachaat* in national (and nationalistic) conservation discourse (Laungaramsri 2001; Jonsson 2006). *Thamachaat* more closely resembles the Western idea of nature as pure, virtuous, and untrammeled by humans. However, *thamachaat* also carries important Buddhist and ethno-nationalistic connotations, translating as it does to "birthplace of the Dharma"[12] and sharing the same root as *chaatthai* ("Thai nation" or "Thai ethnicity"), both of which add to its moral weight in this overwhelmingly Buddhist and ethnically Thai country (Laungaramsri 2001; Roth 2004; Jonsson 2006). Whether as a resource to be managed or as *thamachaat* to be conserved, these reframings of the forest sanction only certain types of people and activities in forest spaces, while at the same time condemning others whose location in and uses of the forest violate these morally and politically infused conceptions of what a forest should look like and how—and by whom—it should be used.

As *thamachaat* was replacing *paa* in national(istic) forest conservation discourse, and as the so-called "problems of the hill tribes" dominated public discourse and state policies in the hills, the language used to identify upland groups—and to position them in relation to the forest and to the Thai nation—also underwent a transformation. Although the longstanding categorization of upland people as *chaopaa* ("forest people," "wild people") carried negative connotations in the eyes of lowland Thais (Winichakul 2000; Laungaramsri 2001; Jonsson 2006), it nonetheless located upland people discursively and conceptually *in the forest* (Laungaramsri 2001). In the latter half of the twentieth century, however, the term *chaokhao* ("mountain people," "hill tribe") came into popular usage, gradually replacing the term *chaopaa*. While the linguistic shift to *chaokhao* may at first seem benign, Laungaramsri (2001) argues that, in fact, it serves to linguistically and conceptually separate upland groups from the forest, and to simultaneously "other" them vis-à-vis ethnic Thais though its implied linguistic binary coupling with *chaorao*, meaning "we" or "us people." Furthermore, as forest conservation and the "problems of the hill tribes" intensified in public discourse and as a focus of state interventions in the uplands, *chaokhao* came to signify "unruliness, illicit practices, and a threat to the country's borders," argues Jonsson (2006: 45). Whereas *chaopaa* "suggests a deficiency in civilization and Thai-ness . . . [*chaokhao*] suggests various obstacles to progress and threats to national integration." This linguistic severing of upland people from both the forest and the national "we" has reinforced the idea among the Thai public and policymakers that the very presence of upland groups in the forested mountains poses a threat to the nation's forests, and thus to national well-being (Laungaramsri 2001; Jonsson 2006).

Affixing Identity to Bodies

Keyes (1994, 2002) and Laungaramsri (2001, 2003, 2014) argue that ethnic categorization is both a project and technology of state power, and that the categorization of upland groups as "hill tribes" (*chaokhao*) has been part of a process of locating these geographically peripheral groups within the nation-state while at the same time ensuring that they remain fixed at its literal, discursive, and political margins. Just as the ethno-nationalist project of defining "Thainess" excluded upland peoples from a constructed national identity, and as the discursive repositioning of uplanders in relation to the forest has informed exclusionary forest policies, the state's project of forging a Thai citizenry has explicitly excluded upland people by legally and discursively mooring Thai citizenship to highly problematic notions of a "Thai race" (Jonsson 2006). With roots dating back to the late nineteenth century and to the historical spatialization of ethnic identity, "the conflation of race and citizenship" (Jonsson 2006: 46–47) continues to inform the social and political marginalization of upland people.

Although discrimination by lowland ethnic majorities against upland minority groups is commonplace throughout mainland Southeast Asia, only in Thailand were upland minority people systematically excluded from citizenship in the country of their birth and residence (Saffman 2007). The systematic exclusion of uplanders from Siamese nation and state building can be seen as early as 1904, with the first national census. Consistent with pre–nation-state cosmological views of mountainous regions and peoples as lying beyond the purview of civilization and state power, most upland border regions were purposefully excluded from the surveys altogether (Grabowsky 1996). Indeed, until the 1960s, upland people were largely excluded from censuses and civil registration campaigns, which are critical steps in the conferral of formal recognition of legal status.

Perhaps as racializing and politically marginalizing as total exclusion were the ways in which upland groups were eventually and selectively *included* in civil registrations and given legal status. When the Thai state officially surveyed and registered upland villagers in 1969, they were not included within broader civil registration campaigns as nationals of Thailand, but rather as part of special registrations of the "hill tribes" (Morlaeku 2010; Flaim 2015). From 1969 through 1999, the state undertook several rounds of "hill tribe surveys" to formally register, count, and account for the diverse groups it had excluded for decades. Through these initiatives, the state registered and mapped upland villages and issued standard household registration documents (*tabienbaan*), which listed demographic information of each resident, such as name, age, and "nationality" (*sanchaat*). Yet, despite the fact that Thailand recognized the right to citizenship by birth in the country (*jus soli*) since the 1909 Nationality Act, the nationalities of uplanders were registered not as Thai but according to their respective ethnicities (Hmong, Akha, Lisu, etc.). As such, they were issued household registrations that marked them as "non-citizen" residents (Morlaeku 2010). Similarly, individuals who registered in the "hill tribe" surveys were issued "hill tribe" identification cards, which officially marked their possessors as non-Thai, semi-permanent residents, whose rights to work, live, and even travel within the country were heavily restricted (Laungaramsri 2003, 2014; Morlaeku 2006, 2010; Toyota 2005; Sakboon 2009). A "hill tribe" ID card marked its holder as a less-than-full member of the Thai nation-state. In other words, uplanders were marked as being legally *in* Thailand but not *of* Thailand. In an extension of processes described by Btihaj (2013) in her research on technologies of identification and surveillance in the UK, once officially registered as a "hill tribe" in the state bureaucracy, individuals become prisoners of their assigned identities as non-Thai others.

By the early 1970s, amidst fears of communist insurrection in the northern uplands, the government revoked the right to citizenship by right of *jus soli*. The move, which was recently but only partially overturned, effectively undermined uplanders' claims to Thai nationality by virtue of their birth and residence in the country, and simultaneously strengthened the notion of Thainess as a category of belonging passed on only by blood (*jus sanguinis*) (Flaim 2015). As most uplanders were born in their homes until recently (Flaim, 2015), and as unknown thousands of uplanders were excluded from or inaccurately accounted for in the "hill tribe surveys" (Morlaeku 2010; Sakboon 2009), the lasting effect of these measures was to ensure that uplanders would be perpetually excluded by virtue of their "selective integration" as non-Thai residents (Vaddhanaphuti 2005).

By the end of the century, the combined effects of protracted political exclusion, ill-conceived state "development" projects, restricted prospects for legal work outside the village, and severe land use restrictions imposed in the name of forest conservation had largely decimated upland village economies and livelihoods (McKinnon 1997; Laungarmasri 2001; Sturgeon 2005; Ahlquist 2015). Within this context, uplanders mobilized for state recognition of their citizenship as a way to ensure access to rights and livelihood possibilities within and beyond their villages (Morlaeku 2010; Sakboon 2009). As a result of this movement, approximately 75 percent of upland residents included in the UNESCO Highland Peoples Survey II are now recognized as citizens (Flaim 2015). However, in most cases, their non-Thai names and ID numbers denote a *naturalized* citizenship and leave the indelible trace of an identity that cannot be reconciled as fully and completely Thai.

Discussion and Conclusion

Over the past half century, the Thai state has denied upland people land rights and curtailed their land use practices through a combination of policies and narratives that officially "other" upland people as non-Thai. Those same policies and narratives define the uplands as state spaces—as forest and border spaces critical to the nation's well-being and in need of state protection—and thus as off-limits to individual ownership and non-sanctioned uses of the land (Laungaramsri 2001; Sturgeon 2005; Forsyth and Walker 2008; Usher 2009). Given these logics behind the exclusion of upland people from state-recognized land rights, one might reasonably expect that the state's restrictions would apply equally to all people seeking land rights in the northern uplands. However, our analysis of the HPS data reveals that ethnic Thais living in the uplands are gaining legal land title at over *five times* the rate of their upland neighbors, and have also proven far more successful in gaining usufruct rights (see figure 3.1). We have argued that the pronounced disparity between ethnic Thais and uplanders in securing state-recognized land rights in the northern uplands is a symptom of a historically specific and ongoing process of racialization, wherein once-fluid ethno-spatial differences have become naturalized and formally affixed to the bodies of upland people—and, by extension, to the bodies of ethnic Thais. That is, in contrast to the spatial conceptions of ethnic difference that predominated in the region until at least the mid-twentieth century, ethnic status is now both fixed and portable. Today, people carry their ethnic identity with them wherever they go, regardless of whether they live in the uplands or lowlands, what language they speak, or how they dress. Whether they are physically located in upland villages or lowland towns, upland people are marked as *chaokhao* ("hill tribe")—as *less Thai*—by their names, their hill tribe identity cards, and their accents, leaving them vulnerable to discrimination, loss of rights, and, in the cases of noncitizens, deportation. On the flip side of the same coin, ethnic Thais now carry with them both the rights of their citizenship and the privileges of their Thainess: their full membership in the Thai nation.

Yet, to deny the continued salience of space in the restrictions placed on upland people's rights and livelihood prospects, and in the emerging inequality between ethnic Thais and upland people in securing land rights in the northern uplands today, would be to leave intact the veil concealing the state's persistent exercise of exclusionary power on the basis of racialized ethno-spatial otherness. Even as ethnic identity has become affixed to bodies, those marked as *chaokhao* remain burdened by their historical association with upland spaces long perceived as fundamentally non-Thai. After centuries of being cast as "wild" and "uncivilized" precisely because of their association with upland forests, uplanders seeking land rights today must contend with a new and highly politicized narrative that frames forests as central to the national well-being, and that leaves no place in the forest for upland people or their livelihoods.

Notes

1. The 2010 UNESCO Highland Peoples Survey II included more than seventy thousand people—over fifteen thousand households—living in the upland border villages in five northern Thai provinces (see Flaim 2015).

2. Of note, these findings are not weighted for population differences. When accounted for, these differences in population subsamples actually reveal the advantage of ethnic Thais over upland groups to be much greater.

3. Due to a fire, the museum was recently renovated. The description here depicts the museum before the fire.

4. We borrow the term "geo-body"—referring to the nation's "most concrete definition," including "its territory [and] its related values and practices"—from Winichakul (1994: x).

5. In swidden systems, farmers cut and (usually) burn trees and shrubs prior to planting crops. After cultivating a single field for a few years, farmers move on to a different field site and let the original field site lay fallow for several years. Most swidden systems in northern Thailand were rotational, meaning that farmers rotated through the same few field sites in cycles lasting from a few years to a few decades.

6. For more in-depth analyses of the definitions and evolution of the terms *chaat* (also transliterated as *chat*) and *chonchaat* (*chonchat*), see Winichakul (1994: 134–135) and Jonsson (2006: 44–55), respectively.

7. Owen (2005: xxii) suggests that the name "Thailand" (*prathetthai*) is "a neologism, combining the traditional ethnic identity 'Thai' with 'land' (*prathet* in Thai). As the word 'Thai' also means 'free,' some people translate the country's name as 'Land of the Free,' but it is unlikely that that was the original meaning."

8. *Siwilai* is the Thai transliteration of the English word "civilized."

9. Bunchuai Srisawat (1950: 32), describing the northern Thais (*khonmuang*), as quoted in Jonsson (2006: 53).

10. The Thai word for "forest" can be transliterated as *pa, paa,* or *bpaa.*

11. National forest cover had by this time been reduced from around 75 percent in 1900 to less than 29 percent (Usher 2009).

12. In Buddhism, Dharma (or Damma) can mean a state of nature, the conditions of existence, or the Buddha's teachings.

References

Ahlquist, D. B. 2015. "Losing Place in the Corn Mountains: Forest Conservation, in situ Displacement, and Agrarian Change in Upland Northern Thailand." PhD diss., Ithaca, NY: Cornell University.

Anderson, Benedict. 1991. *Imagined Communities: Reflections on the Origin and Spread of Nationalism*, 2nd ed. London: Verso.

Anthias, F., and N. Yuval-Davis. 1992. "Racialized Boundaries: Race." *Nation* 303.

Bonacich, E., S. Alimohamed, and J. B. Wilson. 2008. "The Racialization of Global Labor." *American Behavioral Scientist* 52 (3): 342–355.

Braun, B., and J. Wainwright. 2001. "Nature, Poststructuralism, and Politics." In *Social Nature: Theory, Practice and Politics,* edited by B. Braun and N. Castree, 41–63. Malden, MA: Blackwell Publishers Ltd.

Chupinit, K. 1994. "Dubious Concepts in the Thai Highlands: The Cha Khao in Transition." *Law and Society Review* 28 (3): 673–686.

Dunn, E., and J. Cons. (2014). "Aleatory Sovereignty and the Rule of Sensitive Spaces." *Antipode* 46 (1): 92–109.

Ergin, M. (2014). "The Racialization of Kurdish Identity in Turkey." *Ethnic and Racial Studies* 37 (2): 322–341.

Flaim, A. 2015. "No Land's Man: Sovereignty, Legal Status, and the Production of Statelessness among Highlanders in Northern Thailand." PhD diss., Ithaca, NY: Cornell University.

Forsyth, T., and A. Walker. 2008. *Forest Guardians, Forest Destroyers: The Politics of Environmental Knowledge in Northern Thailand.* Seattle: University of Washington Press and Chiang Mai: Silkworm Books.

Ganjanapan, A. 1996. "The Politics of Environment in Northern Thailand: Ethnicity and Highland Development Programs." In Seeing Forests for Trees: Environment and Environmentalism in Thailand, edited by P. Hirsch, 202–222. Chiang Mai: Silkworm Books.

Grabowsky, V. 1996. "The Thai Census of 1904: Translation and Analysis." *Journal of the Siam Society* 84 (1): 49–85.

Hall, S. 1997. "The Spectacle of the 'Other.'" In Representation: Cultural Representations and Signifying Practices, edited by S. Hall, 223–290. London: Thousand Oaks.

Hart, G. 2006. "Denaturalizing Dispossession: Critical Ethnography in the Age of Resurgent Imperialism." *Antipode* 38 (5): 977–1004.

Hirsch, P. 1990. "Forests, forest reserves, and forest land in Thailand." *The Royal Geographic Society* 156 (2): 166–174.

Jonsson, H. 2006. *Mien Relations: Mountain People and State Control in Thailand.* Chiang Mai: Silkworm Books. (Originally published in 2002 by Cornell University Press.)

Kammerer, C. A. 1987. "Minority Identity in the Mountains of Northern Thailand: The Aka Case." In *Southeast Asian Tribal Groups and Ethnic Minorities*, 85–96. Cambridge, MA: Cultural Survival.

Keyes, C. F. 1987. "Tribal Peoples and the Nation-State in Mainland Southeast Asia." In Southeast Asian Tribal Groups and Ethnic Minorities, 19–26. Cambridge, MA: Cultural Survival.

———. 2002. "The Peoples of Asia: Science and Politics in the Classification of Ethnic Groups in Thailand, China, and Vietnam." *Journal of Asian Studies* 61 (4): 1163–1203.

Luangaramsri, P. 2001. *Redefining Nature: Karen Ecological Knowledge and the Challenge of the Modern Conservation Paradigm.* Chennai: Earthworm Books.

———. 2003. "Ethnicity and the Politics of Ethnic Classification in Thailand." In *Ethnicity in Asia*, edited by C. Mackerras, 157–173. New York: Routledge Curzon.

———. 2014. "Contested Citizenship: Cards, Colors, and the Culture of Identification." Chapter 6 in *Ethnicity, Borders, and the Grassroots Interface with the State, Studies on Southeast Asia in Honor of Charles F. Keyes*, edited by J. A. Marston. Chiang Mai: Silkworm Books.

Leach, E. [1954] 1970. *Political Systems of Highland Burma: A Study of Kachin Social Structure.* London: The Athlone Press, University of London.

McKinnon, J. 1997. "The Forests of Thailand: Strike up the Ban?" In *Development or Domestication? Indigenous Peoples of Southeast Asia*, edited by D. McCaskill and K. Kampe, 117–131. Chiang Mai: Silkworm Books.

Morlaeku, C. 2006. "Problems Concerning the Laxity of Legal Status within the Thai Highland Population." Internal report. Bangkok: UNESCO.

———. 2010. "Addressing the Remaining Legal Status Question." Internal report. Bangkok: UNESCO.

O'Connor, R. A. 2000. "A Regional Explanation of the Tai Muang as City-State." In *A Comparative Study of Thirty City-States*, edited by M. H. Hansen, 431–447. Copenhagen: Royal Danish Academy of Sciences and Letters.

Omi, M., and H. Winant. 2014. *Racial Formation in the United States.* New York: Routledge.

Roth, R. 2004. "On the Colonial Margins and in the Global Hotspot: Park-People Conflicts in Highland Thailand." *Asia Pacific Viewpoint* 45 (1): 13–32.

Safman, R. M. 2007. "Minorities and State-Building in Mainland Southeast Asia." Chapter 2 in *Myanmar: State, Society, and Ethnicity*, edited by N. Ganesan and K. Y. Hlaing, 4–31. Hiroshima: Hiroshima Peace Institute.

Sakboon, M. 2009. "Citizenship and Education as the Basis for National Integration of Ethnic Minorities in North Thailand." PhD diss., Sydney: Macquarie University.

Scott, J. C. 1998. *Seeing Like a State: How Certain Schemes to Improve the Human Condition Have Failed.* New Haven, CT: Yale University Press.

————. 2009. *The Art of Not Being Governed: An Anarchist History of Upland Southeast Asia*. New Haven, CT: Yale University Press.

Silverstein, P. A. 2005. "Immigrant Racialization and the New Savage Slot: Race, Migration and Immigration in the New Europe." *Annual Review of Anthropology* 34: 363–384.

Stuart-Fox, M. 2003. *A Short History of China and Southeast Asia: Tribute, Trade and Influence*. Crow's Nest, NSW: Allen & Unwin.

Sturgeon, J. 2005. *Border Landscapes: The Politics of Akha Land Use in China and Thailand*. Seattle: University of Washington Press.

Tooker, D. E. 1996. "Putting the Mandala in its Place: A Practice-based Approach to the Spatialization of Power on the Southeast Asian 'Periphery'—The Case of the Akha." *Journal of Asian Studies* 55 (2): 323–358.

————. 2004. "Modular Modern: Shifting Forms of Collective Identity among the Akha of Northern Thailand." *Anthropological Quarterly* 77 (2): 243–288.

Toyota, M. 2005. "Subjects of the Nation without Citizenship: The Case of the 'Hill Tribes' in Thailand." In *Multiculturalism in Asia*, edited by W. Kymlicka and B. He. Oxford: Oxford University Press.

Trouillot, Michel-Rolph. 1995. *Silencing the Past: Power and the Production of History*. Boston: Beacon Press.

Usher, A. D. 2009. *Thai Forestry: A Critical History*. Chiang Mai: Silkworm Books.

Vaddhanaphuti, C. 2005. "The Thai State and Ethnic Minorities: From Assimilation to Selective Integration." In *Ethnic Conflicts in Southeast Asia*, edited by K. Sritwongse and W. S. Thompson, 151–166. Singapore: Institute for Southeast Asian Studies.

Vandergeest, P. 2003. "Racialization and Citizenship in Thai Forest Politics." *Society and Natural Resources* 16: 19–37.

Vandergeest, P., and N. L. Peluso. 1995. "Territorialization and State Power in Thailand." *Theory and Society* 24 (3): 385–426.

————. 2006a. "Empires of Forestry: Professional Forestry and State Power in Southeast Asia, Part 1." *Environment and History* 12: 31–64.

————. 2006b. "Empires of Forestry: Professional Forestry and State Power in Southeast Asia, Part 2." *Environment and History* 12: 359–393.

Walker, A. 2004. "Seeing Farmers for the Trees: Community Forestry and the Arborealization of Agriculture in Northern Thailand." *Asia Pacific Viewpoint* 45 (3): 311–324.

Walker, A., and N. Farrelly. 2008. "Northern Thailand's Specter of Eviction." *Critical Asian Studies* 40 (3): 373–397.

Winichakul, T. 1994. *Siam Mapped: A History of the Geo-body of a Nation*. Honolulu: University of Hawaii Press.

————. 2000. "The Quest for 'Siwilai': A Geographical Discourse of Civilizational Thinking in the Late-Nineteenth and Early-Twentieth-Century Siam." *Journal of Asian Studies* 59 (3): 528–549.

Wittayapak, C. 2008. "History and Geography of Identifications Related to Northern Thailand." *Asia Pacific Viewpoint* 49 (1): 111–127.

Wolters, O. W. 1982. *History, Culture and Region in Southeast Asian Perspectives*. Singapore: ISEAS.

Wyatt, D. 2003. *Thailand: A Short History*. Chiang Mai: Silkworm Books.

4

Making Things for Living, and Living a Life with Things

Olivia Maria Gomes da Cunha

Mi be go a foto, ma mi nai seli mi sani ("I went to the city but I didn't sell my things").

—From *A Be De Kaba—Mi Nai Seli Mi Sani*, vol. 1, CD recorded in French Guiana (year not indicated)

Maroons living on the Eastern Coast of Suriname, in the small town of Moengo and in Maroon villages close to the Cottica River and its tributaries, often refer to their self-denomination, *Cottica Ndyuka*, when they wish to explain why they think, speak, live, and perform rituals differently to other Maroons, especially those they call *Ndyuka sama na Tapanahoni*,[1] the Ndyuka people who live to the south in dozens of villages spread along the Maroni, Tapanahoni, and Lawa rivers. This distinction also involves various local histories of conflicts and fissions, the range of which may vary considerably, producing what we could call a process of Ndyuka deterritorialization in the region.[2]

As the ethnographic material presented later reveals, gender plays an important role in these ongoing processes of differentiation. The lives of many of the women that I met during fieldwork assumed new configurations after they and their parents returned to the Cottica region at the end of the Interior War (known in Dutch as the *Binnenlandse Oorlog*: 1986–1992). The eruption of this conflict, which affected thousands of Maroon people, was accompanied by the invasion of villages and the destruction and contamination of plantation fields and rivers by the Surinamese army.[3] After the war, Moengo, a small settlement founded on the shore of the Cottica River in 1916 as the base for an industrial plant, and later transformed into a modern center of bauxite production, became home to tens of thousands of returning Maroon refugees, especially women who had fled with their families to the interior and to refugee camps in French Guiana during the war. Upon their return to Moengo at the start of the 1990s, Cottica Ndyuka refugee families transformed the landscape of the industrial town. The buildings and semipaved streets of what was once the heart of the twentieth-century South American bauxite empire were now taken over by bananas, plantains, mangos, ackee and calabash trees, medicinal bushes and crops planted in small plots next to the invaded houses. Moengo's landscape was not just "ruralized," it was transformed into, in the words of a non-Maroon critic, a "Maroon village." The transformation of the space was the result of the way Cottica Ndyuka people, particularly the women, had turned it into a "place for living" (*peesi fu libi*), a space where the living must be fabricated from domestic and agricultural work. This implies not cutting but carefully maintaining the connections between the house (*osu*) and agricultural work in the *goon*—the small plots of terrain where Maroon women and men grow food and cultivate healing and spiritual plants. These activities range from clearing the fields to selling food produce, medicinal herbs, and processed food in the cities. In so doing, they mobilize and reinforce a set of work, kinship, and neighborhood relations, as well as ecological and spiritual ties (Andel 2010). In the Cottica, these are relations "infused with social and cultural meaning" (R. Price 1991:123) that also increasingly involve non-Maroon interlocutors (*bakaa*).

From the viewpoint of some of my interlocutors, working in the *goon* and selling produce in the streets and markets of Saint Laurent du Maroni (French Guiana), Paramaribo, Albina, and Moengo are not in any sense radically opposed to the traditional forms of living, working, and interacting with kin and non-Maroon people well described in Maroon ethnography (Köbben 1967, 1979; Thoden van Velzen 1988, 2004). On the contrary, the persistence of these practices and, at the same time, their reconfiguration within the dynamics of the local markets and the relations of the Cottica Ndyuka with agents outside the village spaces enable them to continue their obligations and to observe the traditional rules (*gwenti*) and rights operating in their traditional territory, as well as the contacts and negotiations with the gods and spirits of the forest. For many women, going to the *goon* means more than producing their own sustenance and observing the traditional rules, customs, rights, and logics that govern life in many of the Cottica villages: it also means controlling a set of potential relations with the world of the *bakaa*. As I shall show in the following sections, these relations were very much part of the history of Ndyuka people and their close contact with non-Maroon (*bakaa*) throughout the twentieth century.

This chapter focuses on two Cottica Ndyuka experiences of making things for the living and their relations with the *bakaa* world. Based on archival and ethnographic material, I describe how the work in the traditional gardens and planting grounds (*goon*), as well as the manufacturing and selling of craftwork, clothes, and personal and decorative objects form part of the lives of Ndyuka women and their families in Moengo. I show that from the perspective of my interlocutors, being engaged in these activities does not mean living "as if" in a Maroon village. Cottica Ndyuka recognize that Moengo is a non-Maroon territory (*bakaa peesi*) that requires them to live under different rules. As Maroon persons, however, their connections to their villages and ancestors (or those of their kin) are unbroken. They are very much alive and renewed daily through family obligations to deceased affines and other healing and purification rituals. This implies a dynamic circulation between the villages, the family's *goon*, and the city markets. It has contributed to the continual transformation of Maroon villages in the region—since the mid-twentieth century affected by development projects and occupied by churches, new buildings, basic water supply and sanitation infrastructures, satellite dishes and telephone antennae—as well as, following the slow decline of industrial activity and the return of Maroon refugees, a visible change in the urban structure and in the ways of living in Moengo. But these are not inexorable processes. Neither are Maroon villages being "modernized," nor Moengo "ruralized." Cottica Ndyuka differentiate the meanings associated with living in each place. However, after the Interior War, and due to their interlocutions with people and their involvement in the production and circulation of things, Maroon women became key protagonists of the relationships that make up the Cottica Ndyuka experience and their way of living in Moengo.

As I argue in the next section, these transformations have important historical antecedents and have been produced by the Cottica Ndyuka themselves, based in their engagements with non-Maroons since the mid-nineteenth century, and hence must be understood in their own terms.

A Ndyuka Territory

Cottica is the name of the river on which important Ndyuka Maroon villages were established throughout the nineteenth century. When the first Ndyuka men from the Tapanahoni and Sara River areas began to arrive in the region, the Cottica area was the site of colonial prosperity, but also of wars against runaway slaves. Occupied by plantations since the seventeenth century, the east coast of the former Dutch colony, traversed by the Cottica, Comewijne, Courmotibo, and Wane rivers and their affluents, was the setting for slave rebellions and flights. References to camps situated close to the region's rivers and marshlands appear in accounts of the wars launched against the villagers and new fugitives, typically by militias formed by farmers and colonial troops. Palgrave wrote that these fugitives "seem perfectly at home, without strangeness or even shyness of any kind. Nor, indeed, are they strangers from far off; their villages on the banks of the Upper Cottica itself, and of its tributary stream, the Coermotibo, are almost contiguous to the European Estates" (Palgrave 1876: 141). In an account of his travels published in 1854, Augustus Kappler described the region's rugged terrain, affluents and mangrove swamps, and the innumerable villages lining the shores of the Cottica and the Courmotibo from where, "for years," people said, "Aucaner-Boschnegers" would set out to sell timber, sometimes exchanging the wood for food produced by slaves, since they themselves saw agricultural work as "humiliating" (1854: 78, 79, 130–131). The Cottica—once home to settlements of fugitives who, throughout the last century, settled in inaccessible marshy areas, in some cases including survivors of wars between Maroons considered "pacified" and recently formed groups of runaways—became the setting for a bloody war involving the Ndyuka, the colonial forces and numerous groups of fugitives, then referred to as *Boni-neggers* (Hoogbergen 1990). In 1863 when slavery was abolished in the Dutch colony, the migration of Maroon people to the region intensified. No longer sustained by slave labor, the colonial economy became extremely dependent on the timber extracted and marketed by Maroons, a population skilled in the construction of boats capable of navigating powerful rivers filled with obstacles, as well as techniques for transporting timber logs over large distances.[4]

Colonial officers ("posthouders") who had the mission of controlling the villages and the movements of Maroons, as well as ensuring observance of the treaty signed between the Ndyuka and the colonial government in 1760, which granted autonomy to Maroon settlements, have described the unsuccessful attempts to prevent or convince Maroons to return to their villages. Later treaties made observations on encampments on the coast created as temporary places to stay while working on logging, transporting and selling timber, as well as selling and exchanging objects and food with other fugitives and slaves working in the region's plantations (Boon-acker 1916; Wong 1938).[5] "Old" and "new" Maroons settled in mangrove swamps along the coast, close to the plantations and Paramaribo. This proximity not only entailed new relations with non-Maroons, but also led to various strategies for interacting with groups of recent runaway slaves, spiritual authorities, and chiefs from their traditional clans and matriclans in the interior. Indelibly associated with a hegemonic matriclan, the maternal village is the place where the Maroon person establishes connections with the land, the forest, and the river (nonhuman beings) and their *bee sama* (relatives from the same matrilineage).[6]

Far from Diitabiki, the village inhabited by the paramount chief or *gaaman*, the Cottica River villages established relations dominated by the power of certain clans and matriclans and their villages on the Tapanahoni. As van Lier and Köbben observed, local decisions were generally dependent on consulting oracles in order to divine the wishes of the gods and ancestral spirits. The same dynamic deter-mined the distribution of clan members and the control of the Cottica Maroon villages (van Lier 1940: 158–159; Köbben 1969). Whether forming the abode of important oracles and gods, as in the case of Wanhatti, one of the oldest villages in the Cottica region, or functioning as a satellite node of the power and control of Diitabiki, the Cottica River villages reterritorialized in their own way—and fol-lowing the dynamics of new local alliances—the clashes, conflicts, and hegemony of certain clans and villages on the Tapanahoni (Köbben 1967).[7]

Aside from their impact on the configuration of Cottica Ndyuka territory, the conflicts involving village authorities and clansmen in the Tapanahoni also affected the complex relations with the colonial government, missionary groups, and representatives of extractivist and mining companies who arrived in the coastal area at the beginning of the twentieth century—people with whom the Maroons had to negotiate spaces where they could stay, work, and find ways to support themselves. As Groot observed, "as far as wage labor was concerned the Maroons simply refused even to consider working on plantations. Lumbering and river transport already formed part of their activities and they only intended to extend their work as they themselves thought fit" (2009: 161). Although Ndyuka and indigenous groups from villages along the Cottica River and the lower Marowijne had worked in plantations producing timber to supply the building industry and in temporary logging jobs since the 1850s, the traditional peoples were to experience a significant socioeconomic and demographic change in the 1920s.

Bauxite Landscape

The Cottica flows past a hillside on the site of a previous Maroon village known by Ndyuka historians[8] as Mungo. Occupying the two shores of the river, Mungo had sacred sites and several houses to provide accommodation to the first Ndyuka men and women arriving from the Tapanahoni region. However, in the early twentieth century the place was abandoned. According to myth, Mungo's residents disregarded sacred taboos on working after sunset. This disobedience incited the fear of punishment from the gods. After hearing a sudden strange noise, like an explosion, coming from the earth, all the inhabitants fled into the forest along the Cottica and its affluents, where clansmen established new temporary encampments (*kampu*) and villages (*kondee*). Mungo still lives today as a site and name associated with the presence of Ndyuka Maroons on the coast. Among some old headmen (*gaan sama*), the Cottica River is designated *Mungo Liba*, the Mungo River (Cunha 2018).

When the *bakaa* arrived in Mungo, they discovered an abandoned village and an enormous bauxite deposit. In 1916 an industrial settlement was founded by the North American mining company ALCOA (Aluminum Company of America)[9] in the middle of the forest, close to the shores of the Cottica. The bauxite economy boosted colonial development and a demographic transformation, including impacts in the Maroon villages near to the plant. A small town was planned and built to house workers (Javanese, Creole, and Chinese) involved in the extraction, storage, and shipping of the mineral along the Cottica River to Paramaribo on the coast. Hired workers, their Dutch superiors and a small contingent of US technicians came to live in Moengo,[10] requiring an expansion in the infrastructure supplying water and sanitation, and the implantation of regimes to organize the time and spaces for work, movement, education, leisure, and meals (Oudschans Dentz 1921; Hesseling 1974; Koning 2011a, 2011b; Hoefte 2013). The work of felling and clearing the large areas of forest and swamps was undertaken through informal agreements and one-off contracts with Ndyuka living in the Maroon villages nearby or new migrants from the Tapanahoni.[11] The Cottica Ndyuka were the main workforce used in logging and for opening large holes in the ground prior to planting explosives (Hesselink 1977; Lamur 1983).

Only in the 1950s did the company begin to hire a few Maroon men. They received low-status housing in an outlying neighborhood where their families were also allowed to live. A small portion of Maroon workers who settled on the periphery of the concession descend from occasional workers who had been allowed to settle temporarily in certain areas in order for them to work, avoiding the long distance, difficulties, and time involved in traveling to the villages. Women coming from villages along the Cottica River could also be seen selling produce in the urban area, but had to return to the villages before nightfall (Hesselink 1974). The company's ban on Maroons living or staying in the concession area led to small groups of families settling nearby, on the other side of the Cottica River—as in the case of the encampment then called Happyland. They also established small *kampu* in some areas of the mostly Javanese district named Wonoredjo, or close to the rail track where a road would later be opened and named Bursideweg (Burside's Road), after a company employee. In his study of the company town, Hesselink (1974) provided detailed information on the production of food in the Wonoredjo and Bursideweg in 1970, the existence of Maroon residents and their children frequenting schools in an area controlled by the Javanese community, and the Maroon villages, *kampu*, and *goon* founded along the Moengo-Albina highway at the end of the nineteenth century. In the 1970s, Maroon crops produced in the *goon* and sold on the roads and markets also helped supplement the supply of agricultural food to the families of Suralco employees. Whether living in formal or informal conditions, the number of Maroon residents in Moengo and Wonoredjo was always low compared to the Javanese and Creoles, employees who had the right to a house, education, and health care and access to goods subsidized by the company. At the same time, services connected to mining operations in nearby areas (principally along rivers and in terrains close to the villages) that lacked workers with experience in forest tasks, were carried out with the help of Ndyuka from villages on the Cottica, in particular those settlements with a strong Catholic and Moravian missionary presence, such as Tamarin and Wanhati.

Working for *Bakaa*

Despite the ecological and social impact of the mining industry in the region, including in sacred and traditional territories of the Cottica Ndyuka, caused by the arrival of "development," schools, and work, by the mid-twentieth century the gap between their world and that of the *bakaa* was still considerable. In 1962, the village of Langa Uku was separated from Moengo by an eight-hour journey in a traditional Maroon boat (*boto*). So when one of anthropologist Andre Köbben's interlocutors returned to the village surprisingly quickly after a period of working for *bakaa,* the event stirred a lot of local people's interest. After three years working for a timber company in Commewijne without once returning to the village, Ti Vallisi[12] made the journey back in a modern boat with an outboard motor, bought with his savings. His arrival showed the other villagers that a boat trip to Moengo could now be made in just two hours. Ti Vallisi contemplated turning this new mode of river transport into a business, but, as Köbben observed, his evident keenness to make money from the venture was censured. Another of Köbben's interlocutors, Da Tengi, was concerned to keep his life modest.

> Da Tengi has been buying timber in various villages for a number of years. He is an intelligent man with a commercial talent and when he starts supplying a big factory his transactions grow to a comparatively great volume. He is careful not to change anything in his way of life. His hut remains just as sober as everyone else's. He discharges his kinship obligations more than generously. All the same people are jealous, for they can see that he is rising considerably above them financially and they somehow feel it is at their expense. Tengi feels the hostile sentiments and thinks himself threatened by witchcraft. When one of his grandchildren dies and another takes ill soon afterwards, he stops his timber transactions for a few years. (Köbben 1967: 51)

Ethnographic data on the sudden wealth acquired by Ndyuka working for the *bakaa* on the coast also appears in studies of conflicts in villages along the Tapanahoni River (Thoden van Velzen and Wetering 1983, 2004; Vernon 1980, 1985). Particular attention is given by these authors to describing and explaining the confrontations and dramas observed in the Cottica villages as outcomes of their relations with non-Maroons (Köbben 1967). Examples of similar problems to those faced by Da Tengi, Ti Vallisi, and one of the latter's wives, Sa Lomina, reveal the constant flow of Maroon people between villages and the relations involving men's work in the forest, whether in logging, selling and transporting timber, or in the sale of produce grown in the *goon.* Disputes, envy, and witchcraft accusations are listed as some of the causes of "disunity" among the Cottica Ndyuka and—just like the intra- and inter-village affinities—reaffirm the relevance of these tensions in the Cottica's cosmopolitics.

From their first experiences of evangelization in Maroon villages in the Cottica region, Catholic missionaries quickly perceived these tensions and realized that their work would have to be accompanied by different strategies of persuasion. First, they needed to acknowledge that the Ndyuka in the Cottica were subject to other relationships and economic pressures that threatened their "unity" as "one people." Second, evangelization should be accompanied by the creation of work and income opportunities proximate to those of a peasant economy controlled by the church. The life of the "new Christians" would have to involve the transformation of Maroon children—and, by extension, their parents—into rural workers.[13] As Father Coppelmans, a Catholic missionary who worked among the Ndyuka in the Cottica and Tapanahoni river areas in the 1950s, said: for the Maroon, the *bakaa* world—its rules, practices, things, and languages—were a single entity. The word *lanti* in Ndyukatongo—meaning the government or "their (*bakaa*) power"—was used to refer both to the colonial state and to the Christian missions. All foreign rule related to work or the evangelization imposed on their society was seen to be determined by the *lanti*. Discussing one conversion methodology used among the *bosnegers*, Coppelmans points out that the "creation of jobs [. . .] with any company or individual" was a way to transform them into "workers" under missionary guidance.[14]

Inspired by the Jesuit reductions among Guarani Indians in nineteenth-century Brazil, Dutch Redemptorist missionaries set up a self-sustaining Catholic community. Tamarin village was chosen by Father Wortelboer as the site for a boarding school for indigenous (Galibi) and Cottica Ndyuka boys, combined with a factory for processing timber logged and brought by the Maroon men. The income would be used to run the school. The chosen village had 1,860 residents and was situated close to other important Maroon villages: Wanhati and its counterpart, Agiti-Ondo. The first, the site where the Moravians had built their school and started missionary work in the early twentieth century; the latter, one of the oldest and most populous Ndyuka villages in the region and where the cult of the oracle *Gaan Tata* attracted a lot of visitors from the Cottica and migrants from the Tapanahoni (Thoden van Velzen and Wetering 1988, 2004).[15]

The boarding school in Tamarin opened in 1915. The wood-processing plant and a trading post selling *goon* produce were used as strategies to make the village more "attractive" to the Ndyuka (Vernooij 1996: 49). The arrival of Rosendaal nuns to set up a school for children and women in 1925 was also accompanied by new machinery: one of the most modern sawmills in the colony was installed there. According to missionary accounts, the interest of the Cottica Ndyuka was considerable. By the end of the 1950s, Father N. C. Spruijt could observe that moral control of Tamarin had been achieved: "nobody enters the village if they are not in accord with Christian morality." More than half a century after the association between missionary activity and the introduction of mechanized agriculture and, at a smaller scale, livestock breeding, the same pattern is observable in all the villages where Catholic priests work or run schools. As well as Tamarin's timber yard and aviary, the Maroon villages of Ricanaumofo and Pilgrimkonde produce rice and other food.[16]

Although important, this was not the only initiative pursued by the Christian missions to transform the Maroon into productive rural workers, nor the only attempt by companies with transnational links to control their ephemeral extractivist activities. The construction of the Afobaka dam in central Suriname in the early 1960s, responsible for the destruction of villages and sacred territories belonging to the Saamaka and Ndyuka, also had an impact on development programs that saw "agriculture" as a form of controlling the Maroon population living in villages throughout various parts of the interior and turning them into "productive" workers.[17]

The role of missionary action among the Maroons in the first attempts to relocate the Cottica Ndyuka to peripheral areas of the bauxite mining concession is evident not only in the labor practices introduced in the villages, but also in the opening of schools in Moengo. In the 1950s the Catholic missionaries working on the Cottica River would discuss inter- and intra-village politics when planning new schools. One of the most important factors considered was the existence of nearby work sites.[18] The proximity of the schools—today no longer exclusively religious—is still a strong reason for children and old people to leave the villages and live temporarily or definitively in the bauxite town.

Living with *Bakaa*

In Maroon matrilineal societies, the place where women and their kin from the same matrilineage (*bee*) and matrisegment (*wan mama pikin*) live and produce their sustenance is also the temporary dwelling place of men. These particular Cottica Ndyuka modalities of dwelling that connect spaces traditionally seen as "urban" (marked by the complexity of manual work and spatial occupations, the wider availability of transport, new modalities of habitation and market organization) and "rural" (characterized by rural work and dwellings, modes of consumption, and familiar and labor organization) reveal the proliferation of what Köbben described as "neolocal" forms of habitation: the establishment of households in localities distinct from the couple's original villages. In the Cottica region described in Köbben's ethnography, this modality was fairly unusual. Unlike the frequency of uxorilocal and ambilocal arrangements, and, less frequently, residential patterns labeled virilocal (in the husband's village), autolocal (the couple staying temporarily in alternating villages), and endolocal ("intravillage marriages, husband and wife living together, both in their own village," 31), the rise in neolocality involves an important spatiotemporal transformation related to the "life histories of individuals" (1967: 32). Rarely permanent, between 1961 and 1962 neolocality afforded some degree of symmetry in terms of the localization of the new residence for both spouses. The building of the new dwelling reaffirmed the ties with (their) equally symmetric villages.

Not coincidentally, the example of neolocality on the Cottica River provided by Köbben describes the arrival of members of the Pata-*lo* to the company town. He mentions the settling of three Pata people (*Pata sama*) in a "camp" close to the "mining town of Moengo," but "outside of tribal villages." Among them was "Sa Lomina, a woman from Langa Uku," married to Ti Valisi, who was temporarily "working on a timber concession" (1967: 51). Settling in Moengo or on its outskirts, albeit temporarily and precariously, allowed proximity to jobs, markets, and schools, but also a greater distance and freedom from the political and spiritual control of the villages. The existence of analogous forms of neolocality and polylocality in the material studied by Köbben and Thoden van Velzen (1966) in the Cottica and Tapanahoni regions, respectively, do not suggest any kind of continuity or "pattern" per se, but rather a complex mode of establishing continuous relations between affines in discontinuous spaces. Köbben's examples from the early 1960s concerning the decisions and factors that determined residence, how houses were established, the ways of assuring sustenance and work, and the obedience to local authorities and the designs of gods and ancestors, indicate an enormous complexity and, above all, a constant flow of persons between the different villages and between the latter and nontraditional localities.

In Moengo, the residential units comprising a house and a small yard, which were built by Suralco for its employees in the mid-twentieth century but abandoned during the war, are today occupied by households headed by Cottica Ndyuka women. Generally speaking, they comprise distinct habitational units and family configurations encompassing the first generation of refugees and their descendants. Each house (*osu*) typically contains three generations: a mother, her daughters, and her grandchildren. Older relatives often stay in the villages from where they travel to obtain medical treatment in Moengo, Paramaribo, and Saint Laurent, or to receive small quantities of money in *Foto* (Paramaribo).

After school and between homework and spending leisure time with friends, young men sometimes help their mothers with more physically demanding tasks or help them look after the smaller children. After obtaining some schooling, they migrate to Paramaribo where they live with their young wives in outlying districts largely inhabited by other Maroon people. Some work in civil engineering, for freight companies or providing informal passenger transport.[19] Adult men remain away for days or weeks, circulating between Moengo, the *goon*, *Foto* (Paramaribo), and *Soolan* (Saint Laurent du Maroni), where they may undertake sporadic work connected to gold mining in the interior, or mineral prospecting for Chinese and Korean companies subcontracted by Suralco or concessionaries of the Surinamese state. In these wanderings, the men inhabit—also temporarily—the houses of their other wives or their own *mama osu pikin* (the house of their mother, the matriseg-ment to which they belong) in the cities or villages. In other words, various men of different ages circulate through and provisionally inhabit various *osu*. This does not mean that women do not themselves move about. On the contrary, it is precisely the proximity to those tasks that make their spatial fixation possible—owning a house where they live and raise their children, and obeying the temporality of planting and harvesting in their *goon*—that enables their circulation too and, with it, a higher concentration of resources in their *osu*.

In the next section I explore the experiences of Sa Mari and Sa Yani, whose parents were temporary workers for Suralco and other mining contractors during the last century. Sa Mari's and Sa Yani's itineraries, personal histories, modes of circulation, and forms of access to worlds full of things are associated with the repercussions of the Interior War. The histories of the two women and their rela-tives are connected to the complex relationships between Cottica Ndyuka Maroon villages and the *bakaa*.

Two Women

Sa Mari lives in the *kampu* with other *pa pikin*, children of her father, Da Dumee, a worker who was informally hired by Suralco for forest work during the first half of the twentieth century. The location served as a temporary residence on the outskirts of the imposing industrial plant built to extract, process, and load bauxite onto ships that would then transport the cargo down the Cottica River to Paramaribo. After Da Dumee's death in the 1970s, and especially following the Interior War, many of Sa Mari's sister's children (*sisa pikin*) built houses there. A place of residence, conviviality, and domestic work that interconnects the house spaces. Part of the work begun in her *goon*—located between the Wane Creek (*kiiki*) and the lower Marowijne River (*Mawina*), approximately 100 kilometers from Moengo—is completed back at the *kampu* before fatigue sets in at the end of her long working day, begun before sunrise. In her *goon* Sa Mari plants and harvests her crops in the company of other women doing the same in nearby strips of land. In the *kampu*, she also lives with children and grandchildren, as well as neighboring relatives. The dwelling area is not the only difference between these two spaces, although having a place to live (*wan peesi fu libi*) is very different to working on a garden (*wooko na goon*).

The terrain surrounding Sa Mari's house is populated by numerous things: hoes, spades, boots, pots, sacks and plastic bags, metal and plastic containers of all shapes and sizes, a small wooden and aluminum wheelbarrow used to cart soil, a clay grinder, plants, and heavy items. Fruit trees provide shade to the yard and the houses of her recently deceased sister and their children. The space provides Sa Mari's grandchildren with an area to play after school until their mothers get back from work. While at home, Sa Mari spends much of her time in a small open-walled shed, close to the small veranda, full of shoes and clothing draped over some improvised washing lines. This is also where her *pikin kuku* (literally, small kitchen) is found, the place where she processes the vegetables grown in her *goon* and house backyard. She cooks all the bitter cassava on an open wood and charcoal fire, transforming the root crop into flour and bread (*Baka Kassaba*), which is then sold or shared out among her family. Other crops like eggplant, *kosubantu* (black-eyed peas), *taya*, plantain, *callalo*, bananas, yam, watermelon, *pountayer*, and okra are shared with her daughters, sometimes given away, or swapped for other foodstuffs with relatives living near her in the *kampu*. Most, though, will be sold to other vendors or directly traded by Sa Mari herself in the markets of *Soolan* and *Foto*. This merchandise, sometimes left in consignment, is resold by other Cottica Ndyuka women for a negotiated price.

Sa Mari's day-to-day life is mostly shared with other women of her generation, keeping alive traditional customs of the Ndyuka villages where a substantial portion of the work of planting and harvesting crops is carried out by women in the *goon* located relatively close to the villages. Men are generally, albeit not exclusively, responsible for heavy tasks like clearing land and burning or felling the trees in preparation for planting crops in the *goons*, or constructing small straw huts to store machetes, axes, knives, shovels, water pumps, and produce (Lier 1940: 253–279; R. Price 1975, 1991; S. Price 1993). As in other nearby villages in the Cottica region, work in Moengo's *goons* primarily involves men and women over the age of fifty who have few alternatives to ensure their families' sustenance. Each day they set out to the *goon* areas in cars, by boat, or on foot, leaving the villages virtually empty for much of the day. The children and young people, meanwhile, head off to school in other forms of transport. Youths, many people lament, refuse to accompany their parents and grandparents to assist with work in the *goon*. Some youngsters combine school with helping their relatives with various tasks in the *goon* from time to time, or receive small sums of money from other families for a day's work. Most, though, prefer to try making some money by helping sell produce, or working in the markets and transport services in Albina, Saint Laurent, and Paramaribo.

Although the children of Sa Mari and Sa Yani were born in Moengo, the place is not conceived as a point of origin and does not impede them from identifying the villages of their parents—in general the village of the matrilineage—as the place where they come and go, the locale to which they return when a funerary ritual occurs, or whenever a family conflict needs to be resolved or spiritual treatment obtained. Polylocal forms of habitation form a significant part of the experiences of people who settled in Moengo after the civil war. In his own ethnography, Köbben mentions the fact that Maroons went to Moengo to obtain medical care. Sa Yani, now around sixty years old, recollects the visits to the modern hospital run by the company when she was small. Everything changed with the war, though, and the hospital was closed. The deactivation of bauxite mining operations in Moengo[20] led to a rapid vacation of the factory's installations. It also, though, had a pronounced effect on the villages and on the supply of casual labor. The company ceased to invest in the locality (the town has little or no state presence: road cleaning and housing repairs were undertaken by the employees and the company), and some of its building assets were simply abandoned. Sa Yani occupies one of these houses, invaded with the help of kin.

After some years living on the outskirts of Paramaribo because of the war, Sa Yani came to live in Moengo, where she gave birth to her daughter and, a while later, moved in with Ba Elesi. Sa Yani's mother is from Manja Bom village on the lower Cottica, and her father worked in sporadic jobs for Suralco. Her relatives never lived in Moengo, though. Ba Elesi's mother was from Morakondee and his father from Adjumakonde, where he worked as a teacher in a *RK sikoo* (a Catholic school). When the war (*féti*) broke out they had to leave the Cottica. While Sa Yani and her parents took refuge in Paramaribo, Ba Elesi allowed his family to flee to *Faansi* (French Guiana) while he himself joined one of his mother's relatives as a *soldati* from the Jungle Commando.

Ba Elesi's knowledge of the forest, and especially the earth and bauxite mining, led to him being hired on a temporary basis by various mining companies subcontracted to Suralco. After working for some days in the forest (*na busi*), Ba Elesi would return to Moengo and Sa Yani's house. From time to time he accompanies her to the *goon*, helping with heavier work, but it is still Sa Yani who produces their sustenance. Their oldest daughter, a teacher married to a Creole man, lives in *Foto* where Sa Yani left her relatives and friends during the period of exile. Almost every week, Sa Yani goes to *Foto*, meets up with her siblings in Moengo, and sells the surplus produce grown in her *goon*. When necessary, and despite lacking the necessary documents (*pampila*), she crosses the Maroni River to sell produce in *Soolan*'s markets. Despite these comings and goings to urban markets, the *goon* and the villages, she still feels very much an inhabitant of Moengo.

About four years ago, after working with a close relative selling packed hot meals, Sa Yani decided to run her own business with her children. She mixes the crops planted and harvested by herself with industrial items bought in Moengo to "make meals to sell" (*boli njan fu seli*), variations of Surinamese Creole dishes with a strong Javanese influence. To run the business, the configuration of Sa Yani's house differs only a little from Sa Mari's *osu*. Next to the building containing her large room, bedrooms, and a kitchen, facing the yard, is a shelter thatched with leaves of *maipa* (*Attalea Maripa Palmae*) with two wooden benches inside. From time to time, employees from concessionaries and companies linked to Suralco—generally, Maroon men—drive up and buy food. When I met her, she was working in the *goon* and selling food as a livelihood. On my most recent return to Moengo, though, Sa Yani told me that she no longer sells food. She did not become wealthy, but she no longer needs to work so much: what she produces and earns from the *goon* produce is sufficient to buy the things (*sani*) she wants. Her membership in a cooperative of women associated with "people from the church" (*keleki sama*: a group linked to the Moengo Wesleyan Church)[21] helps her to *libi bun* (live well) and be protected from envy.

Sa Mari was raised in a village with a Christian presence and went to Catholic schools, though she never learned how to write or speak Dutch. Her relation to Catholicism is limited to sporadic visits to Sunday Mass. In Peetondo, the village where she lived with one of her father's wives, there was also a weekly presence of priests and missionaries, as well as sanctuaries for the gods and spirits of the Pinasi-*lo*. Sa Mari later moved to Moengo and married a Maroon man employed at Suralco; they were one of the few Maroon families to live in a house officially granted by the company prior to the war. It was there that her four daughters and three sons were all born before the war broke out and they were forced to cross the forest and rivers, her youngest child still a baby, with the help of the men from the Jungle Commando, eventually finding refuge in *Faansi*. Sa Mari lived in Acarouny and Charvein, two refugee camps set up by the French government. In Charvein her fourteen-year-old daughter gave birth to her first grandchild. When she returned to Moengo in 1992, Sa Mari moved into a larger and more comfortable house with her children. She left a few years later when a family conflict led to her occupy the *kampu* of Ba Dumee, where her daughters had already started to build their own houses. Three teachers, working in areas with a strong Maroon presence, help them and are in turn helped by Sa Mari. They share food, care of the children, and dividends from produce sold at fairs and kermesses. From her daughters she sometimes receives presents likes earrings and necklaces, as well as news about the habits of *Foto*.

Things for Living

Whenever there is a trip from Moengo to the markets to sell new produce, Sa Mari first collects the agreed asking price from the vendors with whom she had left her produce to sell. Some are able to settle their debts in full, others only partially. Sa Mari usually manages to obtain some return from the trust she invests in the sellers. Working with this uncertain income, Sa Mari saves some of the money to purchase another batch of the important raw materials from which she obtains much of her income. Each week she pays an acquaintance to fill sacks with ball clay (*pemba doti*), extracted from riverbanks and areas already mined by Suralco, and takes them to the *kampu*. In the past *pemba doti* was collected from river shores that had large quantities of white sand.

Following the abandonment of Suralco's mining pits, it can now be collected close to Moengo itself. The availability of *pemba* and the fame of the spirits and women of the Cottica gives the product a high market value. "Everyone likes it, it's good for your health, it's sweet (*ala sama lobi, dem bon fu sikin, de suiiti*) [. . .] they call it Moengo pemba (*den kay en Moengo Pemba*)," Sa Mari remarked as she worked one rainy afternoon. The *pemba* has curative effects and is associated with the treatments administered by specialists (*obiaman*) and the *papa* and *komanti* spirits (Thoden van Velzen and Wetering; Vernon 1992: 57, 61; Wetering 1992: 119; Andel 2010; Bilby 1989: 256). However, it is also used as a valued food for children and, especially, pregnant women.[22] If the weather is good, the next day she will travel to *Soolan*, where she is famed for selling *pemba*. When necessary she stays the night in the house of one of her daughters who still lives in Charvein with her four children and her Guianese Creole husband. Between Charvein, *Soolan*, and Moengo she mobilizes an extensive network of traders, vendors, border police, and employees with whom she shares kinship, friendship, and sometimes a few euros. They are all Cottica Ndyuka *sama* (people).[23] Sa Mari and her acquaintances do not speak French.

Sometimes when she returns to the *goon* in the late afternoon, Sa Mari processes the clay left in the *kampu* on her own. Her daughters do not do this work, nor do her grandchildren. After being passed through an old grinder, pounded in a *mata* (a wooden pestle to crush grains), sieved, and mixed with water in huge plastic basins, the *pemba* is carefully molded. This is slow work, performed as she converses with her neighboring kin, or sometimes when engaged in the everyday work of looking after her grandchildren. When a thick mass is obtained that begins to stick together, Sa Mari squeezes handfuls of the clay and shapes them into almost uniform balls. When ready, these are placed on a flat wooden, plastic, or aluminum surface and left in a dry and covered space while waiting for sunny days. Obtaining a compact white ball without cracks is essential to maintaining the properties of the *Moengo Pemba*—which, as well as knowing the seller and origin, is one of the factors making it recognizable in the markets.

Sa Mari says that *pemba* is the product that sells the most: good for cures and bodily health, it assures spiritual "efficacy" when used to make artifacts and substances for spiritual and curative procedures known as *obia*. These varied uses make the substance enormously attractive to some people and repulsive to others. She knows that *keleki sama* tend to avoid contact with *pemba*, at least publicly. For this reason she emphasizes its positive effects on the skin and the fine taste of the product, the sale of which provides for a large portion of her sustenance. She knows that not everyone who purchases *pemba* from her uses it for *obia* practices.

This does not mean that all the consumers understand the meanings and effects of the substance and its associated practices in the same way. The term serves to designate both the practices and their spiritual and artifactual effects.[24]

Conclusion

The epigraph that opens this chapter is taken from a song on an album of music performed by Ndyuka women of the Cottica River region. *Sani* (thing) in this song has a clear sexual connotation. Sung and accompanied by a female chorus, it tells the story of a woman who describes everything that she bartered on her trip to the city. The refrain is also an observation: to obtain all the goods, she sold many things but not her body. Women like Sa Mari, Sa Yani, and their daughters, who circulate on the road between their *goon*, the villages, and urbanized areas such as Moengo, Paramaribo, and Saint Laurent du Maroni, make their living out of things and relationships that connect different places, times, and things: Maroon villages and cities, ancestors and children, spiritual and *bakaa* materialities. As women, they are also mediators of the circulation of blood, wealth, and spiritual powers. But, differently from their kin from older generations or those living in Maroon villages in the interior, they are Cottica Uma, whose "reputation" is associated with their capacity to circulate through diverse worlds and make their own life. Cottica Uma is a constant reference in the Maroon musical styles sung in Okanisi, in particular aleke, originally from the Cottica River (Bilby 2001). The lyrics—generally composed and sung by men—tell of love stories, but also allude to situations involving modern women (*uma*) who decide to head to the city, either abandoning their men or returning to them later, women remarkable for both their beauty and their audaciousness.

Describing the relations between Saamaka men and women in 1983, Sally Price observed that "one of the most important contrasts between Saramaka men and women is their differential involvement in the world beyond their tribal territory. This involvement has left its mark on their respective material lives, sexual histories, linguistic patterns, personal styles, and philosophical orientations" (1983: 462). This important observation, explored in other texts on the incorporation and fabrication of artifacts in the Maroon universe, skillfully captures the places, objects, and relations in which gender is produced (1983, 1993, 2003). Along the same lines, the relations between bodies and persons appear traversed by events involving the incorporation of things brought from outside the villages. The movements of Sa Yani and Sa Mari—wandering through the markets, working in the *goon*, or taking care of the children in the *kampu*—signal important discontinuities with the experiences of Maroon women living in the villages. On the other hand, as I showed in the previous sections, they seem to reinforce the relations between the Cottica Ndyuka and the world of the *bakaa*.

Moengo is not a village, but neither is it quite an urban territory. This ambiguity means that the movements toward what pertains to the territories, beings, and forces that inhabit the villages never cease to affect the lives and bodies of the people who inhabit the former bauxite town. As shown by the example cited in the second part of the text, the fear of Da Tengi, Köbben's informant, that returning to the village after years making money in the timber trade would expose him to witchcraft is, in fact, a recurrent theme in the ethnography on the Ndyuka. Similar references appear in the narratives of missionaries and colonial government employees, as well as cases observed by anthropologists who studied the impact of migration on Maroon men from the nineteenth century onward (Thoden van Velzen and Wetering 1982, 1983; R. Price and S. Price 1989; R. Price 2007; Lenoir 1975). Women were responsible for the houses, swiddens, and children, while their bodies were the preferred vehicle for the presence of the gods—"the main channel through which they could improve their social position" (Thoden van Velzen and Wetering 1982: 62). Their permanence in the villages contrasted with the constant circulation of men.

The theme of migration and its impacts in the villages has always been treated from the viewpoint of men and their activities in the world of the *bakaa*. Since the women stayed in the villages along with the elderly and children, they received the local and spiritual reflexes of men's wanderings. As the object of the action of spirits and gods through possession, women captured the designs of nonhuman agencies sometimes directed toward their matrisegment or clan. The anthropologists Wilhelmina van Wetering (1966, 1992) and Diane Vernon (1980, 1985) described cases in which the much feared *Baku* (or Bakulu)—beings who would exchange forms of submission and impersonalization through coercive labor for sudden wealth among the *bakaa*—were held responsible for the outbreak of conflicts, sudden illnesses, or witchcraft involving women as soon as their husbands returned from the coast or from the mines bringing money and presents. The cure for these beings' actions was spiritual cleansing and exorcism. Although these strange creatures were depicted as small beings who inhabited the forest, their associations with money (Vernon 1980, 1985), goods, wealth, and "things" (*gudu sani*)—modern objects brought from the coast—arrived via the agency of men and affected the bodies of women and men and the relations between them.

In the cases of Sa Mari and Sa Yani, the work in the *goon* determines where the women need to travel: to the markets. From these urban places where they sell and buy things, they return to their houses and from there head back to the *goon*. In the Cottica, women no longer wait for the men to return to be affected by the forces that accompany the latter; rather, they mobilize resources and time and establish relations so as to control them. Sa Yani not only sometimes receives Ba Alesi's help to transport vegetable crops and clear the *goon*, she also has a small business. Both activities provide her with the security and resources to expand and improve the house and buy consumer objects. Her husband and business are equally important. In a social world where polygamy is traditionally accepted—albeit contested by many women converted to Christian churches, especially Pentecostal denominations—to have *wan man* (a husband) means having someone to help in the tasks essential to the family's sustenance. Moreover, Sa Yani is over fifty years old and, as Sally Price (1983: 462) observed, her chances of finding a husband are slight. Sa Yani had studied little but enough to sing and read pamphlets in Sranantongo, Dutch, and English, and to live in *Foto* like other young Ndyuka. Even so, her life with Ba Elesi does not appear to be one of dependence or marked by a division of tasks and commitments that distinguishes women's spaces from those of men (S. Price 1983). In Vernon's words, a "payment" for the "restriction" of women's movements:

> [. . .] although what men are specifically paying for are her favors, what they are paying for in a more general sense is the advantage of being men: of being able to enjoy the freedom to move about, live about, seek employment, and earn salaries without answering to anyone, and of being free to enjoy sexual promiscuity and multiple marriages. What they are in a broad sense paying women for is her subjection to a double standard that limits her freedom of movement and her economic activity to the fields and obliges wives to remain sexually faithful to husbands away for sometimes a year at a time without a return, who are off indulging in other relationships and other matches. (1985: 16)

In a sense, the work in the *goon*, the markets, the village, the congregation, and church services (which take up several days per week) lead Sa Yani to circulate through different places and relations with Maroon and non-Maroon people alike.

Ba Elesi spends days in the forest (*na busi*) and less time in Moengo or in the places that Sa Yani frequents—in other words, his movement away from the house shared with his wife mostly occurs in the opposite direction to the one traditionally involving migration from the forest to the coast. With the arrival of different multinational companies in the forest regions (R. Price and S. Price 1989), non-Maroon money (*bakaa moni*) is also found in the forest, not just on the coast.

Although it is difficult to know for sure how much Sa Yani earns from growing and selling her crops, Ba Elesi does not seem to be a traditional provider. In other words, the activities of the Cottica women who make a living from the produce cultivated in their *goon* not only afford access to money and consumer goods, they also enable their circulation and engagement in other work and cooperative activities. This, in turn, allows us to rethink the idea of the dependency of Maroon women on men who migrate—an idea that shaped an important critical and feminist reading of gender in Maroon socialities. We can focus instead on the viewpoint of Cottica women like Sa Yani who call themselves "free" (*fii*). Not coincidentally, this term cropped up many times in our conversations and included diverse themes such as the increasing flexibility of menstrual seclusion rules, women traveling to work in the cities, and the rules governing life in the villages. "Having a husband" (*abi wan man*) does not always imply subjugation, especially among those who, like Sa Yani, congregate in Pentecostal churches that condemn practices associated with Maroon tradition (*traditie*) and culture (*kulturo*), such as polygamy and various alimentary and sexual taboos.

The return of Maroon families to the Cottica River and Moengo, the vast majority headed by women, enabled the modes of occupying houses, yards, and *kampu* to become associated with domestic work and the commercialization of vegetable crops, processed food, *podosiri*, and *kassaba baka*, as well as the sale of beauty services: the work of women who "make hair" (*meke a uwiii*), manufacture natural cosmetics, and sell clothes brought from Paramaribo. The funds obtained through these activities tend to be used to make house improvements, to pay for food and school transportation for children, and to buy clothes, jewelry, and even cars. The relationship between mimicking a consumption pattern typical of Creole women in *Foto* and agricultural work undertaken in the *goon* is reaffirmed in the ways in which people live in Moengo, but also in how they circulate in *Faansi* and the villages. The ability to access and make use of resources in different currencies—vegetable sellers often swap Surinamese dollars for euros or vice versa—is also a target of accusations.

Figure 4.1. Bolls of *pemba doti*. Author's photo, September 2015.

Figure 4.2. Foodstuffs from the *goon* in the Cottica, after a workday. Author's photos, September 2015.

The increasing circulation of money and consumer items through the hands of women seems to have altered the dynamic and impact of the kinds of male migration observed in previous centuries. As a result, the relation between men's mobility and the spiritual effects on women cannot be described as a pattern. The motives—not only made explicit by my interlocutors in Moengo, but also cited in research conducted from the 1990s onward in Suriname and French Guiana—are directly associated with the war and foreground Cottica women as the leading protagonists. Wetering (1992), for example, described a series of events involving consultation of oracles and treatment for possession by *Bakuu* spirits in an encampment set up on the French side of the Tapanahoni River where the Cottica Ndyuka sought refuge during the war. Called *Mongo kampu*, in 1991 this site was the venue for a series of attempts to expel the harmful effects of "demons." The novelty now, though, was the possibility that they had been "brought" by women who migrated and circulated through places like Paramaribo and Saint Laurent du Maroni. Commenting on the impact of her informant, Erna, being accused of buying a *Bakuu* from a Ndyuka man in the city, Wetering observes: "Many demon-ridden young women, likely candidates for exorcism, make a timely escape to Saint-Laurent. Young women like Erna are not only aware of what townspeople think of the rustic Ndyuka but they secretly share these views. Though born and bred in the upriver area and living in a rather worldly camp now, Erna is apparently fearful of being thrown back into the life of the past and resents all attempts to bring her back into a traditional fold" (1992: 123).

Thoden van Velzen and Wetering, for their part, call attention to the singular situation of the Cottica women and their supposed association with nonhuman agencies responsible for their wealth. "Women who lived in the makeshift settlements along the lower Marowijne could earn some money by producing foodstuffs. [. . .] This became quite profitable for those who lived relatively close to the Coast. But the demons riding women urged them . . ." (2004: 232). The relative proximity to Albina and Saint Laurent du Maroni where the earnings, albeit modest, are in euros, is important not only in terms of the speedy access to markets, but also because of the circulation of consumer goods of every kind in the Cottica villages and their impact on the matrimonial market. According to Khoesial, "since it is possible to trade agricultural products in French Guiana for foreign exchange, men have become increasingly involved in farming. They may hire labor or marry more women to take care of the plots" (1996: 74). In Moengo, my female interlocutors observed with a mix of irony and concern, unions between older women and men without an occupation are commonplace.

The residence in a *kampu* and the almost daily journeys to the *goon* and the markets connect activities that form a vital part of the everyday life of numerous Cottica Ndyuka women living in Moengo today. The women are responsible not only for making the things necessary for living—through agricultural work and the sale of *goon* produce—but also for acquiring other things required for 'living well':[25] the objects that transform persons and their relations, the acquisition of objects that express prosperity and decorate their houses, bodies, and hair. Important differences exist in relation to the places of circulation, age, levels of schooling, and the religious affiliations of these women, especially those modalities that Joel Robbins called "Pentecostal-charismatic Christianity" (Robbins 2004).[26] As Heermerske observed apropos the impact of the mining economy on Maroon socialities in recent decades, distinct situations have precipitated important transformations in the relations of Maroon men and women with non-Maroon people.

In the villages located in the interior, difficult and expensive to access, women have limited mobility beyond journeying to their *goon* and the nearby villages, and are subject to rules and taboos associated with menstrual seclusion. Living conditions are difficult in these villages, which are often semi-abandoned or face serious problems of desertification and soil contamination due to mining activity and the illegal extraction of timber by transnational concessionaries. By contrast, on the Cottica River and on the outskirts of cities close to the coast with a strong Maroon presence—like Paramaribo, Moengo, and Saint Laurent du Maroni—women epitomize the connections between mobility, freedom, consumption, and prosperity (2000: 11). The relative freedom of circulation and the potential to make larger earnings from *goon* produce continue to make the *Cottica uma* (Cottica woman) the object of attraction and danger.[27]

Acknowledgments

This chapter is a substantially revised version of the paper "A 'Peesi fu libi': The Cottica Ndyuka families in the spacetimes of Moengo," presented at Duke University and the Symposium Race and Rurality in the Global Economy, organized by Michaeline Crichlow and Ann Maria Makhulu. I thank the participants and audience for their questions, which helped me to reformulate the first version of my paper. Special acknowledgment goes to Juan Giusti-Cordero and Sally Price for their comments and careful suggestions on the manuscript, and to David Rodgers for the editing. My research is funded by CNPq (National Council for Scientific and Technological Development).

Notes

1. When transcribing Ndyuka names, places, and rituals, I give preference to the language spoken by my interlocutors—Okanisi (also Ndyuka and Aucaner)—over the equivalents in Sranantongo and Dutch. These terms appear in italics. Given the orthographic variations and the lack of any consensus concerning how the words should be written, I use the grammars produced by Huttar and Huttar (1994) and Goury and Migge (2003).

2. The Ndyuka (also known as Aucaners, Okanisi, or Ndyukanengee), Paamaka, Aluku, Saamaka, Kwinti, and Matawai are the six Maroon societies, formed by descendants of African slaves who fled from captivity and began to settle in isolated and semiautonomous villages located in the interior of the Dutch colony from the seventeenth century. With some differences, these groups shared a common structure, based largely on matrilineal kinship and affinity. Each group is subdivided into clans, exogamic groups called *lo*, whose members descend from the same female ancestor. In turn, each matriclan is subdivided into matrilineages, designated *bee*. Members of different *lo* are distributed in different villages, although each *bee* has its own village, since it is in the village of a particular *bee* that gods, spirits, ancestors, and sanctuaries are worshiped and, most importantly, kin are buried (Thoden van Velzen 2011: 50 and passim; Polimé 2007).

3. Moengo was semi-destroyed during the Interior War, a dramatic process that marked the culmination of a series of events involving Maroon groups and urban non-Maroon groups from the coast. This comprised a major shift away from the complex relations of avoidance and approximation involving traditional Maroon authorities and the state since the signing of treaties in the eighteenth century, described by Scholtens as a "state within a state" (Scholtens 1994:147). In the 1980s, migration, schooling, and jobs in the city, combined with the attraction policies promoted by Surinamese political parties following independence and the creation of the Republic of Surinam in 1975, had substantial impacts on the Maroon villages, especially in the Marowijne region (R. Price and S. Price 1989; Kruijt and Hoogbergen 2005; MacKay 2006). Criminalization and persecution of young Maroon in the coast contributed to the formation of an armed uprising of, in particular, Cottica Ndyuka, against the Desi Bouterse government. The first armed actions undertaken by Cottica Ndyuka against army soldiers began in 1984 on the roads in the Eastern Coast region. The persecution of the insurgent Maroons involved armed assaults on the villages. A guerrilla group composed of

hundreds of Maroons and a few Amerindians, called Jungle Commando (hereafter JC), was formed to protect Maroon territories from attacks by the Desi Bouterse government and the Surinamese army. The beginning of the "war" in the "Interior" was officially recognized, and the actions of the Surinamese Army began to target Maroon villages in Ndyuka, Saamaka and Paamaka territories. As the JC was led by a Cottica Ndyuka man from the village of Morakondee, Cottica Ndyuka Maroons saw their agricultural fields destroyed and houses burned down, as well as violence against children, women, and the elderly. In 1986, a *kampu* nearby Mungotapu, a village "owned" by a Ndyuka clan (*lo*) associated with the main JC's leaders was invaded, its crops were destroyed, and twenty-one civilian Maroons were killed (Kambel and MacKay 1999; MacKay 2006). Terrified, hundreds of Cottica Ndyukas fled to French Guiana and sheltered in refugee camps. My interlocutors and their families in Moengo witnessed these events directly or were descendants of the victims.

4. The timber transported by Maroons was sold by them for more attractive prices than those practiced by the *houtenplantages*—plantations producing and extracting timber on a large scale for use in civil construction (Kappler 1854).

5. The treaties allowed momentary interruptions to the attacks on plantations and granted the autonomy of the village settlements in the territories already occupied by fugitives. The accords were signed first with the Ndyuka (1760), and subsequently with the Saamaka (1762) and Matawai (1767). Later, in the decades prior to the abolition of slavery in 1863, these treaties were renewed (in 1835 and 1838) with the addition of new terms (Boonacker 1916; Groot 2009; Bilby 1997).

6. Maroon socialities in the Guianas are composed of matrilineal-descent kin groups, organized in matriclans (*lo*) and matrilineages (*bee*). Affiliation to a common ancestor informs a person's obligations, defines the relations between affines and non-affines, and determines the modes and rights of occupying space, knowledge transmission, the appropriation of goods, and above all the control of spiritual, magical, and divinatory practices.

7. Polimé estimates that the first villages and *kampu* that resulted from the migration of Ndyuka from the Tapanahoni River were founded between 1820 and 1915 (2004, 2007). There are important clues in the available sources corroborating this estimate. Coster, for example, who traded timber with Maroon villagers on the Cottica between 1851 and 1857, mentions negotiations with a *kabiten* called Sparri Passi from Manja Bon village (1866: 3).

8. This expression was used by Thoden van Velzen and van Wetering (2004: 267) to describe old Ndyuka men recognized as "specialists" or "connoisseurs" of facts, events, myths, and sacred histories about places, gods, and spirit, by their own or younger generations. These men are considered specialists in the histories (*toli*) of the "first-times" (among the Saamaka Maroon, *Fési-ten*, or *Fositen Toli* among the Ndyuka) that tell of the conflict, fissions, and taboo restrictions among clans and matrisegments, which, due to their power and potential effects on the present, are rarely revealed (R. Price 1983; Pakosie 1989).

9. Suralco (Suriname Aluminum Company), the local subsidiary of ALCOA (Aluminum Company of America), succeeded SBM (Surinamische Bauxite Maatschappij).

10. Although old maps refer to the place as "Moengro" and old Cottica Ndyuka people use "Mungo," in this text I use the official name of the locality as it appears in contemporary government publications and is used by local inhabitants.

11. The posthoulder R. W. van Lier, for instance, ended up acting as a mediator, reconciling the interests of the bauxite company in attracting workers and resolving the conflicts on the Cottica over the implantation of schools, immunization campaigns, and the transportation of deceased employees (Lier, cited in Groot 1969: 207, 217).

12. The name of Köbben's interlocutor is fictitious (1967: 367).

13. The presence of churches, missionary work, and conversion to different forms of Christianity have been part of Maroon experience in Suriname since the eighteenth century (Thoden van Velzen 1988; Vernooij 1996).

14. Coppelmans, C. J. M. et al. 1953. "Specifieke voor Hinderpalen bij Missionering der Bosnegers." Bisdom Archief, Paramaribo, 2.

15. It was not uncommon to find missionaries of both groups working in neighboring villages and, later quite frequently, even in the same villages. This is the case of villages such as Peetondo and Adjumakonde, the first to have both EBG (Broadergemente) and RK (Rooms-Katholiek) churches and school.

16. Spruijt, N. C. 1957. *La Mission chez les Noirs de l'intérieur*, Bisdom Archief Paramaribo, 4. See, for example, the expeditions of the medical biologist and Interior Affairs Department officer, Dirk Cornelis Geijskes, between February and April 1952 (Geijskes 1955). Catholic missionary activity not only supported projects like the transfer of residents of Maroon villages to new "villages" in Brokopondo, it also won state resources for the opening of Catholic schools. "Aantekeningen naar aanleiding van het bezoek aan de Boven-Cottica en het Brokopondo-gebied op resp [16 maart 1966 en maart 1966]," n/a. Bisdom Archief, Paramaribo. See also (1950), "24 Jaar naar Tamarin: een jubileum in het oerwoud." Bisdom Archief, Paramaribo.

17. In 1947 the opening of a pre-molded construction factory, using timber extracted by Maroon labor, the *Bruynzeel Surinaamse Houtmaatschappij*, attracted Maroon families to areas close to the Patamaca region. After delivering the timber, the Maroon would spend the night sleeping by the river shore before returning to their villages on the Cottica (Helman 1977: 190).

18. In a letter to his superiors in Paramaribo, Father Spruijt, for example, refers to the plans of the "Americans" to mine bauxite in an area close to Ofiaollo village and their negotiations with the *kapiten* Asinga. See Spruijt, N. C. (1953). Brief [Tamarin, 25 mei 1953], Bisdom Archief, Paramaribo.

19. Just as river transport on the Maroni has been controlled by the Maroon—in particular Ndyuka—since the nineteenth century, the passenger road transport connecting Paramaribo to Albina is controlled by Cottica Ndyuka. On the conflicts over control of river transport and, after the war, control of the roads in Eastern Suriname, see Hoogbergen and Polimé (2002).

20. Though it has continued in nearby areas with serious environmental and human impacts, causing harm and destruction to villages created in the nineteenth century like *Ajumakonde.*

21. Since women and matrilineages have no rights over the land on which they traditionally live and plant (the *goon*), they receive no resources from the state. Sa Mari had already participated in women's cooperatives and groups—such as *A Sa Yepi* in Peetondo—that organize to provide resources for planting, transporting, and selling their produce, as well as to promote community forms of investing profit.

22. White clay associated with medicinal and spiritual powers capable of protecting the body against outside forces (Bilby et al. 1989: 256).

23. On the presence of the Cottica Ndyuka in French territory, see Jolivet and Vernon (2007) and Leobal (2014).

24. The notion of *obia* among the Maroon of the Guianas shows important semantic convergences and divergences vis-à-vis seemingly analogous practices in the Anglophone Caribbean known as *obeah*. On this topic, see Bilby and Handler (2004). The concept of *obia* can be taken to refer to the transformative potency of persons themselves and, therefore, their bodies and relations with other beings, human and nonhuman. However, it is also a concept that articulates the approximation of worlds in constant and mutual relation.

25. Here I am making a direct analogy with the idea of "living well" found in the ethnological literature on Western Amazonia, in particular in Peru and Ecuador, with its evocation of rules and values of conviviality (Gow 1991). Among my interlocutors in Moengo, it was common to hear expressions in Okanisi combined with terms in Dutch such as *mi de rustig* ("I am at peace").

26. In the Cottica area, besides the Moravian and Catholic presence and a few Baptist and Adventist churches and schools in villages, over the last decade Moengo has seen the arrival of several branches of the *Volle Envangelie gemeente* (Full Gospel movement) and the Wesleyan Church from Paramaribo and United States (van der Pijl 2010: 181).

27. *Cottica Uma* is also a context that involves young Maroon women in Suriname and French Guiana. Each year Moengo hosts "miss" competitions in which not only the beauty but also the clothes and knowledge of young Maroon women are judged. Cash and travel prizes are offered to the winners.

References

Amoksi, M. 2009. *De Marronvrouw in de Stad: Een historische analyses van de gevolgen van de urbanisatie voor de marronvrouen in Suriname.* Amsterdam: Ninsee/Amrit.

Andel, T. R. v. 2010. "How African-based Winti Belief Helps to Protect Forests in Suriname." In *Sacred Natural Sites: Conserving Nature & Culture*, edited by B. E. A. Verschuren. London, Earthscan.

Besson, J. 2007. "Squatting as a Strategy for Land Settlement and Sustainable Development." In *Caribbean Land and Development Revisited*, edited by J. Besson and J. H. Momsen, 135–146. New York: Palgrave Macmillan.

———. 2002. *Martha Brae's Two Histories: European Expansion and Caribbean Culture-Building in Jamaica.* Chapel Hill: University of North Carolina Press.

Bilby, Kenneth M., and Jerome S. Handler. 2004. "Obeah: Healing and Protection in West Indian Slave Life1." *Journal of Caribbean History* 38 (2): 153.

———. 2001. "Aleke: New Music and New Identities in the Guianas." *Latin American Music Review* 22 (1): 31.

———. 1997. "Swearing by the Past, Swearing to the Future: Sacred Oaths, Alliances, and Treaties among the Guianese and Jamaican Maroons." *Ethnohistory* 44 (4): 655–689.

———. et al. 1989. "L'Alimentation des noirs marrons du Maroni: Vocabulaire, pratiques, représentations." Institut français de recherche scientifique pour le développement en coopération, Centre ORSTOM de Cayenne.

Bonne, C. 1923. "Hygiannische Ervaring te Moengo." *Nieuwe West-Indische Gids*: 395–404.

Boonacker, J. 1916. "Politieke Contacten met de Boschnegers in Suriname." *Bijdragen tot de taal-, land-en volkenkunde/Journal of the Humanities and Social Sciences of Southeast Asia* 71 (1): 371–411.

Cadena, M. de la. 2010. "Indigenous Cosmopolitics in the Andes: Conceptual Reflections beyond 'Politics.'" *Cultural Anthropology* 25 (2): 334–370.

Carney, Judith. 2005. "Rice and Memory in the Age of Enslavement: Atlantic Passages to Suriname." *Slavery and Abolition* 26 (3): 325–348.

Coster, A. M. 1866. "De Boschnegers in de kolonie Suriname. Hun leven, zeden en gewoonten." *Bijdragen tot de Taal-, Land-en Volkenkunde van Nederlandsch-Indië*: 1–36.

Cunha, Olivia M. G. da. 2018. "(Re)creating Spaces and Times: The Cottica Ndyuka in Moengo" In *Ethnographies of U.S. Empire*, edited by J. Collins and C. McGranahan. Durham, NC: Duke University Press.

Dijck, P. van. 2001. Continuity and change in a Small open economy: External dependency and policy inconsistencies. 20th Century Suriname. Continuities and Discontinuities in a New World Society, edited by R. Hoefte and P. Meel, 48–70. Leiden: KITLV Press/Kingston: Ian Randle.

Geijskes, D. C. 1955. "De landbouw bij de bosnegers van de Marowijne." *New West Indian Guide/Nieuwe West-Indische Gids* 35 (1): 135–153.

Goury, L., and B. Migge. 2003. *Grammaire du Nengee: Introduction aux Langues Aluku, Ndyuka et Pamaka.* Paris: IRD Editions.

Groot, S. W. de. 1969. *Djuka Society and Social Change: History of an Attempt to Develop a Bush Negro Community in Surinam 1917–1926*. Amsterdam: Van Gorcum.

———. 2009. *Agents of Their Own Emancipation: Topics in the History of Surinam Maroons*. Amsterdam: de Groot.

Heemskerk, Marieke. 2000. *Gender and gold mining: The case of the Maroons of Suriname*, vol. 269 of *Women in International Development*. Ann Arbor: Michigan State University.

Helman, A., and E. Abendanon-Hymans. 1977. *Cultureel Mozaïek van Suriname*. Zutphen: Walburg Pers.

Hesselink, G. 1974. *De Maatschappijstad Moengo en haar omgeving*. Amsterdam: Geografisch en Planologish Instituut van Vrije Universitëit.

Hoefte, R. 2013. *Suriname in the Long Twentieth Century: Domination, Contestation, Globalization*. New York: Palgrave Macmillan.

Hoogbergen, W., and T. Polime. 2002. "Oostelijk Suriname 1986–2002." *OSO—Tijdschrift voor Surinamistiek en het Caraïbisch gebied* 21 (2): 225–242.

Huttar, G. L., and M. L. Huttar. 2003. *Ndyuka*. New York: Routledge.

Jolivet, M.-J., and D. Vernon. 2007. "Droits, polygamie et rapports de genre en Guyane." *Cahiers des Études Africaines* 187: 733.

Kambel, E.-R. 2007. "Land, Development, and Indigenous Rights in Suriname: The role of international Human Rights in Suriname." In *Caribbean Land and Development Revisited*, edited by J. Besson and J. H. Momsen, 69–80. New York, Palgrave Macmillan.

Kappler, A. 1854. *Zes jaren in Suriname: Schetsen en tafereelen uit het maatschappelijke en militaire leven in deze kolonie*. Utrecht: W. F. Dannenfelser.

Khoesial, Sheela. 1996. *Women Food Producers in Suriname: Technology and Marketing*. San Jose, Costa Rica: Inter-American Institute for Cooperation on Agriculture/Inter-American Development Bank.

Köbben, A. J. F. 1967. "Unity and disunity-Cottica Djuka as a kinship system." *Bijdragen tot de Taal-, Land-en Volkenkunde* 123 (1): 10–52.

Koning, A. 2011a. "Shadows of the Plantation? A Social History of Suriname, a Bauxite Town Moengo." *New West Indian Guide/Nieuwe West-Indische Gids* 85 (3–4): 215–246.

———. 2011b. "Moengo on Strike: The Politics pf Labour in Surinama's Bauxite Industry." *Revista Europea de Estudios Latinoamericanos y del Caribe* 91: 31–48.

Kruijt, D., and W. Hoogbergen. 2005. "Peaceful Relations in a Stateless Region: The Post-War Maroni River Borders in the Guianas." *Tijdschrift voor Economische en Sociale Geografie* 96 (2): 199–208.

Lamur, C. 1983. *The American Take-over: Industrial Emergence and Alcoa's Expansion in Guyana and Suriname: With Special Reference to Suriname, 1914–1921*. Leiden: Brill.

Léobal, C. 2014. "Politiques urbaines et recompositions identitaires en contexte post-colonial: Les marrons à Saint-Laurent du Maroni (1975–2012)." Rapport de Recherche. Paris Cité, Université Paris-Descartes, Sorbonne.

————. 2013. *Saint-Laurent-du-Maroni: Une porte sur le fleuve*. Matoury: Ibis Rouge Editions.

Lier, W. F. v. 1940. Notes sur la vie spirituelle et sociale des Djuka (Noirs Réfugieés Auca). (Trad. avec la introdution de C.H. de Goije). MS. L. University. Leiden University, KITC.

MacKay, F. 2006. *Moiwana zoekt gerechtigheid: De strijd van een Marrondorp tegen de staat Suriname*. Leiden: KIT Publishers.

————. (2002). "Mining in Suriname: Multinationals, the State and the Maroon Community of Nieuw Koffiekamp." In *Human Rights and the Environment Conflicts and Norms in a Globalizing World*, edited by L. Zarsky. London: Earthscan Press.

Mintz, S. W. 1974. *Caribbean Transformations*. Chicago: Aldine Publishing.

Oudschans Dentz, F. 1921. "De Bauxietnijverheid en de stichting van een nieuwe stad in Suriname." *De West-Indische Gids* (1921): 481–508.

Palgrave, W. G. 1876. *Dutch Guiana*. London: Macmillan.

Pakosie, A. R. M. 1989. "Orale traditie bij de de Bosneger." *OSO—Tijdschrift voor Economische en Sociale Geografie* 8 (2): 159–165.

Pijl, Y. v. d. 2003. "Room to Roam: Afro-Surinamese Identifications and the Creole Multiple Self." *FOCAAL*: 105–116.

Polimé, T. 2007. "Het traditioneel gezag op een tweesprong: De Ndyuka-marrons." In *Ik ben een haan met een kroon op mijn hoofd. Pacificatie en verzet in koloniaal en postkoloniaal Suriname*, edited by W. Hoogbergen, 55–74. Amsterdam: Uitgeverijn Bert Bakker.

————. "Reproductieve Rituelen van de Ndyuka." *Tijdschrift voor Surinamistiek en het Caraïbisch gebied* (OSO) 19 (2): 241–259.

Polimé, T., and B. Thoden van Velzen. 1988. *Vluchtelingen, opstandelingen en andere Bosnegers van Oost-Suriname, 1986–1988*. Utrecht: Instituut voor Culturele Antropologie.

Price, R. 1975. *Saramaka Social Structure: Analysis of a Maroon Society in Surinam*. Puerto Rico: Institute of Caribbean Studies.

————. 1991. "Subsistence on the Plantation Periphery: Crops, Cooking, and Labour Among Eighteenth-century Suriname Maroons." *Slavery and Abolition* 12 (1): 107–127.

————. 2007. "Liberdade, Fronteiras e Deuses: Saramakas no Oiapoque (c. 1900)." In *Quase-Cidadão: histórias antropologias da pós-emancipação no Brasil*, edited by Olivia M. G. Cunha and Flavio S. Gomes, 119–146. Rio de Janeiro: Fundação Getulio Vargas.

Price, R., and S. Price. 1989. "Working for the Man: A Saramaka Outlook on Kourou." *New West Indian Guide* 63: 199–207.

Price, S. 1993. *Co-wives and Calabashes*. Ann Arbor: University of Michigan Press.

————. 1983. "Sexism and the Construction of Reality: An Afro-American Example." *American Ethnologist* 10 (3): 460–476.

————. 1994. "The curse's blessing [menstruation]." *Frontiers: A Journal of Women Studies* 14 (2): 123–142.

————. 2003. "Always Something New: Changing Fashions in a 'Traditional Culture.'" In *Crafting Gender: Women and Folk Art in Latin America and the Caribbean*, edited by E. Bartra, 17–34. Durham, NC: Duke University Press.

Stengers, Isabelle. 2011. *Cosmopolitics II*. Minneapolis: University of Minnesota Press.

Thoden van Velzen, B., and W. van Wetering. 1983. "Affluence, Deprivation and the Flowering of Bush Negro Religious Movements." *Bijdragen tot de Taal-, Land-en Volkenkunde La Haye* 139 (1): 99–139.

————. 1988. *The Great Father and the Danger: Religious Cults, Material Forces, and Collective Fantasies in the World of the Surinamese Maroons*. Dordrecht and Providence: Foris Publications.

————. 2004. *In the Shadow of the Oracle: Religion as Politics in a Suriname Maroon Society*. Long Grove, IL: Waveland Press.

Tomich, D. 1991. "Une Petite Guinee: Provision Ground and Plantation in Martinique, 1830–1848." *Slavery and Abolition* 12 (1): 68–91.

Toren, Christina. 1995. "Seeing the Ancestral Sites: Transformations in Fijian Notions of the Land." In *The Anthropology of Landscape: Perspectives on Place and Space*, edited by Eric Hirsch and Michael O'Hanlon, 163–183. Oxford: Oxford University Press.

Vernon, D. 1980. "Bakuu: Possesing Spirits of Witchcraft on the Tapanahony." *New West Indian Guide* 54 (1): 1.

————. 1985. *Money Magic in a Modernizing Maroon Society*. Tokyo: Institute for the Study of Languages and Cultures of Asia and Africa (ILCAA), Tokyo University of Foreign Studies.

Vernooij, J. 1996. *Bosnegers en Katholieke Kerk: Van confrontatatie naar dialog*. Paramaribo: Stichting Wetenschappelijke Informatie.

Wetering, W. van. 1992. "A Demon in Every Transistor." *Etnofoor* 5 (1/2): 109–127.

Wetering, W. van, and B. Thoden van Velzen. 1982. "Female Religious Responses to Male Prosperity in Turn-of-the-century Bush Negro Societies." *New West Indian Guide* 56 (1/2): 43–68.

Wong, E. 1938. "Hoofdenverkiezing, stamverdeeling en stamverspreiding der Boschnegers van Suriname in de 18e en 19e eeuw." *Bijdragen tot de Taal-, Land-en Volkenkunde* 97 (3): 295–362.

5

Race and Class Marginalization in the Globalization of the Rice Industry

Wazir Mohamed

This chapter explores the dynamic relationship between increasing globalization and the marginalization of small-scale rice farmers by considering some of the ongoing changes in the rice industry in Latin America and the Caribbean, but pays special attention to the experience of Guyana and Honduras.[1] I use the term "race and class marginalization" to demarcate the specificities of social class relations and racialization in the Caribbean that emerged as these societies evolved under racial rule in the colonial period but which are now being covertly deepened under neoliberal globalization. Colonial power relations marginalized Amerindian, Afro-Guyanese, Indo-Guyanese, and the other nonwhite peoples and generally subordinated them in rural space through their dependence on plantation agricultural labor regimes, or by their displacement from indigenous land entitlements. Despite these power relations, marginalized groups still developed attachments to specific food crops through which they wove their lives' purpose and around which specific cultures and rituals emerged conditioning particular experiences.

Neoliberal globalization operating through neoliberal structural adjustment policies in the Global South during the 1980s has reconfigured rural and agricultural sectors by expelling small farmers and rearranging their attachments to food crops and the rice industries they created since the colonial period. The central point of departure in this chapter is the expulsion of small rice farmers in Guyana and Central America as neoliberal globalization processes unfold. Two processes of expulsion are being witnessed. In Guyana, lands used by small farmers are swallowed up by larger farmers; while in Central America as the millers and marketing companies benefit from increased imports of subsidized US rice, small farm production is unable to compete and is pushed out of contention. From this standpoint, this chapter adds to and complements the work being done by scholars, as well as international agencies such as Oxfam and Christian Aid, critical of neoliberal policies (Sumner 2011; Paasch, Garbers, and Hirsch 2007; Germain 2009), who have examined these policies and their effects since 1980. Despite policy shifts in prescriptive adjustment regimes led by the IMF or World Bank, these neoliberal trends continue through patterns of open regionalism, as recently exemplified in the Dominican Republic Central American Free Trade Act (DR-CAFTA), which was signed into law in August 2005 and governs trade between the United States of America and those countries covered by the agreement. Apart from the expulsion of small rice farmers due to the impact of neoliberal globalization, this chapter highlights, or brings into sharper focus, the damaging asymmetries of these liberalizing trade regimes given the effects of continued US agricultural subsidies on small farmers in the countries to be discussed, mainly Honduras and Guyana. This chapter first traces the historical footsteps of rice in the Americas and its connection to the lives and survival of historically marginalized minority groups. Next, the chapter examines the changing political economy of regulation and competition in agriculture. After that, the chapter describes the politics of rice in the era of liberalization, marginalization, and displacement. This is accomplished by examining what actually happened to small rice farmers in Honduras and Guyana after structural adjustment policies were adopted and implemented.

The Historical Footsteps of Rice

Rice and its history in the Latin American and Caribbean (LAC) region is bound up with resistance and the search for spaces of survival as carried out by slaves, indentured servants, and the indigenous peoples marginalized by the colonial projects. Thanks to the research of Carney (2001a, 2001b, 2004, 2005), Castanha (2011), Steiner and Rodriguez (1975), Todorov (1999), Littlefield (1981), Wood (1974), Robert Voeks and John Rashford (2013), and others, we are able to make sense as to why rice became part of the communities of the poorest sections of Central and Latin America and the Caribbean. Rice, a staple of the rice coast of Africa, was one of multiple food crops that crisscrossed the Atlantic in what became known as the Columbian Exchange (Carney 2001b: 377–396).[2] The proliferation of rice as a crop of those marginalized by the colonial economy proved to be integral to the life and survival of slaves, the descendants of slavery, indentureship, and the Amerindians in many parts of the region. For example, in Spanish America runaway slaves joined with Amerindians who had established communities far away from the plantations, and in these communities strains of rice that were native to South America and to Africa survived into the postcolonial period (Castanha 2011: 72). It was thus among the crops around which resistance as well as accommodation communities emerged in the Americas during the long colonial period.[3] In most of the region under discussion, as these communities expanded their livelihoods, culture and history became intertwined with rice. Rice growing became established as an ancestral tradition across the region. It is a cultural lifestyle of the poor in which all members of the family are involved.[4] Small-scale rice farming, which much of the literature of the region categorizes as peasant farming, emerged then from the bowels of slavery, racism, and colonialism and is a lasting testament of the struggles against plantation agriculture and to the capacity of humans to find ways and means of survival against all odds. The point I make here is the need to recapture this history, and to recognize as James Scott (1985: 36) does, that history as written has conspired to expunge everyday forms of resistance from memory.

Rice, one of the resistance crops that survived monoculture, is today one of the important staple foods of working peoples in South America. For several centuries it was produced primarily on miniscule patches of land by small-scale farmers (variously described as proto-peasants, paddy proletariat, and small-scale farmers) who make up approximately 75 percent of rice producers in the region.[5] The evolution of rice production has also been directly connected to the diffusion of African and Amerindian knowledge systems in the Americas during the long period of colonial conquest, slavery, and indentureship. Over the period 1492 to the end of the illegal slave trade in the 1860s, food crops and knowledge systems crossed the Atlantic between the Americas and Africa. The diffusion of rice and rice production systems is deeply embedded and connected to this Columbian exchange (Carney 2001b: 5–7).

Rice farming in the region of the Americas has therefore been coexistent with slavery, slave plantation production, slave subsistence production on plantations, slave resistance, with Amerindian resistance to the conquistadors, and with the survival of slave runaway communities. The production and proliferation of rice farming as a small farming crop by small-scale producers is no accident of history. As Judith Carney concluded in her article "Grains in Her Hair," "rice cultivation provides a signature of the black (nonwhite) Atlantic, linking the Upper Guinea

Coast" to the Americas (Carney 2004: 22). Africans, Amerindians, and African and Amerindian knowledge systems in the production of rice shaped the early development of the rice industry both as a plantation and subsistence crop (Carney 2001a). From excavations and the emergence of new evidence, we are now also learning that there was some fusion of African and Amerindian knowledge systems in the production and proliferation of subsistence crops including rice in the highlands of Central and Latin America (parts of Spanish America). The history of rice in Central and Latin America, especially among the indigenous communities, can deepen our understanding of its role in shaping endogenous development trajectories. We know, for example, from the research of Judith Carney and others that Amerindian and African crops were exchanged during the period of the slave trade. Resulting from this exchange, rice slowly became a staple in the diet of much of the region of the Americas outside of the United States and Canada. This is especially true with respect to the cultural connection reflected in the fusion between rice and beans in the region into the dietary cuisine of the black and indigenous communities.

Rice and beans is a coveted part of the history and memory of dietary and cultural life in all areas of the region—Spanish, French, Portuguese, Dutch, and English. The history and memory of these staple foods combined in a single dish that proliferates across the region is captured in a recent text, suitably titled "Rice and Beans: A Unique Dish in a Hundred Places" (Wilks and Barbosa 2012). This work helps to showcase the contribution of the indigenous Amerindian, African, and East Indian communities to regional and global cuisine. The fact that this text brings together articles that discuss the different ways rice and beans is cooked and presented also gives us the opportunity to learn that the diffusion of food systems that is tied to rice as a staple has regional variations depending on specific colonial histories. The point here is that in each area, transplanted peoples developed and created ownership of specific aspects of what has become culture, and the Amerindians have contributed enormously to this culture located in food. But while rice is enormously connected with the history and survival of the African and indigenous communities, in Guyana it is also bound up with the food, history, as well as the survival of poor rural dwellers among the East Indian indentured community who partly or completely separated themselves from the sugar plantations. The process of proliferation of rice in Guyana is thus different from the other colonies.

In Guyana, rice did not survive the vagaries of the plantations' demands on the slaves' time. Because of sugar's command over land and labor in the age of sugar's dominance, the slave population was prevented from planting rice officially, and they were also prevented by force of arms to do so unofficially. Due to the relative scarcity of labor in the colony in the final decades of slavery, the planter class did not permit or sanction the development of a diversified agriculture in the colony. They curtailed the growth of slave provision grounds and smashed attempts by slaves who wanted to and who had established runaway African communities in the interior (Viotti da Costa 1994: 80–81; Thompson 1987: 129–152). On the heels of the denial of Africans to engage in rice production, because of the demands on the labor time of the slaves in the period of the beginnings of the sugar revolution of the nineteenth century in Guyana (1815–1838), East Indian indentured servants recruited to supplant the freed African labor force as a means of cheapening the cost of labor were grudgingly allowed to plant rice on the margins of the sugar plantations (1865–1897) as a means of subsidizing and reducing the cost of food imports. From this early beginning, the rural East Indian population that emerged out of indentured servitude in the twentieth century established what Lesley Potter (1992) describes as the "paddy Proletariat," a rural-based, small-farm rice peasantry that is now being phased out as market forces take over. The history of sugar and rice in Guyana offers a unique opportunity for us to understand the workings of capital and the evolution of the structural dimensions of racial and ethnic marginalization. In Guyana, Africans as slaves and Africans after slavery were denied the possibility of economic independence through production of a rival commodity to sugar. As a result, although Africans are involved in the rice industry, the bulk of producers in the industry are the descendants of East Indian indenture.

This history teaches us that rural nonwhite peoples (Africans, East Indians, and indigenous Amerindians) created a space of partial independence as subsistence producers of rice within the construct of the plantation economy in the first instance, and then later in the colonial and independence period, as producers of one of the major staples within the region. During the course of the twentieth century, these communities of subsistence producers emerged to become an important sector of national economies. They either satisfied the local requirement of rice for domestic consumption and/or added to exports from particular countries of the region. This served to reduce the food import bill, bring in much needed foreign exchange, and provide employment and livelihoods to vast areas in the rural communities.

The Changing Political Economy of Regulation
and Competition in Agriculture

In the rice-producing countries of Central America and the Dominican Republic, rice provides jobs for approximately 1.5 million people, and livelihood to tens of thousands of farmers who make a living from growing the crop (Oxfam UK 2004: 4). This figure does not account for the tens of thousands of people in Haiti (93,000 families, McGuigan 2006: 12) and Guyana who make a living as small farmers (in 1996 20,000, *Guyana Review* 1989:11) and the jobs that result from the industry—in 1996 150,000 jobs out of a total population of 800,000 (Oxfam Canada 2001:1). In these countries rice was protected because of its importance to domestic consumption and the savings these countries made through the reduction of the food import bill.

Trade protection mechanisms were specifically designed by the majority of national governments of poor Third World countries during the period 1945–1970, to shield local producers, including rice producers and rural peoples from international and global competition (McMichael 2004: 18–71). For example, import controls were put in place in most of these countries, and mechanisms, such as high import tariffs, made it difficult for foreign rice to penetrate local markets.[6] These controls began under colonial relations and both the colonial economy and European metropolis benefited from this structure of protection in several ways—for example, they did not have to expend monies to import the main provision for the diet of the majority of the populations of these subject countries. As such, after the formal end of colonialism in the latter half of the twentieth century, in order to continue to benefit from access to rice and other products, new counterpart agreements were developed that allowed for preferential access of these products to their markets. In the case of the African, Caribbean, and Pacific group (ACP) of countries the counterpart arrangements titled the Lomé Conventions (1, 2, 3, and 4, 1975–2000), which defined trade relations between these countries and the European Union (EU), were put in place. These acted as a disincentive for national governments to diversify their economies, and hence these countries became trapped within the colonial structure of production and dependent on one or two crops even as agricultural trade was globalized.

Notwithstanding the presence of protective and preferential agreements present in developing countries, small-scale farming in these areas has been under the threat of global capitalist agriculture, especially from the US, in the Latin American and

Caribbean region since 1945. The growing power of big capitalist farmers is not a new phenomenon; it is a continuation of what was experienced in England, many parts of Europe, and in the US in the twentieth century. Several scholars, but for brevity I will reference only three, in particular, Farshad Araghi, Eric Hobsbawm, and Phillip McMichael, point to these most massive social changes accompanying globalization that has affected and continue to affect the structure of rural society and in particular small farm agriculture. For example, Eric Hobsbawm (1992) explained that in the period between the Second World War and the onset of neoliberal globalization in the 1980s, this type of agro-industrial concentration had been quickening in pace. He noted that between 1945 and 1980 the world "saw the most spectacular, rapid, far-reaching, profound, and worldwide social change in global history. . . . [It] is the first period in which the peasantry became a minority, not merely in industrially developed countries, in several of which it had remained very strong, but even in the Third World countries" (Hobsbawm 1992: 56). Farshad Araghi (1995) highlighted this trend in his essay "Global Depeasantization," which artfully demonstrated that in the period 1945–1990, the world, specifically the Third World, witnessed a massive movement of people from rural to urban areas. This movement was concentrated in the relocation and/or migration of people whose lives were organized around agriculture as the mainstay of their subsistence (Araghi 1995: 338). In the shadow of such structural changes, some Third World govern-ments implemented protective mechanisms between 1945 and 1970 that sheltered small farmers against encroachment from foreign produce in the local marketplace. In Guyana, apart from protective tariffs that served to debar, and/or limit the pos-sibility to import rice, several mechanisms were established by the government to help small farmers. These included government-funded and -managed agricultural machinery pools that allowed for easy access to small farmers; extension services that brought improved knowhow to the farm; marketing facilities (rice silos—for storage), improved drainage and irrigation, agricultural banks, and so forth. Such state-supported mechanisms were important to the survival of small farm agriculture, and this was an important aid to the rapid expansion in the number of rice farmers between 1955and 1968 (the approximate increase ranged from 26,983 to 45,000).[7]

The establishment and survival of support mechanisms for small rice farmers was not only related to the preferential access agreements between former colonies and their former masters, but extended to independent governments, which saw protection of their small farming population as a necessity for internal development and growth.[8] Hence, within most of the Third World, after political independence many of these countries sought for and developed local instruments to control and manage their economies. These included but were not limited to provision of subsidies and cheap sources of finance for farmers (in Guyana, the Guyana Agricultural and Industrial Bank, or GAIBANK, an agricultural bank was established that offered cheap and readily available financing), and public ownership of enterprises such as telecommunications, electricity generation, water, health, education, and other services that were deemed public goods. These in effect helped to stem the tide of the complete erosion of rural culture, located in small farm agriculture until the 1980s.

The Politics of Rice in the Era of Liberalization, Marginalization, and Displacement

In the decade of the 1980s, debt-strapped national governments in the Third World, having been forced by the International Monetary Fund (IMF) and the World Bank to choose between continued fiscal crises or accept enforced and managed structural adjustment, agreed to the latter course. Acceptance of the structural adjustment packages, which in real terms meant the imposition of adverse and harsh conditionality, which included the dismantling of protections. Within the affected countries class cleavages and inequalities began to expand, and at the global level the old historical economic and political asymmetries were deepened in favor of the dominant North and European powers. Development goals from this backdrop were no longer national, but liberal. Vulnerable groups were sacrificed, and the prescriptions of the IMF and World Bank—through which global capital imposes the neoliberal economic system—exacerbated and widened the structural divisions between large and small producers. Structural inequalities that originated in the colonial period widened, intensifying the gap between the haves and have-nots. The process of neoliberal change that began with the imposition of structural adjustment policies in the decade of the 1980s was further enhanced with the promulgation of the World Trade Organization (WTO) in 1995. The push for implementation of "free trade" in agriculture under the aegis of the WTO reinforces the ever-widening chasm between large and small farmers. The primary issue with the implementation of the WTO's Agreement on Agriculture clause is unevenness in outcome for producers from the rich countries of the North, which continue to receive generous producer and price support subsidies, while producer and price support subsidies for farmers of the Global South are dismantled (McMichael 2004: 172–178). The United States is the biggest beneficiary of this lopsided policy. The US projects the ideology of the free market, while it protects its farmers through subsidies and price supports that distort and make a mockery of its free market mantra.

The Impact of US Policy on the Rice Industry

Subsidies and producer support programs for the big farmers in the United States create an artificial market for low rice prices in the region. This US agricultural policy harms the developing world by picking on the poor, according to Daniel Sumner (2011: 1–2), director of the University of California Agricultural Issues Center and the Frank H. Buck Jr. Professor in the Department of Agricultural and Resource Economics, University of California, Davis. He points out in his publication, "How US Agricultural Policy Hurts the Developing World," that: "In many ways, US agricultural policy is harmful to the global poor. Farm-commodity and related subsidies reduce world prices, especially when prices are already low." Further farm-commodity and related subsidies distort the global market and permit the US to dump its agricultural products, thereby undercutting local production in Third World countries.

Rice is one of the agricultural commodities that is so highly subsidized by the United States that it is creating havoc for small producers in the countries of Central America and the Caribbean. According to Griswold (2006) and OXFAM (2005), US farmers were given an average of $1 billion in rice subsidies from 1995 to 2004, which amounted to at least 72 percent of the cost of production. This made US rice one of the most subsidized commodities in that period. Sumner (2005: 21) estimates that because of such huge subsidies, rice farmers in the United States are in a position to produce rice below world market cost, thus depressing rice market prices by 4–6 percent globally. Through this process, the US has created for itself a coveted position in the regional rice supply market. Such artificial penetration of markets is permitted through several instruments. Among these are the US government's Public Law 480 (PL 480 or Food for Peace) and the structural adjustment programs that lay the basis for long-term change in developing countries' market structure.[9] To complete the cycle, these are accompanied by the near complete eradication of local tariffs and longstanding preferential access agreements between countries of the North and their former colonial possessions.

To emphasize the impact of these structural shifts on the poor and poor small-scale rice farmers, the impact of the Dominican Republic Central American Free Trade Act (DR-CAFTA) on Central America, and the cases of Honduras and Guyana are helpful in understanding the dilemma faced by small farmers. Although space does not permit for an expansion of the discourse with regard to Haiti, note is taken that through the combination of US rice as food aid and structural adjustment in Haiti in the 1980s and 1990s, Haiti moved from being self-sufficient as a net producer to a net importer of rice. Haiti, a country recognized for its revolution against imperial racial power and slavery, is now dependent on US rice imports. Taste and consumption of rice in Haiti is tied to US production, as it became the fourth-largest market in the world for rice that originates in the United States of America. The "Miami rice" variety produced in the United States has taken over the market (Germain 2009: 99). This saga is being repeated over and over across the region, as the Honduran experience demonstrates.

Structural Adjustment and Honduras

Honduras is a classic case study, which demonstrates the impact of liberalization on small-scale farmers. Rice is a key product for food security for the rural economy and survival of the poor in Honduras as it is the third-major staple food, and is among the basic grains upon which the people in the rural communities depend for their basic calorie intake, the others being beans and maize (Paasch, Garbers, and Hirsch 2007: 60). It is thus a key source of nutrition in several regions of the country. Karl Weber of Food Inc. (2009: 247–248) sums up the current rice crisis for small-scale producers as follows: "Due to the opening of markets [Honduran rice market] and the eradication of public services in the agricultural field, Honduras has been repeatedly affected by import surges of rice from the United States since around 1992 . . . [Economic liberalization] had a far greater impact on domestic rice production than natural disasters such as Hurricane Mitch [1998]." Weber goes on to explain that "while there were a reportedly 25,000 rice farmers in Honduras at the end of the 1980s," their numbers have been reduced to less than 1300 rice farmers in the country, according to the official estimates for 2009 (Webber 2009: 247).

Pressures to open up the economy came from the IMF and from large rice-importing companies operating within the country (Oxfam 2004: 13). These pressures were placed on the government in 1991 against the backdrop of the impact of El Niño, which had temporarily restricted local production, thus offering an opening for the importation of rice. Accordingly, long-established protection tariffs against foreign imports were reduced. What was significant here was the permanence of the dismantling of regulation, which allowed for almost unfettered importation of rice. Hence, although farmers had recovered from the harsh effects of El Niño by the end of 1991, which is described as a good year for the rice harvest in the country, the government reduced the tariff on imported rice to 1 percent and began to import rice from the US. Rice shipments in that year amounted to 32,000 metric tons of milled rice and 12,500 metric tons of paddy rice (Paasch, Garbers, and Hirsch 2007: 59–64; Oxfam 2004: 13–14). This measure was implemented even though local production in that year amounted to 54,000 metric tons of paddy rice. The fact that the annual import was almost equivalent to yearly consumption meant that farmers found themselves with no market, and this produced the biggest crisis seen in the industry up to that time. This is what Hondurans call the "Arrozazo" (rice scandal). This shock forced many farmers out of production, since they could not market their rice. Small farmers in many parts of Honduras, especially in areas such as Santa Cruz de Yojoa, Cuyamel, and Cortes, are dependent on rice for their livelihood. Rice is integral to their heritage and culture. This is how Cuyamel rice farmer Jose Candido Sanchez, in an Oxfam (2004:16) interview, described the importance of rice in their heritage and culture: "We live off rice because we do not have dry land." This gives a graphic picture of the connection between rice cultivation and rural food security.

The replacement of local rice, in most cases the primary source of family income for rural communities, exacerbated the already volatile food security problems in the country. The decade of the 1990s brought fluctuating fortunes for farmers as they wrestled with competition or the threat of competition from processed rice (milled rice) or paddy rice (raw material for processing by local mills). A combination of factors led to the gradual reduction in the price of rice on the local market, which forced local farmers to try to compete with imports. However, in the face of increased imports in 1991 and between 1995 and 1997, along with the equalization of the tariffs for milled and paddy rice, it became less attractive and profitable for local millers to purchase from farmers. As it was cheaper for millers to buy imported paddy rice for processing, they refused to purchase at least one-third of the crop from local farmers (Oxfam 2004: 14). This was another blow to the local community of small farmers, as many of them were pushed aside due to pressure from rice and paddy imports from the United States.

To make matters worse, the cheaper rice on the market also created the conditions for the reduction in the ability of millers to engage in competition, and pushed many of them out of contention. Local processing facilities and millers were accordingly pushed aside as wholesalers and supermarkets imported finished rice.[10] As milling capacity was reduced small farmers were pushed to cut production, and a significant number stopped producing altogether. Hence, even before Hurricane Mitch devastated the country in 1998, rice cultivation had already been reduced from 16,000 hectares to 10,000 hectares (Paasch, Garbers, and Hirsch 2007: 63–64; Oxfam 2004: 14). Hurricanes Mitch (1998) and Michelle (2001), combined with the impact of US rice as aid, ensured that the rice industry had no possibility of recovery after the turbulent decade of the 1990s—when it suffered the devastating impact of the "Arrozazo," natural disasters, and increased importation of US rice into the market. Faced with this dire situation, by 2002 Honduras resorted to reliance on 95 percent imports of either milled or paddy rice from the US. This was yet another country that had been self-reliant (Stenzel 2010: 691). The gravity of the crisis for small rice farmers in Honduras is captured in this comment in the 2004 Oxfam briefing paper on DR-CAFTA, "[F]aced with this difficult situation, the majority of rice farmers have opted to migrate, either to the cities or to the US" (Oxfam 2004:16), with upwards of 500,000 Hondurans now living in the United States.

The perversity of this neoliberal global disorder is highlighted by the subsequent rice agreement of 2003 between the government of Honduras and local millers, an agreement that essentially established an oligopoly (Paasch, Garbers, and Hirsch 2007: 68). Rather than involve local rice producers, the millers were given the ability to control the entire industry from production to marketing. They essentially became the main supply channel for national demand, including imported and national production (Paasch, Garbers, and Hirsch 2007: 68). The catch here was the reduction in imports of milled rice, and an increase in the imports of paddy rice for milling and processing by the millers. This action demonstrates the neoliberal emphasis of investment in the merchant classes rather than the rice cultivators. The rice agreement saved the rice sector but was, at the same time, disastrous for small-scale rice farmers. The basic structure of the industry was altered. Consumers no longer were expected to rely on local production for rice. Imports of subsidized US rice and paddy rice served as a roadblock to the future development and expansion of the local rice-farming sector. National production was effectively sacrificed. Farmers were sacrificed, as the millers' piggybacked on the subsidies paid to US producers.

The shift in emphasis away from local production to local processing of imported paddy rice as raw material for processing represents one of the most important shifts in global economic relations in agricultural trade for the rice sector. Millers and rice marketing companies operating in Honduras were able to benefit directly from subsidies paid to US producers. To compete in this market, producers are now required to become more efficient than their counterparts in the US. This can only be achieved through high-yielding production operations. The report from Oxfam (2004: 37–38) argues that this plays into the requirements of the DR-CAFTA arrangement, which Honduras negotiated between 2003 and 2004, and which was ratified by the parliament in 2005, and began its implementation in 2006.

DR-CAFTA and Its Impact

The situation in Honduras offers an important entry point to the discourse as to the climate within which the DR-CAFTA was negotiated and is being implemented. This agreement was entered between the United States of America, Guatemala, El Salvador, Honduras, and Nicaragua in 2006, and then with the Dominican Republic in 2007 and Costa Rica in 2009. According to the terms of this agreement, 100 percent of US consumer and industrial goods exported to these countries will be free of tariffs by 2015, and all tariffs on agricultural products will be phased out by 2020 (http://www.export.gov/fta/cafta-dr/).

While the jury is still out with respect to the full impact of DR-CAFTA on small rice farmers in Central America, the Honduran example shows that instruments such as the rice agreement of 2003 laid the structural basis for takeover of the rice-producing market by large farmers and rice companies as DR-CAFTA is implemented. Though the rice agreement ended as DR-CAFTA came into being, it was an important instrument in the transition phase to more unfettered penetration of the local market by subsidized rice from the US. Another central issue that arises in this process of economic neoliberalization is not just competition from milled rice, but unfair competition from paddy rice. The import of paddy rice helps millers to force down the cost of local production. This was demonstrated earlier in the discussion of the situation in Honduras. It is through this mechanism that DR-CAFTA picks winners and losers. The primary winners are on both sides. They are the large-scale US exporters, and on the Central American side they are the importers. According to the Oxfam (2004: 37) report, "marketing in Central America is concentrated in the hands of a few companies with the means to influence the governments' trade policies and modify the rules of the game." The report goes on to explain that in many instances the local rice companies are subsidiaries or maybe partially owned by US exporters as well. Thus, As Paasch, Garbers, and Hirsch (2007: 82) point out, "By signing the DR-CAFTA, the Honduran state has given up the policy space which is necessary for it to protect the right to food of domestic rice producers." Outcomes such as this are not new. Under NAFTA (North American Free Trade Act), which opened up the Mexican economy to a massive dose of subsidized imports of US rice, 30,000 small rice producers, or approximately two-thirds of small-scale rice farmers in Mexico, were forced out of the rice industry. Indeed, since 1985 many have abandoned farming (Oxfam 2004: 25).

As in Mexico, the people who stand to lose more as DR-CAFTA is implemented are the small rice producers of Central America and the Dominican Republic. Seventy-five percent (19,500) of the 26,000 rice farmers in Guatemala are small farmers whose farm size varies from one to seven hectares (Oxfam 2004: 11). Incidentally, it is in the areas of small rice farm concentration that poverty rates are very high. According to Oxfam (2004) in the rice valleys of Guatemala, poverty rates average between 73 and 80 percent. In Nicaragua, there are 17,000 rice farmers of which there is a preponderance of small-scale farmers, the bulk of whom, that is 34 percent or 6,000, are concentrated in the Autonomous Region of the North Atlantic (RAAN)—home to the Miskito and Mayagna Native populations. As in Guatemala and Honduras, small rice farmers in the RAAN in Nicaragua were already suffering from crisis situations and were abandoning production even before DR-CAFTA (Oxfam 2004: 39). The structure of DR-CAFTA, which is favorable to larger farmers and local rice companies, is likely to further create the conditions for more indigenous, and typically nonwhite small farmers, who have been impoverished by the systematic class discriminatory policies of a hegemonic global neoliberalism, to abandon production. The trend of abandonment of small-scale rice farming prevalent in Central America is not limited to that region. This has been the case in Guyana since the 1980s also. In the late 1980s Guyana liberalized its economy by agreeing to an IMF structured program in 1989 called the "Economic Recovery Program." This was equivalent to the structural adjustment programs alluded to earlier in this chapter. This program represented the final stage of the dismantling of the state-regulated social system established by succeeding governments before 1980. As a result, significant changes have been noted with respect to the rice sector and in particular the condition of these rice farmers.

The Case of Guyana

Guyana offers an interesting study into globalization, the impact of economic neoliberalization, and local dimensions of global change. Guyana has a peculiar history of race and class oppression as it emerged out of slavery and indentureship and became the largest rice producer in the Anglophone Caribbean. For almost one hundred years, between 1897 and 1980, rice cultivation was predominantly small-farmer based. But a slow transition from small- to large-farmer holdings that started in the 1980s has become a deluge as small farmers are expelled due to the exigencies of globally driven market conditions. While many countries in the former colonial world are in the midst of land-grabbing projects from the encroachment of foreign capital as highlighted by the 2012 issue of the *Journal of Peasant Studies*, and the GRAIN (2014) report, in Guyana with regard to rice cultivation, a different and less spectacular sort of land grabbing is occurring. Lands formerly owned and cultivated by small landholders are either acquired and are being cultivated by larger farmers either through purchase, prescriptive rights acquisition, or rental. Through these processes, the numbers of actual farmers/cultivators are being reduced, while the acreage under cultivation has either remained constant or has increased.[11] What is clear is that the Guyanese rice industry is fast becoming one based on large-scale enterprises, which is changing the racial and demographic profile of rice farming in that country.

Guyana openly embraced neoliberal economics and politics under the rubric of the Economic Recovery Program (ERP) in the decade of the 1980s. The ERP opened the floodgates to the market economy and liberalized the institutional controls of the previous decades, and in so doing further dismantled the long-established framework of a small-farmer-based and controlled rice industry. For most of the twentieth century the rice industry was organized around small farmers. It was heavily invested with public assets in the form of modern rice silos, mills, credit facilities, and machinery pools that aided the possibilities for the survival of the small farmer in a rapidly globalizing world economy. The most damaging impact of liberalization has been the privatization of modern rice silos and mills, and complete dismantling of machinery pools that for decades allowed small farmers easy access to tilling, harvesting, and transportation machinery.

Since the ERP was implemented, the small rice-farming sector has had fluctuating fortunes. After a period of rapid decline in the 1980s, even in the shadow of the World Trade Organization (WTO), there was limited recovery in the period from 1990 to 1997. In the latter period farmers took advantage of the relaxation of controls over their ability to sell in the European and the Caribbean Community and Common Market (CARICOM) on account of preferential access.[12] Apart from the benefits of the rice quota to the European market under the Lomé agreements due to the rice production shortfall in the rice industry in some parts of Europe at the time, a much larger bulk of Guyana's rice also entered the European market through a back route, called the Other Countries and Territories Route (OCT, Ministry of Agriculture Report, Guyana, August 1997, "Economic Impacts of the Overseas Countries and Territories Rice Quota"). On account of this, both production and profits skyrocketed until the shocks of 1996–97, when this route was closed. (See discussion on the EU agreement and the OCT route in *The National Development Strategy* 2000: 109.)

Unbridled access to the CARICOM and European markets in this period forestalled the hemorrhaging of farmers experienced in the earlier decade. Lands that had become idle as a result of abandonment by farmers in the earlier decade were returned to active cultivation (*Guyana Review,* August 1999). This was not an accident of history. As a former colony of Europe, Guyana's agricultural sector was organized and structured to respond to the demands of the European economy. But this short honeymoon ended as the rice sector of Europe rebounded from the effects of El Niño, and as Guyana was forced to contend with the changes required under the liberalization of agriculture agreements of the WTO. Hence beginning in 1996 Guyana's rice access to the European market was curtailed, and preferential trade and access to markets with its Caribbean neighbors were also curtailed, as its quota to the EU began to be phased out (Guyana, Ministry of Agriculture report on impact of trade curtailment of European access, 1997; *Guyana Review*, August 1999). The crisis for farmers on account of this curtailment was further exacerbated by the incursion of US paddy rice into the Jamaican market in 1997 (Gafar 2003: 149–151). The Jamaican market at the time was home to 30 percent of the Guyanese rice crop under preferential and protected regional arrangements by virtue of Guyana's membership in CARICOM (Gafar 2003). The capitalization by the US rice industry of Grains Jamaica Limited, the beneficiary of PL 480 paddy rice shipments for milling, threw a wrench in the ability of Guyanese farmers to access the favorable Jamaican market and consequently served to undercut the small farming sector of Guyana (de Groot 1999). The export of paddy rice to Jamaica from the United States is now being repeated in Nicaragua, Honduras, and other Central America countries.

The result was catastrophic for small-scale farmers in Guyana. By 1999, according to Fazal Ally (late general secretary of the Guyana Rice Producers Association), the number of farming families had declined from 45,000 in 1970 to between 15,000 and 20,000 in the late 1990s, and 70 percent of the acreage of approximately 200,000 was under the control of "fewer than five large companies" (*Guyana Review*, August 1999).[13] Since 1999 the number of rice farmers has continued to decline. Based on the analysis of the 2009 farmer's register of the Guyana Rice Development Board (GRDB) for the first crop, the number of farmers had declined to 5,324. (This latter figure represents the number of farmers who cultivated the spring crop of 2009. This number, though somewhat higher when the number of cultivators for autumn 2009 is considered, does not alter the downward trajectory.) It represents a reduction since 1999 of approximately 10,500 farmers, and since 1970, approximately 39,500. These figures correspond with a changing pattern of land concentration and related demography of the rice industry, as is gleaned from a comparison between landholding patterns in 1954/1955 and 2009. As tables 5.1 and 5.2 demonstrate, the average farm size in 1954/55 was six acres

Table 5.1. Number of rice farmers in Guyana, 1954, autumn crop

	Berbice	Demerara	Essequibo	Total
32+ Acres	35	229	10	274
16–31.9 Acres	207	388	31	626
8–15.9 Acres	1,365	1269	944	3,578
4–7.9 Acres	4,383	1,869	2,283	8,535
2–3.9 Acres	5,119	1,182	1,245	7,546
Under 2 Acres	4,229	1,363	832	6,424
Total Farmers	15,338	6,300	5,345	26,983

Source: Extracted from Carleen O'Loughlin, "The Rice Sector in the Economy of British Guiana," *Social and Economic Studies* 7 (1958): 121.

Table 5.2. Number of rice farmers/cultivation area in Guyana, first crop, 2009

	Region 2	Region 3	Region 4	Region 5	Region 6	Total
100–1,000+ Acres	38	32	8	108	124	310
51–100 Acres	93	40	24	110	111	378
31–50 Acres	111	67	24	156	114	472
1–30 Acres	1,905	893	382	487	497	4,164
Total Farmers	2,147	1,032	438	861	846	5,324

Source: Extracted from Wazir Mohamed, "Guyana's Rice Industry Responds to Global Change, 1992–2014," http://grdb.gy/index.php?option=com_content&task=view&id=98&Itemid=1.

per rice-farming family, while in 2009 it had risen to 29 acres per rice-farming family. What is more revealing, when the statistics provided by O'Loughlin (1958: 121) are compared with the Guyana Development Board's (GRDB) register for 2009, is that while in 1954 there was a maximum of 274 rice landholders planting acreages in excess of 32 acres; in 2009 there were 1,160 rice landholders (farmers) who planted acreages between 31 and in excess of 1,000 acres. Further to that in comparison to 1954/55, the number of farmers cultivating between 1 and 31 acres in 2009 declined from an approximately 26,709 (1954) to 4,164 (2009).

These figures give a snapshot of the growing trend, and demonstrate that the rice industry, which came into fruition in the aftermath of the global cane sugar crisis in the 1880s, has now fallen victim to trade liberalization. The small farmer, once the backbone of the industry between 1900 and 1970, has become the casualty as the industry reorganizes and transitions to more large-scale farms. This level of reorganization represents what economists and others are now calling "land grabbing," which in Guyana is taking place under the radar as it is more localized.[14] Accordingly, the rice industry in Guyana, which emerged at the dawn of the twentieth century as a small farmer crop primarily among the rural-based Indo-Guyanese population (the descendants of indentured labor), is well on the way to becoming a large-farmer-controlled industry.

Conclusion

In conclusion, I would like to make three points. First, globalization and its current form, neoliberalism, as applied in countries that were historically dependent on small farm rural agriculture, pushes small rice farmers out of production. Within the former colonial enclaves in Central America and the Caribbean the people most affected are the descendants of slaves and indentured laborers, as well as the Native Amerindian communities whose history predates the coming of the Europeans to the region. In Guyana the local impact of globalization has been the displacement of the possibilities for Africans (Afro-Guyanese) to claim and plant rice as their crop of choice in the nineteenth century. As I have argued in another essay (Mohamed 2000), Afro-Guyanese were "not only prevented from planting rice officially, [they] were also prohibited . . . unofficially." This was due to a process of racialization endemic to the colonial relations of power. Guyana's coveted position as a player in the nineteenth-century sugar revolution "played a crucial role in the marginalization of [Afro-Guyanese] from land and from participation in the rice industry" (Mohamed 2000). In similar manner globalization is now consuming the very class of people, small-scale Indo-Guyanese rice farmers, who were given land at very concessionary prices as a means of cushioning the impact of the crisis-ridden sugar industry on labor at the end of the nineteenth century and is replacing them with a new stratum of large-scale class of local farmers (predominantly Indo-Guyanese) in the rice sector (Mohamed 2000). In Central America and in Haiti, the rural indigenous and Afro-Haitian populations, respectively, who for centuries organized their economic and food security interests around the production of rice, are now losing their grip over a crop that was central to their survival. Their place in the economies of their respective countries is being taken by middlemen and rice-milling and processing companies, the beneficiaries of importation of finished and paddy rice, especially from an imperial United States.

The second point of note is the way in which neoliberal globalization policies have produced changes in the outcomes for rural small farmers. Since the 1980s, the space in national economies and production systems formally occupied by small rice farmers are being encroached upon and taken over by agricultural rice companies, large-scale farmers, and rice millers. Indeed, national governments are acting as the business managers of the rice companies, big farmers, and millers. In this unfolding process, rural rice culture is being reshaped, and rural communities (which had been for centuries the preserve of small-scale farmers) are becoming the economic stomping ground of rich and powerful big farmers, rice millers, and rice companies. Under the aegis of the IMF and the World Bank, which laid the foundation for DR-CAFTA, the countries of Central America and the Dominican Republic have been encouraged to open their markets to imported rice and paddy rice from the United States. This is problematic from two standpoints. Firstly, imported rice from the US is highly subsidized, and this presents the dilemma of unfair competition for local producers, millers, and so forth. Secondly, and perhaps the most important dilemma for local production, is the importation of paddy rice, or rice as raw material for processing. This undercuts local producers who are expected to compete with subsidized paddy rice. The drastic reduction in the number of farmers in Honduras is directly connected to the preference of millers for the cheaper imported paddy rice. This fits into the neoliberal approach, which is the creation of local middlemen catering to transnational capitalist classes. In the case of rice, a rural, hegemonic class—of large farmers, millers, and traders—is being created at the expense of those marginal and racialized groups who have historically operated as small farmers.

My third and final point in conclusion is that this status quo is only possible because the Global North continues the long-established practice of control over subject peoples with the complicity of their governments. The US espouses the idea of free and open markets; at the same time, however, they close their markets through protective mechanisms (Oxfam 2004: 26–31). The time has come for the US to end subsidies to its rice farmers. The complex and implicitly racially discriminatory processes of marginalization being experienced by small-scale farmers in the Caribbean (Haiti, the Dominican Republic, and Guyana) and Central America (Nicaragua, Costa Rica, El Salvador, Guatemala, and Honduras) is a direct result of the ability of the US to dump its highly subsidized rice, produced by and large by white agro elites, into the market. Subsidies to rice farmers in the US are practically killing the poor and erasing these marginalized small-rice farming communities in the Caribbean and Central America.

Acknowledgments

I acknowledge the contributions of Patricia Northover (Mellon Visiting Professor, Duke University) and of Michaeline Crichlow (Professor of African American Studies, Duke University). Their timely suggestions and interventions helped in the production of this chapter.

Notes

1. Debates on what is or how to think about globalization are ongoing. For the purpose of this article, the term is used to delineate the manner in which decisions to maintain subsidies in the production of rice in the United States have far-reaching consequences for rice-producing countries, who, through international agreements imposed by the International Monetary Fund and the World Bank, are prevented from doing the same. See *Global Transformations* by David Held, Anthony McGrew, and David Goldblatt.

2. In the period after Columbus first landed in the Americas, thousands of food crops crossed the Atlantic, including rice, which came with African slaves. Judith Carney in "African Rice and the Columbian Exchange" chronicles the journey of rice from Africa to the Americas. Through this research, we are now certain that it became an established crop from the late 1800s until the early 1980s.

3. The term "resistance and accommodation" was introduced by Sidney Mintz in the literature on Caribbean slave societies to explain independent subsistence production. Mintz

delineated these spaces as resistance spaces through which slaves organized limited "freedom." See Mintz 2007: 146–157.

4. I spent the formative period of my life as a member of a small-rice-farming family and was a small rice farmer in Guyana until the1997.

5. See in particular Sidney Mintz's discourse on the question of "Caribbean Peasantries," in *Caribbean Studies* 1: 31–34, 1961. Also see Lesley Potter's "The Paddy Proletariat and the Dependent Peasantry," in *History Gazette* 47.

6. An example of this type of mechanism was provision in the treaty of Chaguaramas of 1973 establishing the Caribbean Community Common Market (CARICOM) and imposed external tariffs on imports of goods originating outside the region.

7. See Laughlin 1958: 121, and Thakur 1978: 113.

8. Note is made that several countries and regions were able to protect local production through counterpart agreements. This was the case for the many African, Pacific, and Caribbean countries that entered into the Yaoundé and Lomé conventions with Europe beginning between 1960 and 2000. This was also true for the rice, sugar, and banana industries in the Caribbean, the Pacific, and Africa.

9. The PL 480 program was first established in 1954 by the US government as a foreign policy mechanism to stimulate foreign agricultural trade through the export of surplus agricultural commodities as aid.

10. Rice ready for consumption.

11. This observation is based on my research over a twenty-year period, and on the spot field interviews, research, and surveys conducted between 2008 and 2010.

12. Access to the European and CARICOM markets was easier because of preferential access quota in the case of Europe and the imposition of the Common External Tariff on rice originating outside the Caribbean. Farmers also benefited from the access loophole that allowed for the importation of Guyana's rice into Europe through the Other Countries and Territories Route (OCT).

13. These base figures are approximations of officials in the industry.

14. Land grabbing is carried out by national capitalist classes, who are more socially acceptable than foreigners. For further explanation on the rise of localized land grabbing, see Saturnino et al. 2012.

References

Ali, Fazal. 1999. "A Bright Future for Rice." *Guyana Review* 7 (79): 11–12.

Araghi, Farshad A. 1995. "Global Depeasantization, 1945–1990." *Sociological Quarterly* 36 (2): 337–368.

Carney, Judith. 2001a. *Black Rice: The African Origins of Rice Cultivation in the Americas.* Cambridge, MA: Harvard University Press.

———. 2001b. "African Rice in the Columbian Exchange." *Journal of African History* 42 (3): 377–396.

———. 2005. "Rice in the Memory in the Age of Enslavement: Atlantic Passages to Suriname." *Slavery and Abolition* 26 (3): 325–347.

———. 2004. "With Grains in Her Hair: Rice in Colonial Brazil." *Slavery and Abolition* 25 (1): 1–27.

Castanha, Tony. 2011. *The Myth of Indigenous Caribbean Extinction*. New York: Palgrave Macmillan.

de Groot, Peter. 1999. "The Rice Industry in Guyana." *Stabroek News* (Sunday Stabroek Perspective, April 18).

Gafar, John. 2003. *Guyana: From State Control to Free Markets*. New York: Nova Science Publishers.

Germain, J. C. 2009. "Trade Liberalization and Globalization: The Experience of Haiti." (Order No. 3392053). Available from ABI/INFORM Complete; ProQuest Central; ProQuest Dissertations & Theses A&I; ProQuest Dissertations & Theses Global (305170611). Retrieved January 11, 2015. http://search.proquest.com/docview/305170611?accountid=11648.

Griswold, D. 2006. "Grain Drain: The Hidden Cost of U.S. Rice Subsidies." Washington, DC: Center for Trade Policy studies, Cato Institute. Retrieved January 9, 2015. http://www.cato.org/pub_display.php?pub _id=6801.

Held, David, Anthony McGrew, and David Goldblatt. 1999. *Global Transformations*. Stanford, CA: Stanford University Press.

Hobsbawm, Eric. 1992. "The Crisis of Today's Ideologies." *New Left Review* 192: 55–64.

Kotz, David M. 2002. "Globalization and Neoliberalism: Rethinking Marxism." *A Journal of Economics, Culture & Society* 14 (2): 64–79.

Littlefield, Daniel C. 1981. *Rice and Slaves*. Baton Rouge: Louisiana State University Press.

McGuigan, C. 2006. "Agricultural Liberalization in Haiti." Retrieved January 11, 2016. http://www.christianaid.org.uk/images/ ca-agricultural-liberalisation.pdf, 1–43.

McMichael, Phillip. 2004. *Development and Social Change: A Global Perspective*. London: Pine Forge Press.

Mintz, Sidney. 2007. *Caribbean Transformations*. New York: Columbia University Press.

———. 2001. "The Question of Caribbean Peasantries: A Comment." *Caribbean Studies* 1: 31–34.

Mohamed, Wazir. 2015. "African Labor in Guyana and the Expansion of the Second Slavery." In *New Frontiers of Slavery: Publication of Collection of Papers on the Study of the Second Slavery*, edited by Dale Tomich and Rafael Marquese. Albany, NY: State University of New York Press.

———. 2015. "Guyana's Rice Industry Responds to Global Change, 1992–2014" (Power Point slides). Retrieved from http://grdb.gy/index.php?option=com_content&task=view&id=98&Itemid=1.

———. 2000. "Guyana's Rice Industry: A Historical Perspective." Retrieved January 5, 2016. http://www.guyanajournal.com/Wazir_Mohamed_Guyana_Rice_Industry.html.

O'Loughlin, C. 1958. "The Rice Sector in the Economy of British Guiana." *Social and Economic Studies* 7 (2): 115–148.

Oxfam. 2002. "Rigged Rules and Double Standards: Trade, Globalization, and the Fight against Poverty." Oxford, UK. Retrieved January 5, 2016. http://nghiencuuquocte.net/wp-content/uploads/2014/01/cr-rigged-rules-double-standards-010502-en.pdf.

———. 2004. "A Raw Deal for Rice Under DR-CAFTA: How the Free Trade Agreement Threatens the Livelihoods of Central American Farmers." Oxfam briefing paper. Retrieved from https://www.oxfamamerica.org/static/oa3/files/a-raw-deal-for-rice-under-dr-cafta.pdf.

———. 2005. "Kicking Down the Door: How Upcoming WTO Talks Threaten Farmers in Poor Countries." Oxfam briefing paper. Retrieved January 5, 2016. http://www.oxfam.org/en/policy/bp72-wto-subsidies.

Paasch, Armin, Frank Garbers, and Thomas Hirsch. 2007. "Trade Policies and Hunger: The Impact of Trade Liberalization on the Right to Food of Rice Farming Communities in Ghana, Honduras and Indonesia." Produced for the Ecumenical Advocacy Network. Retrieved January 8, 2016. http://www.e-alliance.ch/typo3conf/ext/naw_securedl/securee492.pdf?u=0&file=fileadmin/user_upload/docs/EAA_TradePoliciesHunger-RiceResearch_FullStudy_Letter_EN.pdf&t=1433875438&hash=5717b3b6036b9e0aad6eee1ffa3f8706.

Potter, Lesley M. 1992. "The Paddy Proletariat and the Dependent Peasantry: East Indian Rice Growers in British Guiana, 1871–1921." *History Gazette* 47.

Saturnino, Borras, Jr., Jennifer C. Franco, Sergio Gomez, Cristobal Kay, and Max Spoor. 2012. "Land Grabbing in Latin America and the Caribbean." *Journal of Peasant Studies* 39 (3–4): 845–872.

Saturnino, Borras, Jr., Ruth Hall, Ian Scoones, and Wendy Wolford. 2012. "The New Enclosures: Critical Perspectives on Corporate Land Deals." *Journal of Peasant Studies* 39 (3–4): 619–647.

Scott, James. 1985. *Weapons of the Weak: Everyday Forms of Peasant Resistance.* New Haven, CT: Yale University Press.

Shujiro Urata. 2002. "Globalization and the Growth in Free Trade Agreements." *Asia-Pacific Review* 9 (1).

Singh, Jagnarine. 2009. "The Guyana Rice Industry." (PowerPoint slides.) Retrieved from http://legacy.iica.int/Eng/regiones/caribe/guyana/IICA%20Office%20Documents/risk_symposium_2009/Day%201/Overview%20of%20the%20Agricultural%20Sector%20in%20Guyana/The%20Guyana%20Rice%20Industry%20-%20Jagnarine%20Singh.pdf.

Steiner, Stan, and Geno Rodriguez. 1975. *The Islands: The Worlds of Puerto Ricans.* New York: Harper and Row.

Stenzel, Paulette L. 2010. "Free Trade and Sustainability through the Lens of Nicaragua: How CAFTA-DR Should Be Amended to Promote the Triple Bottom Line." *William & Mary Environmental Law and Policy Review* 34 (3): 652–743.

Sumner, Daniel A. 2011. "How US Agricultural Policy Harms the Developing World." Paper published by the American Enterprise Institute. Retrieved January 7, 2016. https://www.aei.org/wp-content/uploads/2011/11/-picking-on-the-poor-how-us-agricultural-policy-hurts-the-developing-world_15192995761.pdf.

Thakur, Andra. 1978. "The Impact of Technology on Agriculture: A Study of the Mechanization of Guyana's Rice Industry." Unpublished PhD diss., University of Alberta, Edmonton.

Thompson, Alvin O. 1987. *Colonialism & Underdevelopment in Guyana 1580–1803*. Bridgetown, Barbados: Carib Research & Publications.

Todorov, Tzvetan. 1999. *Conquest of the Americas*. Norman: University of Oklahoma Press.

Viotti da Costa, Emilia. 1994. *Crowns of Glory, Tears of Blood: The Demerara Slave Rebellion of 1823*. New York: Oxford University Press.

Voeks, Robert, and John Rashford. 2013. *African Ethnobotany in the Americas*. New York: Springer.

Weber, Karl. 2009. *Food Inc: How Industrial Food Is Making Us Sicker, Fatter, and Poorer— And What You Can Do About It*. Philadelphia: Perseus Books Group.

Wilk, Richard, and Livia Barbosa. 2012. *Rice and Beans: A Unique Dish in a Hundred Places*. New York: Bloomsbury Press.

Wood, Peter H. 1974. *Black Majority*. New York: Alfred A Knopf.

6

At the Margins of Citizenship

Oil, Poverty, and Race in Esmeraldas, Ecuador

Gabriela Valdivia

The Ecuadorian State is indebted to black and indigenous peoples. . . . Where we black people live, where indigenous people live, is where you find the greatest hunger, the greatest misery, the greatest poverty. This means that there is racism, exclusion. . . . This is the conversation that we need to have. The Ecuadorian State is indebted to us. Racism, xenophobia, we will only be able to overcome this if we invest more in ethno-education . . . but the government imposes a generalized education . . . this is the terrain of struggle.

—Ernesto Estupiñan, interviewed
on February 15, 2015, in *Ecuadorenvivo*

This is a problem of citizenship. . . . Slavery, poverty, exclusion, have not allowed us to become citizens.

—John Antón Sánchez, in response to
Estupiñan's remarks on February 15, 2015

Over the last fifty years, uprisings, protests, and marches against widespread inequality have marked the beginning of a "new century of revolution" in Latin America (Grandin and Joseph 2010). Latin American states have revamped economic plans, constitutions, and institutions in response to demands for better and more dignified living conditions (Escobar 2010; Gudynas 2009; Hylton 2007). The subject of this chapter, Ecuador's *Revolución Ciudadana* (Citizens' Revolution), fits within this paradigm of state-led response to citizen demands. Established by the government of Rafael Correa (2007–present), the *Revolución* is based on a capabilities framework (Sen 1997) that recognizes the individual's ability to live the life she or he values as a liberating and emancipatory force that will reduce massive inequality. Freedom from economic inequality, under the *Revolución*, is promoted by nurturing the individual's capability to do the things she or he "has reason to value" (Sen 1997: 1959), regardless of who the individual is. In Ecuador, this approach has translated into heavy investment in public infrastructure and social assistance to "awaken" citizen participation and so individuals can *choose* to "love life," as a national slogan of the *Revolución* states on radio and television ads, and on the public faces of many state government buildings.[1]

While all Ecuadorians are expected to participate in the *Revolución*, "the poor," those without a voice in how the economy is managed or how the legal system is designed, are framed as its prime subjects. In the state-sponsored television campaign, "For the people, Revolution," for example, smiling young children in modest rural and urban backgrounds run to meet industrial infrastructure that then melts away into modern homes, schools, and hospitals to be held on the palm of the hand. The message is that citizens of disadvantaged backgrounds can transcend the particulars of their current existence; indigenous peoples, workers, middle-class urban dwellers all have the potential to engage with the modernity mediated by the state, when they "transform natural resources into permanent resources." "This is revolution," states the Correa administration–sponsored ad, "for the people, what belongs to the people, for the people, Revolution." Such media campaigns underpin the principles of state-citizen relations under the current administration. The *Revolución* is envisioned as a sort of great equalizer that levels out differences in worldviews, material needs, and desires, and encapsulates them within the more universal "citizen." In this political imaginary, all Ecuadorians have the opportunity to make themselves better citizens by supporting the state apparatus. Rurality, race, poverty *should not be* obstacles for citizens to participate in the "project of life"; these forms of difference must be subsumed to the universal citizenship of the *Revolución*.

Bringing attention to the geography of identity politics, this chapter examines how these processes of citizenship-making unfold in one of Ecuador's most strategic economic locations: the coastal city of Esmeraldas, in northwest Ecuador. The city of Esmeraldas is the capital of the canton of Esmeraldas, and of the province of Esmeraldas.[2] It houses the largest oil refinery in the nation as well as the maritime terminus for the country's two largest oil pipelines: the state-owned *Sistema de*

Oleoducto Transecuatoriano (SOTE) and the privately owned *Oleoducto de Crudos Pesados* (OCP). As such, Esmeraldas is crucial to Ecuador's revenue generation: the oil sector generates about one-quarter of total government revenue and about half of exports.

Despite this pivotal economic role, the province of Esmeraldas is a "state margin" (Das and Poole 2004) in the Ecuadorian political imaginary: a space excluded from full citizen recognition through practices of state abandonment (e.g., limited investment, at times deliberate disinvestment) but also a space of threatening difference, of subjugated, racialized rebelliousness (Handelsman 1999).[3] During the colonial period, Esmeraldas was home to Maroon communities, and until the mid-twentieth century, hacienda and plantation production. In the 1940s and 1950s, Esmeraldas became a center of banana production. The largest plantations were worked by black laborers and European owners. Of these, Swedish entrepreneur Folke Anderson was the largest banana magnate in Esmeraldas. By 1953, his Astral Fruit Company had turned Esmeraldas into a top banana exporting site: more than one in every four bananas shipped overseas from Ecuador moved through the port of Esmeraldas (Southgate 2016), generating various formal and informal employment opportunities for many. A crash in the banana market in the mid-1950s ended the short-lived banana business in Esmeraldas, forcing the abandonment of large-scale banana plantations and massive rural and urban unemployment.

Toward the end of the twentieth century, the main political economic centers of Guayaquil and Quito actively isolated Esmeraldas to minimize its economic competitiveness. In the 1980s, for example, they successfully lobbied against the export of Esmeraldeño commodities through the provincial port, and in favor of concentrating its exports through the ports of other provinces. During this timeframe, and coinciding with the rise of leftist politics, labor mobilizations and economic strangulation, a black political consciousness began forming in Esmeraldas. Echoing regional movements for decolonization, such as in Colombia and the Caribbean (Miranda 2010), and the independence of African nations, renowned Esmeraldeño poet and activist Antonio Preciado suggests that at the time, Esmeraldas was paying to attention to Africa's awakening, "like a bright light, we will go towards bread, and work, towards the distributed land, towards the equality of all humans, because we are the same to the sun and the breeze, to mother Earth" (Preciado 1992: 28).

Today, the *Revolución* has forcefully expanded the presence of the state in Esmeraldas. This chapter argues that in the quest for the universalization of citizenship, the *Revolución* is a differentially implemented government project that overlooks the role of sociohistoric conditions and associated citizen-subjectivities in how individuals engage with the *Revolución*. I examine how the political legibility/illegibility practices that produced Esmeraldas as a state margin continue to inform individual choices to participate, as well as constrain their participation, in the *Revolución*.[4] I use two locations in Esmeraldas as case studies of how the *Revolución* unfolds in areas influenced by oil extraction (map 6.1): 15 de Marzo, a neighborhood in the urban parish of Simon Plata Torres, abutting the refinery; and Tabete, a community in the rural parish of Chinca, which coexists with the OCP. Both cases highlight different oil-infused positions from which to examine how the *Revolución* is implemented. The former is an urban proletariat collective with an acute sense of black and poor redistribution politics vis-à-vis the national government, while the latter is a rural space where identity politics are tied to questions of displacement and landed production. The cases are not oppositional or illustrative of an urban-rural divide but of how the rural and urban textures of place in Ecuador shape the unfolding of the *Revolución*.

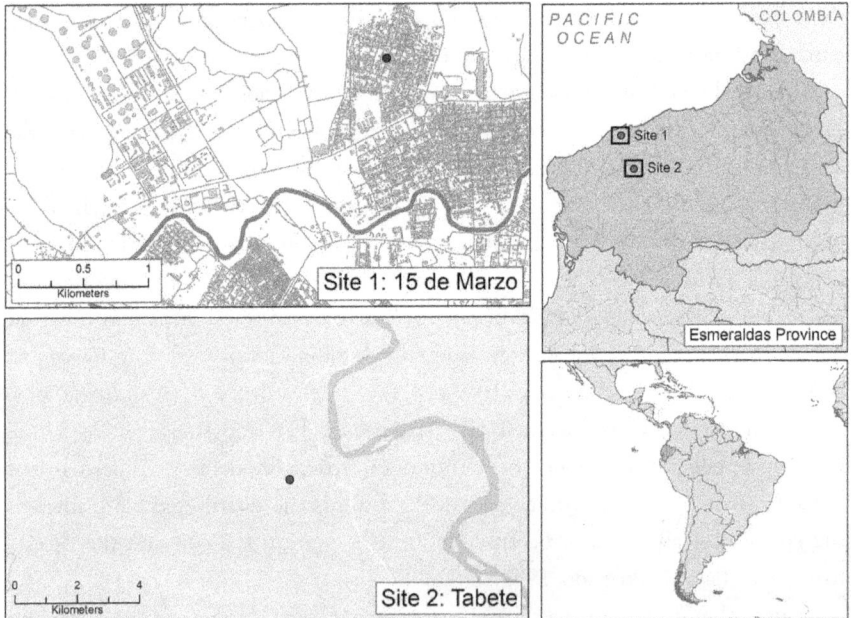

Map 6.1. Map of location of case studies.

The chapter is structured as follows. The next section is an overview of state strategies of citizenship improvement under the *Revolución Ciudadana*: public infrastructure and social assistance. The subsequent section builds on ethnographic observations in 15 de Marzo and Tabete, between 2011 and 2016, to offer a "sense of place" of the *Revolución*—how experiences of movement, connection, and subordination influence the freedom to participate in the national project of development. The section illustrates how state response and categorization of citizen claims structure political visibility and action in urban and rural areas. The chapter concludes with a situated critique of projects such as the *Revolución*. The analysis is conjunctural as both the *Revolución* and place are ongoing processes, and is not intended as a conclusive prediction of the fate of state-led development projects.

For the People, Revolution

Twentieth-century social movements in Ecuador have demanded the right to a dignified way of life: a life that is not determined by poverty and stagnation but by the enhancement and protection of rights for individual and collective improvement. Former Minister of Economy Rafael Correa won in the 2006 presidential elections with a campaign responding to these demands, calling for radical change that "returned" the state as overseer of development. Heavy investment in public infrastructure and income supplements are two main strategies put in place to jumpstart this change. Both are widely applied in Esmeraldas Province.

Public Infrastructure

In 2011, President Correa created the Public Enterprise Ecuador Estratégico, an institution tasked with building infrastructure to ameliorate the effects of "strategic" extractive activities on nearby areas and peoples.[5] A rapid and spectacular expansion of service infrastructure followed in urban and rural areas affected by large-scale, resource-extraction activities, under the belief that they had been historically abandoned by the state and this was a problem to be addressed. By 2016, US$ 943.5 million had been invested in more than twelve hundred projects in thirteen provinces affected by oil and mining extraction (Ecuador Estratégico 2016). The *Revolución* underscores that this infrastructural investment is a state response to the dual geography of uneven development evident in Ecuador—the result of a national division of labor through which resources of the periphery (rural and urban) are extracted and channeled through capitalist networks to enhance wealth accumulation in the economic cores of Quito and Guayaquil. Such uneven development, Neil Smith (2008) reminds us, is the product of historical relations of capitalist production, where racialized and classed divisions of labor reproduce internal territorial inequalities while remaining functional to global capitalist accumulation (Dussel 2008). To address this unevenness, the *Revolución* built highways and bridges that more forcefully connect areas of oil, mineral, and timber extraction to the larger network of commodity exchange, as well as make more feasible the future intensification of these very same practices.

The building frenzy also included health and education centers that consolidate smaller services and generalize the provision of basic services for youth, disabled, and elderly, and the provision of services that connect citizens to the larger national grid, for example, water and sewage services, transport accessibility, schools, and housing. Through these projects, access to drinking water, paved roads, schools, and health centers become the channels to revolutionize political subjectivity—the ways in which an individual chooses to live a life she or he "has reason to value." Fourteen percent of Ecuador's Gross Domestic Product (GDP) was destined to this form of public spending—a tremendous difference from the 3 percent allotted during the period of neoliberal restructuring.[6]

The spectacular infrastructure of the *Revolución Ciudadana* reached the city of Esmeraldas around 2009, with the inauguration of a four-lane bridge that dramatically shortened the travel distance from the airport to the city center and improved its connections to major national transport corridors. Furious destruction and construction followed. Roads were upturned and paved at lightning speed, trees in the city center were dug out while water and sewage pipes were put in place, and bulldozers dug enormous holes in the neighborhoods surrounding the refinery to build the foundations for new health centers. Between 2012 and 2014, large billboards announcing "La Revolución Ciudadana Avanza" ("the Citizens' Revolution Progresses") pointed to the transportation routes, paved neighborhood streets, and schools and health centers built as examples of "real change." The overwhelming presence of these billboards insisted that change was palpable: the facts spelled out on each billboard named the sidewalks, road paving, installation of water pipes and sewage lines, schools, and health centers; the contractors carrying out the projects; and the amount of dollars invested as evidence of the *Revolución*.

Income Supplements

While not spectacular like state-sponsored infrastructure, income supplements (*bonos*) are also a broadly applied policy of the *Revolución*. *Bonos* are received by families in both rural and urban areas where access to basic public works and formal employment resources are insufficient. In the city of Esmeraldas, for example, every month, long lines of women form outside of banks and other authorized disbursement businesses (stores and pharmacies) to collect *bonos*. Some come from rural areas, others are from the city. For these women, *bonos* are a constant form of income in an otherwise highly variable household economy. *Bonos* provide immediate cash to fund aspects of everyday social reproduction: school uniforms and materials, routine doctor visits, food provision, and household care. One of the most talked about *bonos* is a monthly, conditional cash transfer called the *Bono de Desarrollo Humano* (Human Development Supplement, or BDH), available to female heads of household below the poverty line who care for children, elderly, and people with disabilities. This *bono* was originally introduced in 1998 and amounted to US fifteen dollars as a "solidarity supplement" to compensate for the rolling back of state gas and electricity subsidies in urban areas during neoliberalization in the 1980s. In 2007, President Correa increased the amount of the *bono* to US thirty dollars per month and increased it again, in 2009 to thirty-five dollars and fifty dollars in 2013, both times coinciding with election periods.[7] Approximately 85,773 Esmeraldeños benefit from this *bono* (La Hora 2011).

Bonos strengthen biopolitical relations of dependence between citizens and the state in rural and urban locations.[8] For example, de la Torre points to the story of a rural resident from Pachagsí, Chimborazo Province, who thanked "God and President Correa" for taking care of his family through the *bono*, with which he could purchase food, pay for electricity, and buy things for his children. As this resident added, "the government takes care of us, we should correspond" (Tuaza 2010; cited in de la Torre 2013). Similar stories linking dignity, citizenship, and the everyday work of *bonos* are regularly present in the media, as evidence of how the *Revolución* "touches" the lives of those who most need help, regardless of their political and cultural identities.

Bonos are contentious poverty-alleviation strategies. Ecuadorian sociologist Luis Verdesoto (2015), for example, calls the BDH a policy of "non-poverty" because it "artificially" maintains households above the poverty level but does not necessarily break the cycle of poverty.[9] As such, *bonos* perpetuate the state's domination over (poor) women's bodies and agency. On the other hand, according to Pabel Muñoz, ex-director of the National Secretary of Planning and Development (SENPLADES), one of the premier institutions of the *Revolución Ciudadana*,[10] *bonos* help poor people alleviate some of the weight of actually existing structural poverty, that is, poverty related to everyday basic needs. In this reading, *bonos* facilitate the possibility of alternative futures with a "touch of dignity" (Unda 2009), a way to support poor people in their struggle to attain the kind of life they value.

The Margins of the State

Approximately 530,972 people live in Esmeraldas Province. The most urbanized and densely populated canton is Esmeraldas Canton, with 189,500 people, of which 81.3 percent live in urban and 18.7 percent in rural parishes (Secretaria Nacional de Informacion 2014). According to the 2010 national census, 20.9 percent of the economically active population is involved in commercial activities, from large-scale trade (import and export) to small-scale entrepreneurial activities (e.g., car repair, laundry services, restaurants, transportation, street vending). Twenty-five percent is self-employed; 13.9 percent work for the state; 19.7 percent are wage laborers; and 28.4 percent are day-wage and flexible-labor workers. Fifty-seven percent of the population in Esmeraldas Canton does not have access to public services (e.g., water sanitation, garbage collection, electricity, etc.). In 2013, over 20,300 females heading poor households received the Human Development Bono, of which approximately 60 percent lived in urban and 40 percent in rural households (MIES 2013).

Esmeraldas Province is the southernmost end of the Chocó-Darién bioregion, which runs the Pacific Coast from Panama to northwest Ecuador, and the historical home to one the longest-lasting Maroon societies in Latin America. In 2010, the province was home to 44 percent of Ecuadorians who self-identify as Afro-descendant. During the early sixteenth century, slaves shipped between the nations known today as Panama and Peru fled into the dense tropical forest of Esmeraldas and coexisted with indigenous peoples, initially adapting and later becoming a dominant group that was not subject to the Spanish Crown (Rueda Novoa 2001). Over the next couple of centuries, runaway slaves and freed peoples from other parts of Ecuador and Colombia migrated to Esmeraldas, attracted by the sovereign black community that developed there. In the twentieth century, two waves of post-abolition Colombian black migrants contributed to the growth of Esmeraldas: one wave was associated with the tagua nut boom and the other with the banana boom in the 1940s. In the 1960s, the construction of the Quito-San Lorenzo railroad and the Quito-Esmeraldas city highway brought more black migrants, from Colombia and the Caribbean, in search of labor opportunities. Today, Esmeraldas is considered the southernmost extremity of a vast cultural area that includes the Pacific lowlands of Colombia and the Panamanian province of Darién (Rahier 2013).

Long seen as a space of rebellious blackness, Esmeraldas was often marginal to projects of integration and development in the mestizo-dominated nation. Though a highway was planned during the colonial period to integrate Esmeraldas to the seat of government, Quito, it wasn't until 1972 that it was actually built; black resistance to mestizo domination and then rivalries between Quito and Guayaquil elites fought against this increased connectivity. Similarly, when the refinery was built in 1977, the state invested in gated compounds for workers and roads that connected the refinery to the main highways, but not to the city, which largely continued in isolation. The current conditions of poor access to potable water, sewage, and garbage collection services are understood as everyday reminders of historical state abandonment (United Nations Environment Programme 2006). During the rainy season, for example, it is not unusual to see sewage systems spilling onto streets like fountains of waste and dirt roads on the hillsides turn into rivers of mud because of poor urban planning. Unpaved roads limit access to emergency and security vehicles into some areas, which, according to residents, explains the high levels of criminality in some neighborhoods.

This extended history of resistance in the face of marginalization is often recognized by locals as an Esmeraldeño trait, so much so that when the first black mayor of the city of Esmeraldas, Ernesto Estupiñan, was elected in 1999, he promptly commissioned statues and a mural to commemorate the rebellious and entrepreneurial black origins of Esmeraldas. Such memorials had been missing in the city until the turn of the twentieth century, most likely because no other governmental administrator considered such recognition worthwhile. One of the best-known murals showcasing this black history pride is located on the second floor of the municipality of the city of Esmeraldas. Commissioned in 2000 and titled "Libre por Rebelde, y por Rebelde Grande" ("Free by Its Rebelliousness, and for Its Rebelliousness, Great"), this mural offers a black-subject rendering of the national narrative of Esmeraldas. It traces the arrival of African slaves, their coexistence with indigenous peoples, their role in battles of independence, labor in banana plantations, and the arrival of the oil refinery. While this rendering of citizenship is representative of how blackness is recognized and remembered in the city, it also showcases how it is entangled with struggles over freedom of choice in how to exist in relation to subjugation to a capitalist class and to the coloniality of power dominated by the centralized state.

The city of Esmeraldas is also a node of national energy logistics: it is home to Ecuador's largest oil refinery, its largest thermoelectric plant, Termoesmeraldas, and the terminus of the two major pipelines that bring oil from fields in the Amazon. This node secures a national development project based on oil rents that began with the commercial exploitation of oil in 1967. The oil complex that emerged, along with the rents it generated, produced a general sense of progress and modernity for the nation (Carriére 2001; Gerlach 2003), though not so for Esmeraldas. In 2013, Vice President Jorge Glas called the refinery "the pillar of a new era of energy production in Ecuador," and the key to a change in the "national energy matrix"—from nonrenewable to renewable energy. In light of depleting reserves and the boom and bust effects of oil prices, the *Revolución* proposed a "post-oil" energy transition where hydroelectric energy, perceived as more stable and permanent, is promoted to meet a larger proportion of everyday citizen needs.[11] The Esmeraldas refinery was retrofitted in 2014 to meet this goal, and to meet the needs of the thermoelectric plant, which sits across from the refinery.

The Revolution Is Here

The *Revolución* is entangled with these histories of poverty, blackness, and oil in the city of Esmeraldas. Residents of neighborhoods surrounding the refinery, for example, often complain of skin rashes and respiratory ailments. Some believe these ailments are linked to the refinery, which they say is "killing them slowly." Those who are highly conscious of the health effects of emissions, point to how inequality is reproduced through refinery operations—how Afro-descendant communities in Ecuador continue to suffer the colonial logics of resource extraction, bearing the burdens of air and river pollution in exchange for oil profits for the state. But the refinery is also a site for building relations of dependence with the state. Residents describe the refinery as a hopeful site of advancement, either via direct and indirect employment, or through lobbying for favors and compensation that minimize historical state abandonment. Rural residents, who live with its pipelines and witness their frequent leaks, tell similar stories of the potential burdens and opportunities linked to coexisting with oil infrastructure. Many of those who recognize the environmental burdens of the refinery and pipelines are quick to qualify their responses, adding that responsible refinery operations require an obligation toward the well-being of residents at the poorest margins of the state: investing in the creation of green areas, public recreation spaces, contributions to celebrations and community building, better schools and health services, and so on.

Thus, the infrastructural investment of the *Revolución* is welcomed by many as a positive change. For some, it even echoes the efforts of black political activists who, after the installation of the refinery, recognized that participation in the practices of state-making, for example, elections, was a way of becoming legible to the state. Reflecting on this black consciousness, Preciado (1992: 14) states that from Esmeraldas came the idea to "not stay behind the progress of the masses" and that electoral participation is "indispensable." But Marxist militant allies at the time denounced this idea, accusing Esmeraldeños of putting personal interests ahead of revolutionary change, of wanting to return to being the black "caciques" (strongmen) of Esmeraldas Province.

A closer look at the geography of state-sponsored development demonstrates that these racialized tensions underpin the unevenness of citizenship today, deepening existing divides within the Esmeraldeño body politic, and making some claims for development more visible for groups with greater political weight versus others. To elaborate on the point, next I draw on interviews and participant observation to compare the experiences of two neighborhoods in Esmeraldas Canton: 15 de Marzo, a densely inhabited neighborhood in an urban parish abutting the refinery, and Tabete, a rural parish about twenty kilometers outside the city.

15 de Marzo

As a largely Afro-Ecuadorian neighborhood abutting the refinery, 15 de Marzo was among the neighborhoods that experienced the full power of the *Revolución*. The land on which 15 de Marzo sits today was initially zoned as part of the industrial buffer zone of the refinery, but by the 1980s people escaping economic depression in the surrounding rural areas, and who could not afford to live in the city proper, settled it. 15 de Marzo was a hotbed of political demands for recognition. Residents were evicted from the refinery's buffer zone time and time again, but rural migrants, pushed by economic loss and agro-industry dispossession, continued to settle these "empty" spaces. This struggle over land in the periphery of the city became pivotal to a change in the political regime in the city, which until the early 1990s was dominated by center-right political parties. The MPD (*Movimiento Popular Democrático* or Popular Democratic Movement), one of Ecuador's radical leftist parties, harnessed the political capital of neighborhoods like 15 de Marzo, and used it to gain local presence. Self-identified as the party that fought "the people's fight" throughout the 1980s, 1990s, and 2000s, it stood out for its grassroots support in severely economically depressed Afro-Ecuadorian neighborhoods like 15 de Marzo. Many young people joined their ranks, seeing the promise for change.

Part of the attraction of the MPD for young, black Esmeraldeños was that Jaime Hurtado, one of Ecuador's best-known black politicians, led the MPD in the 1980s and 1990s. Hurtado was born and raised in *Barrio Caliente*, one of Esmeraldas's most politically active black neighborhoods, where banana workers settled during the banana market boom and crash.[12] He was the first Afro-Ecuadorian to be elected to Congress in 1979 and the first one to run for president in 1984, coming in fourth with the support of the left. Hurtado was known for his work with labor unions and farmers, his opposition to privatization policies, and for leading strikes and protests against market liberalization, accusing the Ecuadorian government of keeping poor people poor. As the chairman of the Parliamentary block of the MPD, he ran for president again in 1999 but was assassinated in the streets of Quito in February 1999, leaving a leadership vacuum in the left. Today, Hurtado's image is found in various governmental offices and public areas, a proud Esmeraldeño reminder of the struggle for dignity and a better life.

One of the MPD's young militants who looked up to Hurtado was Ernesto Estupiñan, a black community organizer, also born and raised in Barrio Caliente—in fact, across the street from where Hurtado lived. In the 1980s, he became a high-profile refinery operator who at one point led strikes against locally unpopular state interventions. In 1999, Hurtado's death still fresh in voters' minds, he ran for the major's office and won in a landslide. Upon taking the municipal leadership, he transformed the underground infrastructure of city life: he established erosion control measures that ended the buildup of mud in city streets, built water and sewage systems, paved roads, and set up a limited garbage-collection service that gave the sense of a cleaner city. Estupiñan's "underground" public works were oil-infused: during his first term, he pushed for agreements with then-president Gustavo Noboa to channel oil rents toward the municipality.

In 2003, during election campaign times, Estupiñan annexed areas surrounding the refinery, 15 de Marzo included, into urban parishes under municipal management, enabling the extension of basic services to these. Estupiñan understood the lively history of racialized state abandonment in Esmeraldas. As a resident of 15 de Marzo explained, people identified with "Ernesto [because he] knew how to take care of his people." He is remembered as "assisting" neighbors with cultural enhancement and city beautification works, which 15 de Marzo residents qualify as supporting a more "dignified way of life." The central government, on the other hand, was regarded with suspicion. Estupiñan was reelected in 2005 and again in 2010. Though his popularity declined, he continued to provide basic public works to "assist" people in exchange for their electoral backing. By the 2010s, political fatigue settled in, as well as increasing accusations of corruption in electoral processes against his administration.

The experience of 15 de Marzo illustrates how Estupiñan's "assistentialism" paved the way for the *Revolución*. By August 2012, 15 de Marzo had fallen into disrepair: people called it a "red zone," an unsafe place where one is likely to get robbed. Emergency vehicles do not usually enter these neighborhoods, I was told, since it is difficult to follow suspects and the vehicles can get stuck in the numerous potholes that plague the dirt and loose rock streets of the area. By June 2013, 15 de Marzo felt different; the *Revolución Ciudadana* was everywhere. Heavy-duty machinery furiously dug out roads and paralyzed movement, schools were brightly painted in the blue and white colors associated with the state-owned oil company, Petroecuador, their white walls giving the sense of clean and inviting space. And in January 2014, 15 de Marzo looked spectacular: smooth, slick roads and freshly painted billboards proudly showcased how much appeared to be invested. Every billboard bore a patriotic flag and the signature of President Rafael Correa (or his name), as a reminder of state presence. Cars and buses entered the neighborhood without trouble and bus stop sites facilitated public transport, and residents complained about how cars drove too fast through these streets. According to a resident, this was an improvement over what life used to be like. We were not in a red zone anymore.

This transformation of 15 de Marzo was linked to an electoral war between state and local government tangled with race. In 2013, Alianza País, the formal party led by President Correa, was seeking to oust opposing parties from provincial and municipal seats throughout the country, which included seats dominated by the MPD in Esmeraldas. First, a media war broke out between Alianza Pais and the MPD during campaign time; Correa called Estupiñán a *cacique*, echoing historical racialized critiques against black sovereignty, and called his almost fourteen-year-old administration lazy and slow, terms often used to refer to the inferior nature of blacks and Indians in colonial plantations, and not worthy of receiving state funding. This racialized language diminished the importance of the work performed by Estupiñán. Meanwhile, Estupiñán called the Correa administration imperialist, and advised Esmeraldeños to be wary of losing local control through an Alianza Pais "puppet government" in Esmeraldas.

Long-term residents of 15 de Marzo help illustrate how this political war unfolded in the terrain of everyday political agency. For example, Leonor, an Afro-Ecuadorian woman in her fifties and one of the original settlers of 15 de Marzo, defines her life as constantly enduring risk: "se juega la vida" (risks living everyday). She is the head of her household and main income earner. Her seventeen-year-old house, donated by a Catholic group, fell down in 2013, and since then she has invested whatever capital is available to her to build it back again. Her main income is derived from informal activities. Over the last ten years, she has run a food business that involves roasting *maduros* (sweet plantains) in the morning and taking them to the nearby flea market and/or bus terminal using her "business cart," a bicycle that she adapted into a three-wheel vehicle. She used to own a larger fleet but with age, sickness, and rising insecurity, she decided to scale down. During the electoral campaign season, her informal economic activities brought about twenty to thirty dollars a week to the household. Her seventeen-year-old son was a bricklayer at the new school built by the *Revolución Ciudadana*—a source of income that she is thankful for—and her husband was occasionally hired to do welding jobs for the booming construction of state-sponsored infrastructure. Leonor's most constant income comes from the "bono de la dignidad," the colloquial term for the BDH, which she readily admits is the only way to keep things afloat. Though she is professionally trained as a teacher, she prefers her independent activities because they allow her to stay close to her family and to escape the routine of wage labor—to choose to live the life she has reason to value.

Meanwhile, the city streets where Leonor conducts her everyday business were plagued with potholes and rubble during the campaign year of 2013. These obstacles were "frictions" to the successful accomplishment of her economic activities. She called the municipality to fix these but received little response. In contrast, the smooth roads brought by the *Revolución* were a positive change for her and contributed to her success. It would be easy to say that the potholes that Leonor experienced were indicative of Estupiñan's ineffective "assistance" and corruption. A deeper analysis suggests that these potholes exemplified how Estupiñan was disarticulated from his constituency by the *Revolución*. Throughout the electoral campaign season of 2013, state agencies stopped channeling oil funds to the municipal government, which directly affected the municipality's ability to finance public works maintenance and repair. As an Ecuador Estratégico representative reflected in 2013, no infrastructural improvement scheme by the municipality would be funded until Alianza Pais won the election. Furthermore, some of the works sponsored by the state during election times destroyed those built by the municipal government, which sat as political statements about *who* actually serves the people: the state or the municipality. The city, it appeared, was being tuned by oil funds to the time and space of the Correa *Revolución*. Conversations with residents and election results in 2014 confirmed that citizens understood and condoned this strategy: The Alianza Pais candidate, a new politician with close connections with Correa, received 46 percent of the vote in the parish where 15 de Marzo is located. The MPD received 11 percent, effectively erasing it from the municipal government.

Tabete

The experience of Tabete residents with the *Revolución*, about twenty minutes south of the city by car, is dramatically different. Access to Tabete is through a two-kilometer dirt road off the main highway, its entrance framed by a now fading billboard supporting the MPD. Established in the 1980s, Tabete is home to rural migrants from the neighboring province of Manabí. Some came to Esmeraldas in the 1950s, when the *paja toquilla* hats (Panama hats) market crashed; others came in the 1980s to escape drought and the high cost of land associated with the establishment of a revamped banana industry in Manabí. In 2013, Tabete was home to about seventy dispersedly settled mestizo families making a living off the land, and seasonal wage workers in nearby haciendas, some hinting at strong social dependence on absentee landlords. As in other rural areas, population density is low in Tabete; a few homes are placed close together in the community center, close to the school, while the majority is dispersed throughout the valley and closer to their plots of land.

Despite its relative proximity to the main highway, Tabete is regularly isolated. Seasonal heavy rains can destabilize the clayish hillsides, causing landslides that can block roads for days. Residents rely on horses and communally rented transport to take their produce on the two-kilometer dirt road that is the main point of access to the closest paved road. On this road, roughly halfway to Tabete, signs mark the underground presence of the heavy-crude pipeline, the OCP, which travels perpendicular to the road and follows the up-and-down features of the land. This pipeline is operated by a private Ecuadorian group, and is expected to be transferred to the Ecuadorian government in 2023. In its journey from Amazonian oilfields to maritime port, the OCP crosses Esmeraldas, sometimes visibly along rolling green hills, other times only evident by the markers that indicate its underground location. In Tabete, the OCP is a sort of specter; it is sometimes present, for example, when worker crews drive oil company cars through local roads to conduct pipeline maintenance, but often it is part of the everyday, like the markers that indicate its buried location or the vibrations of the flow of oil.

In 2012, a nongovernmental organization approached the residents of Tabete to promote a sustainable agricultural project in the community. Tabete residents produced organically grown high-quality Arabica coffee as well as avocado trees. Both the coffee and the avocados are sources of income for Tabete agriculturalists. They sell the coffee directly to an intermediary and either take the avocados to the city market or wait for an intermediary to sort the dirt road and reach the community. Residents were excited about the possibility of certifying their coffee production practices and envisioned the possibility of improving their transportation networks to facilitate economic connections. Investing in the value-added elements of their production also fit well with the existing push by the *Revolución Ciudadana* to activate and support local production entrepreneurial schemes.

In April 2013, Tabete endured a nighttime landslide that buried thirteen people alive and demolished a portion of the community. The exact cause of the landslide is unclear: some claim it was due to heavy rains and unstable soils, others blame land clearing and deforestation as sources of soil destabilization. Yet others believe it was triggered by the pulsating activity of the OCP, which runs along the top of the valley where Tabete is situated. Some residents believe that the pipeline stresses the hillside by increasing impervious surfaces on high areas and increasing the rate of water flowing toward Tabete. Identifying this concern as a political matter, community leaders wrote to the OCP management on several occasions, expressing their concern over the infrastructural risks of the pipeline. They received no response. Tabete residents stepped up their political presence. Days after the event, an activist ally from the city even appeared in the weekly news program hosted by Correa, raising questions about the poor state response received and blaming the oil complex for irresponsible planning and for contributing to the tragedy.

Soon after, municipal officials from the MPD poured in with assistance to rebuild the community. Though Tabete is not under municipal jurisdiction, officials were present to help this nearby community, but also to show support for the provincial government, also an MPD administration. This was election campaigning time. Estupiñan and several members of his administration appeared in front of cameras, rubber boots–deep in the recent mudslide, decrying the human losses in Tabete. President Correa also visited, about a week later, although to promote a different message. Bringing national attention to this remote place for the first time, he told residents that his ministries of risk management and housing would help secure land *elsewhere for their relocation*. Residents explained that Correa labeled Tabete "too risky" for human settlement and promised them land for their productive activities and new housing in a different location. He asked them not to resist. The possibilities of slope stabilization, infrastructural strengthening, and better evacuation routes were not even considered in this case.

But by early 2014, the land promised for relocation had not materialized. Agricultural activities had declined; I observed abandoned avocado plots that were being reclaimed by the nearby forest. Following the old dirt road that led to the more distant homes showed regrowth; remote homes that used to be located along the path, further up on the mountainside, were abandoned. Residents did not want to build on the slopes anymore and moved closer to the community center. This, in turn, increased their distance from plots. Some residents were told that the area would be turned into a wildlife sanctuary. In a newspaper interview by the local newspaper *La Hora* (2014), Tabete residents expressed concern over when and if relocation would ever happen. Some had already moved to the city in search of more stable sources of income. The local school, a hot spot of the community, was closed to make sure kids were not at risk of exposure to another avalanche. And yet others heard rumors that if they wished to take advantage of the relocation program, they would have to pay a portion of the costs, and that this payment would come from their *bono*.

By April 2014, relocation had not taken place, and the Ministry of Housing concluded that in order to qualify for a new plot of land, Tabete residents could apply for a titling *bono* of four hundred dollars (US), a supplement that helps minimize the costs of registering for land. But many Tabete residents did not have legal title to the land or access to resources to secure this. By 2014, Tabete residents seemed to have engaged in a politics of waiting (Bourdieu 2000), where making people wait, without crushing their hopes for change, is a form of power *inac*tion that facilitates the domination of the poor. Tabete residents waited for roads, assistance, and land. They were trapped by state inaction: they did not have the political or economic capital to articulate their demands for recognition as political subjects; many did not know exactly who to contact to have their claims addressed outside of the frame of relocation, which in turn appeared to have been forgotten. By March of 2016, about forty families still remained in Tabete and strong rains had caused another landslide, though no residents were affected at that time.

Conclusion

Twenty-first century Latin American state-led revolutions are not all the same (Castañeda 2006; Coronil, Craig, and Derluguian 2011; Dickovick and Eaton 2013; Foster 2007), but they all were initiated by citizen demands for a different political economy of life. This chapter offered insights into how the *Revolución* is experienced in Esmeraldas, one of Ecuador's most strategic sites of the oil complex, demonstrating the entanglements of oil's circulation with the Esmeraldeño body politic. The 2014 elections timeframe offered a conjuncture of democracy to examine the uneven urban and rural dynamics of the *Revolución*. Where the urban needs of 15 de Marzo became functional to the national political project, and thus preferred sites of political action, rural spaces like Tabete, which do not carry the same visibility, were largely ignored. The slow and vanishing response from both the municipal and central government demonstrates that rural claims continue to be peripheral to state-led citizenship projects. At the same time, the historical trajectory of 15 de Marzo, specifically the struggles over land and identity expressed by its residents, problematizes the fixity of urban-rural distinctions, and points to the entangled relations between devalued rural spaces and the intensification of urban politics under shifting political economies.

Many Esmeraldeños have benefited from the political moment of the *Revolución Ciudadana*. It would be disingenuous not to recognize that *bonos* and infrastructure works are broadly evident investments in citizenship making, a promise of transformation from citizen-lacks (e.g., insufficient income or limited access to infrastructure that connects individuals to the larger economy) to citizen-ideals. But it would be equally incorrect to gloss over the *Revolución's* role as a project of subordination and dependence in its push for liberation from poverty. The participation of poor Esmeraldeños in the *Revolución* has happened through well-trodden patron-client relationships with political parties and electoral politics, not through a radical commitment for "real change" in the hegemonic context of extractive economies.

For example, 15 de Marzo constitutes a population that must be attended; their claims matter to the everyday operations of the refinery and thermoelectric facilities. The risks borne by its residents (toxic exposure) are minimized in relation to everyday urban needs. Fixing infrastructural capital in urban projects not only pacifies local demands but produces state clients that use their political capital to back up state power. The *Revolución* effectively nurtures relations of dependence with these urban groups. Yet, this process is only possible because of the historical devaluation of Esmeraldas, where black populations were seen as peripheral and threatening to white-mestizo interests in dominant cities. While urban blackness in Esmeraldas had at one point meant isolation and marginalization, under the *Revolución* the devalued conditions of existence became a space of opportunity for capturing electoral publics, a potential site of colonization under the new regime of liberal improvement for all.

The rural community of Tabete, overlapping with the OCP pipeline, does not hold the same electoral or political capital. The risks borne by its residents mark them as a population to be removed (or worse, forgotten) rather than attended to. In the current race politics of Esmeraldas, their rurality does not hold the same political capital; they are not urban black citizens nor do they have the population density to sway electoral results. Removing Tabete residents from the spaces of the pipeline and moving them to state-built homes was a strategy of risk amelioration but also of minimizing the value of their claims against the oil complex. The state effectively stopped responding to Tabete's needs when the electoral period passed and the desired candidate was elected. While the equalization of citizenship is the intended goal of the *Revolución*, place specificity inflects the form and work of social change, differentiating some citizenship claims and risks as more relevant and thus accountable than others.

Estupiñan's and Sánchez's arguments, cited at the beginning of the chapter, point to the historical articulation of race with citizenship in Ecuador: how these forms of sociality underpin who counts as a citizen, as well as how an individual is recognized as a citizen in the current *Revolución*. Their reflections on state-citizen relations speak to the problematic universalization of the *Revolución*, which privileges one metric of citizen value—participation in and support for the political establishment as the way to improve life—while at the same time negating other forms of value that do not fit with the goals of the Correa administration. This chapter paid attention to the uneven geography of these state-citizen relations, specifically, how race and rurality politics infused the realpolitik of the 2014 elections, and deepened the divide between urban and rural political bodies in Esmeraldas.

It is too early to conclude on the accomplishments and failures of the *Revolución Ciudadana*. It remains a fruitful terrain and space for reflection on Ecuador's and, more generally, Latin American twenty-first-century political economic transitions. Questions on positioning and epistemology remain (for whom does the *Revolución* work, how does it work, and at what cost for whom?) as well as ontological questions (what worlds and options are created and which are removed or ended). As the television campaign "For the people, Revolution" suggested, the *Revolución* did bring urban services to citizens, but it did so by recognizing citizen needs and capabilities in some places and ignoring them in others. Transcending the particulars of existence in order to achieve dreams of dignified living is not currently available to all citizens, opening questions about the scalability of such projects of social transformation. Place-specific differences, existing prior to and during the revolutionary project, inflect the form and work of the *Revolución*, leading to a differentiation of which citizenship claims count and which are invisibilized.

Postscript. By June 2014, soon after Alianza Pais secured the mayor's seat, the potholes returned to 15 de Marzo. With decreasing oil prices, the state is no longer funding the upkeep of these infrastructural projects. Local governments are not able to tap on the oil bonanza and are expected "to sort out" things on their own and not expect state handouts. The political capital of black neighborhoods has receded in importance, perhaps until the next election cycle. Meanwhile, in Tabete, a bus sponsored by the national government to pick up children to take them to school, as the local school was closed due to the risk of another landslide, stopped showing up after a few months. The kids now have to walk several kilometers to make it to the closest school. Bracketing these spaces of rurality so that their claims can be resolved at a later time appears to have suspended them temporally from state view—perhaps long enough to exhaust their political voice. A remaining resident who does not wish to leave Tabete and who lost a family member in the 2013 landslide mentioned that a new pipeline might be in the works on the other side of the valley. Removing his community, he thought, might have been a tactic to control any possible future risks for the pipeline.

Acknowledgments

The material presented in this chapter is based upon work supported by MUSAM (Mujeres Apoyando a Mujeres), an Esmeraldeño grassroots organization support-ing local livelihoods, and by a grant from the National Science Foundation. Any opinions, findings, and conclusions or recommendations expressed in this material are those of the author and do not necessarily reflect the views of the National Science Foundation.

Notes

1. In public speeches, President Correa explicitly links the funds available for the "revolution" to a recent law that assigns 12 percent of oil exports income for infrastructure building, an enormous boost due to the historically high price of oil, and from increased taxes on financial institutions to help finance a suite of cash-transfer programs. By 2011, $US 943.5 million had been invested in 1,200 public works, mostly in areas of intense resource extraction (oil and mining) (Ecuador Estratégico 2016), and from 2006 to 2011, social spending (pensions, insurance, education, housing, social security, and cash transfers) doubled, reaching 12 percent of the GDP (Llerena et al. 2015).

2. In Ecuador, provinces, cantons, and parishes are administrative divisions of land. Esmeraldas Province is divided into seven cantons, which are further subdivided into several urban and rural parishes.

3. See Minda (2002), Miranda (2010), Rueda Novoa (2001), and Whitten (1965) for the contextualization of struggles over land and blackness in Esmeraldas Province.

4. While indigenous struggles and their intersections with coloniality are often examined in regard to oil-producing areas of Ecuador (e.g., Kimmerling 2001; Sawyer 2004; Valdivia 2005), the Afro-Ecuadorian experience is not. This chapter is not focused on oil-producing areas, a site prioritized since the establishment of the national industry, but on the other spaces of the oil complex, specifically refining areas, where racialized subaltern identities are also reproduced but conspicuously absent in scholarly analyses of oil.

5. The term "strategic sectors" refers to sectors that weigh heavily on national economic, social, political, and environmental decision making. Energy, telecommunications, nonrenew-able natural resources, hydrocarbon refinement, and biodiversity and genetic patrimony are some of the strategic sectors most often discussed by the Correa administration.

6. The drop in oil prices in 2014 translated into a reduced public budget, and a con-sequent reduction in projects. By 2015, Correa had declared a moratorium on any new

public works projects, prompting questions about future strategies of capability building. This chapter focuses on the years before the drop in oil prices (2008–14).

7. Funding for the BDH was secured through a $60 million loan from the World Bank (World Bank 2006). New taxes levied on banks and the elimination of certain financial-sector tax exemptions financed over 50 percent of the 2013 increase (Weisbrot, Johnston, and Lefebvre 2013). In 2016, the total amount allocated to cover *bono* disbursements was $US 6.21 billion, $129 million less than in 2015 (Menendez Torres 2016).

8. In Ecuador, chronic structural poverty tends to be higher in rural areas, while relative poverty—associated with booms and crisis—tends to be higher in urban areas.

9. Poverty in Ecuador is measured according to income, consumption, and "unmet basic needs" (inadequate access to water, sanitation, education, health, and housing infrastructure). "Chronic poverty" is a measure of the cyclical oscillations of poverty: how many people leave and how many return to poverty within a designated time period.

10. SENPLADES coordinates strategic policies to meet the goals stated under the new Constitution of 2008: integrated development across all territories of Ecuador (not solely urban areas), public investment in the democratization of the state, participatory citizen-ship, and transparency and efficiency in public funds governance. For more information, see http://www.planificacion.gob.ec/la-secretaria/.

11. To this effect, the Correa administration plans a reduction in the consumption of oil derivatives (which in 2014 was close to 95 million barrels), along with a reduction in subsidies for these (Reyes 2016).

12. Antonio Preciado, another well-known political activist, also lived in Barrio Caliente and was militant in the MPD, though he later broke off due to ideological differences.

References

Bourdieu, P. 2000. *Pascalian Meditations*. Stanford, CA: Stanford University Press.

Carriére, J. 2001. "Neoliberalism, Economic Crisis and Popular Mobilization in Ecuador." In *Miraculous Metamorphoses: The Neoliberalization of Latin American Populism*, 132–149.

Castañeda, J. G. 2006. "Latin America's Left Turn." *Foreign Affairs* 85 (3): 28.

Coronil, F., C. Craig, and G. Derluguian. 2011. "The Future in Question: History and Utopia in Latin America (1989–2010)." *Business as Usual: The Roots of the Global Financial Meltdown* 1: 231–292.

Das, V., and D. Poole, eds. 2004. *Anthropology in the Margins of the State*. Santa Fe, NM: School of American Research Press.

De la Torre, C. 2013. "El tecnopopulismo de Rafael Correa: ¿Es compatible el carisma con la tecnocracia?" *Latin American Research Review* 48 (1): 24–43.

Dickovick, J. T., and K. H. Eaton. 2013. "Latin America's Resurgent Centre: National Government Strategies after Decentralisation." *Journal of Development Studies* 49 (11): 1453–1466.

Dussel, E. D. 2008. *Coloniality at Large: Latin America and the Postcolonial Debate*. Durham, NC: Duke University Press.

Ecuador Estratégico. 2014. "Rendicion de Cuentas." Quito, Ecuador: Ecuador Estratégico.

———. 2016. "Proyectos Estratégicos." Quito, Ecuador: Ecuador Estratégico. Retrieved from http://www.ecuadorestrategicoep.gob.ec/proyectos/proyectos-estrategicos.

Ecuadorimediato. 2015. "Debate por la sanción impuesta por la Supercom a Bonil" (February 15). Retrieved from http://www.ecuadorenvivo.com/sociedad/189-videos/27348-el-presidente-correa-me-ha-ridiculizado-en-las-sabatinas-y-los-movimientos-afro-donde-estuvieron-reclama-exalcalde-de-esmeraldas-debate-por-la-sancion-impuesta-por-la-supercom-a-bonil.html#.VyIqvFYrIQ9.

El Telégrafo. 2012. "La banca financiaría el 54% del incremento del Bono de Desarrollo." Retrieved from http://www.telegrafo.com.ec/noticias/informacion-general/item/la-banca-financiaria-el-54-del-incremento-del-bono-de-desarrollo.html.

Ferguson, J. 2015. *Give a Man a Fish: Reflections on the New Politics of Distribution*. Durham, NC and London: Duke University Press.

Foster, J. B. 2007. "The Latin American Revolt: An Introduction." *Monthly Review* 59 (3): 1.

Gerlach, A. 2003. *Indians, Oil, and Politics: A Recent History of Ecuador*. Lanham, MD: Rowman & Littlefield.

Grandin, G., and G. M. Joseph. 2010. *A Century of Revolution in Latin America: Insurgent and Counterinsurgent Violence in Latin America's Long Cold War*. Durham, NC: Duke University Press.

Handelsman, M. 1999. *Lo Afro y la Plurinacionalidad: El Caso Ecuatoriano visto desde su Literatura*. Romance Monographs, 54. University of Mississippi.

Hernández, J. 2012. "Balance de la revolución ciudadana." In *Gobierno de la revolución ciudadana*, edited by S. Mantilla, S. Mejía, and J. J. Paz y Miño Cepeda. Quito, Ecuador: Centro Latinoamericano de Estudios Políticos/Editorial Planeta del Ecuador S.A.

Kimerling, J. 1991. *Amazon Crude*. New York: Natural Resources Defense Council.

La Hora. 2011. "Por aporte al IESS se quedan sin bono," (September 27). Retrieved from http://lahora.com.ec/index.php/noticias/show/1101211083/-1/Por_aportes_al_IESS_se_quedan_sin_bono_.html#.Vy_1c4QrIQ8.

———. 2014. "No nos olviden, por favor," (March 26), A2. Retrieved from http://issuu.com/la_hora/docs/esmeraldas260314.

Llerena, F. P., M. C. Llerena, M. A. Llerena, and R. Saá. 2015. "Social Spending, Taxes and Income." CEQ Working Paper No. 28. Retrieved from http://www.commitmen

toequity.org/publications_files/Ecuador/CEQWPNo28%20SocSpendTaxIncome
RedistEcuador%20Feb%202015.pdf.

Menéndez Torres, T. 2016. "Bono de Desarrollo Humano, 1 de los 4 subsidios que se ajustarán en 2016." *Ecuavisa*. Retrieved from http://www.ecuavisa.com/articulo/televistazo/noticias/121326-bono-desarrollo-humano-1-4-subsidios-que-se-ajustaran-2016.

MIES. 2013. "Reporte Nacional Mensual." (December). Quito, Ecuador: Ministerio de Inclusion Economica y Social.

———. 2014. "Del Bono hacia el emprendimiento productivo: el caso de doña Betty." *MIESpacio* (March). Retrieved from http://www.inclusion.gob.ec/wp-content/uploads/downloads/2014/05/MIESPACIOO-20.pdf.

Minda, P. 2002. *Identidad y conflicto: La lucha por la tierra en la zona de la provincia Esmeraldas*. Quito, Ecuador: Ediciones Abya Yala.

Miranda, F. 2010. *Hacia una narrativa afroecuatoriana: Cimarronaje cultural en América Latina*. Havana: Fondo Editorial Casa de las Américas.

Rahier, J. M. 2013. *Kings for Three Days: The Play of Race and Gender in an Afro-Ecuadorian Festival*. Urbana: University of Illinois Press.

Reyes, R. 2016. "El terremoto y la refinería." *El Comercio*. Retrieved from http://www.elcomercio.com/cartas/terremoto-refineria.html.

Rueda Novoa, R. 2001. *Zambaje y autonomía: Historia de la gente negra de la provincia de Esmeraldas: siglos XVI–XVIII*. Esmeraldas, Ecuador: Municipalidad de Esmeraldas.

Sawyer, S. 2004. *Crude Chronicles: Indigenous Politics, Multinational Oil, and Neoliberalism in Ecuador*. Durham, NC: Duke University Press.

Secretaria Nacional de Informacion. 2014. "Ficha de Cifras Generales Canton Esmeraldas." Esmeraldas, Ecuador.

Sen, A. 1997. "Editorial: Human Capital and Human Capability." *World Development* 25 (12): 1959–1961.

Southgate, D. 2016. *Globalized Fruit, Local Entrepreneurs: How One Banana-exporting Country Achieved Worldwide Reach*. Philadelphia: University of Pennsylvania Press.

Unda, M. 2009. "Hacia la segunda fase de la 'revolución ciudadana.'" *Alai*. Retrieved from https://www.alainet.org/en/node/133917.

United Nations Environment Programme. 2006. *GEO Esmeraldas: Perspectivas del medio ambiente urbano*. Ecuador: PNUMA: FUDAMYF.

Valdivia, G. 2005. "On Indigeneity, Change, and Representation in the Northeastern Ecuadorian Amazon." *Environment and Planning A* 37: 285–303.

Verdesoto, L. 2015. "¿Realmente ha bajado la pobreza en el país?" *Plan V*. Retrieved from http://planv.com.ec/historias/entrevistas/realmente-ha-bajado-la-pobreza-el-pais/pagina/0/2.

Weisbrot, M., J. Johnston, and S. Lefebvre. 2013. *Ecuador's New Deal: Reforming and Regulating the Financial Sector*. Washington, DC: Center for Economic and Policy Research.

Whitten, N. E. 1965. *Class, Kinship, and Power in an Ecuadorian Town: The Negroes of San Lorenzo.* Stanford, CA: Stanford University Press.

World Bank. 2006. "Report 35064: Project Appraisal Document on a Proposed Loan in the Amount of US $60 million to the Republic of Ecuador for a Support to Reform of the Bono de Desarrollo Humano Project in Support of the First Phase of the Bono de Desarrollo Humano Reform Program." Retrieved from http://documents. worldbank.org/curated/en/535711468026951408/pdf/35064.pdf.

7

Racing the Reservation

Rethinking Resistance and Development in the Navajo Nation

Dana E. Powell

A merican Indian reservations are political, legal territories, distinct from—but also intimately interior to—the United States. These territories embody the contradiction implicit in the "domestic dependent nations" legal framework enacted in United States law in Supreme Court cases in the 1830s, under Chief Justice John Marshall, laying the foundation for settler-native treaty making and legal relations (Deloria and Lytle 1983).[1] Simultaneously sovereign *and* dependent, reservations thus occupy a liminal ontological space: their existence speaks to the future, inasmuch as they lay claim to lands based upon political integrity predating European settlement, and yet the enactment of that claim is always already constrained by the contours of colonial violence—in this case, the geopolitical boundaries drawn up by empire. In another register, reservations are one very particular kind of indigenous political space that complicates and challenges "modular" or uniform conceptions of the nation-state (Biolsi 2005). They pluralize, multiply, overlap, and ultimately challenge the modern nation-state's claim to unity and legitimacy. The degree of their threat, however, as materializations (in land, infrastructure, and citizens' bodies) of an alternative political assemblage, becomes most legible in recent spectacular land claims conflicts like the Standing Rock Sioux's challenge to the Dakota Access Pipeline or transnational social movements like Idle No More[2] mobilizations that articulate the possibility of new forms of reclamation as resistance.

Though indigeneity circulates, shapes, and refashions through transnational diaspora, for many communities in North America, the reservation-homeland in the United States remains the consistent point of reference for all other types of indigenous political space (Belin 1999; Smith 2009; de la Cadena and Starn 2007). These are spaces of desire and self-authoring, even as more than 60 percent of American Indians reside primarily outside of reservation lands (Utter 1993). As predominantly rural geopolitical spaces, reservations and other tribal jurisdictional territories embody many contradictions, two of which are particularly relevant for thinking through their racialized dimensions. First, although sovereign in name, the land title itself is held in trust by the federal government, with specific benefits to Nations (e.g., socialized medicine through the Indian Health Service) ensured by nineteenth-century treaties. Second, though federally recognized tribes are granted reservations on the basis of a particular Native Nation's historical and political occupation of lands prior to European contact, the logics and technics of settler colonialism frequently repackage this difference in racialized terms, in biological lexicons of blood and skin. My concern here, as a non-Native scholar, ally, collaborator, and writer deeply concerned about the ongoing lived effects of colonialism, is to illuminate and critique ways in which non-Native perceptions of indigenous geopolitical spaces are shaped and limited by modes of racialization smuggled into environmental discourse and practice.

Racial logics that overplay phenotype and ideas about "blood" at the expense of *political* distinctiveness work to erase, or at least silence, the historical violence and trauma that led to the establishment of these spaces (see Noble 2015; Simpson 2014; Tuck and Yang 2012). Such biological and phenotypic emphasis also serves to undermine claims to land and territory, generating as Jean Dennison shows, "logics of recognition" that privilege skin and blood over long land tenure and occupation (Dennison 2014). The persistent (and highly problematic) imaginary of reservation spaces as fundamentally ethnic enclaves is grounded in longstanding settler notions of individual natives as ethnic or racialized "others"—rather than seeing Native Nations as *political bodies*. This racialized move (enacted in the settler gaze) serves the coloniality of power relations, constitutive of modernity (Mignolo 2000), thereby disguising territorial politics with body politics. Technologies of the state have enacted, regulated, and managed this kind of biopolitical rendering of indigenous difference as racial instead of political. In other words, indigenous difference is produced, by the imperial settler state, as ethnic/racial rather than political/historical.

Critical legal scholars note this nefarious sleight of hand: "Federal Indian law has consistently constructed identity in its naming of indigenous groups by decontextualizing and remapping identity to a fixed map of race" (Gooding 1994: 1181; see also Allen, Daro and Holland 2007; Inwood and Yarbrough 2010).[3] This decontextualization has everything to do with the history of Anglo colonialism and westward expansion, in which settlers reconfigured diverse indigenous spaces to meet the growing, land-based requirements of settlement in a particular historical moment. Legal scholar Rebecca Tsosie critically rethinks the meaning of Lewis and Clark's "explorations," as a foundational American narrative, illuminating the twin logics of discovery and conquest that underpinned the duo's Jefferson-mandated study and mapping of Native peoples west of the Appalachians (Tsosie 2007). Such voluntary migration, against the backdrop of the violent *in*voluntary migrations of millions of enslaved Africans and millions of dispossessed Native Americans during Removal, was nothing if not a power/knowledge enactment of territorial control and population management. Through such spatial transformations, these remappings of place produced racialized landscapes, with diverse Nations consolidated as "Indians" in the non-Native imagination, by the 1890 massacre at Wounded Knee.[4] The West's layered failures of acknowledgment, as Michel-Rolph Trioullot has shown, is an operation of power in which certain narratives (and their attending experiences) are produced as dominant, as other stories are strategically silenced (Trouillot 1995).

In this chapter I address the Navajo (Diné) Nation reservation as a racialized, rural space, historically particular, and yet also emblematic for indigenous experiences today, given the challenges facing tribal leaders as they negotiate the future of tribal sovereignty in a settler colonial context. In particular, I wish to consider the mode of racialization through the materiality of coal and the gendered nature of natural resource management on the Navajo reservation. How does an object such as coal, with its own political-ecological history, actively assist in the configuration of not only human-environment relationships, but of human-human relationships in broader networks of power? How does coal undermine politics as usual, putting into question mainstream environmentalist assumptions about indigenous difference, as read through "race" rather than history? I approach these questions through critical political ecology, particularly its feminist and environmental justice trajectories with their emphasis on difference, and how it is enabled, produced and deployed in environmental struggles (di Chiro 2008; Escobar 2006, 2008; Rawwida and Harcourt 2015; Rocheleau et al. 1996). In this case examined, difference materializes not only in racialized and gendered bodies, but through landscapes: the indigenous reservation as a historical-political-cultural territory emerges as a geographic indicator, a spatial practice of differentiating indigeneity, regulated by the hegemonic settler state.

Settler-Mapping and Counter-Mapping Indigenous Difference

In the American Southwest, displacement and resettlement of Natives resulted in the creation of mostly reservations with large land bases: modern spatial enclosures that, in their remove from urban centers, established a landscape of largely rural indigenous territories. The reservation-as-homeland in the Southwest serves as a dense site of meaning in contemporary configurations of Native subject position and identification. Yet moreover, the continued occupation of the land itself serves the very ground for indigenous claims to political as opposed to racial difference in settler society. At times, the politics of indigeneity often hinges on proving authenticity through geographic proximity: for many Diné people, a widely held, but often challenged, belief is that "real" Indians come from, and reside on, "the rez." On the Navajo Nation, this spatial claim to authenticity is often more salient than the contemporary and contentious blood quantum debates troubling Native Nations in other locales. Yet despite these very situated, local, and dynamic indices of belonging, American Indians have become a "racial minority" category, available for self-reporting on US census forms despite the diverse policies regulating tribal membership established by particular Native Nations' governments. This is striking, given that many Native scholars consider American Indian identification a fundamentally political rather than racial category. Starting with the 2010 US census, self-reporting as American Indian has been able to coexist with another identification, allowing for multiracial ethnicities, resulting in a 39 percent statistical increase in the American Indian population of the country (Norris et al. 2012).[5]

Census categories can be seen as what Michel Foucault called an operation of biopower, wherein the state engages in regulating and managing subjects of a population in order to both subjugate and promote its longevity (Foucault 1978, 2003). As such, biopolitical technologies of the state, when working through racial classifications as modes of writing bodies, silenced and flattened diverse indigenous identifications, which are legally and importantly complicated. As Andrew Curley argues, "Navajo" identity as such was only rendered legible by the state by making a diverse indigenous group in the Southwest that called themselves Diné ("the people") into a "standardized and simplified ethnic group within the United States" that could be a "decipherable population subject to the control and sometimes manipulation of a colonial authority" (Curley 2014: 129). Yet also, as Curley illuminates, these technologies of making Diné into Navajo—and thus making a collectively independent people into a "tribe"—were resisted in sometimes overt, but often less obvious ways (ibid.). Such mechanisms of making indigenous difference legible through standardized markers of multiraciality is part of broader racializing discourses and distracts from the historically particular experience of Diné and other Native peoples as *political subalterns* in settler society. The effect of this framing thus depoliticizes the long land tenure of indigenous peoples in North America. This erasure further elides the ever-present cultural and political threat of dispossession of Native territories by the settler state (as in midcentury policies that "terminated" particular Native Nations as political entities), which lays penultimate claim to indigenous reservation lands.

Historically, to mitigate the insecurities of tribal sovereignty under settler colonialism, Diné leaders in the US Southwest have pursued mining and exporting nonrenewable energy resources (oil, natural gas, uranium, and coal) from Navajo territory as a method of revenue for the tribal economy, rendering the 27,000-square-mile Navajo reservation just as "global" as it is "local," as I and others discuss elsewhere (Powell and Curley 2009; Powell and Long 2010). However, meeting the endless energy demands of Phoenix and other Sun Belt cities is at least partially a historical response to decades of exploitation under the Cold War economy for uranium and coercions into below-market coal deals during the termination era of the 1950s. As such, the Navajo reservation's complicated political ecological history poses a challenge to standard scripts of modernity that see development as an "attack" on indigenous peoples, who are, in turn understood through two main tropes: as either "victims" of development (passive, lacking agency, sacrifices of Manifest Destiny) as often presented in dependency theories, *or* as "resisters" to development (natural revolutionaries, liberatory agents, the return of the Noble Savage) as often presented in social movements theories. These tropes—and the many forms of violence they produce—are persistent elements in the genealogy of development discourse (Escobar 1995; Edelman and Haugerud 2005). In both cases, these tropes present anti-modern subjects: indigenous peoples are presented as either overcome by technology, *or* inherently opposed to technology. And crucially, in both cases, "development" is a pressure and a possibility that can only come from the outside.

Rather, I propose we attend to the complexities of simultaneous suffering *and* renewal, of disavowal *and* embrace, in the lived experience of the racialized, rural space of the Navajo Nation (Moore 2005).[6] These complexities are entangled with reservation landscapes and the "natural resources" these lands produce, which have, customarily, been managed by elder women. They are part of twenty-first-century nation-building processes of American Indian Nations more broadly, where "development" is never a unilateral or homogenous moral project, as many contemporary examples illustrate. And where, increasingly, development (or alternative practices some might call "development") is being taken up endogenously as a way to transform the enduring structural violence of settler colonialism.

Of course, urban-rural and developed-undeveloped distinctions are neither universal nor self-evident. Just as Stacy Leigh Pigg shows how "the village" and "the villager" were discursive constructions of development discourse in Nepal (Pigg 1992), and Paige West details the discursive and material practices that transformed a rural mountain in Papua New Guinea into a globalized "conservation site" (West 2006), we can see the Navajo reservation as a social and political construction of rural space and rural subjectivities, spurred by decades of contradictory federal programs to "develop" Native peoples, by curtailing movement, retooling them as farmers, and working to assimilate through education and other governmental technologies. Critical reflections in indigenous studies direct our attention to the ways in which modern reservations are the material consequences of settler colonialism's spatial practices: first accomplished through federal policies such as nineteenth-century forced removal of southeastern indigenous peoples, known by settlers as the "Five Civilized Tribes," and later through twentieth-century programs to relocate Natives away from rural territories and into urban territories, where—as the ideology proposed—they would culturally assimilate through urban modernization, and through geographic distance from their quintessentially "anti-modern" rural homelands. Development-by-assimilation was thus a spatial and legal practice, resulting in midcentury legislation that terminated the recognition of certain tribes, such as the Menominee. Mishuana Goeman shows us the figurative and material significance of the reservation that emerged in the post-termination era, reading poet Esther Belin's ruminations on being Diné in urban Oakland and Los Angeles. Registering impacts of settler-mapping through poetry, Goeman tells us she aims to interrogate "the impacts of spatial policies in our cognitive mapping of Native lands and bodies" (Goeman 2009: 170). Belin's memories of Diné homeland, Goeman suggests, reveal the power of routes that are both physical and mental, a kind of transit between urban relocation and rural homeland that subverts the "dominant spatial norms of fixity of Native peoples in time and space and allows for a potential spatial restructuring" (Goeman 2009: 171).

Emphasizing experiences of displacement, diaspora, and movement as counter-narratives to various technologies of cartographic and territorial enclosure has been the pivotal turn of new spatial imaginaries of indigeneity in the early twentieth century. Within this refreshed imaginary of place, movement, and identity, indigenous modernities emerge as diversely positioned, poly-vocal, multi-sited, mobile, hybrid, and networked. I want to suggest, however, that the material significance of the reservation as an identifiable place—to which one might travel physically and/or mentally, as Goeman points out—remains a spatial imaginary of the utmost significance today for understanding the complex articulations of race, place, ecology, and political economy in understanding indigenous difference in the United States. Among Diné people, being "on the rez" or "off the rez" is a defining kind of boundary politics, bound up with what one can say, know, and do. Globalization is a displacement in which the reservation is not erased or eclipsed, but in fact becomes more salient precisely because of relocation and the "deferred return" of diaspora (Clifford 2007). So within this moment of theorizing mobility and global citizenry, I want to re-ground us, so to speak, in the materiality of the reservation, as a space where the ambiguous autonomy of tribal sovereignty and Diné subjectivity are worked out through particular interactions with infrastructure and the environment, and where discourses of race often occlude the deeper politics at stake for Native people.

I take Goeman seriously in this call to think about the "cognitive mapping of Native lands and bodies" and in what follows, do so through discourses of racialization that work as a kind of cognitive *remapping*. In this case, the discourse deployed repackages "the Indian problem" (as it was derisively known for two centuries by US lawmakers) as a problem of ethnic difference in an attempt to subvert the fundamental political difference that enables American Indian Nations to challenge the legitimacy of state power and, at the same time, to rework the environmental politics of coal, in unexpected ways. Belin's poetics, read through Goeman's literary analysis, offers rich terrain for rethinking the spatiality of race, gender, place, and politics more broadly.

Ethnography, I contend, can offer similarly fertile ground for productive cognitive remapping, posing situated surprises of everyday life that complicate well-worn narratives of human-environment relations. In what follows, I first map the historical terrain of Diné homeland then turn to describe one particular ethnographic revelation that suggests broader implications for understanding how gender, race, and place sometimes collide in unexpected ways, enlivening our understanding of how livelihoods on "the rez" are both politicized, and lived, in our contemporary moment.

Dinétah: Navajo Homeland

Of course reservations-as-homelands have been differently configured, in historically particular and diverse ways: for instance, Oklahoma was established as "Indian Territory" precisely through a geopolitics of violent dispossession, displacement, and relocation of East Coast refugees. For many Native Nations, nineteenth-century land allotment under the 1887 US General Allotment Act (also known as the Dawes Act) was the calculated disintegration of Indian commons; and later twentieth-century real estate maneuverings created "checkerboard" or "patchwork" geographies, where reservations include or are immediately contiguous with longstanding white settlements, with competing claims to shared territory. For other Nations, the reservation is a tiny fraction of their customary homeland, wherein land claims remain contested. For instance, in 2002 the Inter-American Commission on Human Rights (part of the Organization of American States) ruled in favor of the Western Shoshone in a challenge they brought before the commission, on the grounds that the United States had violated due process, property, and equality under the law, for the US's illegal squatter claim to what is unceded Shoshone territory.[7] Each Nation has a historically particular, legal, and cultural relationship to a specific place, or *places* in the case of relocated tribes, so we cannot use "homeland" and "reservation" interchangeably, in all cases. In a similar vein, nor can we allow the imagined geographies of the only occasionally lucrative, modern-day American Indian casino enterprises to eclipse our radical remembering of the sheer violence of settler colonialism.

For the Navajo, *Dinétah* roughly translates as "among the people" and indicates the customary homeland oriented by four sacred mountains, a place defined by stories and geologic formations, more than any precise boundary. This rural, homeland territory maps roughly onto the contemporary boundaries of the modern jurisdiction of the Navajo reservation. This is, of course, a matter of treaty making: negotiations with federal Indian agents in 1868, following four years of incarceration at a military camp near current-day Albuquerque, enabled the Diné to return to the land between the four mountains. Yet as Gooding (1994) demonstrates, the treaties themselves, and treaty litigation, can be deeply racializing forms of legal discourse, displacing and forcing oral and customary identifications with names and places, into specific racial modes of representation, grounded in blood quantum and/or visual politics sanctioned by the US state.

The newly established reservation for the Diné suffered under a politics of indigenous deterritoriality (Kuletz 1998)[8] in the late nineteenth century: that is, an abandonment by the imperial settler state, based on the assumption that the desert plateau of northern Arizona and New Mexico was economically worthless for settler state interests. Only five decades after the final treaty between the Diné and the United States, in 1868, which allowed the survivors to return to their homeland territory between the four sacred mountains, the reservation was reincorporated into US homeland state interests. Rich reserves of easily accessible oil were discovered in the late 1910s and early 1920s, with such promise that in 1924, the federal government engineered the organization of the Navajo Nation as a recognizable, centralized political entity under the leadership of a very few delegates (notably male, in a culture with longstanding matrilineal land tenure practices). This restructuring of leadership and power enabled the United States to broker deals between oil companies and Diné representatives—though this was a rupture from customary forms of environmental governance and leadership, already disrupted by 1860s relocation of Navajos and their subsequent resettlement. Thus from the 1920s onward, the Navajo Nation and its territorial land base, geopolitically bounded by federal agents, offered the United States a site of subterranean mineral resources indispensable for growing industrial capitalism. Standard Oil Company was first, tapping oil reserves on the reservation to fuel industrial growth in urban centers. Then came the Uranium Corporation of America, in partnership with the US Department of Energy, to establish uranium mines across the 27,000-square-mile reservation, ensuring a steady supply for nuclear weapons production during the Cold War. In the 1960s, US competitiveness in the emerging global economy came to depend upon coal and the Navajo reservation's rich deposits of subbituminous coal (the "glittering" dark coal outcrops which gave the sacred "Black" Mesa its name) literally powered the new Sun Belt cities of the Southwest. As Andrew Needham details, the history of modern Phoenix (its air-conditioners, in particular) is nothing other than a history of Navajo coal and its attending exploitations (Needham 2014). In the early twenty-first century, perhaps no element has raised the ire of global environmentalism more than coal, creating a confluence of complex identifications among Navajo people on and off the reservation, national conservation groups, and transnational social movements for climate justice.

In the midst of this international uproar over controversial science, planetary limits on carbon pollution, and the rights of indigenous peoples who often occupy geographies of intensive extraction *and* of intensive carbon sequestration, a racialized discourse has emerged. For instance, Native peoples are romantically heralded by many outsiders as both the "first environmentalists," who carry secrets to the pressing climate challenges of our time, and as tragic victims (the other side of this modern/colonial trope), in which they service the world as "canaries in the mine," alerting wider publics about imminent risks to public health. Indeed, this trope is global, and still dangerous (see Bessire 2014). In the American Southwest, what some call the insidious "racial triangulation" of Native Americans, Hispanos, and Anglos has produced narratives of difference and belonging that both challenge and at the same time, inadvertently reproduce the dominant environmental and racial order (Wilmsen 2007; Kosek 2006). In this context, reservations remain quintessential imaginaries of a kind of difference structured through race, space, and time: these places are commonly viewed as ethnically, spatially, and temporally *separate* from the modern Southwest. This otherness is of course precisely what has always made them objects of desire for elite, Anglo, East Coast consumption: the history of New Yorkers in Santa Fe (along with East Coast feminist anthropologists) is the fascinating subject of other studies (Lavender 2006).⁹ But with coal production as a relatively new and increasingly contentious vector of environmental difference, oppositional tropes of "Noble Savages" versus "money-hungry sellouts" work to script regional environmental politics of the Navajo Nation in equally racialized, equally violent ways: the resistance of some Navajo people to increased coal production gets read as the "natural" work of "first environmentalists," a kind of ethical project that is presented as simply inevitable, ingrained in the very essence of a specific ethnic identity (in this case, "Indian"). Or, other Navajo tribal members' embrace or promotion of coal gets read as a transgression of this "naturally" ingrained proclivity, as the work of "race traitors" (to use an older pejorative), or as the cunning opportunism that only the most abject poverty and population could produce. Both are racialized and colonial discourses, intimately linked to the decontextualized rural geography of the Navajo Nation, and the subterranean mineral resources it happens to possess. As Paul Chaat Smith warns, both are also romantic discourses, detached from the everyday realities facing subordinated Native peoples—racialized Indians—today. And if we accept that settler romanticism about Native peoples is a uniquely, perversely twentieth-century form of racism, as it dehumanizes Indian people by exalting and flattening the complexity of their place in the United States (Smith 2009), then we can begin to deepen our understanding of what sort of politics and subjects are being produced, as well as elided, in environmental debates over coal production on the Navajo Nation.

To think through this confluence of racialization processes and development projects in subject and place formation a little more empirically, I want to reflect upon an ethnographic surprise that emerged from my longstanding fieldwork in Dinétah. I had been working with Navajo environmental organizations on energy development politics for over a decade and had worked with a group of women, in particular, on their struggles to halt the construction of a new coal-fired power plant on reservation land, before I realized how I, too, was caught up in what Dennison (2012) aptly calls the "colonial entanglements" of the contemporary United States.

Carbon's Contradictions: Grandma Alice and the Everyday Life of Coal

On December 6, 2006, Diné community members established a "resistance camp" and road blockade in the rural community of Burnham in the northeastern edge of the Navajo Nation, protesting the tribal government's proposal to build a large-scale, coal-fired power plant and expand the nearby Navajo Coal Mine required to feed it. The movement assembled around a core group of four or five elderly women, holders of permits to the grazing lands slated for new coal development. These "grandma-ladies," as they were colloquially and affectionately known, became famous among anti-coal activists and government officials alike for their highly vocal, public denouncements of the proposed project. Among them, Alice Gilmore figured centrally and very publicly, as she was the most senior in age and the holder of the grazing permit for the land in question.

Gilmore's connection to this badlands landscape is anchored through memory, long-term land tenure, and knowledge of food and water sources that are less visible to outsiders. In a discursive intervention to make the mine expansion and power plant seem more plausible, the Houston-based developer named the project "Desert Rock." However, local place-names for this region include: Ram Springs, Little Water, Crystal Springs, Owl's Water, and *Tiis Tsoh Sikaad* (or, "spreading of cottonwood tree"), recognizing a vibrant ecology, known through the presence of water and nonhuman forms of life. Local residents like Gilmore still give directions in reference to washes rather than road numbers. And despite the environmental impacts of the existing Navajo Mine, the Gilmore family continues to collect and use wild vegetables from their grazing land, such as parsley, rhubarb, and onions.

Gilmore describes this landscape's significance historically, as the ground for life to reemerge, following the trauma of forced removal and federal incarceration that Diné people experienced in the 1860s. At the proposed site for the power plant, just one hundred yards or so south of the Navajo Coal Mine, sit remnants of two stone houses: one was built in 1868 by Gilmore's father's mother, upon her return home from the war camp at Bosque Redondo that same year. Gilmore's father built the second house, where he and Gilmore's mother raised their children and established their sheep camp in the badlands desert. Her daughter translates her mother's story this way:

It was her daddy's land. Her father's mom gave birth right there. They came back from Bosque Redondo, from the war, and were given two sheep at Fort Defiance. They gave birth to a little girl right there. That became her father's mother. She gave birth to a boy there, named David, and he became her dad. Me, my mom, David, and David's mother were all born there. Four generations since Bosque Redondo.[10]

Today, Gilmore keeps about eighty sheep corralled in this area, although she and her husband now live on a small farm thirty miles to the north, just down the road from the Four Corners Power Plant, another controversial giant of the 1960s Navajo coal boom, and the industrial agriculture fields of the Navajo Agricultural Products Industry. Gilmore visits her flock almost daily, especially during lambing season. "They're my happiness," she explains. "They know me."[11] She continues to make the arduous journey even though she is now over eighty-five years old, in a wheelchair, and must rely upon a family member to cover the precious cost of gasoline to drive her forty-five minutes to her grazing land.

At her home one recent spring day, after seven years of knowing the family and several interviews with Ms. Gilmore on her anti-coal activism, I was surprised to see a metal pail containing rough-hewn coal chunks on the ground outside her front door. That same afternoon, we took a detour on our way to her sheep camp, and I was speechless when she and her adult daughter showed me the source of their household coal: the Gilmore's personal coal mine. The women wanted to check on Mr. Gilmore, who had been working out at the mine all day, by himself, chiseling coal from an open seam, one sledgehammer swing at a time. We found his pickup truck backed into the sixty- or seventy-foot-wide ravine, cut about eight feet deep. Glittering outcrops of coal encircled him. Mr. Gilmore tossed one hunk at a time into the bed of the truck. Ms. Gilmore's daughter, Bonnie, explained that her mother and father depend upon coal as their sole source of heat at home, and they used to use it for cooking before they got electricity at the farm. They also collect extra coal to give away to extended family members. She expressed deep concern that her relatives now expect "a free supply of energy, never offering to help" her father haul it to town, or to pay him for his gasoline or labor. She tells me she finds this to be "an unsustainable situation . . . he is getting old, it takes all day to get a truck load, no one pays him, and he can't keep working like this much longer."[12]

On this pivotal afternoon, I began to see the Gilmore's coal activism in far more complicated terms than the emphasis of media, documentary, and environmentalist discourses had ever allowed. Bonnie reminded me that she herself had worked as heavy equipment and coal dragline operator at both the Navajo Mine and the San Juan Mine and, over the years, her mother pressured BHP for additional jobs for her other children. Ripping a sheet of paper from my notebook, she drew a map showing the proximity of all of these projects in the Gilmore's permit land: she described, sketched, and showed me how medicinal herbs, coal, sheep, draglines, wild onions, water towers, corrals and fences, and weathered potsherds tensely coexist in a landscape named for water and trees—though the landscape appears devoid of them now. I learned that several years ago, BHP Billiton covered up her family coal mine as part of the Mine's planned territorial expansion for the new coal plant, reigniting the family's activism. This time, they challenged the company's land lease boundary. Ms. Gilmore met with the local land committee and then traveled to the tribal government offices in Window Rock to reestablish her permit to the land and reopen her family coal mine, a project, she explained, that was part of her cultural heritage to this landscape.

This was not the family's first boutique coal operation. Many years before, Ms. Gilmore's father had harvested coal from a hole dug out in the side of a steep hill, just east of their old stone house. This kind of micro-extraction was not unlike many other Diné small-scale coal producers from the 1920s through the 1940s (O'Neill 2005: 31). The arrival of coal-burning stoves (replacing wood-burning stoves), coupled with the economic devastation of livestock reduction in the 1930s, fueled an indigenous coal-mining industry across the reservation, and it was most active in the Eastern Agency, south of Fruitland and along the Chaco Canyon Wash—the very site of the Gilmore's grazing land, over which she has primary dominion, as the eldest woman in the extended family (ibid.: 32). Ms. Gilmore abandoned her father's steep hillside mine at some point in the 1950s because she and her first husband considered it unsafe. The family has been harvesting from the present family coal mine ever since. Today, there are few other active personal coal mines in the area: the Gilmore family's mine is now rare as a livelihood practice, in a much larger, global economy of coal production across the reservation.

Romanticism as a Form of Settler Racism: Reconsidering the Subject of Resistance

It is striking to see these women on the front lines of two seemingly incompatible coal struggles: protesting the expansion of the Navajo Mine and the construction of the Desert Rock power plant, *while at the same time* demanding continued access to their family's personal coal mine for household use and gifting to their extended family. Much of the press, scholarship, and even much of the activist discourse surrounding coal debates on the Navajo Nation have vilified coal itself as the core problem, a material incarnation of exploitation and contamination. These discourses also advance women activists (like the Gilmores, and many others) as embodiments of "Mother Earth," whether through their traditional knowledge of the land or their work in environmental justice struggles. For decades, women have figured centrally in the struggle against big coal in the Navajo Nation. Diné matrilineal descent has, customarily, placed women in powerful positions as land managers. Spanning generations, elders and youth alike have challenged companies like BHP Billiton and Peabody Coal for their impacts on Diné water sources, especially aquifers. Leaders point out the ecological impacts of large-scale extractive industry, as well as impacts on livelihoods, labor, and culture, in a landscape in which coal is understood to be the liver of the earth and, as such, should remain intact (Begaye 2005).

Despite their role as powerful grassroots leaders, these women are rarely considered in their full and complex humanity: in Gerald Vizenor's terms, these are the real people, of lived experience, or what he calls the "postindians" that contradict the hyperreal image of Native peoples manufactured by Hollywood films, American literature, and other media tropes of indigeneity (Vizenor and Lee 1999). Returning to gender, contradictions within racialized and gendered notions of belonging are manifold in Diné society, where authentic "womanhood" within a matrilineal descent system is often signaled by voice and skilled practice (Jacobsen-Bia 2014) as much as by blood quantum or heteronormativity (Denetdale 2008). In similar ways, "Mother Earth" discourses produced and reproduced in environmental activism restrict these more nuanced views of gender and praxis alike. In doing so, they inadvertently elide possibilities for a deeper, more robust kind of place-based politics, where economic practices like the Gilmores' small-scale coal operation suggest a political and historical difference that cannot be contained by the convenient, romanticized, and gendered tropes of environmentalism.

Coal's well-documented devastating impacts on local well-being and global climate change are established at this point: I do not intend to contest those here. What I propose, however, is that the Gilmores' complex entanglements with coal consumption suggest that what really interests this family, and perhaps others in their situation, is not coal at all. When asked, Ms. Gilmore, Bonnie, and others acknowledge no contradiction in their work to fight big coal while harvesting from their own mine. In fact, there is a remarkable coherence in descriptions of their interactions with the reservation's coal landscape. Rather, their central concern is the destruction of the land and food resources on which their sheep depend, brought on by the large-scale dragline operations of the Navajo Mine. The elderly Ms. Gilmore is concerned over changes in the land: "The land my sheep used to graze is all torn up. It's been dug up and turned up and turned into little mountains [by the mine's dragline] all over the place. Where the sheep used to graze is now destroyed. So we grow a lot of alfalfa [at the farm] to feed our sheep, because there's just nothing for them to eat out there."[13]

I want to suggest that the supposed ethical dissonance in these coal struggles does not lie in the Gilmores' lived experience of this landscape, but rather, in the ongoing processes of settler colonialism and its racializing discourses, with its romantic and entangled conceptions of nature and of indigeneity. Coal—despite its significant negative environmental effects well recorded locally and globally—is positioned as an integral part of local ecological and economic practice on the reservation. In this case, her interest is ensuring the economic and cultural benefits of keeping sheep *and* keeping small-scale coal. If we read this scenario beyond the presumed politics of coal and beyond the presumed tropes of Native identity, we can then see Alice Gilmore as a complexly situated person, dwelling in place. She was involved in a historical and political struggle for recognition both within her own community and as part of a much broader, global struggle for recognition of the political difference of American Indian and indigenous peoples.

Replacing the Gilmore contradiction with "'entanglement' to highlight these moments of complexity" (Dennison 2014: 7) poses a critical challenge to environmental narratives and their rhetorical strategies for defending against the layers of racial governmentality in which the Navajo Nation is implicated. Within these entangled discursive worlds, deeply racialized understandings of indigeneity often take hold, perhaps unwittingly or uncritically, by those who deploy such tropes—even as they work to defray environmental and social harm. Rhetorical strategies of many environmentalists often cohere as narratives that bear the mark of colonial settler logics, inasmuch as they make certain kinds of conceptual *excisions* (such as the inherent political and historical difference of Native peoples) followed by perverse *inclusions*, such as the "natural" sustainability held to be embodied by Native peoples. These dominant narratives are echoes of what Patrick Wolfe describes as the historic and ongoing process of settler colonialism: the historic movement that connects the trans-Atlantic trafficking of enslaved Africans with the conquest of the New World, both land-based, economic, and territorial projects (Wolfe 2006). Settler colonialism's "logic of elimination," following Wolfe, is the simultaneous destruction of difference and then reincorporation of difference in other, less fantastic—and more persuasive—registers of violence. In this case, certain rhetorical strategies and modes of practice in otherwise well-intentioned environmental politics serve the ongoing process of conquest by working to sever Diné rights to Diné land (such as mining coal, however problematic that might be) while also making moral claims about protecting indigenous rural land rights. The complexities of life and place-based politics are erased when families like the Gilmores are heralded only as resisters to big coal power, and not also for their (seemingly contradictory) struggle to maintain a boutique coal mine as an economic act of subsistence and gifting as well as a meaningful act of land tenure, connecting them to earlier generations. Throughout the 2008–2009 apex of the struggle over the 1,500-megawatt Desert Rock coal plant, which would have been built just down the highway from the Gilmores' farm, environmental NGOs and the Navajo Nation courted the family (and other families in similar positions) as spokespersons for their cause: for environmentalists, it was to stop construction on the new coal plant; for tribal officials, it was to secure Ms. Gilmore's signature on a grazing permit that would allow the company access to construct on territory under her land management and oversight. The complicity of tribal entities (such as the Diné Power Authority, charged with securing the permits in tandem with the developer Sithe Global Power) cannot be underestimated in positioning this family (and other residents of the impacted area) as standing in the way of development. Environmental groups positioned the family as beacons of defiance to extraction. No one in the debate, among elected, grassroots, or appointed leaders, spoke of the deeply layered politics of place involved in the Gilmores' historical defense of their backyard coal mine at the same time they resisted massive infrastructural projects like the Desert Rock Energy Project (Powell 2018).

The Gilmores' entangled coal struggles challenge environmental narratives that tend to focus on wilderness preservation and conservation in ways that excise some humans from their landscapes, while deeply entrenching other humans as categorically "of" nature, following the "Great Divide" of nature and culture, us and them, manufactured by moderns (Latour 1991). Much of the rhetoric tends to treat nonhumans (coal, sheep, edible or medicinal plants) as natural resource objects, as moveable parts in a mechanistic ecology, rather than vibrant actors in a complex web of political relationships. These actors—Ms. Gilmore and the coal her husband harvests, the fading botanicals, and the smog blanket of particulate matter from existing coal industry, are not intrinsically resistant, culpable, pure, or dangerous: the reductionist and simplistic moralizing grammars that have constructed them as players in environmental dramas have removed them from their deeper histories of place and practice. The result, among other things, is the alienation of coal from its historical landscape and set of ecological relations (at the same time that extracting and burning it threatens those relations) and the glossing of the human dimensions of development, when matters of scale, subsistence, and extended kinship networks come into play. As in the Gilmores' struggle, small-scale coal for local consumption is very much a part of what is to be defended.

Conclusion

Ultimately, struggles like the Gilmores' challenge settler colonial narratives of indigeneity at the same time they challenge dominant notions of "sustainability." We all know these narratives of indigeneity as embedded in broader colonial relations of power, and how they tend toward the confusing, contradictory "double bind" Jessica Cattelino (2010) asserts in her discussion of the political economy of Native sovereignty, gaming, and citizenship. In this analysis, romanticized notions of indigeneity deploy imaginaries of Native people as intrinsically resilient and revolutionary, as heroes of environmental protection for always being resistant to fossil fuel development; *or* they deploy imaginaries of Native people as essentially weak and dependent, duped by capitalism and its shiny promises. Both positions entail a whole set of racialized and gendered claims about indigenous politics and agency, equally flat and equally violent, and equally dismissive of the political and historical difference that American

Indian subject positioning asserts. Neither notion of indigeneity can account for the Gilmores' intensive investment of labor and personal resources in land-based activities that are not strictly governed by the logic of capitalism *or* environmentalism: in these activities, neither sheep nor coal is a commodity. Ms. Gilmore's anti–power plant activism, as well as her family's solitary coal collection, challenge these narratives, especially their troping of indigeneity as global capitalism's "other."

A final note on sustainability: as Escobar (2006), di Chiro (2008), and certain social movements have argued, the dominant emphasis on technological and economic variables has yet to fully include the complicated role of social and cultural conditions in achieving real and lasting sustainability. Likewise, the trifecta in sustainability studies known as the "three E's"—environment, economics, and equity—does not usually engage the question of difference and culture in the situated, radical terms that it might. Moreover, the "three E's" of sustainability not only falls short in its critical analysis of cultural conditions, it has no rubric for considering the political difference embodied by Nations such as the Diné, and other American Indians, where any sustainability project—if it has any hope of success—absolutely must address the question of sovereignty and settler colonialism. There is no sustainable development in Indian Country without a profound, historically particular consideration of tribal sovereignty and self-determination; and the complexity of the political stakes in this situation abound.[14] As such, if ambiguous concepts such as "sustainability," "equity," and "culture" are to serve our common struggle for an enhanced framework for flourishing and understanding the relationship between difference and justice, we must work vigilantly against any simplistic racialization of indigenous peoples and reservation spaces (including their romanticism, viz. Smith) as a move that plays into dominant, modern/colonial tropes of racial difference in the United States, tropes that can work to debase what are fundamentally political, historical claims to land and identity.

Engagements with coal, much like the history of Navajo identity, are complicated and situated processes—processes still under negotiation as Diné autonomy gains momentum in the early twenty-first century, as Lloyd L. Lee and other Diné scholars have discussed (Lee 2014). Given that within settler societies, the issue of dispossession of indigenous lands remains unresolved (Shaw, Herman, and Dobbs 2006), it is time we rethink the reservation as an indigenous political space that is insidiously undermined through racializing discourses that work to displace politico-historical difference with racial difference, translating indigenous difference into a seemingly unresolvable, uniquely American mode of racism.

Acknowledgments

I am indebted to many people whose analysis of the political ecology of Dinétah has shaped my own thinking, over many years. Yet the critical reflections in this chapter are my own, and I am fully responsible for any errors or oversights. This chapter, however, would not exist without the co-labor of my colleague Bonnie Wethington (Diné), artist, map maker, machinist, activist, and translator. I am also grateful to the extended Gilmore family, to Diné Citizens Against Ruining our Environment, and other environmental justice activists whose labor decries the settler colonial tendencies of uncritical mainstream environmentalism. This work was carried out with approval and ethnographic research permits from the Navajo Nation Historic Preservation Department. Funding from the Appalachian State University Research Council made the final stages of this ethnographic fieldwork possible, following earlier research grants from the National Science Foundation and the Wenner-Gren Foundation. Finally, I am grateful to colleagues at Duke University and the University of North Carolina-Chapel Hill who brought me into this important conversation on race and rurality in the global economy, and to Patricia Northover and Andrew Curley for their careful, insightful comments on earlier drafts of this chapter.

Notes

1. More specifically, it was Spanish theologian Francisco de Vitoria in the early sixteenth century, in his consultation to the Spanish Crown, that argued for the "rationality" and "natural freedom" of New World native peoples, establishing the philosophical impossibility of outright slaughter or bondage, and the basis for treaty making between the Spanish, later the English, and the diverse peoples they encountered. Judge Marshall's rulings in the 1830s cases known as the "Marshall Trilogy" effectively overturned Vitoria's more humanistic position (a position that, however lofty, did not prevent centuries of slow genocide) and set the stage for Andrew Jackson's violent policies of Indian Removal.

2. Idle No More is an indigenous-led movement that began in Saskatchewan (Canada) and rapidly spread throughout First Nations, calling for recognition of treaty rights, Native sovereignty, and indigenous rights to water and territory.

3. Beyond this important legal scholarship, it is of course now well established in critical anthropology and geography that while race is biologically meaningless, with human skin

pigmentation being shaped by evolutionary and solar factors (see Nina Jablonski 2015), it remains socially salient, inextricably linked with place, reconstituted in geographically and culturally particular practices of everyday life.

4. Paul Chaat Smith argues that 1890 was the year that invented "the Indian," a cultural move many decades in the making, but secured by the military defeat marked by the massacre of Sioux people by US Cavalry at Wounded Knee, South Dakota.

5. For example, a short excerpt from a 2010 census brief illustrates this emphasis on *racial* identification: "According to the 2010 Census, 5.2 million people in the United States identified as American Indian and Alaska Native, either alone or in combination with one or more other races. Out of this total, 2.9 million people identified as American Indian and Alaska Native alone. Almost half of the American Indian and Alaska Native population, or 2.3 million people, reported being American Indian and Alaska Native in combination with one or more other races" (accessed at www.census.gov).

6. This motif of "suffering for territory," is developed deeply by Donald S. Moore in his studies of Zimbabwe. Moore's analysis of what he terms the "ethnic spatial fix" is particularly relevant to my work, as it also follows Foucault in apprehending how colonial power "disciplines and fixes," and develops regimes of rule over subjugated bodies in order to "anchor ethnicity in a bounded locality" for the benefit of colonial rule (2005: 154).

7. Following a longer history of extractive interests, federal incursion into parts of Shoshone territory is anchored in a pursuit of gold: more than one-half of US gold mining is done on Shoshone lands (primarily Nevada), 10 percent of global gold production. See Julie Ann Fishel (2006) for analysis of the legal significance of the international human rights challenge, led by the Western Shoshone Defense Project.

8. To Valerie J. Kuletz, whose ethnographic work was situated in Shoshone territory and federal weapons test sites, deterritoriality is about abandonment: a retreat of oversight that carries a dark underside of state investment in these "wasteland" spaces, as sites of dangerous technological research and design, testing and experimentation, and toxic waste storage.

9. This is a historical discussion of elite New Yorkers'—and early feminist anthropologists'—desires to encounter otherness and thus become transformed, in Santa Fe.

10. Interview with Bonnie Wethington, Upper Fruitland, NM, April 8, 2014.

11. Interview with Alice Gilmore, Upper Fruitland, NM, April 8, 2014.

12. Interview with Bonnie Wethington, Upper Fruitland, NM, April 8, 2014.

13. Interview with Alice Gilmore, Upper Fruitland, NM, April 8, 2014.

14. Elsewhere, I explore through more detailed ethnography the valences of these political stakes in energy development and how they are entangled with ethical projects related to expertise, landscapes, and cultural production. See Powell 2015, 2017a, and 2017b.

References

Allen, Kim, Vinci Daro, and Dorothy Holland. 2007. "Becoming an Environmental Justice Activist." In *Environmental Justice and Environmentalism: The Social Justice Challenge to the Environmental Movement*, edited by Ronald Sandler and Phaedra C. Pezzullo. Cambridge, MA: MIT Press.

Baksh, Rawwida, and Wendy Harcourt, eds. 2015. *Handbook of Transnational Feminist Movements*. Oxford: Oxford University Press.

Begaye, Enei. 2005. "The Black Mesa Controversy." *Cultural Survival Quarterly* 29 (4): https://www.culturalsurvival.org/publications/cultural-survival-quarterly/black-mesa-controversy.

Belin, Esther. 1999. *From the Belly of My Beauty*. Tucson: University of Arizona Press.

Bessire, Lucas. 2004. *Behold the Black Caiman: A Chronicle of Ayoreo Life*. Chicago: University of Chicago Press.

Biolsi, Thomas. 2005. "Imagined Geographies: Sovereignty, Indigenous Space, and American Indian Struggle." *American Ethnologist* 32: 239–259.

Cattelino, Jessica. 2010. "The Double-Bind of American Indian Need-Based Sovereignty." *Cultural Anthropology* 25 (2): 235–262.

Clifford, James. 2007. "Varieties of Indigenous Experience: Diasporas, Homelands, Sovereignties." In *Indigenous Experience Today*, edited by Marisol de la Cadena and Orin Starn, 197–224. New York: Bloomsbury.

Curley, Andrew. 2014. "The Origin of Legibility: Rethinking Colonialism and Resistance Among the Navajo People, 1868–1937." In *Diné Perspectives: Revitalizing and Reclaiming Navajo Thought*, edited by Lloyd L. Lee, 129–150. Tucson: University of Arizona Press.

De la Cadena, Marisol, and Orin Starn, eds. 2007. *Indigenous Experience Today*. New York: Bloomsbury.

Denetdale, Jennifer Nez. 2008. "Carving Navajo National Boundaries: Patriotism, Tradition, and the Diné Marriage Act of 2005." *American Quarterly* (60) 2: 289–294.

Dennison, Jean. 2012. *Colonial Entanglement*. Chapel Hill: University of North Carolina Press.

———. 2014. "The Logic of Recognition: Debating Osage Nation Citizenship in the Twenty-First Century." *American Indian Quarterly* 38 (1): 1–35.

Di Chiro, Giovanna. 2008. "Living Environmentalisms: Coalition Politics, Social Reproduction, and Environmental Justice." *Environmental Politics* 17 (2): 276–298.

Edelman, Marc, and Angelique Haugerud, eds. 2005. *The Anthropology of Development and Globalization: From Classical Political Economy to Contemporary Neoliberalism*. Malden, MA: Blackwell.

Escobar, Arturo. 2008. *Territories of Difference: Place, Movements, Life, Redes*. Durham, NC: Duke University Press.

———. 2006. "Difference and Conflict in the Struggle Over Natural Resources: Outline of a Political Ecology Framework." *Development* 49 (3): 6–13.

———. 1995. *Encountering Development: The Making and Unmaking of the Third World*. Princeton, NJ: Princeton University Press.

Foucault, Michel. 1978. *The History of Sexuality, Volume I*. New York: Random House.

———. 2003. *Society Must Be Defended: Lectures at the College de France, 1975–1976*. New York: Picador.

Goeman, Mishuana R. 2009. "Notes toward a Native Feminism's Spatial Practice." *Wicazo Sa Review* 24 (2): 169–187.

Gooding, S. S. 1994. "Place, Race, and Names—Layered Identities in United States v Oregon, Confederated-Tribes-of-the-Coleville-Reservation, Plaintiff-Intervenor." *Law and Society Review* 28 (5): 1181–1229.

Inwood, J. F., and R.A. Yarbrough. 2010. "Racialized Places, Racialized Bodies: The Impact of Racialization on Individuals and Place Identities." *GeoJournal* 75 (3): 299–301.

Jacobsen-Bia, Kristina. 2014. "Radmilla's Voice: Music Genre, Blood Quantum, and Belonging on the Navajo Nation." *Cultural Anthropology* 29 (2): 285–410.

Kosek, Jake. 2007. *Understories: The Political Life of Forests in Northern New Mexico*. Durham, NC: Duke University Press.

Kuletz, Valerie. 1998. *The Tainted Desert: Environmental and Social Ruin in the American West*. New York: Routledge.

Latour, Bruno. 1993. *We Have Never Been Modern*. Cambridge, MA: Harvard University Press.

Lavender, Catherine J. 2006. *Scientists and Storytellers: Feminist Anthropologists and the Construction of the American Southwest*. Albuquerque: University of New Mexico Press.

Lee, Lloyd L., ed. 2014. *Diné Perspectives: Revitalizing and Reclaiming Navajo Thought*. Tucson: University of Arizona Press.

Manuel, George. 1974. *The Fourth World: An Indian Reality*. Don Mills, ON: Collier-Macmillan Canada.

Moore, Donald. 2005. *Suffering for Territory: Race, Place, and Power in Zimbabwe*. Durham, NC: Duke University Press.

Moreton-Robinson, Aileen. 2015. *The White Possessive: Property, Power, and Indigenous Sovereignty*. Minneapolis: University of Minnesota Press.

Needham, Andrew. 2014. *Power Lines: Phoenix and the Making of the Modern Southwest*. Princeton, NJ: Princeton University Press.

Noble, Brian. 2015. "Tripped Up by Coloniality: Anthropologists as Instruments or Agents in Indigenous-Settler Political Relations?" *Anthropologica* 57: 427–443.

O'Neill, Colleen. 2005. *Working the Navajo Way*. Lawrence: University Press of Kansas.

Pigg, Stacy Leigh. 1992. "Inventing Social Categories through Place: Social Representations and Development in Nepal." *Comparative Studies in Society and History* 34 (3): 491–513.

Powell, Dana E. 2015. "The Rainbow is Our Sovereignty: Rethinking the Politics of Energy on the Navajo Nation." *Journal of Political Ecology* 22: 53–78.

———. 2017. "Toward Transition? Challenging Extractivism and the Politics of the Inevitable on the Navajo Nation." In *ExtrACTION: Impacts, Engagements, and Alternative Futures*, edited by Kirk Jalbert, Anna Willow, David Casagrande, and Stephanie Paladino. New York: Routledge.

———. 2018. *Landscapes of Power: Politics of Energy in the Navajo Nation*. Durham, NC: Duke University Press.

Powell, Dana E., and Dailan J. Long. 2010. "Landscapes of Power: Renewable Energy Activism in Diné Bikéyah." In *Indians & Energy: Exploitation and Opportunity in the American Southwest*, edited by S. Smith and B. Frehner. Santa Fe, NM: School of Advanced Research Press.

Powell, Dana E., and Andrew Curley. 2009. "K'e, Hozhó, and Non-Governmental Politics on the Navajo Nation: Ontologies of Difference Manifest in Environmental Activism." *World Anthropologies Network E-Journal* 4. Special issue, guest edited by M. de la Cadena and M. Blaser.

Shaw, Wendy S., R. D. K. Herman, and G. Rebecca Dobbs. 2006. "Encountering Indigeneity: Reimagining and Colonizing Geography." *Geografiska Annaler: Series B, Human Geography* 88: 267–276.

Simpson, Audra. 2014. *Mohawk Interruptus: Life Across the Borders of the Settler States*. Durham, NC: Duke University Press.

Smith, Paul Chaat. *2009. Everything You Know About Indians Is Wrong*. Minneapolis: University of Minnesota Press.

Rocheleau, Dianne, Barbara Thomas-Slayter, and Esther Wangari, eds. 1996. *Feminist Political Ecology*. New York: Routledge.

Tuck, Eve, and K. Wayne Yang. 2012. "Decolonization Is Not a Metaphor." *Decolonization: Indigeneity, Education & Society* 1 (1): 1–40.

Vizenor, Gerald, and A. Robert Lee. 1999. *Postindian Conversations*. Lincoln: University of Nebraska Press.

West, Paige. 2006. Conservation Is Our Government Now: The Politics of Ecology in Papua New Guinea. Durham, NC: Duke University Press.

Wilmsen, Carl. 2007. "Maintaining the Environmental-Racial Order in Northern New Mexico." *Environment and Planning D: Society and Space* 25 (2): 236–257.

Wolfe, Patrick. 2006. "Settler Colonialism and the Elimination of the Native." *Journal of Genocide Research* 8 (4): 387–409.

8

Rediscovering Afro-American Ruralities

The Mississippi Delta and Loíza (Puerto Rico) as Cultural Hot Spots

Juan Giusti-Cordero

In this chapter, I explore critical periods of plantation expansion in the Mississippi Delta and Loíza, Puerto Rico, in the nineteenth century in order to better understand how race, labor, and culture shape, and are shaped by, an evolving rurality. I address these themes by contrasting the Mississippi Delta and Loíza along several dimensions, from ecological transformations and reorganization of production to the creation of new cultural forms.[1] In my analysis, I draw on debates on cultural identity in the African diaspora (Lovejoy 2009; Hall 2005; Gomez 1995; Mann 2001);[2] on creolization, particularly in the Caribbean context (Mintz and Price 1992; Trouillot 1998; Price 2001; Palmié 2006; Khan 2001, 2007); and on race-labor-ecology interactions (Carney 2009; Morris 2012; Giusti 2015).

The Mississippi (or Yazoo-Mississippi) Delta (see map 8.1) is known as the birthplace of early blues music and is often called (or misrepresented as) "the most Southern place on Earth" (Cobb 1991; see Woods 2000; Lomax 1993; Palmer 1981; Ferris 1970) and "Mississippi's Mississippi" (Willis 2000: 4, 185; Helferich 2007).[3] The municipality of Loíza, and particularly its barrio Medianía (see map 8.2), is known for its Fiestas de Santiago Apóstol, an icon of Afro–Puerto Rican culture; Loíza calls itself *La Capital de la Tradición* (Alegría 1954; Hernández Hiraldo 2006; González 2004; Calderón 2002).[4] The importance of the Delta blues in African American culture is comparable to the Santiago celebrations in Loíza. Envisaging the Delta and Loíza as complex, layered ruralities allows a deeper understanding of

Map 8.1. The Mississippi Delta. US Geological Survey. United States (Washington, DC: US Government Printing Office, 1972). In common usage, "the Delta" principally comprises the Mississippi River floodplain in northwest Mississippi, southeast Arkansas, and the southwest corner of Tennessee (including Memphis).

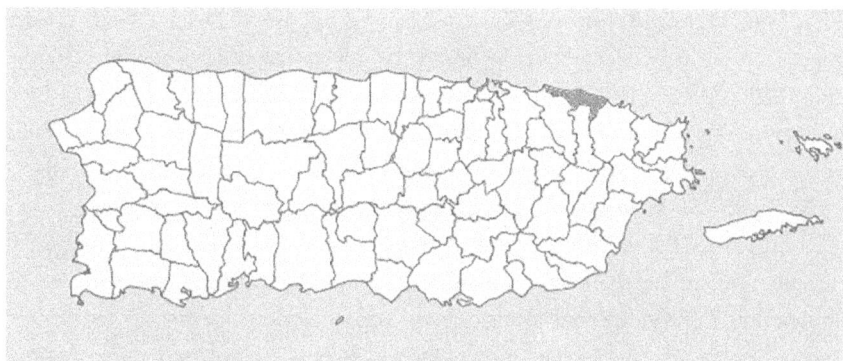

Map 8.2. Puerto Rico, showing the Municipality of Loíza. Wikimedia Commons. Nord-NordWest, CC BY-SA 3.0.

how these sites became "an amalgam of landscape, tradition, and place" (Hinrichs 1996: 259) in their wider national contexts as heartlands of, respectively, African American and Afro–Puerto Rican culture and history.

We need to go back in history to understand how these images were formed and reshaped. In this chapter, my focus is on the origins of the blues in the Mississippi Delta, and of Loíza's Santiago tradition. I attempt to connect the development of the blues form and of the Santiago festivities, as creolization processes, to their socio-environmental context. My threshold approach to the matter is that in the nineteenth century, in both the Mississippi Delta and Loíza, black folk, slave and free, interacted with rapidly changing wetland ecologies under social and political conditions that were themselves in rapid transformation, toward more intensive plantation regimes. I argue that the Santiago tradition in Loíza and the blues tradition in the Delta originated, in different time frames, immediately after a period of expanded freedom in these zones when there was easy access to land and local ecologies, and just as harsher plantation regimes took shape.

Both in the Delta and Loíza, slavery existed previously but had not dominated the region. Loíza's period of expanded freedom began in the late 1790s, when the town's black militias helped defeat the British invasion (1797) and slave production—locally less important than sugar—entered a period of disarray, due in part to the Haitian Revolution and related warfare in the eastern Caribbean. Loíza's expanded freedom ran until the 1820s, when slave plantations grew once again and ate away at land and forests used by the area's smallholders. In the Delta, the few slave plantations that penetrated its forested wetlands were upended by the

Civil War. During Reconstruction, the sparsely populated Delta offered greater opportunities than elsewhere in the South. However, Reconstruction ended by the mid-1870s, followed by a harsh, "reconstructed" plantation regime. In Loíza and the Delta, the key period for cultural creation—1830s–1840s in Loíza, 1880s–1890s in the Delta—followed the years of expanded freedom.

As Clyde Woods argued regarding blues epistemologies (2007), and Juan Flores regarding Afro–Puerto Rican musical tradition (2000), indigenous intellectual currents presented a challenge to plantation domination in ways that we need to understand. These indigenous forms of knowledge underlie contemporary challenges to neoliberal, market-based flattening of identities and social space, themselves often linked to "neoplantationist" forms of racial/class/gender dominance and demonization. It is no accident, for instance, that throughout the twentieth century Mississippi was the epicenter of racial and class schism in the United States (Loewen and Sallis 1974, quoted in Wood: 56), or that Loíza remains a touchstone of racial/cultural resistance in Puerto Rico (Calderón 2003; Ungerleider 2000; Giusti 1994). Exploring Loíza and the Delta as cultural "hot spots" offers a better understanding of the ways in which such spaces may come about and the forms of knowledge and social action that they express (Abrahams 2001).

These issues are not, of course, bounded by specifics of time and place, not even by so-called rural contexts generally. There are other examples of "freedom periods" and radical social-spatial transformations that are associated with new cultural forms. Close to our time, and in an urban milieu, hip-hop arose beginning in the mid-1970s in the vortex of urban decay and the "brownfielding" of major US cities that brought to a nightmarish end the momentous advances of the civil rights era. A "freedom generation" that was born in the climate of expanded freedom of the 1960s collided head-on with the neoliberalism of the following decade. Minority youth now had to figure out social reality amidst the rubble of urban disinvestment, recession, and repression. The South Bronx became the hot spot for hip-hop, as it was there that African American and Puerto Rican musical traditions intersected; so did Jamaican and other Caribbean traditions (Woods 2007; Flores 2000). These are the kinds of transitions and transformations that we need to see not just happening in our own epoch, but in major iterations in the past.

In this inquiry, the large differences in scale between Loíza and the Delta may actually be advantageous. The comparison allows us to view processes in Loíza in a magnified way, as it were, in the Delta. The opposite path from the Delta to Loíza shows up "a sharply defined historical miniature," a phrase that James

Cobb used to illustrate the value of studying the Delta as a microcosm of the US South (1992: ii). I might also add that my "macro" analysis of the Delta may fall short on ground-level evidence, while the "historical miniature," Loíza, needs more "macro" context. Hopefully, in the pages that follow, the respective contexts will mesh to some degree and make sense as an ensemble.[5]

Hot Spots and Creolization

In a comparison between the historical development of Afro-American music and dance in the US South and the Caribbean, Roger D. Abrahams called attention to "cultural hotspots" where "culture is produced locally," trending new styles that are later "caught up in the development of a public sphere, and international popular culture" (Abrahams 2001: 99). Abrahams considered that students of Afro-America have overstated the significance of place, out of an adherence to "the pan-European Romantic nationalist attitude toward territory and land-based traditions" and to a belief in "local genius emerging from the land, the language, and the grounded lore of a race." For Abrahams, the heart of the matter is, rather, "the danced and sung occasions in which the idea of community and spirit arise in performance, celebration, and worship. . . . [It is] not that these black expressive forms are not associated with specific places." In Afro-America, "the festive and religious music and dance provides a greater organizing force than territory or language" (Abrahams 2001: 97–98, 100).

In a register not unlike Abrahams's, studies of creolization have emphasized cultural creation as largely indifferent to specific places. As historical process and analytical approach, creolization refers to cultural interaction and change shaping new cultural forms that embody resistance and transformation, (re)encounters and negotiations with modernity (Trouillot 2002). Studies of creolization thus tend to foreground processes where "adaptation, cross-cultural contact, multiplicity, and the existence, simultaneously, of similar and dissimilar types" (Khan 2001: 278), "where two or more populations, of markedly different origin, historical trajectory, and even phenotypes come into unequal contact." (Balutansky and Sourieau 1998). "Creolization" perspectives have been disputed by other students of Afro-American culture, who lean toward emphasizing African origins and identity (Gomez 1998; Lovejoy 2011; Hall 2005). Kristin Mann's call for historical specificity and a sense of processes that span the Atlantic (2001) has rarely been put into practice. More importantly, despite important and provocative steps toward examining the material and variable conditions of creolization (whether or not the term itself is used), its specific sociohistorical *contexts* (Mintz 2010; Carney 2009; Trouillot 1998; Khan 2014), the discussion has not moved much beyond methodological statements.

Michel-Rolph Trouillot, for one, was on the right track regarding creolization: "The knowledge of creolization can benefit from a more ethnographic approach that takes into account the concrete contexts within which cultures developed in the Americas" (Trouillot 1998: 8); to which he added: "My main point is that we need to rehistoricize creolization" (1998: 27). Trouillot's approach suggests a reconsideration of place, and indeed of cultural hot spots, that dispenses with notions of "local genius" and avoids the overemphases on territorial identity that Abrahams considered misleading.

In Trouillot's call for a "rehistoricized" approach to creolization, context was crucial.[6] His ethnographic view analysis of creolization contexts underscored (1) labor regimes, (2) the frequency with which their denizens had outside contacts, and (3) the extent to which they were subjects of history, that is, in terms of their cultural ideals and their attentiveness to the facts of power on the ground (1998: 16). Hence, Trouillot translated "context" as a broader and thicker "place" inseparable from local social interactions and their "ensemble of other meanings." A fourth aspect of creolization contexts is implicit: ecological transformations, which of course exist in close connection to labor regimes. An important reference is the work of Alfred Crosby, whose "enduring legacy" (in Judith Carney's words) "was to place culture and environment in a new relationship through the dramatic transformations that occurred in Atlantic world ecosystems" (2009: 5). As historical process, creolization thus becomes a "place-making" process (Crichlow and Northover 2009: 21) that may be partly deliberate or, indeed, a strategy (Mintz 1995).

The Delta and Loíza

On first impression, the Mississippi Delta and Loíza are as different as places can be. For one, there are huge contrasts in scale. The Yazoo-Mississippi Delta (7,000 miles)^2 is many times larger than the Loíza municipality (66 miles)^2 and than the even smaller semi-urban coastal fringe of Loíza Pueblo and Medianía.[7] The periods that are most relevant for comparison are chronologically distinct: the early nineteenth century in the case of Loíza, the later part of that century in the case of the Mississippi Delta. The Delta's historical swamp wilderness and subsequent industrial-scale cotton production also contrasts with Loíza's mix of mangrove forests and sugarcane fields. Race and class in the Delta, where Jim Crow and sharecropping prevailed in the late nineteenth century, differed significantly from Loíza's racially more diverse slave and free labor force in the early decades of that century.

Yet the Delta and Loíza also shared major affinities. The two zones were not new to plantation production, but during the periods under study both underwent processes of significant plantation expansion and transformation. The wetland and forest ecologies of both zones, once drained, offered rich soils that were key to the expansion of their plantation regimes. Partly as a result of these processes, both the Delta and Loíza had black demographic concentrations that were exceptionally high in their respective national contexts.

And crucially in terms of rethinking "cultural hot spots," the importance of the Delta blues in African American culture is comparable to Loíza's Santiago celebrations.

Stated succinctly, my analysis takes up the following points of comparison and contrast between Loíza and the Delta:

1. A wetland, forested river-floodplain ecology of uniquely fertile soils

2. Plantation expansion and sharp transformations in labor regimes after a period of expanded freedom

3. Interaction with a shrinking non-plantation periphery

4. Black demographic concentration and relative "isolation"

5. Production/consolidation of new cultural forms

1. A Wetland, Forested River-Floodplain Ecology of Uniquely Fertile Soils

A major similarity between the Delta and Loíza is rather liquid—their amphibious original ecology. Like the Delta, Loíza had a pre-plantation ecology of forest and wetlands. The term "wilderness," while historically/ecologically inaccurate as a characterization of the nineteenth-century Delta (Saikku 2005), does capture the density of forest growth in that region especially in post-indigenous times. Technically, the Delta is not a delta but a basin created by annual river flooding over four millennia. These annual floods, which have been periodically calamitous, are a recurrent "natural disaster" reminiscent of the Caribbean's annual encounters with hurricanes. Prior to large-scale levee construction ("reclamation"), floods were as endemic to the Delta as hurricanes to the Caribbean (or, indeed, river flooding to Loíza), and far more regular. Recurrent flooding played a major role in the forest ecology of the region (Barry 1996: 96–98). "Until after the Civil War, most of the Delta was a subtropical jungle of forests" (Lomax 1993: 68–69) with an immense variety of trees and where "everyone got around on canoes and skiffs" (Brandfon 1967: 13, 29, 30). "The delta had been a frontier until very recently"; there were only "a few ruined plantations perched precariously on bluffs and Indian mounds." Less than one-tenth of the Delta region was cultivated before 1880. Two decades later, only a third of the Delta was under cultivation. Though still a wilderness of sorts, a bright future was predicted for the region as the "garden spot" of the South and indeed of the nation (Lomax 1993: 65, 68–69).

Beneath forest and water, the Delta had uniquely fertile soils. The wetter the terrain, the flatter, blacker, and more fertile the soil. The Delta was as famous for its thick, almost impenetrable forests as it was for the "unsurpassed fertility" of its soils once cleared and drained (Brandfon 1966: 28). Massive organic layers deposited over millennia by the world's mightiest river formed a layer of black alluvial soils fifteen to twenty meters deep.[8] No commercial fertilizer was used in Delta (Brandfon 1966: 132). The Delta was often compared with Egypt's Nile valley, whose unique fertility was also the result of annual floods. The rich black soils of the Delta, as of Loíza, were an ironic counterpoint to its poor black denizens.

Loíza has a similarly complex and prolific ecology. It lies on both sides of the mouth of the Río Grande de Loíza, Puerto Rico's largest river. Loíza is an estuarine delta—hence a "delta" in the more familiar sense. On the east side of the river, cane fields bordered the coastal "coconut fringe." On the west (Piñones) side of the river, in Los Frailes, cultivation was along the riverbank. Before extensive drainage works in the nineteenth and twentieth centuries and dam construction on the Río Grande de Loíza, over two-thirds of Loíza was underwater most of the year. This was partly because of the Río Grande flooding, and partly on account of its mangrove forests/wetlands/lagoon system, the largest in Puerto Rico, which swelled during the rainier months of the year.

Like the Delta, much of the Loíza plain consists of alluvium, mostly silt loams and clays, in contrast with the easily drained, sandy loams of the coconut fringe (Mississippi State University Extension Service). On the banks and lower river basin of the Río Grande de Loíza, alluvium deposits are of variable thickness but—quite remarkably—may be as great as one hundred meters deep (Monroe 1977), indeed far deeper than the Mississippi's alluvium bed. Beyond the immediate riverbed area, Loíza had large areas of seasonally flooded *poyal* soils that were amenable to draining. When well drained, *poyal* soils produced high yields.[9] In the Loíza region *poyal* soils were proportionately more important than anywhere else in Puerto Rico. Sugar plantation production expanded from the more inland portion of Loíza (Canóvanas barrio) to the borders of the coastal east-west fringe of smallholders (barrio Cacique, adjacent to Medianía). An early-twentieth-century soil survey in the wider Canóvanas zone determined that about a third of the soils were "recent alluvium, deep silt and clay loam." The proportion of alluvium is much higher in the long belt of Loíza Pueblo and Medianía on both sides of the Río Grande near its mouth (see map 8.3). Similarly, the prevailing soil type on the Mississippi River's alluvial plain was alluvium ("loam, sand, gravel, and clay"). The attractions of the Delta and Loíza's soils were a magnet for plantation production and for the rapid transformation of social relations. The onset of plantation expansion and the transformation of labor relations are addressed in the next section.

Map 8.3. The Municipality of Loíza, reflecting present-day urbanization. Areas on both sides of the river near its mouth remain unbuilt, in large part because of their tendency to flood. Piñones includes barrios Torrecilla Baja and Torrecilla Alta. Google Earth. Image © 2016 CNES / Astrium. Image © 2016 DigitalGlobe.

2. Plantation Expansion and Sharp Transformations in Labor Regimes after a Period of Expanded Freedom

In both the Delta and in Loíza, a history of black land ownership and occupation—more recent in the Delta, older in Loíza—was overturned by the onset of plantation dominance. In both zones, this process resulted in legally complex and sometimes violent struggles over landownership and titles. Dispossession, displacement, resistance, cultural creation—and race—are at the heart of the historical experience of the Delta and Loíza. Both zones have been linked to plantation slavery and large-scale export agriculture; both entered their most intense transformation in the nineteenth century.

Until the advent of flood control and drainage works, the dense forests and annually flooded wetlands of the Delta and Loíza limited plantation development. Historically, the Delta was as wet, forested, and amphibious as the Mississippi River's many mouths below New Orleans. However, unlike the Mississippi River's mouths—its estuarine delta—the interior delta was more easily subject to large-scale drainage.

The Delta had only a marginal role in the antebellum "Cotton Kingdom." At the time of the Civil War, 4 million acres of Delta wetland forests (the "bottoms") lay undeveloped, and only 10 percent of Delta land was cleared (Woodruff 2003: 10). The particular ecological barriers that forested, wetland zones initially posed to large-scale plantation agriculture also shaped a borderland of runaway slaves, free blacks, and freedmen.

After the Civil War, drainage and plantation development impacted growing portions of Delta territory, but large extensions remained in swamp forest. After the war and during Reconstruction, former slaves made important gains in land occupation and even landownership. "For all its disappointing aspects, the Reconstruction experience nonetheless left Delta blacks better off than they would have been otherwise" (Cobb 1992: 70). Even in the times of the so-called Redemption in the 1870s, when the planter elites literally recovered much of their lost terrain, they still did not have the black population quite under control.

According to Cobb, until the 1880s, "the blacks had been able to capitalize on their labor" and to advance materially, politically, and even socially. The 1880s, however, saw a sharp reduction in their fortunes and set the stage as well for the legal and extralegal measures whereby whites regained control" (Cobb 1992: 94). The federally funded levees and the new railroad connections to Memphis and New

Orleans opened up the Delta fully to the world market, and the onrush of black migrants to the Delta itself weakened the position of its laborers. The Delta was soon at the forefront of white-against-black violence in the South, and was the site of more than a third of the ninety-three lynchings that occurred between 1888 and 1901. The quarter-century that followed would be, in Cobb's words, "a period of unrelenting frustration" (Cobb 1992: 102). Statistics on the acreage of "improved," that is., cleared and drained land in the core Delta counties in the period 1850–1900 reflect the accelerated pace of ecological transformation and plantation/sharecropping development, particularly in the 1870s and 1880s. State-subsidized levee construction went hand in hand with the expansion of the Delta plantation economy. Opportunities for black landownership, along with its political power, were fast receding.

Issaquena, and then (after the Civil War) Bolivar and Coahoma counties—which border the Mississippi River—led the way until the 1870s, followed by Washington and Tunica counties, also on the river. Of these five counties, Washington was the last to experience massive land improvement but led in acreage by 1890. Sunflower, Leflore, Tunica, and Sharkey counties (which are all in the interior of the Delta, except for Tunica) followed, with smaller acreages but a rapid pace of acreage expansion in the 1880s.

In the post-Reconstruction "Alluvial Empire," former slaves, many of them autonomous peasants and woodsmen for some years, became renters, sharecroppers, and itinerant laborers. Labor was, of course, an important part of the context of

Table 8.1. Cultivated acreage (improved land) in the core counties of the Yazoo-Mississippi Delta, 1850–1900 (Saikku 2005: 136)

County	1850	1860	1870	1880	1890	1900
Bolivar	16,973	85,188	39,629	74,072	161,337	185,746
Coahoma	11,478	39,139	28,959	52,490	95,019	121,905
Issaquena	27,631	56,596	35,286	32,928	68,837	55,052
Leflore	—	—	—	40,981	80,182	117,013
Quitman	—	—	—	5,714	15,827	23,363
Sharkey	—	—	—	24,824	44,994	61,115
Sunflower	5,966	—	30,264	14,170	35,587	73,696
Tunica	6,015	29,341	14,141	39,558	58,796	93,438
Washington	59,126	—	70,119	99,887	199,001	197,896
TOTAL	127,189	210,264	218,398	384,624	759,580	929,224

cultural creation in the changing physical and social environments of the Delta. Sharecroppers were by far the majority of the tenants. In season, most of the sharecroppers—besides harvesting their own crop—became itinerant laborers.

> The agonies of the 1870s and the blues are permanently intertwined. The turmoil generated by the overthrow of the Reconstruction governments created homeless families and orphans. The former "slave catchers" now travelled the roads of the South looking for men and boys to kidnap for the levee camps, where a man could be killed for injuring a mule. (Woods 2007: 59)

The black laborers' "unreliability" was often attributed to their "migratory habit." There was also labor on the levees, river docks, and land/forest clearing. Crews on both plantation and non-plantation labor were often organized forcibly. These were the "rivermen," "roustabouts," or "rousters," men who often led a very mobile life. The terms were commonly used for and by male workers and musicians (Lomax 1993: 146–147, 153–155, 233). Delta levee work "was the last American frontier, even more lawless than the Wild West in its palmiest days, partly because there was, so to speak, open season on blacks" (Lomax 1993: 216).

Woods's notion of "freedom generations" usefully highlights an approximate age group of one or two generations (Woods 2007: 55) that lived through the period of expanded freedom and then saw its hopes dashed. The Delta's "freedom generations" were primarily slaves born around 1840 who were freed by Emancipation, and who lived through years of plantation collapse, freer access to land, and the hopes and then the demise of Reconstruction. The blues may have condensed in the Delta in the midst of the span of its "freedom generations . . . led by cultural rebels from a generation that witnessed the overthrow of the Reconstruction" (Woods 2007: 58), and which extended roughly to the first decade of the twentieth century.

Loíza's "freedom generations" were comprised of slaves, free blacks, and *agregados* (customary tenants) and spanned from around 1780 to 1850; the Fiestas de Santiago appear to originate in the 1830s. The creolization contexts that existed in these two zones were not simply scenarios of plantation consolidation, but of plantation regimes *re*consolidated and expanded through the defeat (more overt and violent in the Delta, more muffled in Loíza) of a "freedom generation" that went hand in hand with large-scale spatial/ecological transformation.

In Loíza, sugar production on slave landholdings was relatively unimportant until the early nineteenth century. The cultivation of manioc and other food crops, produced mostly by customary tenant *agregado* labor, was far more important. This, at a time when sugar reigned over the English, French, and Danish islands. Interestingly, the supposedly "blackest" zone in Puerto Rico was the leading producer of the basic Arawak crop and of the cassava bread made from manioc, using an indigenous process (Abbad 1959 [1788]).

*Agregado*s and free laborers interacted with freeholders as well as the last generations of slaves. Beginning in the 1820s, Loíza combined a modest expansion of slave-based sugar production with an influx of African slaves, as well as an expansion of wetland drainage. The slave population of the *partido* of Loíza (probably concentrated in Loíza Pueblo/Medianía and Canóvanas) increased from 266 (O'Reilly 1765: 188 men, 78 women) of a total population of 938, to 425 in 1775, of a total population of 1,146. The 1775 total of 425 slaves comprised 329 male and 96 female slaves. This was the most skewed male-to-female ratio on the island, nearly 3:1 and suggests recent importation. In 1775, Loíza also had 358 *agregados*, a number that overlaps with the number of free colored (336) and free blacks (36).[10] The largest increases in the number of slaves were between 1791 and 1812 (617 to 696), and from 1820 to 1828 (from 673 to 742).[11]

In 1828 with only 324 *cuerdas* planted in cane (and 276.4 tons of *muscovado*), Loíza was in eighth place among island *municipios* (De Córdova 1833; 1 *cuerda* is approximately 1 acre or .393 hectares). In the 1820s the slave population of Loíza (at 18 percent of the total population) declined but was not far behind Ponce (22 percent) and Mayagüez (21 percent), the fast-growing, sugar-producing *municipios* in the south and west coast. (Guayama, also on the west coast, was the leading producer at the time, with 30 percent of the total slave population.) Cassava production declined as a consequence of flour imports (now allowed legally by Spanish commercial reforms), perhaps due to the expansion of sugarcane cultivation itself. Loíza's coconut production grew, and seems to have had a steady demand in St. Thomas. Labor was employed in smallholding, drainage, and in all phases of sugarcane cultivation (land clearing, planting, cutting, loading) and sugar-mill work.[12]

3. Interaction with a Shrinking Non-Plantation Periphery

The coexistence, over several decades, of the half-wilderness of the Delta with a fast-expanding plantation regime, and the successive subordination of Delta zones to the plantation economy, suggests both an escape valve and unequal competition between social regimes. A similar conjunction existed in Loíza. The slave plantations of the lower Mississippi valley were often close to forests, marshes, and rivers. As Christopher Morris notes, these plantation edges, or ecotones, were very important for both the slaves and the slaveholders' diet, especially in the Delta and elsewhere in the lower Mississippi valley. The ecotones represented a vital space of slave autonomous activity. In the ecotones, ecologists have found the most prolific and diverse environments, with "combined resources from adjacent ecological zones" (Morris 2012: 125–6). In the densely "populated" subtropical wetlands, the ecotones horizontally compressed ecological zones that were layered horizontally, in contrast with the vertical zones that John Murra discerned in the Andes (Murra 2002 [1972]). Water "regulates" the Delta's horizontal ecological zones and ecotones (as in Loíza), somewhat like altitude does in the Andean highlands. On the edges of the plantations, slaves "found themselves squarely within the natural world" (Morris 2012: 132). One is reminded of Trouillot on creolization as "culture on the edges" (1998), a spatial connotation that Trouillot evidently intended. In the Delta, according to one ex-slave, "the woods were full of game, deer, bear, wild cows, panthers, turkeys, geese, ducks, possums, rabbits, squirrels, birds and everythin'" (Cobb 1992: 16).

> The woods also harbored and sustained runaways, who lived on the planta-
> tions' edges short and long term. Well into the nineteenth-century, camps
> of runaways were discovered on Mississippi River islands and marshes along
> the Ouachita River. (Morris 2012: 129)

Archaeological research has unearthed deer, raccoon, opossum, squirrel, rab-bit, and fish (especially catfish) remains in slave quarters. "Fish and wildlife were so abundant that some planters integrated them completely into the plantation economy, for instance by assigning slaves the full-time task of hunting for meat to supply the entire plantation population" (Morris 2012: 130). "The legacy of the edges between plantation and wetland forest persisted in the culture who lived there" (Morris 2012: 136). Clearly, the accessibility of wetland ecologies had major implications for plantations, in the Delta region as elsewhere, particularly in contrast to later developments.

The lumber industry and the new plantations in the Delta attracted the already diverse ex-slave population of the Cotton Kingdom, as well as a new influx of ex-slaves looking for frontier-type opportunities in the Delta (a flow partly promoted by Delta planters). The result was probably the most amalgamated, diverse, and mobile free black population in the South and in the nation. Following Emancipation, many freed people purchased land in the Delta backcountry. In the 1870s and 1880s, they were joined by hundreds of African Americans who had migrated from the flagging cotton economy of the southeastern states to the labor-hungry Yazoo Delta in search of better opportunity.

> Landowners, eager to find labor to clear the outlying acreage on their plantations and to increase their cotton production, rented land to black farmers for cash rents [. . .] Many renters, black and white, became part time backwoodsmen, selling the tree they felled to lumber mills in Delta towns. (Woodruff 2003: 21)

In Loíza, the most remarkable instance of ex-slave and historically free black occupation of land was in Los Frailes (Piñones), just across the Río Grande de Loíza river on its west side (administratively, barrios Torrecilla Alta and Torrecilla Baja). Los Frailes ("the Friars") was named after the friars of Dominican order, which owned most of Piñones between the mid-sixteenth century and 1837. It was by far the largest Dominican estate in Puerto Rico and was originally called "el Hato Los Frailes" (Hernández Ruigomez 1987: 109). The *hato* extended over 8,000 *cuerdas* and may have reached 10,000 (10,000-*cuerda hatos* were common at the time, Godreau and Giusti 1993; 1 *cuerda* = .97 acres). The fertile but partially flooded land of Los Frailes excited planters' imagination with its expanses of potentially productive soils.

The trajectory of Los Frailes exemplifies the quiet, even non-deliberate resistance that plantation development met in Loíza on both sides of the river (see Mintz 1995). Because of its particular history, Los Frailes is a well-documented case. The Dominican presence in Piñones had been desultory and was limited to the area next to the Río Grande; after the late eighteenth century, that presence was almost nil. By the nineteenth century, the name "Los Frailes" generally referred only to 3,000 *cuerdas* between Punta Vacía Talega and the Río Grande de Loíza, including several hundred *cuerdas* of pastures and cropland by the river. Its soils were virtually virgin, so to speak.

Los Frailes was the largest extension of cultivable land in Loíza not yet held in private property, and had alluvial soils that were exceptionally suitable for sugar cane. Los Frailes's soils were "unsurpassable for any crop" (*inmejorable para toda*

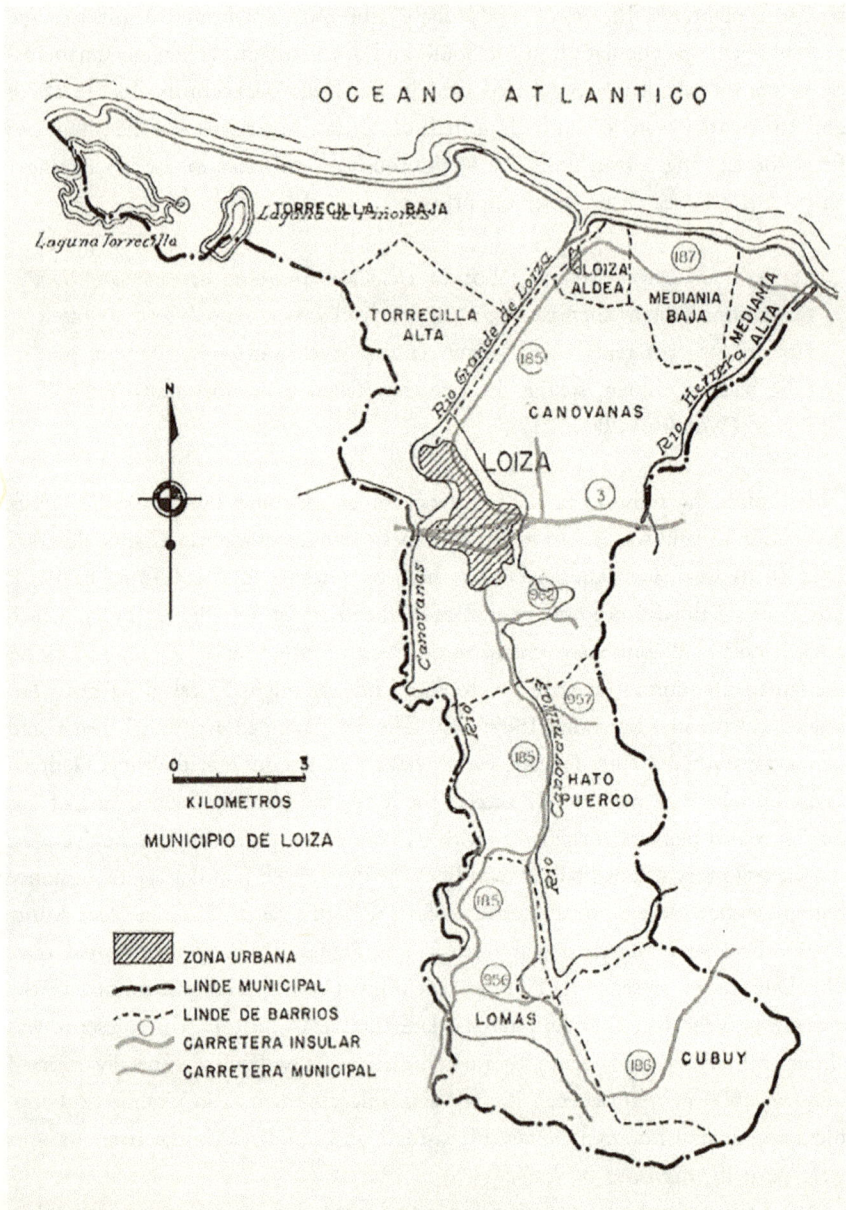

Map 8.4. Barrios in the Municipality of Loíza, showing the Los Frailes area (*barrios* Torrecilla Alta and Torrecilla Baja). Puerto Rico Planning Board, Municipio de Loíza. Memoria suplementaria al Mapa de límites del municipio y sus barrios. Memoria Núm. 72 (1957).[13]

clase de siembra), in the words of an 1847 report.[14] Los Frailes harbored ex-slaves of the Dominican order and free blacks from Loíza who took over parts of the Dominican estate even before its expropriation, and surely some runaway slaves. Maroons or their descendants probably lived in Piñones, but so far their presence has not been documented. The maroons could have originated in slave haciendas that operated in the immediate zone as early as the sixteenth century, and the Dominican estate was itself a slave hacienda.

Beginning in 1837, Spanish Liberal regimes intermittently embarked on expropriation of friars' lands as part of *desamortización* (disentailment) policies. The expanse of Los Frailes, the fertility of its soils, and the Dominicans' weak presence turned the estate into a key arena of conflict over land occupation and resource use. The colonial state's initial attempt to take over Los Frailes "was not consummated because the land was occupied by some blacks who cultivated the land and who refused to leave it, even though they did not pay any rent" (*nunca llegó a consumarse por encontrarse los terrenos ocupados por unos negros que cultivaban la tierra y que se negaron a abandonarla, a pesar de no pagar ningún tipo de renta*) (Hernández Ruigomez 1987: 112). Between forty-four and seventy families lived there, including fifteen persons who were, or claimed to be, descendants of the slaves owned by the Dominican friars. Those who were indeed former slaves in the Dominican estate may have felt some entitlement—or at least some attachment to the area—for that reason.

The colonial authorities considered that the dwellers of Los Frailes were not even "squatters" but rather "intruders" (*intrusos*), "usurpers" (*usurpadores*), and "prowlers" (*merodeadores*).[15] Of course, these terms construed and constructed Los Frailes politically, and expressed the officials' own optic.[16] The so-called "usurpers" were settled in Los Frailes "on their own authority" (*avecindados de su propia autoridad*)[17] . . . that is to say, without any that the authorities would respect. In the eyes of the colonial elites, Los Frailes was an annoying backwoods that was difficult to watch over (*es como un despoblado de difícil vigilancia*) and "a lair of acts harmful to the moral, good order, and to public security" (*madriguera de actos perjudiciales a la moral, al buen orden y a la seguridad pública*).[18]

In Los Frailes, little heed was paid to official denunciations or to the 1837 decree. Several dwellers entered into sublease arrangement with a planter to whom the Real Hacienda rented Los Frailes. By 1847—almost a decade after the initial *desamortización* of Los Frailes and almost three decades before slave emancipation—

there were more than sixty family and individual households in Los Frailes. From the state's point of view, Los Frailes was *un caos insondeable de misteriosos enredos* ("an unfathomable chaos of mysterious entanglements").[19] Once the authorities announced a new round of *desamortizaciones*, some twenty individuals and families left with their livestock. An 1848 report indicated that forty-four households remained in Los Frailes.[20]

While most of the peasants in Los Frailes moved out of the central portions of the estate by the river, most remained within its boundaries and simply moved closer to the seashore and to the cove in Torrecilla Baja at Vacia Talega. Moreover, they continued to make use of the fecund cropland, forest, lagoons, and coastline. Diverse food-crop cultivation (with predominance of manioc) combined with substantial livestock raising, crab catching, fishing, hunting, and so forth, characterized settlement in Los Frailes in the decades that followed, as in much of the Loíza coast. Ricardo Gallardo, who formally acquired two shore lots in Los Frailes (about 400 *cuerdas*), complained in 1882 that on "his" land there were still "intruders who were destroying the timber on it" (*intrusos que estaban destruyendo el maderage en ellos existente*).[21] At the same time, Gallardo noted that on those lots there remained several dwellings of old tenants of the State (*que en esos terrenos subsisten todavía algunas viviendas de antiguos colonos del Estado*).

A short-lived sugar estate, Hacienda Virginia, was the object of continuing incursions by *merodeadores* who cut down trees, made charcoal, and rustled cattle. In 1879, Virginia's manager complained to the colonial government that on a Real Hacienda lot next to the sugar mill's land:

> the damages to the property increase by the day . . . in the first place due to the many persons [*vecinos*] that have entered it with the livestock, which they turn loose and these go to damage the plantings in the adjoining holdings, which we had acquired, second, that some of those *vecinos* have no known means of subsistence and threaten with theft that land in its crops and cattle and third . . . because it is . . . public land and they are damaging the State's parcel . . . by the cutting of wood and trees to make charcoal that it constantly observed.[22]

A landowner next to the same Real Hacienda lot protested against "the abuses both of cutting trees and making charcoal." The Virginia mill closed in 1880 and was "entirely abandoned."[23] Even into the 1890s, thirty *bohíos* dotted the shoreline among the palm trees east of Vacía Talega, and ten more lay upriver in Hato Arriba. As it turned out, even the mayor of Loíza was a "usurper" and grazed some cattle near Vacía Talega.[24] The rest—some 500 *cuerdas*—was forested.

While plantation slavery and large-scale landholding tightened their grip across the river in the 1820s–1840s, the Los Frailes smallholders had a more autonomous livelihood. The fecund ecology of the Los Frailes "squatters," the extensive mangrove forest and wetlands just behind their smallholdings, and the peculiar legal status of Los Frailes made all the difference. Yet the Los Frailes "squatters" were not immune to the impact of the colonial state and planter power, as reflected in the 1848 eviction. Hence we may infer some of the history of interaction and conflict on the east side of the river from the better-documented and more drawn-out developments on the west side, in the conflict over Los Frailes.

4. Black Demographic Concentration and Relative "Isolation"

The Mississippi Delta is often considered "an isolated, time-warped enclave whose startling juxtapositions of white affluence and black poverty suggested the Old South legacy preserved in vivid microcosm" (Cobb 1992: 13).

> Negroes were more heavily concentrated in the Delta than they were in any other area of the South, and because of the violence of the Mississippi caste system they were kept at an even further distance from the influence of southern white music. With the exception of a few small groups—the people of the sea islands of Georgia and the Carolinas . . . the Delta field hands were less a part of the southern life than any other large Negro group. (Charters 1977: 27)

Brandfon reaffirms the "isolation" argument by characterizing the Yazoo Delta as an "enclave," with the Mississippi River on the west, and the Yazoo River and high bluffs on the east (1967: viii). In the Civil War, "the delta was probably less affected than any other equal area in the south. For this its isolation and inaccessibility easily account" (Stone 1902: 242). Of the three "Deepest Souths" of the US South (the Delta, the Georgia-Carolina Sea Islands, and the Piedmont), the Delta is the "deepest" of them all in terms of contemporary plantation control (Willis 2000).

In a sense, Loíza is a barrier island as much as the Delta is a fluvial island; and "isolation" arguments have been made for Loíza as for the Delta. The eminent

Puerto Rican anthropologist, archaeologist, and historian Ricardo Alegría carried out his early research in Loíza and its Santiago fiestas. Alegría studied with Robert Redfield at the University of Chicago, and went to conferences by Melville Herskovits and William Bascom at Northwestern; he first discussed the Loíza project with Herskovits.[25] Alegría, who founded the Institute of Puerto Rican Culture in 1956, has had an enormous intellectual influence in Puerto Rico (and on its cultural politics), on a scale comparable to Fernando Ortiz in Cuba (who wrote the foreword to Alegría's fundamental book on the Loíza fiestas in 1954) or Gilberto Freyre in Brazil, and shared some of their major conceptions.

In his pioneering work on the Fiestas de Santiago (1954), Alegría described "Loíza Aldea"[26] as a "relatively isolated" community, "a forgotten and distant little town" (*un pueblecito olvidado y alejado*) where there had been a "conservation and articulation of beliefs," including "old Afro-Hispanic practices" (1954: 3, 5, 7–11). Loíza Aldea was "far removed from the equalizing progress of machine civilization, that lives its peaceful and monotonous life, maintaining ancient beliefs and customs as if it ignored the passing of centuries" (Alegría 1954).[27] Alegría explained Loíza's isolation as due to its "antiquity of settlement," "ethnosocial homogeneity," and primary orientation to subsistence agriculture. Despite, or in part because of, Loíza's exaggerated association with slavery (although Ponce, Mayagüez, or Guayama were clearly more important in that regard), Loíza has generally been viewed, as St. John (Virgin Islands) in the nineteenth century, as "a small peasant backwater, which appeared to be an isolated rural idyll" (Olwig 1985: 2); perhaps reinforced by a general understanding that squatters (as many of Loíza's denizens were seen) were historically "marginal and isolated" (Leeds 1977: 236).

In social science, "isolation" gained particular traction in Robert Redfield's dichotomous characterization of the transition (or continuum) from "folk" to "urban" society, which he developed out of his research in Yucatán.[28] For Redfield, "isolation" was a major, independent variable that went hand in hand with "a high degree of genetic and cultural homogeneity, slow culture change, preliteracy, small numbers. minimal division of labor, and simple technology, among other dimensions" (Mintz 1951: 137). Redfield's perspective grew out of the Chicago school's emphasis on physical distance, an "ecological approach to spatial distribution around a dominant center as an outcome of competition among populations" (Silverman 2003: 180). It is in this context that Alegría proposed the notion of "relative isolation" to explain Loíza's social history.

Although Alegría qualified his characterization of Loíza's "isolation" as "relative," in the substance of his account—and, particularly, in the ways that his account has been *read*—Loíza's "relative" isolation has become naturalized, nearly absolute. Physical distance—which does not necessarily equal isolation—is, of course, a major dimension of historical social relations, and figures (or should figure) prominently in analyses alert to environmental history. However, isolation is not "absolute"; all distance is in part socially and historically constructed. Any time that "isolation" is asserted we cannot simply infer it as an assumed, bare consequence of a given physical distance or an ecological configuration (lakes, rivers, swamps, etc.). A relational approach to local or regional space "demands that we distinguish regions, or places, based on a historical understanding of the processes that create distinctive identities, relations, and characteristics" (Woods 2007: 71).

Loíza's physical and historical geography does not necessarily suggest isolation. Loíza is only twelve kilometers from San Juan, on the eastern end of an arc-like hinterland that stretches around San Juan Bay from Toa Baja to Río Piedras to Loíza. Of course, that Loíza's slaves and runaways originally came from Africa or elsewhere in the Caribbean was hardly "isolating," nor was its sugar production, which was mostly directed to overseas markets. And the slaves and planters of the Loíza coast in the nineteenth century were particularly *not* "isolated." Many slaves were recent arrivals from Africa or from elsewhere, while most of the planters (and overseers) were immigrants of Irish background from nearby English islands or from the US; and Loíza was immersed in wide-ranging commercial circuits proximately centered in St. Thomas. Loiza was not "isolated," of course, unless we take "isolation" to be synonymous with Africanness, and, more pointedly, blackness.

Loíza's local economy—which occupied most of its laboring population—was not "isolating" either. The main local crop was manioc, which grew well on the sandy loams that border the beach fringe. Into the early nineteenth century, Loíza was the main cassava-producing zone in Puerto Rico (Arroyo 1981: 33, 39). Free mulatto and black townsmen carried the cassava on horseback on the excellent road from Loíza to the capital that ran the length of the coast, partly behind forty-foot dunes blanketed by sea-grapes.[29] This was the *camino real* ("royal road"), the *ruta del casabe* or "cassava road" as I have called it elsewhere (Giusti 1994). Discussion of Loíza's "relative isolation"—which may have been a significant dimension of Loíza's social history, in some respects, and in some ways and times more than others—has to be historically grounded in these sorts of connections and temporalities.

Historical grounding is also essential to "isolation" arguments on the Delta. James Cobb, Jeannie Whayne (1996), Clyde Woods (1998), and Nan Woodruff (2003), among others, have questioned absolute "isolation" approaches in their work on the Delta. "Many of the human and material extremes that were the keys to the Delta's identity either as the 'South's south,' or 'America's Ethiopia' were shaped not by its isolation but by the pervasive global and national influences" (1992: 333). As Woods wrote, the Delta regime was not the result of "too little capitalism, too little development" (1998: 13), but rather its opposite. Even labeling the Delta as "rural" (synonymous with "isolation" and "homogeneity" in Redfield's approach) is open to question. Contemporary observers such as the planter-sociologist Alfred Holt Stone would agree. In the Delta, "[t]he line of demarcation between rural and urban life is so indistinct and persons pass so constantly from one to the other that there is not much difference between the negroes of the town and those of the country" (1902: 261; on Stone, see Hollandsworth 2008).

The often unspoken keystone of "isolation" arguments on Loíza and on the Delta is their high black demographic concentration, which became socially constructed as "isolation." Both in the Delta and in Loíza, blacks constituted an especially high proportion within the wider national formation. Yet the "high" proportion of Afro–Puerto Ricans in Loíza's population was hardly unique and must also be placed in the context of also largely black and mulatto communities in Santurce (Cangrejos), Río Piedras, Toa Baja, and elsewhere in the San Juan area, which were subject to displacement, fencing in, and early forms of gentrification and "social whitening." If anything, it is not a question of the Loíza littoral "being" isolated in the twentieth century, but of having *become* "isolated" (and "blacker") in some respects through wider historical processes, including the shift of the economic axis and administrative seat of the municipality several miles inland, to Canóvanas (the former Ribera Arriba). At the same time, Loíza became far less "isolated" through acquisition of its estates by one of the largest US sugar corporations in Puerto Rico, incorporation into the San Juan metropolitan region, massive sand extraction for San Juan's urbanization, and migration to Carolina, San Juan, or the United States. This contradictory movement corresponds to wider economic and spatial processes of capital and labor.

Comparable isolating/incorporating processes are also in full view in the Mississippi Delta. The Delta was thinly populated before the Civil War, but already had a substantial black population (mostly enslaved). Since the 1870s, the Delta had one of the nation's highest proportions of African American population. The Mississippi Immigration Bureau encouraged freed-slave migration to the Delta, which, by 1890, was a new "Black Belt" (Brandfon 1967: 136). The Delta became "the 'blackest' of the South's 'black belts,'" with a black-white ratio as high as 16:1 in some of its counties. In the 1900 census, African Americans constituted 11.6

Figure 8.1. Mouth of the Rio Grande de Loíza, with Los Frailes (Piñones) on the west side, and Loíza Pueblo and Medianía on the east, showing the penetration of drainage and sugar cane cultivation by the early twentieth century. Hacienda Grande land can be seen in the lower-right section of the photograph. US Navy, Puerto Rico Aerial Survey, 1930–31. This is the earliest known aerial photograph of the area.

Figure 8.2. North-south view of the cane fields in the eastern section of Loíza, next to the town. The cane fields surround the mogotes (karst hills, monadnocks). The edge of the town of Loíza appears on the right of the photo, which also shows the Río Grande de Loíza and, a short distance upriver, the chimney of Central Canóvanas (upper central part of the photo). On the other side of the Río Grande, Los Frailes. AGPR. Colección Departamento de Instrucción Pública (Charles Rotkin).

Figure 8.3. Western section of Loiza (Piñones), on the west side of the Rio Grande de Loíza, viewed from the south (1948). Cane fields are in the foreground; Torrecillas and Piñones lagoons and the mangrove forest in the background, between the cane fields and the Atlantic Ocean. AGPR. Colección Departamento de Instrucción Pública (Charles Rotkin).

percent of the total population of the United States, 58.5 percent of Mississippi's, and 87.6 percent of the Delta's (Stone 1902: 235, 239). By 1900, seven Delta counties were among the twelve US counties with the highest proportion of African American population and had a constantly growing percentage of America's black population (Stone 1902: 237). The Delta continued this trend until World War I, when demand for black labor in the North began a seismic shift in migration.

5. Production/Consolidation of New Cultural Forms

In both Loíza and the Delta, new, historically rooted cultural forms of music, dance, and communal celebration took shape or were consolidated. While the question of origins is complex, and probably unsolvable, regarding the Delta blues as well as the Loíza fiestas, some circumstances stand out. In the Delta, blues pioneers Charlie (or Charley) Patton, Robert Johnson, and Howlin' Wolf lived and worked in Sunflower County, partly in the Dockery Plantation near the Bolivar and Coahoma county lines. Son House was born in Coahoma and lived in New Orleans before returning to the Delta and eventually becoming a blues musician (Lomax 1993: 205). A striking number of artists in the blues vein and blues-descended genres (mainly rhythm-and-blues) were born and/or raised in the Delta: Bo Diddley, Little Walter, Muddy Waters, B. B. King, Sam Cooke, John Lee Hooker, Otis Spann, Jimmy Reed, J. B. Lenoir, and Diana Ross (Ferris 1970: 20–21). "Legions of organic blues scholars emerged from the Lower Mississippi Valley" (Woods 2007: 60).

> Even with the confusion of sources and influences, however, it does seem clear that it was in the Mississippi Delta counties that the first blues were sung, and of all the Southern areas where the blues became a deeply rooted folk style, it was in the Delta where there was the richest creative growth. (Ferris 1970: 32–33)

The blues took shape in the midst of a rapidly transformed, often devastated landscape. Alan Lomax contends that the blues "came into prominence at the time of the decay of the plantation collectivity and the emergence of individualized effort as the main source of survival for Delta blacks" (Lomax 1993: 232, citing Ferris 1970: 32). It may be more accurate to frame the process in a transformation, rather than a decay, of the Delta plantation regime (Woods 1998), but Ferris's general point about the direction of historical change is persuasive. This transformation occurred in many places at once between Georgia and Texas, but most strongly or at least most visibly among Delta blacks.

One of the earliest and most significant figures in blues history was Charley Patton (born between 1881 and 1891), from the Delta town of Drew in Sunflower County. Patton's influence of the region's musical style is considered "monumental" (Woods 1998: 110–12). To judge from the only surviving photograph, Patton was phenotypically quite mixed, perhaps "Creole." He was sometimes taken for Mexican or Native American or both. Patton's musical style was locally rooted; his showmanship may have been as well.[30] One of his best-known pieces is *High Water Everywhere* (ca. 1930), on the Mississippi River flood of 1927. Many African Americans who lived along the river lost their lives because they were barred from taking refuge in the white hill country.

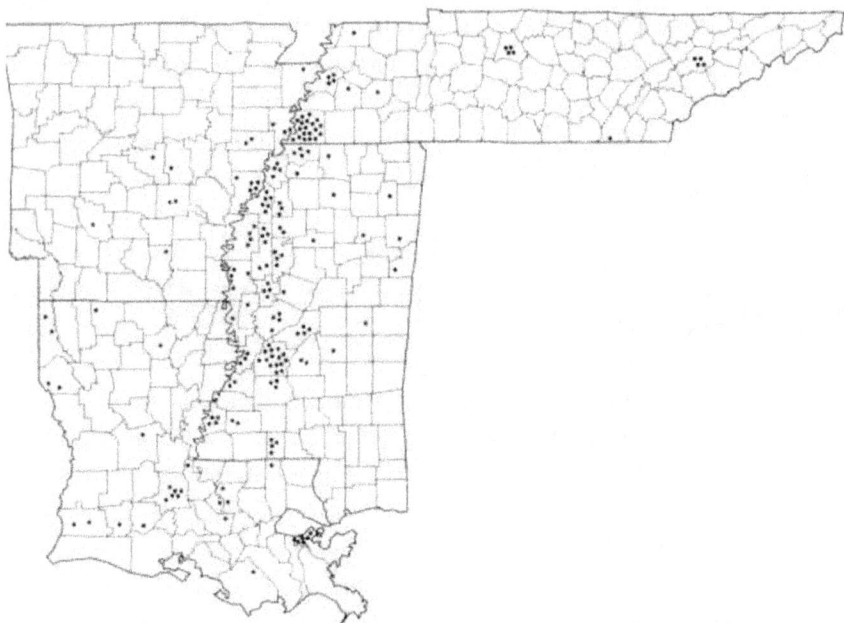

Map 8.5. "Birthplaces of Recorded Blues Performers, 1890–1920," in John F. Rooney Jr., Wilbur Zelinsky, and Dean R. Louder, eds., *This Remarkable Continent: An Atlas of United States and Canadian Society and Cultures* (College Station: Texas A&M University Press, 1982), 243. Reprinted by permission of Texas A&M University Press.

> Lord, the whole round country,
> man, is overflowed
> You know I can't stay here,
> I'll go where it's high, boy
> I would go to the hilly country,
> but, they got me barred[31]

Another, perhaps closer dating of the origins of the Delta blues begins with the outstanding African American musician, songwriter, and musicologist William C. (W. C.) Handy (1873–1958), often known as the "Father of the Blues." Handy toured extensively with a minstrel show through the South and even to Cuba during the 1880s and 1890s. Handy lived for six years (1899–1905) in Clarksdale (Coahoma County), on the Mississippi, which is often known as the heart of the

Delta. Coahoma was "the cotton capital of the Delta," and "one of the capitals of the cotton industry: it was the headquarters for the richest and most efficiently operated plantations in the South" (Lomax 1993: xii).[32]

As Handy narrated it, in 1903 in a train station in Tallahatchie County, he saw "[a] lean loose-jointed Negro had commenced plunking a guitar beside me while I slept. . . . As he played, he pressed a knife on the strings of the guitar in a manner popularized by Hawaiian guitarists who used steel bars. . . . The singer repeated the line three times, accompanying himself on the guitar with the weirdest music I had ever heard" (Handy and Bontemps 1991: 74, 76). Two years later, Handy heard a group that

> struck up one of those over and over strains that seem to have no begin-
> ning and certainly no ending at all. The strumming attained a disturbing
> monotony, but on and on it went, a kind of stuff associated with [sugar]
> cane rows and levee camps. Thump-thump-thump went their feet on the
> floor. It was not really annoying or unpleasant. Perhaps "haunting" is the
> better word. (Scarborough 1925: 269)[33]

Handy's oft-repeated story narrative is on fragile footing, since by 1903 the development of the blues may have been at a fairly advanced stage; but it's about as close as one gets to grasping the hot spot of the blues. On the earlier formative period there is virtually no reliable evidence. For instance, the man believed to be Patton's musical mentor, and who may have been closer to the configuration of the blues, was Henry Sloan (ca. 1870–1948). Sloan was a decade or two older than Patton, though he lived longer. Unlike Patton, Sloan left no recordings. Several key bluesmen were still alive in the 1940s who had known, as children, its earliest periods in the 1880s and 1890s; this includes, prominently, the man who was supposedly Charlie Patton's mentor. Jazz historian Paul Oliver writes:

> It would be possible to continue for several more pages with extracts from
> jazz histories that state, each with disarming certainty, quite conflicting
> accounts of the period when blues developed and how it influenced jazz.
> It is not possible to find a consensus among the jazz historians on these
> matters: blues began, variously, before the Civil War, during the War, after
> Emancipation, during Reconstruction, after Reconstruction, in the 1880s,
> the 1890s. Blues was African in origin, it was not African in character, it

was a rural music, it was a city music, it was part of the pre-history of jazz, it was an influence on the formation of jazz, it was part of a convergence phenomenon in the shaping of jazz, it was assimilated by jazz after its marching phase, it was played with ragtime before jazz bands played jazz, it was adopted by ragtime musicians at a later stage, it was, and is, the essence of jazz expression. (Oliver 1991: 18)

A lack of documentary sources has hindered blues research, though historians like Oliver believe that a great deal of knowledge was wasted by the neglect of valuable informants and by a tendency of secondary sources to quote other such sources.

The broad cultural significance of Loíza turns especially on the Fiestas de Santiago, but Loíza is also important in the more broadly based *bomba* Afro–Puerto Rican tradition of music and dance. The nightly *bomba* dancing is a major feature in the weeks leading up to the fiestas.[34] The Santiago fiestas may have come about as a response by the villagers of Medianía, the rural barrio of the Loíza town next to Hacienda Grande, to a revival of Saint Patrick as patron saint of the town by recently arrived sugar planters.

The origins of Loíza's Saint Patrick tradition, as can be best surmised from fragmentary evidence, may be traced to a sixteenth-century devotion. In the 1520s or 1530s, a plague of worms attacked manioc plants in San Juan and elsewhere on the island. A drawing was held, and Saint Patrick came up. However, since this saint was "little known and extraordinary," the drawing was twice repeated, but Saint Patrick came up both times. The plague ended and a Mass and procession was ordered for the annual commemoration of the "miracle," apparently on the saint's feast day (Alegría 1954: 53–54; Fernández Méndez 1995: 188). The commemoration of Saint Patrick eventually lost devotees. However, a new plague of worms in 1641 led to a revival. After festivities followed by three processions, once again the plague ended (De Torres Vargas 1647: 188). In 1670, an old hermitage (*ermita*) in Ribera Baja, near the river's mouth—where the town of Loíza would develop—was dedicated to San Patricio (Giusti 2006–07: 23).[35]

The patron saint of Loíza at least since 1729, if not earlier, was the Holy Spirit (*Espíritu Santo*). This uncommon patron "saint"[36] had its own roots in the Loíza region's ecology and toponymy. Already in the 1580 *Memoria de Melgarejo*, "Espíritu Santo," was the name of the peak known today as Pico del Toro o del Suroeste (1,074 meters). Pico Espíritu Santo is one of the triad formed by the tallest peaks of the Sierra de Luquillo, which frames the Loíza plain on the east. Pico del Toro rises at the center of the three peaks, when the landscape is viewed from the Loíza coastal plain. The other two peaks of the Sierra de Luquillo "trinity" are known today as Pico del Yunque (1,065 meters), which is on the northern, seaward side of Pico Espíritu Santo, and Pico del Este (1,050 meters), to its south.

The *Memoria* suggests that Pico Espíritu Santo, along with Pico del Yunque, were so named by the local black population. According to the *Memoria*, Pico del Yunque was known as Furidi: "[T]he tallest one [Pico del Yunque] they call Furidi, *so named by the blacks*, which in their tongue means a thing always full of clouds; the other they call the Espíritu Santo. . . ." (Fernández Méndez 1995: 118, emphasis added). Pico del Yunque has a strong profile and does seem to be the tallest of the three peaks, but Pico del Toro is actually higher by a few meters. Pico del Este, the most distant of the three, was named Loquillo after the rebel cacique who fought the Spanish in that zone.[37] "Loquillo" thus originated the name both of the eastern mountain range (Sierra de Luquillo) and one of its tallest peaks.

Pico del Este/Espíritu Santo is the headwaters of the river that was also named Espíritu Santo. The Espíritu Santo River, thickly lined with mangroves, crosses the eastern part of Loíza plain with hardly any tributaries. The combination of mountain and river gave the *Espíritu Santo* an everyday presence in Loíza.

Since the late eighteenth century, Irish planters were a growing presence in the zone around San Juan, then the main sugar-producing and slaveholding area in the island. Irish Catholics were among the few foreigners allowed by the Crown to enter Spanish territories in the eighteenth century, and several came to Puerto Rico usually in or after military or government service to the Crown. Some of them may have been operating in Loíza in the 1790s. A Spanish official who opposed the temporary expulsion of several Irish landowners in the wake of the 1797 British invasion argued in their defense that these planters "were spearheading the conversion of swampy, uncultivated lands into flourishing plantations."[38] Most of the Irish planters, however—like the majority of Puerto Rico's immigrant sugar planters—arrived between 1815 and 1830. Moreover, even though the official's defense of the planters in 1797 suggests that they came from Great Britain rather than by way of other Caribbean islands, several of Loíza's Irish planters came from the Leeward Islands, where sugar production was stagnating and slavery was abolished in 1833.

Given the specialized knowledge required in sugar production, it is not surprising that some of these immigrants were involved in plantation production in the nearby islands, or in the import trade in the United States. Several came to Loíza initially as plantation overseers in Irish-owned plantations. The planters and would-be planters were surnamed Seary, O'Neill, Kearney, Kiernan, Fitzpatrick, Parsons, Fitzsimmons, Viner, and Quigley, and they adopted Spanish first names rather quickly (e.g., "Guillermo" Parsons, "Miguel" Kearney), at least in official documents. "The social segment that established the new sugar economy [in the Loíza region] seems to have been the Irish" (Sued Badillo 1986: 45). Other planters were Danish (mainly creoles from the Danish Virgin Islands) and English. All these planters and would-be planters may have been especially attracted to Loíza by the proximity of the British and Danish Virgin Islands and the very active legal and illegal commerce (including slave trading) circuits with which Loíza's immigrant planters had notable connections.

Loíza's immigrant slave planters had, or formed, intricate marriage and business connections in the anglophone Caribbean. Bernardo Fitzpatrick and Arthur O'Neill are the oldest landowners on record in Loíza. In 1817, Fitzpatrick and O'Neill paid more than all the smallholders of Loíza's Ribera Baja combined (436 pesos total). In 1825, Mary Ann Sarah Cockley Brown, a native of St. John's (Danish Virgin Islands) married "Miguel" Kearney Fitzpatrick (owner of the Hacienda Palma). She brought to her marriage properties and valuables in Loíza, St. Croix, and Yost Van Dick and Spanish Town in the British Virgin Islands . . . and New York (Arroyo 1981).

In Loíza, a reputedly "isolated" and "backward" corner of Puerto Rico, Irish and Danish *hacendados*—among the more dynamic and well-connected planter groups in Puerto Rico before 1850—were actually more conspicuous than perhaps anywhere else in the island. An apparent shift in Loíza's new epoch, whose broader context was the development of the "second slavery" (Tomich 2004, 2016) in the Atlantic, was that the new crop of Loíza planters and overseers established locally unprecedented patterns of hegemony.

In particular, several planters and overseers promoted the restoration of Saint Patrick as the local patron saint. George (Jorge) Seary, a North American of Irish parentage who was one of the earliest sugar planters in the area, played an especially prominent role in the Saint Patrick revival. Seary owned San José del Cacique (later known known as Hacienda Grande). At 900 *cuerdas*, this was by far the largest estate that adjoined Medianía, where the Fiestas de Santiago tradition began. After having spent some time in St. Croix, Seary came to Puerto Rico in 1816 accompanied by Leonor Avery, of Saint Thomas, with whom he had five children. Seary reported bringing 6,000 pesos to Puerto Rico, a considerable sum. Seary's oldest daughter married another Irish *hacendado* in Loíza, Guillermo Parsons. (Neerman 2012: 2, 6).[39]

Data on Hacienda Grande is spotty, and corresponds to a somewhat later period. In 1849 the hacienda was second in importance among Loíza haciendas (along with San Isidro) in paying 6,600 pesos in taxes. Hacienda Grande reached 1,163 *cuerdas* in the late 1850s, when it was joined to an adjacent hacienda, Las Mercedes. In 1859, Hacienda Grande's area in sugarcane was 175 *cuerdas,* and it had sixty-one slaves and twenty free laborers (Arroyo 1981: 39).[40]

The role of George Seary, the proprietor of Hacienda Grande, in promoting the Saint Patrick veneration in Loíza was quite explicit. Seary donated a statute of the saint to the Loíza parish church and may have contributed funds for its construction on the site of an earlier, rustic structure. The former church, built in 1729, was described as "a hut-like structure made of widely separated reeds, covered with royal palms" and was dedicated to the Holy Spirit. The new church, built between 1798 and 1821, was renamed "Iglesia del Espíritu Santo y San Patricio" (Ojeda O'Neill 2001: 5).[41] It had a vaulted structure and "was one of the best in the island" (De Córdova 1968: 27). Seary may have made his bequest to the church soon after his arrival to Puerto Rico in 1816, since he was already the third-largest taxpayer in Loíza in 1818.[42] In tandem with the change in the church's name, in the 1820s Loíza officially became "Pueblo del Espíritu Santo y San Patricio de Loyza."

In the decade after the Loíza church was built and renamed, Saint Patrick's Day plausibly became the officially sanctioned patron-saint celebration, while the Holy Spirit faded in local memory—as did Saint Patrick's earlier association with manioc cultivation and cassava production. Saint Patrick was now at least obliquely linked to sugar growing, an association that the saint already had in Hacienda San Patricio (ten kilometers east of Loíza), the largest slave hacienda in Puerto Rico at the time.[43] Seary, a leading slaveholder and clearly a locally powerful planter, was mayor of Loíza from 1844 to 1846. Hacienda Grande figures as an oppressive worksite in one of the best-known Loíza *bombas,* sung in the Fiestas de Santiago: *En Hacienda Grande botaron a los paleros / porque no hacían los hoyitos barrileros.*[44]

The Saint Patrick celebration appears to have had little if any appeal in Medianía.[45] In the early nineteenth century, the slaves and free black and mulatto residents of Medianía and slaves from the nearby plantations, perhaps in response to the new enshrining of Saint Patrick, themselves "rediscovered" a saint, in the guise of a wooden statue of Santiago. The Santiago statute appeared either under a rubber tree or thrust by an ocean wave, according to the two versions of local tradition. The appearance of the Santiago statute several kilometers away from the Loíza church, in rustic association with nature (land or sea) stands in suggestive counterpoint to the donation by the *hacendado* Seary of the Saint Patrick statue to that church. Instead of reviving the older patron saint, the Espíritu Santo, a new saint was invoked, none other than Santiago, the eminently venerable patron saint of Spain. As it happens, Santiago "outranked" almost any other saint in Spanish Catholic hagiography, let alone one who, like Saint Patrick, was a minor figure in that tradition. Santiago, the symbol of a bellicose Spanish Christianity, became the defender of the people in Loíza (as elsewhere in other Santiago traditions in Spanish America [Harris 2000]). A date that has been mentioned for the approximate beginning of the Fiestas de Santiago, 1832, suggests that the celebration was in some ways a response to encroachment by the recently arrived planters and their revived Saint Patrick (Yurchenco 1971: 50; see Giusti 2006–07: 19).[46]

Loíza's original Santiago was *Santiago de los Niños* (Santiago of the Children, or *Santiago de los Muchachos*, as in Alegría 1955). This is another telling association of *el Santo*, as Santiago is often called in Loíza. There are two other Santiagos: *de las Mujeres* (of the Women) *y de los Hombres* (of the Men). These other "Santiagos" were apparently added in the late nineteenth century. Each saint has his day on July 26 (*Santiago de los Hombres*), 27 (*de las Mujeres*), and 28 (*de los Niños; el Santito, Santiaguito*), which remains the most revered Santiago. Puzzlingly, none of the three Santiagos are commemorated on July 25, the day that the Catholic Church tradition-ally celebrates the saint. (Instead, July 25 features the thoroughly secular celebration of the "Loiceños Ausentes," a formerly massive, now diminished, homecoming event centered on an auto caravan of *loiceños* from the diaspora and their families and friends.)[47] The three statutes are enshrined year-round in Medianía, three kilometers away from the Loíza church, in the homes of their respective "maintainers" (*man-tenedores*). In past decades the "maintainers" have been invariably women, but there have been male *mantenedores* as well.[48]

In the morning of each of the three days of the Fiestas de Santiago, the statute of the saint of the day is taken to the town church in a procession, and then brought back in the afternoon to the *mantenedores'* homes until the next year. Loíza's local space is very important for this construction of identity (Harris 2001). Various char-acters in the procession further define the narrative, including a Spanish caballero and the all-important *vejigantes* (Fiet 2007). The best-known figure is the *vejigante*, which has transcended Loíza and has become virtually a national symbol of Puerto Rico and especially of the island's culture.

Conclusion

Comparison and contrast between the Mississippi Delta and Loíza during different periods of the nineteenth century highlight the significance of ecology/labor transformations in shaping these widely different places as cultural "hot spots" marked by deeply creative processes of creolization. Perspectives on cultural creation such as Abrahams' on "hot spots" and most creolization studies, while illuminating cultural form and performance, need to be complemented by approaches such as Trouillot's emphasis on ethnographic context, on the heterogeneity of processes of creolization, and on their specific historical conditions. These aspects usefully direct our attention to dimensions of space and human-space interaction. In a sense—though my inquiry takes somewhat different directions—such approaches propose "a geographical inquiry into human experience" (Said 1993: 7). More broadly, this study questions renderings of "place" that distance themselves from ecological and material dimensions and concrete human interactions. Such distancing also applies to many current approaches to landscape.

To some degree, my approach also overlaps with geocritical perspectives in literary studies in their attention to spatial data (Westphal 2011; Tally 2011). However, my focus is not on authors and works of literature but on the contextual space itself and human interactions, especially through labor; on rural and historical space more than on urban and contemporary space; and on patterns of spatial interaction more than on their transgressions. After all, the question of land, and of land concentration and distribution, is a major historical issue in the Caribbean as in the US South. George Beckford stated it succinctly for Jamaica: "The struggle of the Jamaican people is essentially a story of the struggle for land" (Beckford 2000: 288). And for place, one might add. Clyde Woods noted the cultural dimensions of that struggle:

> At its most fundamental level, the blues expansion was the expression of the rise of an African-American culture that was self-conscious of its space and time and, therefore, fully indigenous. The South was the space of origin, the African-American hearth. (Woods 1998: 108)

Langston Hughes said just as much in 1943, in portraying blues space:

> [T]hrough the smoke and racket of the noisy Chicago bar [where blues is being played] float Louisiana bayous, muddy old swamps, Mississippi dust

and sun, cotton fields, lonesome roads, train whistles in the night, mosquitoes at dawn.[49]

Beyond specifying creolization contexts, we need to connect such contexts, through a "systematic comparison (among regions and through time)" (Price 2001: 47) that locates them in the changing circuits of the Caribbean *oikoumenê* (Mintz 1995) and the wider spaces of the Atlantic and the world economy (Price 2001: 47; Tomich 2004, 2016). In this framework, we may place the development of Loíza's Santiago feasts and Delta blues music on a common historical stage, inviting comparison and connection between the two creolization processes, and (above all!) framing new and more probing questions.

My study has looked closely at five interrelated aspects of the historical experience in Loíza and the Mississippi Delta: a wetland, forested, river floodplain of uniquely fertile soils; flood control, plantation expansion, and sharp transformations in labor regimes; interactions with non-plantation peripheries; black demographic concentration and relative "isolation"; and production/consolidation of new cultural forms. Both the Delta and Loíza had periods of further expansion and transformation in the twentieth century, but in a sense the creolization die was cast for Loíza in the 1830s and for the Delta in the 1890s.

In studying Loíza and the Delta, this chapter has foregrounded environmental history as a way into aspects of social history—for example, the Dantean work of bottomlands clearing and drainage, the toil and impact of levee and drainage works, the importance of fishing and hunting for laborer subsistence—that otherwise remains blurry or whose significance is little understood when the focus is exclusively on the production process and the plantation unit of production. The Loíza-Delta comparison and its connection of social and environmental history offer a perspective on race, culture, and creolization that goes beyond the usual plantation or urban contexts and raises significant questions about how slaves and free people of color generally related to New World nature and specifically to ecologies beyond plantations and towns.

Spatial/economic/cultural transformations such as the Delta's and Loíza's achieve a particular urgency in our times, as "the particularity of the dominant narratives of globalization is a massive silencing of the past on a world scale, the systematic erasure of continuous and deep-felt encounters that have marked human history throughout the globe" (Trouillot 2003: 34). The selective erasure or silencing of historical memory is closely related to the erasure/reconfiguration of space, and the cult of "placelessness" that has been trending in contemporary culture. The urge to respond to these trends, and to go beyond mere counterpropositions, is the leitmotif of this entire inquiry.

Acknowledgments

Earlier versions of this chapter were presented at the "Race and Rurality in the Global Economy" conference, African and African-American Studies Department, Duke University (March 2015) and in the Latin American Studies Association conference, San Juan, Puerto Rico (May 2015). My thanks to Michaeline Crichlow for comments and suggestions on the earlier LASA paper, which we presented in a panel. The late Sidney Mintz also read the LASA paper and made valuable recommendations. All faults to be found are of course solely my responsibility.

Notes

1. The Yazoo-Mississippi Delta is an interior delta, a basin that is one of the Mississippi's several such aquatic-terrestrial regions. The Delta is not the Mississippi Delta as usually understood, that is, the mouth of the Mississippi, which is three hundred miles south (Cobb 1992: 16). It is, in fact, part of a larger inner delta that includes several Arkansas counties.

2. Despite the varied meanings and often Eurocentric connotations of "creolization," due in large part to its genealogical relationship with "creole," the term has a history in the Caribbean that is at least as robust. Debates on creolization have been "at the heart of historical, social, and literary discussions that have taken place in the Caribbean for several decades" (Balutansky and Sourieau 1998).

3. In William Faulkner's work, the Delta rivals adjacent Yoknapatawpha (Lafayette) County as narrative historical space, though it appears far less frequently and is of a very different order (Loichot 2007). Maya Angelou's *Down in the Delta* (1998), the one film directed by the celebrated poet, follows the tradition of depicting the Delta as an African American heartland/homeland where family bonds and memories help mend lives broken by northern urban chaos.

4. "There are other towns and cities where African traditions are often celebrated (for example, San Juan, Ponce, Guayama, Carolina, and Hatillo), but in the common vernacular Loíza is seen as best representing the African/black component of Puerto Rican culture/ society" (Hernández Hiraldo 2006). Other major literary and cultural references to Loíza

and its region include Fortunato Vizcarrondo's poetry, Julia de Burgos's epic "Río Grande de Loíza" (which however does not address race), and Tego Calderón's "Loíza" (2002). On *La Capital de la Tradición*, the slogan's silence as to *which* tradition seems to reflect Puerto Rico's perennial ambivalence about race and culture.

5. From the vantage point of Puerto Rican social history, the Mississippi Delta also holds considerable interest for its similarity to Puerto Rico's poverty profile. Mississippi is the poorest state of the Union, one is often reminded in political discourse in Puerto Rico. However, Puerto Rico's poverty rate of 45.6 percent is twice Mississippi's. The more apt comparison is with the Delta counties: Humphreys (44.9 percent), Holmes (43.5 percent), Quitman (40.7 percent), Leflore (40.4 percent), Coahuma (38.2 percent), Sunflower (36.1 percent), and Bolivar (34.3 percent). In reality, however, Puerto Rico's poverty indicators are worse, as the federal government established a "special" statistical poverty threshold for Puerto Rico: about $10,000, roughly half the federal poverty level.

6. E. P. Thompson would have agreed: "The discipline of history is, above all, the discipline of context; each fact can be given meaning only within an ensemble of other meanings" (Thompson 1971: 45, quoted in Calhoun 1994: 230).

7. Trouillot's criteria for delineating his three most visible creolization contexts are (1) labor regimes, (2) the frequency with which their denizens had outside contacts, and (3) the extent to which they were subjects of history, that is, in terms of their cultural ideals and their attentiveness to the facts of power on the ground (1998: 16).

8. Watson H. Monroe, "Geomorphologic Notes," Map I-1054, *Geologic Map of the Carolina Quadrangle*, 1977. Base by Geological Survey, 1969. http://pubs.usgs.gov/imap/1054/plate-1.pdf. Accessed November 8, 2015.

9. *Poyal* soils are so named because of the stands of *palo de pollo* trees (swamp blood-wood, *Pterocarpus officinalis*), a landward mangrove associate, that thrive there. *Poyal* soils are heavier and stiffer than true alluvial soils, and have some saline content; but this difficulty could be minimized, and *poyal*-type soils were widely used in Puerto Rico.

10. In 1828, the population of the Loíza township—including its extensive rural zone—was 4,198, classified as 1,133 mulattoes (*pardos*), 742 free blacks, 714 enslaved blacks, 556 whites, and 1,053 *agregados de todas castas* ("tenants of all castes") (De Cordova 1968: II, 25).

11. AGPR, Gobernadores, Censo y Riqueza, boxes 11 and 13. The 1828 figure is from De Córdova 1968: II, 35.

12. Drainage proceeded more quickly toward the end of the nineteenth century, particularly after 1890. By the early twentieth century, the drainage system in the Loíza plain was Puerto Rico's most extensive (Vicente 1931).

13. The map shows the boundaries of Loíza municipality as they stood from the early 1800s to 1971, when the municipality was split in two. The barrio identified as "Loíza Aldea" is actually the historic town center, which lost its status in 1909 when the municipal seat was transferred to the village of Canóvanas, then renamed Loíza (or Nueva Loíza; and again after 1971, Canóvanas). Since 1971, only the coastal barrios constitute the municipal-

ity of Loíza, with the historic town center as its municipal seat, while the inland barrios correspond to the municipality of Canóvanas.

14. AGPR. OP. PP. Box 120. "Informes de que los terrenos denominados 'los Frailes' jurisdicción de Loíza, son de primera calidad. Año 1847," f. 1. These same soils are found just south of Medianía and in Canóvanas, where the slave plantations had been established since the 1820s.

15. AGPR. OP. PP. Box 124. Loíza 1872–73. Exp. 517, f. 71. Governor Pezuela, who established the *libreta* workbook regime in Puerto Rico, said that the free blacks of Los Frailes "supported themselves from the prowling that they carried out in the estates that adjoined their slovenly huts." AGPR. OP. PP. Box 124. Gobernador Pezuela al Ministro de Gobernación (May 1850). The reference was specifically to Los Frailes, where the 1848 mass eviction had recently taken place (see later). AGPR. OP. PP. Box 120. Exp. 1418, f. 78. Tribunal de Hacienda to Superintendent, June 19, 1850. The term *inbasores* (*invasores*, "invaders"), had also been used by the Dominican prior himself in the case of an adjacent Dominican estate, Cangrejos Arriba, some decades earlier.

16. Of course, this has important implications for historians and social scientists who use the word "squatter" and kindred terms (even if nominally less violent than *merodeadores* and so forth) without close deliberation.

17. AGPR. OP. PP. Carolina. Boxes 32 and 120.

18. The nexus between forests and "outlaws" is a recurring pattern in many societies undergoing transformation of their land and forest resources. In England, in medieval times, forests were "the haunt of poachers and brigands, but also the domain of farmers and craftsmen" (Birrell 1980: 85). The farmers, craftsmen, poachers, and brigands may all have been the same people.

19. AGPR. OP. PP. Box 140. Mayor of Loíza to the Governor General, April 8, 1850. Curiously, the mayor's imagery echoed the Count of Cuba, Chairman of the disentailment commission in Spain, who had concluded that the expropriation of friars' properties would be a labyrinthine, hopeless affair. "The *desamortización*, which is here believed to be so easy and valuable, will become in due time *a labyrinth of impenetrable egress*, a seed-bed of claims and complaints that cannot be resolved with violence without risking abuse to the sacred right of property, and to disturb the public peace to a palpable extreme" (Hernández Ruigomez 1987: 100; emphasis added).

20. AGPR. OP. PP. Box 120. "Relacion general de los habitantes q^e residen en la Hacienda que fue de los Frailes Dominicos en Loíza con espresion de los que se han establecido en virtud de contratos escritos, o convenios verbales y las personas que han concedido estos" (1848). These households occupied 362 *cuerdas*, including 123 *cuerdas* under cultivation, 103 in pastures individually claimed by the households, and 135 in commonly used pastures, marshes, and mangrove forest. The Los Frailes dwellers also had ninety-eight head of livestock.

21. AGPR. OP. PP. Box 127. Leg. 33, exp. 1, ff. 4, 7 (verso). See also on "usurper" woodcutting, box 127, "Expediente sobre el arrendamiento del Lote Núm. 17 en Loíza,"

f. 10, Rafael Ramírez de Arellano to the Superintendent, March 26, 1881; box 126, Negociado de Bienes del Estado to the Superintendent, f. 61, February 3, 1873.

22. Barasoain and Cia to the Crown Treasury, February 6, 1879. AGPR. OP. PP. Box 126. Loíza 1979–81. Leg. 35, exp. 18, ff. 1, 9.

23. AGPR. OP. PP. Box 132. Exp. 1481, ff. 25, 31.

24. AGPR. OP. PP. Box 124. Exp. 571, ff. 30, 63.

25. Alegría earned an MA in Chicago in 1946, taught at the University of Puerto Rico for several years, and carried out a number of major projects in history and anthropology, including the video and book on the Fiestas de Santiago. Alegría then went to Harvard for his PhD from 1952 to 1954 (Hernández 2002: 100, 126–8).

26. Alegría, as many others have before and (less so) since, referred to the town of Loíza and Medianía as "Loíza Aldea," the degraded town name that gained currency after Loíza lost its standing as municipal seat. In the past, it was also called "Loíza Vieja" while Canónavanas, where the town seat was moved in 1909, was often called "Nueva Loíza." Ver Tesauro de Datos Históricos, "Loíza."

27. Alegría's views echoed earlier literary perspectives on Loíza. Fortunato Vizcarrondo, intent on depicting the unique aspects of Loíza town and Medianía, underscored their apartness in his poem "Loíza Aldea: de ótroj puébloj alejaoj": "faraway from other towns" ([1942] 1976: 8). In "Pueblo Negro," Luis Palés Matos does not name Loíza, but the landscape he so vividly portrays certainly pertained: "Tonight I am obsessed by the remote/ vision of a black *pueblo*/ Mussumba, Timbuctoo, Farafangana/ it is a *pueblo* of dreams/ lying in my inner mists/ in the shadow of stark coconut palms/ . . . / There amongst the palm tress/ the *pueblo* languishes/ Mussumba, Timbuctoo, Farafangana/ Unreal hamlet of peace and slumber" (Palés Matos 1993: 111–112; my translation). In Spanish, *pueblo* has the double sense of town or village and of "the people."

28. Note, however, that Redfield's typology actually *subverts* notions of isolation by locating "folk" and "urban society" in a common terrain (Mintz 1951: 137). In Mintz's view, the major shortcoming of Redfield's model was less in the typology itself—which did have empirical flaws, for instance the striking absence of Yucatán's henequen plantations—but rather in the ahistorical way it was being understood and applied.

29. AGPR. Gobernadores. Censo y Riqueza, 1812; quoted in Sued Badillo and López Cantos 1986: 47.

30. Jimi Hendrix–style, Patton was known to throw his guitar in the air and play it behind his back.

31. Charley Patton lyrics cited here are from http://blueslyrics.tripod.com/artistswithsongs/charley_patton_ 1.htm#banty_rooster_blues. Accessed May 29, 2016. Many of Charley Patton's songs were more personal and sang of love and fast-changing relations where women were often as independent as the men . . . as in *Bird Nest Bound*:

Oh, I remember one mornin' stand in my baby's door,
(spoken: Sure, boy, I was standin' there)
Oh, I remember one mornin' stand in my baby's door,
(spoken: Boy, you know what she told me?)
"Look-a here papa Charley, I don't want you no more"

32. Coahoma County is notable for several reasons. Willie Lee Brown was born and raised in Coahoma and later lived in Tunica. Muddy Waters was raised in Coahoma County. Coahoma County was chosen for a pioneering Fisk University-Library of Congress 1941–42 project coordinated by Lewis Jones (where Alan Lomax participated as music recorder).

33. As Handy's reference to "cane rows and levee camps" suggests, work songs were an important local breeding ground of the blues.

34. In a larger sense, the Santiago celebration begins on June 23, on the eve of the feast of Saint John the Baptist (St. John's Eve, *víspera de San Juan Bautista*, associated with the summer solstice). On that night, preparatory rituals were held, and the *bomba* was drummed, danced, and sung every night until the Santiago Fiestas. The *bomba* is also an integral part of the Santiago Fiestas during its three days and nights.

Like the blues in the US South, the *bomba* has a far wider scope in Puerto Rico: historically, in the south coast it is *sones de bomba*, in the north *seises de bomba*. The most common *bomba* variants are *sicá*, *holandé*, and *yubá*; *güembé* and *leró* are also common in the south coast tradition, as was the *grasimá* in Cangrejos, just outside San Juan. These are all both drum rhythms and dance variants. Loíza is principally associated with the energetic, rousing *corvé* and the *seis corrido* (however, these associations between *bomba* rhythms and specific Puerto Rican zones continue to be debated). Kindred dance/musical forms exist throughout the Caribbean. *Rumba* in Cuba, *tumba* in Haití, Cuba, or Curazao, *palos* in Santo Domingo, *gwo-ka* in Guadalupe, *bámbula* in New Orleans and Saint Croix, *punta* in Belize and Honduras (Alvarez and Quintero Rivera 2001). The word "*bomba*" originally refers to a drum. In Angola, *mbomba* is a type of dance of mythical significance, while in the historical Congo region *ngomba* is a type of drum beat/rhythm. In St. Thomas, the *bomba* was the overseer in sugarcane plantations, perhaps because at one time a drum was used to regiment the pace of work. The drums in Loíza and the San Juan area were made with barrels of pork fatback (*tocino*), which was imported, while in the south coast the barrels were locally manufactured for use in exporting rum and molasses. In the Loíza *bomba*, unlike the south coast versions, both men and women sing and the güiro was commonly incorporated (only women sang in the south coast plena). *Bomba* drums are also called *barriles de bomba*.

Most importantly, in Loíza—unlike the other main *bomba* region, the south coast—traditionally the *bomba* was danced only in the June–July prelude to the fiestas. Because of its intrinsic association with the Santiago fiestas, the Loíza *bomba* remained "closer to the ritual of symbolic meanings" (Alvarez and Quintero Rivera 2001).

By the late 1940s, the *bomba* was said to be nearly defunct, but Loíza's fiestas (though apparently in decline at the time) may have been its most important ongoing context. The 1950s revival of both the fiestas (partly due to Alegría's film and publications on the fiestas) and of the *bomba* (partly due to its incorporation in the big-band repertoire) is a major issue for another time.

35. According to the 1645 *Synod of the Diocese of San Juan de Puerto Rico*, there were four churches along the Rio Grande de Loíza (*en la ribera de Loyza*): one in the sugar mill in Canóvanas (Canóbana), and others in Canovanilla, Campeche, "and in the estancia that formerly belonged to doña Mayora de Solís" (López de Haro, 1986).

36. The Holy Spirit does, however, appear in place names in Cuba (Sancti Spiritus) and is the name of a state in Brazil (commonly called "ES") that was one of the earliest zones to be settled and named in that colony (1535). Espiritu Santo is also the name of a volcano on the Chile-Argentina border, of a river in Bolivia, and of the largest island in the Vanuatu.

37. As it happens, one of the three peaks links with African culture, another to Taino rebellion, and the third—Espiritu Santo—connects with Christianity, but with a figure that is premised on the interconnectedness of all three.

38. AGPR. Ultramar, leg. 451, July 3, 1797, quoted in Chinea 2007: 178. Note, however, that Bryan Edwards suggests that the English invaders in 1797 had expected internal support in Puerto Rico (Edwards 1819: 85–86) . . . possibly, one would surmise, from the Irish planters.

39. This paper, which was located through Ancestry.com, was generously sent to me by its author, Mr. David Neerman. Ricardo Gallardo, one of the titled landholders of Los Frailes (and mayor of Loíza in 1870), married Elisa Celestina, one of the daughters of Jorge Seary and Eleanor Avery. One of their sons, Félix Gallardo Seary (1863–1889) was the grandfather of Ricardo Alegría (1921–2011) (Neerman 2012: 6). Ricardo Alegría (whose maternal surname was Gallardo) was thus the great-grandson of Elisa Seary Avery and the great-great grandson of George Seary (Hernández 2002: 21–23). Félix Gallardo Seary died young, but Alegría's grandmother, Estefanía Varonne y Lachere (a *viequense* whose parents were natives of France and Guadéloupe) died in 1970 at the age of 102. Alegría remembered Estefanía Varonne as "a formidable woman" who, as a widow, fought hard to retain the 900 *cuerdas* of Hacienda Grande. Adjacent owners and occupants frequently attempted to move the hacienda's boundary markers (*puntos*), perhaps animated by memories of past *hacendado* appropriations of land and wetlands in common use.

40. In comparison, in 1859 Hacienda Punta (the largest in Loíza, later the site of Central Canóvanas) had an *extensión* of 430 *cuerdas,* 232 of those in sugarcane (54 percent) (Arroyo 1981: 39). The largest estate (but not the one with the greatest extension in cane), San Isidro, was immediately inland in Ribera Arriba/Canóvanas. LaRuffa quotes an unspecified census whereby between 1838–58 the leading immigrant group residing in Loíza was from

Ireland (12), followed by Denmark (6), St. Thomas (5), St. Croix (3), and the United States (2), among others (1971: 13).

41. AGPR. Gobernadores. Loíza. 1829. Leg. Loíza 1812, 1822.

42. AGPR. Gobernadores. Box 489. Reparto para Cura (1818). Seary appears in the section "Canobana hasta Casique."

43. Hacienda San Patricio was owned by one of the earliest and most successful Irish Catholic settlers in Puerto Rico, Thomas (Tomás) O'Daly, and later his brother James (Jaime). The area of the slave hacienda continued to be known as San Patricio.

44. "In Hacienda Grande they fired the diggers/Because they didn't make the holes [for planting the sugarcane] large enough" [*barrileros*, "barrel-like"]. This remarkable *bomba* verse appears in the film that Alegría produced on the Fiestas de Santiago Apóstol in 1949. The verse is part of the traditional *bomba* repertoire and is well known by *bomba* musicians; its best-kown version mentions "las Carmelitas," and this *bomba* is known as *la bomba de las Carmelitas*. This is a striking reference due to the fact that in the seventeenth century the Carmelite order owned the Hacienda San Luis in Loíza Arriba (Canóvanas). Moreover, in the 1949 video of the Fiestas de Santiago the bomba is sung in both versions and "Hacienda Grande" alternates with "Las Carmelitas." The *bomba de las Carmelitas* raises significant issues, but the issue is best left for another occasion and further research.

45. To this day, Saint Patrick has his own competing fiestas in Loíza, a tradition that had declined and that the parish priest revived in the 1980s. These draw (if indifferently) the more middle-class, whiter sectors in the old town of Loíza itself (Ungerleider 1992). Indeed, in the 1990s, the Loíza parish priest tried to formalize the patron-saint status of Saint Patrick and attempted to wholly exclude Santiago by not allowing entry to the church of the one procession of the Fiestas de Santiago that had been allowed into the church, Santiago de los Hombres. The attempt was unsuccessful.

46. The 1832 date was offered by the master mask maker for the Fiestas de Santiago and longtime cultural patriarch of Loíza, Castor Ayala Fuentes, in a 1971 interview (Yurchenco 1971). Ayala was also the founder of the Ballet Folklórico Hermanos Ayala de Loíza (see later). The festivities are not mentioned in any nineteenth-century travel account or official reports on Loíza. Ayala narrates that his great-grandfather gave him a piece of a mask "that was so old it crumpled in my fingers. I think it was used when the festival began, around 1830, I saw another old mask in the house of a friend. The colors were nearly erased, so I washed it, guessed the colors, and designed new masks." Elsewhere in the interview, Ayala dated the origins of the fiestas to the 1830s. Ayala was born in 1911 and his father in 1875 (US Census of Population, Manuscript Returns 1920). Ayala's great-grandfather could easily have been born in the 1830s or even in the 1820s.

47. That July 25 is also the date of the US invasion and of the establishment of commonwealth status in Puerto Rico in 1952, both of which appear somehow irrelevant in the context of Loíza's more deeply rooted festivities, only adds to the irony of the occasion.

48. Despite many tangencies with Spanish and Latin American Santiago traditions, the structural originality of the Santiago fiestas in Loíza calls for greater comparative research. The following features of Loíza's Santiago do not, to my knowledge, appear elsewhere in Santiago celebrations: (1) the official feast day of Santiago, July 25, is not observed as part of the festivities, (2) Santiago is "split" into three Santiagos, each one celebrated on a different day (men, women, and children), (3) each Santiago is associated with a different age-gender section of the community, that is, children, women, and men, (4) in order of veneration, the children's Santiago comes first, and the women's before the men's, and (5) in both foundational narratives of the Santiago tradition, the finding of the statute is itself "tripartite," as the statute is found three times. There may be an intriguing connection between the three Santiagos and the veneration of Santiago as the twin brother of Christ (in juxtaposition with the more common belief in Santiago the Older, the fisherman who was Christ's companion and follower). The coupling of Jesus and Santiago as twins was venerated in Ibero-Roman Spain prior to the Muslim conquest. The Jesus-Santiago twins were linked in Ibero-Roman belief as the twin deities Castor and Pollux, where the Pollux was immortal and rose to the heavens while Castor remained on earth (at least for some time) as protector of mankind (Alegría 1954: 15). The Santiago tradition, which began in the early ninth century, that is, long after the Muslim occupation began, founded the importance of Santiago de Compostela as a major site of Christian pilgrimage. The Santiago tradition was radically transformed during the following centuries from veneration of a fisherman/apostle/codeity to Santiago Matamoros ("Santiago the Moor-Slayer"), a Christian holy warrior who rode on a white horse to a victory in the Battle of Clavija (supposedly, 844 AD). It has been established that the Battle of Clavija did not occur, but the myth of the battle was long central to the Santiago tradition in Spain. Santiago was first invoked in battle in the thirteenth century. A deeper level of the twins myth resides in astronomy and even older layers of beliefs surrounding the Gemini constellation.

49. See http://www.birthplaceoftheblues.org/blues.htm. Accessed March 10, 2015.

References

Abbad, Fray Iñigo. [1788] 1959. *Historia geográfica civil y natural de la isla de San Juan Bautista de Puerto Rico*. Río Piedras: Ediciones de la Universidad de Puerto Rico.

Abrahams, Roger D. 2001. "Afro-Caribbean Culture and the South: Music with Movement." In *The South and the Caribbean: Essays and Commentaries*, edited by B. C. Richardson, D. Sullivan-González, C. R. Wilson, and Porter L. Fortune Jr., 97–113. Jackson: University Press of Mississippi.

Alegría, Ricardo. 1949. *La Fiesta de Santiago. Loíza Aldea. Julio 1949*. Video. Center of Archaeological Research, University of Puerto Rico.

———. 1954. *La Fiesta de Santiago Apóstol en Loíza Aldea*. San Juan: Colección de Estudios Puertorriqueños.

Alvarez, Luis Manuel, and Angel Quintero Rivera. 2001. "Bambulaé sea allá, La bomba y la plena: compendio histórico-social." Article published to accompany the DVD of the TV special *Raíces*, produced by the Banco Popular de Puerto Rico. http://musica.uprrp.edu/lalvarez/bambulae_sea_%20alla_files/bomba_plena.html. Accessed December 10, 2015.

Arroyo, Vanessa. 1981. "Estudio socio-económico de la esclavitud en el partido de Loíza: Siglo XIX." MA thesis, Centro de Estudios Avanzados de Puerto Rico y el Caribe, San Juan.

Barry, John. 1997. *Rising Tide: The Great Mississippi Flood of 1927 and How It Changed America.* New York: Simon & Schuster.

Beckford, George L. 2000. "The Social Economy of Bauxite in the Jamaican Man-Space." In *The George Beckford Papers*, 288–322. Mona, Jamaica: Canoe Press.

Benítez Rojo, Antonio. 1992. *The Repeating Island: The Caribbean and the Postmodern Perspective.* Durham, NC: Duke University Press.

Brandfon, Robert L. 1967. *Cotton Kingdom of the New South: A History of the Yazoo Mississippi Delta from Reconstruction to the Twentieth Century.* Cambridge, MA: Harvard University Press.

Calderón, Tego. 2003. "Loíza." From the album *El Abayarde.* Lyrics at http://www.stlyrics.com/songs/t/tegocalderon10809/ loiza569714.html. Accessed July 20, 2016.

Charters, S. B. 1977. *The Legacy of the Blues: A Glimpse Into the Art and the Lives of Twelve Great Bluesmen: An Informal Study.* New York: Da Capo Press.

Chinea, Jorge L. 2007. "Irish Indentured Servants, Papists and Colonists in Spanish Colonial Puerto Rico, ca. 1650–1800." *Irish Migration Studies in Latin America* 5 (3): 171–182.

Cobb, James C. 1992. *The Most Southern Place on Earth: The Mississippi Delta and the Roots of Regional Identity.* New York: Oxford University Press.

Crichlow, Michaeline, and Patricia Northover. 2009. *Globalization and the Post-Creole Imagination: Notes on Fleeing the Plantation.* Durham, NC: Duke University Press.

De Torres Vargas, Diego. 1647. "Memoria de Diego de Torres Vargas," in Fernández Mendez, *Crónicas de Puerto Rico*, post, 171–217.

De Córdova, Pedro Tomás. [1831] 1968. *Memorias geográficas, históricas, económicas y estadísticas de la Isla de Puerto Rico.* San Juan: Instituto de Cultura Puertorriqueña.

Edwards, Bryan. 1819. *The History, Civil and Commercial, of the British Colonies in the West Indies.* Fifth edition. Vol. IV. London: T. Miller.

Fernández Méndez, Eugenio, ed. [1957] 1995. *Crónicas de Puerto Rico: Desde la conquista hasta nuestros días.* Río Piedras: Editorial UPR.

Ferris, W. R. 1970. *Blues from the Delta.* New York: Da Capo Press.

Fiet, Lowell. 2007. *Caballeros, vejigantes, locus y viejos: Santiago Apóstol y los performeros afropuertorriqueños.* San Juan: Terranova Editores.

Flores, Juan. 2000. *From Bomba to Hip-hop: Puerto Rican Culture and Latino Identity.* New York: Columbia University Press.

Giusti-Cordero, Juan A. 2006–07. "El país de Santiago: ecología y producción en la región de Loíza, siglos XVIII–XIX." *Sargasso* II: 19–30.

———. 2015. "Trabajo y vida en el mangle: 'Madera negra' y carbón en Piñones (Loíza), Puerto Rico (1880–1950)." *Caribbean Studies* 43 (1): 3–71.

Gomez, Michael A. 1998. *Exchanging Our Country Marks: The Transformation of African Identities in the Colonial and Antebellum South.* Chapel Hill: University of North Carolina Press.

González, Lydia Milagros. 2004. *Elogio de la bomba: Homenaje a la tradición de Loíza.* San Juan: La Mano Poderosa.

Hall, Gwendolyn Midlo. 2005. *Slavery and African Ethnicities in the Americas: Restoring the Links.* Chapel Hill: University of North Carolina Press.

Handy, William Christopher, and Arna Wendell Bontemps. [1941] 1991. *Father of the Blues: An Autobiography.* New York: Da Capo Press.

Harris, Max. 2001. "Masking the Site: The Fiestas de Santiago Apóstol in Loíza, Puerto Rico." *Journal of American Folklore* 114 (453): 358–369.

Helferich, Gerard. 2007. *High Cotton: Four Seasons in the Mississippi Delta.* New York: Counterpoint.

Hernández, Carmen Dolores. 2002. *Ricardo Alegría: Una vida.* San Juan: Editorial Plaza Mayor.

Hernández-Hiraldo, Samiri. 2006. *Black Puerto Rican Identity and Religious Experience.* Gainesville: University Press of Florida.

Hinrichs, C. Clare. 1996. "Consuming Images: Making and Marketing Vermont as Distinctive Rural Place." In *Creating the Countryside: The Politics of Rural and Environmental Discourse,* edited by Melanie DuPuis and Peter Vandergeest. Philadelphia: Temple University Press.

Hobsbawm, Eric. [Francis Newton]. 1959. *The Jazz Scene.* London: MacGibbon and Kee.

Khan, Aisha. 2001. "Journey to the Center of the Earth: The Caribbean as Master Symbol." *Cultural Anthropology* 16 (3): 271–302.

———. 2007. "Creolization Moments." In *Creolization: History, Ethnography, Theory,* edited by James Stewart, 237–253. San Francisco: Left Coast Press.

LaRuffa, Anthony L. 1971. *San Cipriano: Life in a Puerto Rican Community.* New York: Gordon and Breach.

Leeds, Anthony. 1977. "Some Unpleasantries on Peasantries." In *Peasant Livelihood: Studies in Economic Anthropology and Cultural Ecology,* edited by Rhoda Halperin and James Dow, 227–256. New York: St. Martin's Press.

Loewen, James W., and Charles Sallis, eds. 1974. *Mississippi: Conflict and Change.* New York: Pantheon.

Lomax, A. 1993. *The Land Where the Blues Began.* New York: Pantheon.

López de Haro, Damián. 1986 [1647, 1920]. *Sínodo de San Juan de Puerto Rico de 1645.* Madrid: Centro de Estudios Históricos del CISC.

Lovejoy, Paul E. *Identity in the Shadow of Slavery*. London and New York: Continuum.

———. 2011. *Transformations in Slavery: A History of Slavery in Africa*. Cambridge, UK: Cambridge University Press.

Mann, Kristin. 2001. "Shifting Paradigms in the Study of the African Diaspora and of Atlantic History and Culture." In *Rethinking the African Diaspora: The Making of a Black Atlantic World in the Bight of Benin and Brazil*, edited by Kristin Mann and Edna G. Bay, 3–21. London and Portland: Frank Cass.

Marshall, Wayne. 2001. "The Rise and Fall of Reggaetón: From Daddy Yankee to Tego Calderón and Beyond." In *The Afro-Latin@ Reader*, edited by Juan Flores and Miriam Jiménez Román, 396–403. Durham, NC: Duke University Press.

McKittrick, Katherine, and Clyde Woods, eds. 2007. *Black Geographies and the Politics of Place*. Toronto: Between the Lines.

Mintz, Sidney W. 1951. "The Folk-Urban Continuum and the Rural Proletarian Community." *American Journal of Sociology* (1953): 136–143.

———. 1995. "Slave Life on Caribbean Sugar Plantations: Some Unanswered Questions." In *Slave Cultures and the Cultures of Slavery*, edited by Stephan Palmié, 12–22. Knoxville: University of Tennessee Press.

———. 2010. *Three Ancient Colonies: Caribbean Themes and Variations*. Cambridge, MA: Harvard University Press.

Mintz, Sidney, and Richard Price. [1976] 1992. *The Birth of African-American Culture: An Anthropological Perspective*. Boston: Beacon Press.

Monroe, Watson H. "Geomorphologic Notes." Map I-1054, *Geologic Map of the Carolina Quadrangle*, 1977. Base by Geological Survey, 1969. http://pubs.usgs.gov/imap/1054/plate-1.pdf. Accessed November 8, 2015.

Morris, Christopher. 2012. *The Big Muddy: An Environmental History of the Mississippi and Its Peoples, From Hernando de Soto to Hurricane Katrina*. New York: Oxford University Press.

Moscoso, Francisco. 1999. "La economía del hato y los campesinos agregados en Puerto Rico." *Historia y Sociedad* 11: 9–28.

Neerman, David. 2012. "Don Jorge Seary of Loíza, Puerto Rico, and His Descendants." Unpublished paper.

Ojeda O'Neill. 2001. *Historia de la Parroquia El Espíritu Santo y San Patricio, Loíza, Puerto Rico*. Loíza: Parish of the Holy Spirit and Saint Patrick.

Oliver, Paul. 1991. "That Certain Feeling: Blues and Jazz . . . in 1890?" *Popular Music* 10 (1): 11–19.

Palmer, Robert. 1981. *Deep Blues: A Musical and Cultural History of the Mississippi Delta*. New York: Viking Books.

Palmié, Stephan. 2006. "Creolization and Its Discontents." *Annual Review of Anthropology* 35: 433–456.

Price, Richard. 2001. "The Miracle of Creolization: A Retrospective." *New West Indian Guide/Nieuwe West-Indische Gids* 75 (1–2): 35–64.

Price, Richard, and Sally Price. 1997. "Shadowboxing in the Mangrove." *Cultural Anthropology* 12 (1): 3–36.

Rivera-Rideau, Petra R. 2013a. " 'Cocolos modernos': Salsa, Reggaetón, and Puerto Rico's Cultural Politics of Blackness." *Latin American and Caribbean Ethnic Studies* 8 (1): 1–19.

———. 2013b. "From Carolina to Loíza: Race, Place and Puerto Rican Racial Democracy." *Identities* 20 (5): 616–632.

Said, Edward. 1993. *Culture and Imperialism*. New York: Vintage.

Saikku, Mikko. 2005. *This Delta, This Land: An Environmental History of the Yazoo-Mississippi Floodplain*. Athens: University of Georgia Press.

Scarborough, Dorothy. 1925. *On the Trail of Negro Folk-Songs*. With the assistance of Ola Lee Gulledge. Cambridge, MA: Harvard University Press.

Stone, Alfred Holt. 1902. *The Negro in the Yazoo-Mississippi Delta*. Electronic copy from Hathi Trust. https://catalog.hathitrust.org/Record/100770131. Accessed October 20, 2015.

Sued Badillo, Jalil, and Angel López Cantos. 1986. *Puerto Rico Negro*. Río Piedras: Editorial Cultural.

Tally, Jr., Robert T., ed. 2011. *Geocritical Explorations: Space, Place, and Mapping in Literary and Cultural Studies*. New York: Springer.

Tomich, Dale. 2004. *Through the Prism of Slavery: Labor, Capital and World Economy*. Boulder: Rowman & Littlefield.

———. 2016. *The Politics of the Second Slavery*. Albany: State University of New York Press.

Trouillot, Michel-Rolph. 1998. "Culture on the Edges: Creolization in the Plantation Context." *Plantation Society in the Americas* 5 (1): 8–28. Also in *From the Margins: Historical Anthropology and Its Futures*, edited by Brian Keith Axel. Durham, NC: Duke University Press, 2002.

———. 2002. "The Otherwise Modern." In *Critically Modern: Alternatives, Alterities, Anthropologies*, edited by B. M. Knauft, 220–237. Bloomington: Indiana University Press.

———. 2003. *Global Transformations: Anthropology and the Modern World*. New York: Palgrave Macmillan.

Ungerleider, David. 2000. *Las Fiestas de Santiago Apóstol en Loíza: La cultura afro-puertorriqueña ante los procesos de hibridación y globalización*. San Juan: Isla Negra Editores.

Westphal, Bertrand. 2016. *Geocriticism: Real and Fictional Spaces*. New York: Palgrave Macmillan.

Whayne, Jeannie. 1996. *A New Plantation South: Land, Labor, and Federal Favor in Twentieth-Century Arkansas*. Charlottesville: University of Virginia Press.

Willis, John C. 2000. *Forgotten Time: The Yazoo-Mississippi Delta after the Civil War*. Charlottesville: University of Virginia Press.

Woodruff, Nan. 2003. *American Congo: The African American Freedom Struggle in the Delta*. Cambridge, MA: Harvard University Press.

Woods, Clyde. 1998. *Development Arrested: The Blues and Plantation Power in the Mississippi Delta*. New York: Verso.

———. 2007. " 'Sittin' on Top of the World': The Challenges of Blues and Hip Hop Geography." In *Black Geographies and the Politics of Place*, edited by Katherine McKittrick and Clyde Adrian Woods, 46–81. Toronto: Between the Lines.

Yurchenco, Henrietta. 1971. *Hablamos/Puerto Ricans Speak*. New York: Praeger.

9

Race in the Reconstruction of Rural Society in the Cotton South since the Civil War

Jeannie Whayne

Introduction

Rural African Americans in the twenty-first-century South inhabit a world dominated by the rise of agribusiness and a global reorganization of agriculture. A hundred years ago, black southerners were central to the production of cotton, but the crop has lost its dominance in what was once called the "Black Belt." Stretching from Georgia through Alabama and into the lower Mississippi River valley, the area has modernized and diversified in a manner that left little room for African American laborers.

Although much has changed, rural African Americans in the twenty-first-century South struggle with many of the constraints faced by their predecessors a hundred years earlier: a pervasive poverty that seems intractable; a disease environment that undermines health and well-being; a new threat to the franchise orchestrated by politicians desperate to maintain control in an era of changing demographics; a return to segregation, particularly in the school system; and racist attitudes on the part of the white population and law enforcement officials that sometimes lead to confrontations that end in violence. A recent survey suggests that southern whites, particularly in the old cotton South, exhibit continuing resentment toward African Americans, are the most likely to oppose affirmative action, and are drawn to Republican candidates who use coded language to play on their racist attitudes. Another recent survey establishes that the same area holds one of the most impoverished populations in the country. The poverty rate is 20 percent or higher for the general population and, in some cases, is well over 50 percent for the black population (Acharya et al. 2015; Tarmann 2003; Frey 2013; Scott 2016; Giggee 2008).[1]

Although African Americans in the rural South face many obstacles, they have demonstrated an impressive resilience in the face of staggering odds. Their churches, though dwindling in numbers because of the rural population decline, remain centers of the black community. Many rural African Americans have embraced the "food justice" movement and organized effectively to address issues of hunger. They retain a certain degree of political clout, and, under some circumstances, their votes represent the deciding factor in crucial elections. The power of the black vote, in fact, is partly what motivated white Republicans to engage in gerrymandering election districts. Rural blacks are typically well aware of their political potency, and although they are undereducated in a failing and re-segregated public school system, they are far from unsophisticated in the ways of the white population in their midst. They are conscious of the attitudes of their white neighbors and keenly suspicious of local law enforcement officials. Their ability to understand their situation is born of generations of experience that schooled African Americans in strategies of survival in a hostile environment (Hahn 2003).[2]

This chapter examines certain persistent problems confronting rural African Americans in the Arkansas and Yazoo Mississippi deltas, where the plantation expanded most dramatically in the post–Civil War South. Thousands of African Americans moved from older southern states like Georgia and Alabama, where declining fertility had caused the withdrawal of tens of thousands of acres of land from cotton production. Labor agents promised, and black newspapers reported, that expanded production had increased wages, and that land in certain newly reclaimed (from swamps) delta areas was cheap and plentiful. While some managed to secure landownership, mostly outside the plantation counties, most worked for shares and became a critical component of the cotton enterprise (Wright 1986; Matkin-Rawn 2013, 2014; Painter 1997; Ravage 1997; Woods 1998; Woodson 1969).[3] African Americans' role in the successful operation of cotton plantations was a crucial factor in the cotton economy's rise and fall. As Sven Beckert argues in *Empire of Cotton: A Global History*, one of the most celebrated historical studies of recent years, "The empire of cotton was, from the beginning, a site of constant global struggle between slaves and planters, merchants and statesmen, farmers and merchants, worker and factory owners" (Aiken 1998; Beckert 2014: xii).

The Civil War and Reconstruction

Occurring in the midst of a great civil war, Emancipation seemed to herald revolutionary changes. There were voices in Congress calling for the seizure and redistribution of plantation lands to freed people; African Americans were keenly aware of the role they had played in the Northern victory. They left plantations in such large numbers during the war that it became impossible for the plantation economy to function. Their arrival in Union encampments forced the federal government to address their status, long before the Emancipation Proclamation and the passage of the Thirteenth Amendment. Finally, nearly 200,000 African Americans, the vast majority of them freedmen, took up arms on behalf of the Union Army and engaged in fierce battles for freedom firsthand.

The efforts of radical Republicans to confiscate and redistribute plantation lands to former slaves were doomed, however, because the revenue generated by the plantation economy served the interests of Northern entreprenuers thus American capitalism. In 1860, "raw cotton constituted 61 percent of the value of all US products shipped abroad." Few in national government could envision a system of production more profitable than plantation agriculture, and they were convinced that freedmen were essential to the enterprise (Beckert 2013: 243). Nevertheless, the collapse of slavery in the United States was more radical than emancipation processes elsewhere in the Americas, and the freed people of the American South had reason for optimism. Elsewhere, slavery ended with the grudging approval of sometimes reluctant but acquiescing planters who received some, and often full, compensation. Southern planters fought a bloody civil war and lost. Not only did they not receive compensation for slaves, their former bondsmen enjoyed one distinct advantage not afforded to freed people elsewhere: the right to vote.

Notwithstanding their political rights, the failure of Congress to provide "40 acres and a mule," or any other resources to freedmen upon Emancipation, made them vulnerable to those who held the land and the capital. Only the Freedmen's Bureau, created in 1865 to attend to the transition of African Americans from slavery to freedom, stood between the freed people and their former masters. But bureau agents who attempted to mediate labor contracts more favorable to African Americans were harassed and even murdered. Other agents served the interests of the planters who had ready allies amongst a segment of the southern white population that visited a reign of terror upon African Americans who attempted to leave plantation areas. Many northern entrepreneurs leased plantations and exploited the former slaves just as viciously as did their southern counterparts (Finley 1996, Richter 1991, Schwalm 1997, Crouch 1992, Smith 2000, Williamson 1965, Powell 1980).

The contract labor system implemented in captured Confederate territories by the federal government during the war sometimes worked to the advantage of freed people, but was deeply dissatisfying to them, and they forced a compromise after the war. African Americans began to withdraw their labor when wage offers were insufficient or when planters failed to deliver. Freed people, who really wanted to own land but had not the means to acquire it, desired at least the semblance of independence from planter control. They moved away from the old slave quarters and onto twenty-five- to forty-acre parcels of land that they worked for shares of the crop: the sharecropping system. The planter owned the crop and paid a share of the crop to them as wages. It turned out to be a bad bargain for the freed people. Wages were only delivered once a year—at harvest—and in order to feed and clothe themselves between harvests, they became indebted to merchants or plantation commissaries. Soon planters were providing them with supplies at credit rates ranging from 25 to 50 percent, and given the passage of certain onerous laws that bound them to their planters, freed people found economic freedom to be illusory; leaving a plantation while in debt was foolhardy or even dangerous. At the behest of planters, local law enforcement officials routinely pursued, captured, and returned escaping sharecroppers to the plantations from which they had fled. By 1900 the term "debt peonage" had become synonymous with the corrupt sharecropping system through which African Americans were once again ensnared in the cotton empire's web (Daniel 1972; Blackmon 2008; Reid and Bennett 2012; Petty 2013; Ransom and Sutch 1971; Woodman 1995).[5]

Despite the economic constraints facing them, rural African Americans vigorously contested the reconfiguration of social and economic relations as they sought to establish their political position in the post–Civil War South. They had eagerly embraced the right to vote during Reconstruction even though they faced violent attempts on the part of the Ku Klux Klan to keep them from the polls. They continued to vote even after former Confederate Democrats pushed aside Republican rule and seized control of state legislatures and local governments in the mid-1870s. Once it was clear that the Republican Party was essentially eliminated from power and that only Democrats could secure office, many black political leaders formed "fusion" arrangements with white Democrats, who recognized the power of the rural black vote, securing some minor political positions on the local level. To the extent they were able to deliver the black vote to the white Democratic politicians they "fused" with, black politicians secured election, putting themselves in a position to provide some representation and services to black citizens (Hahn: 1–7).

Agrarian Protest and the Implementation of Segregation and Disfranchisement

An alliance of rural African Americans and whites during an agrarian protest movement challenged the Democratic Party and reflected a willingness to cross racial lines. However, the party embraced a cunning strategy to counter the populists: disfranchisement of African American voters. Facing falling prices for agricultural products, unfair credit practices, and disadvantageous transportation rates, the populists were launching a challenge to the existing economic structure, and some dared to criticize the nature of capitalism itself. Planters and the southern economic elite closed ranks in the face of this threat (Whayne 2011: 55, 2012: 50; Goodwyn 1976; Hahn 1983; Kazin 1995; Postel 2007; Creech 2006). Those championing disfranchisement declared that their intent was to clean up an electoral system made corrupt by the manipulation of the African American vote. Suggesting that African Americans were too unsophisticated to avoid being swayed by dishonest "fusionist" politicians, they also asserted that they were too ignorant and unschooled in democratic politics. In fact, it was precisely because African Americans were politically astute that the Democratic Party establishment sought to disfranchise them.

Promoters of disfranchisement employed a variety of means to do so: The Australian or secret ballot made it necessary for illiterates (of both races) to have their ballots marked by a white election judge, typically a local Democrat. Since illiteracy rates were particularly high among the African American population, they were disproportionately affected. According to historian Morgan Kousser, "21 percent of black voters and 7 percent of white voters in Arkansas ceased to cast ballots" after the passage of the Australian or "secret" ballot. The imposition of the poll tax "curtailed [black] voter participation by an additional . . . 15 percent." Kousser estimates that between 1888 and 1896, the percentage of blacks voting dropped from 72 to 24 percent. For whites the decrease was less precipitous, from 78 to 59 percent (Kousser 1974: 129–131).

The emergence of the Democratic Party "white" primary dealt the final blow to African American political rights. The Democratic Party began employing the primary system in the South in the 1890s and by the early twentieth century began the practice of excluding blacks from voting in their primary elections. Since any Democrat elected in the primary was assured to win in the fall general elections, impoverished African Americans might be characterized as behaving rationally when they ceased to pay poll taxes for the privilege of voting only for a Democrat who would not represent their interests. Such obstacles to voting lasted into the middle of the twentieth century and were only defeated by the unflagging efforts of African Americans on the local level and the National Association for the Advancement of Colored People (NAACP). Simultaneous to the imposition of disfranchisement, southern legislatures passed segregation statutes in the 1890s that together with disfranchisement sought to place African Americans in a separate caste within the South. The first segregation statutes applied to street and railroad train cars but soon expanded to include virtually all public conveniences from hotels and restaurants to hospitals and schools (Woodward 1951; Cecelski and Tyson 1998; Perman 2001; Graves 1990; O'Brien 1998).

By disfranchising and segregating African Americans, southern politicians and their planter allies created a dangerously hostile environment. Democratic Party spokesmen and their newspapermen allies used heated racist language designed to awaken fears of black domination such as had allegedly existed during Reconstruction. The violence that erupted, largely in response to this, was rarely addressed by law enforcement. It came in at least two forms: violence against individuals and attacks on specific groups. Individual African Americans might be targeted because of some alleged criminal offense or because of insufficient deference to whites. Conflicts sometimes arose between a black sharecropper and his planter, usually over the settlement of the crop, that resulted in the injury or death of the sharecropper or sometimes that of the planter. The latter would result in swift and deadly retribution. While many whites justified lynching as a means of keeping white women safe from rape by black men, studies of the so-called offenses of African American lynching victims establishes that rape was rarely involved. Whatever the reason, a record number of African Americans were lynched in the South in the 1890s, and some local law enforcement officials were complicit (NAACP 1969; Beck and Tolnay 1990; Brundage 1993; Whayne 2011: 55–56, "An Explanation" 1897, untitled editorial 1897, "Murder Most Foul" 1897, "Strung Up" 1897).

Violence as a Political and Economic Tool

Violence was also leveled at certain categories of African Americans, such as share-croppers: whitecapping, that is, night riders who harassed African Americans in remote locations on plantations. Black sharecroppers were particularly vulnerable to this kind of activity precisely because they lived in isolated rural settings. The motivations of whitecappers varied from poor whites, who wanted the tenancy posi-tions on plantations, to those who realized that the plantation system represented a threat to their interests. Whitecappers of the latter variety understood that the plantation system typically dominated land and capital in areas in which it was established, and when it appeared in the newly developing areas of Arkansas and Mississippi, it stood to block small-scale producers. Some poor, white agricultural laborers merely sought a tenancy position on the plantations. Because they typically brought mules and implements to the bargaining table, they could secure better wages and had some standing in law.

Riding in the dead of night and wearing white masks to hide their identities, the whitecappers viciously attacked African Americans and sometimes burned their tenant shacks. They occasionally burned plantation barns and buildings, reflecting a different motivation on the part of some night riders: a resentment of plantation agriculture rather than a desire to secure the tenancies for themselves. Planters sometimes became the erstwhile defenders of their black sharecroppers, but were motivated by the desire to protect their cheap source of labor and thus their profit margin. In Cross County, Arkansas, in 1904, planters became so concerned about the successful operations of some night riders that they pooled their resources and hired a white detective force to subdue them. Unfortunately, the leader of the detective force was murdered in the process and the local court refused to bring indictments (Whayne 1996).[6]

The night riders continued their nefarious activities. Even when law enforcement pursued them, they were difficult to identify and apprehend, and impossible to convict in local courts. Federal prosecutors attempted to intervene but obtained only one successful conviction of three white night riders in 1904 in eastern Arkansas—on the basis that they had violated the "right to employment" protected by the Thirteenth Amendment (a brave but dubious assertion). The conviction was overturned by the Supreme Court in *Hodges v. US, 203 US 1* (1906). Some southern legislatures, influenced by planters fearing the loss of black labor, passed state-based night-riding laws, but only an occasional a night rider was convicted (Whayne 2011: 58).

Both the determination of black labor but also its vulnerability in the racist environment of the Cotton Belt revealed itself most dramatically in Phillips County, Arkansas, in 1919. It was there that the largest, rural, race massacre in American history occurred. Local sharecroppers had recently founded the Farmers and Household Union of American and hired a sympathetic white attorney to represent them, in suits they hoped to file against planters who were exploiting them. They were the first group of rural southerners to challenge the plantation system—and thus the way cotton capitalism functioned—since the Populist Party. Planters were incensed by their boldness, and incendiary rumors began to circulate that blacks were planning an insurrection and meant to murder whites and seize plantation lands. In truth, planters were aware that the African Americans had hired an attorney, Ulysses S. Bratton, and were fearful of the consequences. Bratton, a former federal prosecutor who had secured peonage convictions against planters in southeastern Arkansas in 1905, was a force to be reckoned with. By 1919, he had retired from the Justice Department and was in private practice in Little Rock. Playing on the fears of their white allies, planters whipped up a storm of fury that they could not control. By the time the smoke cleared, the Hoop Spur Church, located at a rural crossroads, was burned to the ground and approximately 250 blacks had been killed (Woodruff 1993; Stockley 2001; Whitaker 2008; Whayne 1999: 287; US Justice Department 2005).[7]

The burning of the Hoop Spur Church was not a singular event. From the earliest days of Emancipation, black churches were targeted because they were perceived to represent a challenge to the white community. They were places not only of religious but also of political communion among African Americans, and whites intent upon keeping blacks away from the polls directed their hostility toward them (Hahn 2003: 230–234; Roll 2010: 77–78; Maffly-Kipp 2001). Occasionally, even a black preacher might find himself the subject of violence, particularly if his political declarations were at odds with those of the larger community on certain sensitive matters. During World War I, Elder Jessie Payne, pastor of a Church of God in Christ (COGIC) in Blytheville, Arkansas, incurred the wrath of white vigilantes over statements he made against African American involvement in the war. This spoke to a larger controversy involving the founder of COCIG, Charles Mason, but also reflected heightened tensions engendered by pro-war propaganda. Elder Payne was tarred and feathered but managed to escape (White 2012: 64; Arkansas Church Records Survey 1939).[8]

Even the poorly funded black school was a target of white rage after Emancipation. It was a focal point of black social activities, an educational institution controlled by black teachers and principals, and it provided one of the few opportunities for employment for the best-educated black citizens in the rural South. Like black preachers, black principals could sometimes serve as intermediaries between their community members and the white establishment, and they stood beside the preachers at the top of the rural black social structure. They presided over a "separate but equal" institution that was severely underfunded while its facilities were often remote, dilapidated, and sometimes threatened with closure. Many southern states passed or proposed segregation of funds by virtue of race so that black schools would only be underwritten by the property taxes paid by black citizens. This was disastrous given the impoverishment of the general black population. Although the Julius Rosenwald Fund provided seed money to build black schools throughout the South, ongoing expenses were the province of local governments and based on property taxes. Another challenge, the hostility of the white community to black education, could lead to violence. In 1925 in Mississippi County, Arkansas, a state-of-the-art black school, the Wilson Industrial School, located on the outskirts of a plantation town, was burned to the ground in the early morning hours of the day it was to be dedicated in 1925. A representative of the Rosenwald Fund, which had provided some funds for its construction, was on the scene to attend the dedication and reported that white arsonists had set the fire because they did not believe that blacks deserved such a building. In other words, they found black aspirations for educational advancement to be a challenge to the caste system established by disfranchisement and segregation (Whayne 2011: 113; Hoffschwelle 2006: 262–263).

The Emergence of an Agricultural Bureaucracy

At the same time that African American sharecroppers faced these challenges, they endured a set of obstacles suffered by farmers across the country, regardless of race or ethnicity: the severe recession in the late nineteenth century had only partially and sporadically lifted in the first decade of the twentieth century. The causes of the national recession were multifaceted, but farmers faced the additional burden of increased competition from abroad and discriminatory transportation rates. Added to this was a troubling crisis in agricultural fertility rates, particularly in some sections of the South where imprudent practices and overproduction had so exhausted the soil that hundreds of thousands of acres were abandoned. Many reformers believed that low productivity levels on farms nationwide, which had increased by only 1 percent between 1900 and 1910, was one reason that a rural-to-urban demographic shift was in motion. The Great Migration—usually associated in the minds of most with African Americans but really involving a good many whites as well—was getting under way at that time. While white planters were alarmed at the loss of black labor, many policymakers were concerned that given the rural flight and the low productivity rate, American farmers would no longer produce enough food for the growing urban sector, or at least not enough to keep food costs low (Danbom 2006: 168–169).

The departure of African Americans from the South was met with alarm by many planters, particularly in the new cotton lands of Arkansas and Mississippi. *The Chicago Defender* sometimes received letters from Cotton Belt blacks expressing the desire for information about employment in the North; and the American Colonization Society (ACS) received many entreaties for assistance to immigrate to Liberia, particularly in the 1890s. Although many rural African Americans departed the South for the North, for Liberia, or in the Exoduster movement to Kansas, many others remained, and they did so because of dedication to their rural culture: their communities, schools, and churches. Of those who did remain, they sometimes moved short distances, preferring to stay close to or within the same rural neighborhood. Regardless, if they moved to work for shares for a more promising planter, their debt traveled with them (Barnes 2004).

The black community was itself at odds over the issue of migration out of the South. Great uncertainty existed with regard to what alternatives existed. The back-to-Africa movement revealed divisions within the black community over emigration that sometimes resulted in black-on-black violence. Tensions flared in 1892, for example, when one black itinerant preacher, Brother G. P. F. Lightfoot, began collecting funds from blacks in Woodruff, Jackson, and Cross counties in eastern Arkansas, promising transportation to Liberia. They erupted into violence not only because Lightfoot proved to be a scam artist but because many rural African Americans believed that the emigrationists were calling into question their status as American citizens who had slaved for planters, fought for the North, and earned a place on southern soil. One church in Woodruff County was so divided over the issue of immigration that when thirteen members were implicated in an attack on perpetrators of a gun battle that left Brother Lightfoot dead, they were angered by the criticism and formed their own separate denomination, St. Luke's

Missionary Baptist Church, near the small agricultural town of Augusta (Giggee 2008: 75; Barnes 2004: 104–105; Arkansas Church Records 1940).[9]

The departure of African Americans from the rural South, part of the much larger phenomenon of migration off of American farms generally, alarmed officials in Washington, DC (Danbom 2006: 169–170). The fear that the declining farm population would be unable to provide for city dwellers led to a greater reliance on the agricultural bureaucracy that had been developing within the United States since the passage of the Morrill Land Grant Act in 1862. The act provided grants of lands to states for the express purpose of founding colleges responsible for agricultural and technical education. With the passage of the Hatch Act in 1887, federal funds were funneled to these "land grant" institutions for the purpose of agricultural outreach programs, and cash-starved southern land grant colleges began to provide access to agricultural information and experiments more widely (Nevins 1962; Carrier 1937: 278–288).

African American farmers, however, were at a disadvantage as the agricultural bureaucracy fashioned the program with white farm owners in mind, and white agricultural colleges did not admit African American students. Recognizing that the overwhelming number of tillers of the soil in the South were African Americans, the United States Department of Agriculture (USDA) passed a new Morrill Act in 1890. Although the second Morrill Act led to the creation of new colleges and aided existing black institutions like Tuskegee, the funding source was inadequate. Unlike the Morrill Act of 1862, the black colleges were not funded by grants of land but rather by a cash grant. Under these circumstances, African American agricultural colleges, which rarely received sufficient state support, struggled to fund their programs and address the needs of black farmers. Although they succeeded in implementing some innovative programs, white plantation owners were hostile, for the most part, to any effort on the part of outsiders to approach their sharecroppers. Planters were determined to maintain some semblance of control of their black labor force and were reluctant to allow anything that might interfere with that control (Lovett 2015; Mays 1960; Minor 2008).

The passage of the Smith-Lever Act, which created the Cooperative Extension Service in 1914, marked a new phase in agricultural education, but it too focused on white farm owners and employed a segregated model. The USDA believed it did not have a mandate to change the social mores of the South and, in any case, the agency was eager to gain acceptance with prominent planters and farmers. Agricultural agents understood that in order to secure the necessary matching funds from county governments to pay for their operations, they had to offer programs that met the approval of the most prominent farmers and planters, many of whom set upon the local quorum court in charge of authorizing such expenditures. The agents believed that the problem facing southern farmers was largely the result of overproduction of certain crops, particularly cotton, and that diversification was a solution to two principal problems: low crop prices because of too much cotton on the world market; and ruination of the soil due to the nitrogen-robbing qualities of cotton production. They urged farmers to diversify and, particularly, substitute soybeans for cotton as both a soil-building and a cash crop. Rather than accept this message, planters and farmers wanted to know how to increase cotton yields and how to fight plant pests like the boll weevil. Indeed, the boll weevil threat drove cotton planters into the arms of county agents and was one major factor in sealing the success of the extension program. Recognizing the opportunity and understanding the influence of prominent farmers and planters on the local quorum court, farm agents eventually gave them what they wanted (Giesen 2011; Whayne 1996: 118–120).

Mirroring segregation practices in southern society in general, the Extension Service created a separate black farm agency division, and, like all "separate but equal facilities," it was anything but equal. White agents were housed in county courthouses, where they had ready access to county officials. Black agents occupied inferior facilities elsewhere and were not permitted to interact with white officials. Their underfunded programs suffered as a consequence (Daniel 1985; Whayne 1992, 1998). Black farm agents were tasked with providing programs to black farmers that were designed to enhance the interests of white plantation owners. This put the black agents in an awkward position. They stood between the black farmer and the white agricultural bureaucracy; they understood the limited mandate they had, but they also knew what black farmers wanted and needed: programs that would lead to some economic independence. Their relationship with black farmers was further complicated by their own middle-class rural backgrounds and the racial uplift philosophy of Booker T. Washington. Many sharecroppers bristled at the condescension of black agents, but in the end they often forged an uneasy alliance. Black agents would reinterpret as much as possible the white bureaucracy's directives, and black farmers came to embrace their modest efforts (Jones-Branch 2014: 86–88; Whayne 1998: 523–551).

Whatever its shortcomings, the black extension program introduced a new black leader to the community, one who acted fairly independently of the white extension agency. Although technically under the guidance of the white agent in a given county, they rarely interacted, and this provided the black agent with greater room to maneuver (Alabama Extension Service 1928).[10] A black supervisor at either the regional or state level worked with individual black county agents, but their contact was largely from a distance and often infrequent. On the remote farms and plantations in the old Cotton Belt, African American extension workers, male and female, had sole responsibility for administering their programs. It was not always easy, particularly in the early years when white fears of interference with black labor were easily aroused. After all, of all the leaders in the black community, the African American agent was the one most likely than any other to challenge plantation operations. One black agent in Georgia, Otis O'Neal, reported in 1916 that he had "been through fire," and that "dark clouds of disappointment have obstructed my path. More than once my life has been at stake" (Whayne 1998: 152; USDA 1916).[11] H. C. Ray, the first director of black extension in Arkansas, and his wife, Mary Ray, the first agent in charge of Home Demonstration, "traveled throughout Arkansas demonstrating farming, canning and home improvement techniques." They avoided challenging the racial status quo and "carefully cultivated the goodwill of planters and county officials." Their approach to the power structure hinged on their argument that "the economic health, and sanitation issues plaguing African American communities" presented a threat to the white community's economic viability and good health. The farm and home extension agents assigned by the couple to the heavily black population counties benefitted by their careful stewardship (Jones-Branch 2014: 86–87).

Black agents came exclusively from farming backgrounds, usually in the state in which they worked, and thus they understood the importance of religion to the rural communities they served. They carefully cultivated black preachers and quickly joined forces with them in the effort to speak to the interests of the rural communities they served. They frequently located their offices near—and sometimes in—them and drew on the strength of the black preacher's connections with the rural African American population. They also carefully cultivated white elites, although, because of the prohibition against direct contact, from a distance. For example, in eastern Arkansas in 1922, the three principal representatives of the black community, a preacher, a county agent, and a school principal, shared the stage at a rally with Congressman W. J. Driver, ostensibly to promote a new program of the black farm extension agency, but the congressman was there for quite another purpose. The preacher gave the invocation; the principal, who served as president of the new Negro County Farmers Organization, spoke briefly, and then turned matters over to the congressman. A brutal lynching of a black sharecropper two weeks earlier had the African American labor force on edge, and Driver was careful to make two points: First, that African Americans were safe in the county; and second, that they would find no ready welcome in the North because, in fact, only white southerners were their true friends. While Driver was drawing on his connections to the black community for his own purposes, black leaders were using the opportunity to cultivate their relationship with one of the most powerful whites in the state (Whayne 2011: 135–136; Gregory 2007; *Osceola Times* 1921).[12]

The Home Demonstration program may have had an even greater direct impact on the day-to-day lives of rural black families. These agents were charged with providing assistance to farm women, helping them to design kitchen gardens and create sewing clubs, and instructing them on how to raise better flocks of chickens and can vegetables for the winter. The availability of vegetables throughout the winter could prevent the development of pellagra, a nutritional deficiency that resulted from the lack of vegetables in the diet. Endemic in both plantation and hill counties of the South, it causes skin rashes, lethargy, and can be fatal in extreme cases (Kraut 2003). The home extension agents created special projects with group leaders, but they did not have to create connections among rural women. Their clubs were built upon existing structures of sisterhood launched through the rural church. Women's Mission Societies existed across denominations (Methodist Episcopal, Baptist, Church of God in Christ, etc.) and were probably the most important women's organizations connected to churches. Churchwomen participated in a variety of activities, such as cleaning and maintaining the church and raising funds to purchase bibles or to secure certain accoutrements like church bells, candelabras, or new pews. Few church buildings were painted or had much in the way of adornments, reflecting the poverty of the black population. Alison Collis Greene argues that many rural southerners worshiped in each other's homes or in whatever abandoned building they could locate. Some churches that started in brush arbors evolved into buildings eventually, but many did not (Greene 2015: 43–44). As John Giggee argues, "most churches [in the Arkansas delta] were supported by poor agricultural workers who struggled to raise money to purchase fancy items. Instead congregants usually built simple houses of worship decorated with a few manufactured wall hangings, a string of electric lights, and perhaps a couple of commercially made sketches." Despite their limited means, many rural churchwomen also participated in auxiliaries focused on the problems confronting the rural population, from committees dedicated to serving the sick and elderly of their respective denominations to "jail" committees designed to not merely take Christ to jailed parishioners but also to provide food or even medical attention to them (Giggee 2008: 161; Arkansas Church Records 1939).[13]

Black Fraternal Organizations
and the Henry Lowery Incident

Men had opportunities to organize through their churches as well; but more important, perhaps, were the many fraternal organizations that black men formed. In rural areas, in towns, and in cities, black men engaged in fraternal organizations that were uniquely their own as well as those that had Euro-American origins. They belonged to the traditional Odd Fellows, Prince Hall Masons, Elks, Woodman of the World, Knights of Pythias, for example, and they formed the Mosaic Templars, the United Brothers of Friendship, the Independent Order of St. Luke, and the Grand United Order of True Reformers, to name but a few. Although scholars have devoted most attention to the urban arms of these organizations, all of them had rural counterparts, and since most of the black population continued to reside in the rural South, most of their members were located there. According to Joe William Trotter, "by the late 19th century, an estimated 350 fraternal orders enrolled more than 6 million members, representing well over a third of all the nation's adult men." By the early twentieth century, black Odd Fellows could boast 304,000 members across the country. Like the other organizations, they promoted largely middle-class values "and guarded members against hard times," particularly through the creation of both burial and widows' funds (Giggee 2008: 63–72; Trotter 2004: 1–2).

The black Odd Fellows were particularly active in the Mississippi and Arkansas deltas and engaged in a variety of programs for its members, providing not only fellowship but also assistance for members in need. They provided burial insurance, for example, and built cemeteries, such as one in Starkville, Mississippi, now on the National Register of Historic Places (Savage and Shull 2016).

One Odd Fellows lodge in Arkansas took assistance to one of their members so seriously they attracted the unwelcome attention of the law enforcement establishment after a confrontation between a tenant farmer and his landlord left two whites dead and two others seriously wounded. On Christmas Day, 1920, Henry Lowery, characterized as a "respectable African American farmer" by one white newspaper, demanded a written statement from his employer establishing his freedom from debt so he could feel free to depart a plantation in eastern Arkansas without fear of pursuit by local law enforcement. Heated words were exchanged and then gunfire broke out. Lowery was wounded but escaped, hid in the swamps, and was bandaged and fed by his Odd Fellows brothers. They purchased a train ticket that made it possible for Lowery to reach El Paso, Texas, where he was apprehended and returned to Arkansas. The seven black Odd Fellows and the wife of one of them were arrested and incarcerated but suffered a better fate than that awaiting Lowry. It was Lowery's brutal lynching On January 26, 1921, that inspired Congressman Driver to speak to a meeting of the Negro County Farmers Organization (Whayne 2011: 127–134; Pickens 1921: 426–28; "An American Lynching" 1921; "Fled from a Murderous Sheriff" 1921; "Friends of Lowery" 1921; "Gasoline" 1921; "Governor Would Avert Lynching" 1921; "Henry Lowery Bound to Log" 1921; "Lowery" 1921; "Lynching" 1921; "Negro, Dual Slayer" 1921; "Negro Farmers Meet" 1921; "Negro, Hunted by Arkansas Mob" 1921; "Negro Murderer Burned at Stake" 1921; "Negro Murderer Burned at Stake Should Think of Torture" 1921; Poddy 1921; "Slayer" 1921; "Will Bring Negro Back" 1921).[14]

Another organization that had widespread membership across the country but with a rural wing that was particularly prevalent in the South was the Universal Negro Improvement Association (UNIA), known colloquially as Garvey clubs. It was far more than a fraternal organization, however, and appealed to both men and women. Of the approximately 923 divisions in the country, 423 were in the eleven states of the former Confederacy and the vast majority of those were in rural locations. The greatest number of Garvey clubs existed in the Arkansas and Mississippi deltas. The UNIA espoused self-help, self-defense, and separatism, and called for blacks to embrace their African roots. Their members typically met in churches, and some preachers were closely involved in their founding and operation. The men dressed in regalia, drilled in a military fashion, and often paraded publicly. Their anti-miscegenation position, aimed at the protection of black women, softened white reaction against their activities. Their popularity declined after 1927 when Garvey was deported and other leaders with a more urban focus began directing operations. By that time, in any case, the economic situation had deteriorated and even the small sum required for membership became onerous for poor rural southerners (Rolinson 2007: 3–4, 206–223, 138–139).

The Great Depression and African Americans

The failure of the post–World War I recession to lift undermined the cotton economy and worsened the situation confronting rural southerners, while the election of Franklin Roosevelt as president in 1932 did little to ease the burden of the black rural population in the old Cotton Belt. In fact, the Agricultural Adjustment Administration (AAA) was fashioned with large farm owners in mind, and southern congressmen played a key role in shaping the cotton program. Roosevelt understood that his task was to save American capitalism, and white Democrats in Congress were crucial to his success. Federal works programs permitted wage differentials for the South (based on race) in the works programs it sponsored. Rural African Americans from Alabama to Arkansas protested the ways these programs were implemented, but the AAA came in for special criticism. Planters were paid a sum for "renting" their land to the government in exchange for withdrawing the land from the production of certain crops . . . like cotton. With the encouragement of the county agents, they put those acres in soybeans, a much less labor-intensive crop.

Planters not only evicted sharecroppers whom they no longer needed, they also refused to share crop subsidies with them, despite the fact that they had reduced the acreage allotted to each sharecropper, thus reducing his income. Organizations like the Sharecroppers Union in Alabama, an all-black Communist union, and the Southern Tenant Farmers Union (STFU) in Arkansas, an integrated socialist union, attempted to represent the interests of landless farmers. The STFU was founded in northeast Arkansas and its heaviest membership was in the very areas the Garvey clubs had functioned a decade earlier. The STFU, however, in directly challenging the prerogatives of plantation owners, was thwarted at every turn, first by the violent reaction of local and state officials and white vigilantes, and ultimately by the willingness of the USDA and the federal government to abandon the needs of the landless in favor of securing support in Congress for other New Deal programs. Franklin Roosevelt needed the southern Democrats to keep his fragile New Deal coalition together, and landless black farmers were not going to stand in his way (Hamilton 1991; Koerselman 1977; Daniel 1977; Barry 1997; Woodruff 1985; Kirby 1998; Cobb and Mamorato 1984; Sullivan 1996; Mertz 1978; Mitchell 1979; Conrad 1965; Phillips 2007; Badger 1989; Wright 2011).[15]

Regardless of the odds against them, black and white sharecroppers in Arkansas, Tennessee, Mississippi, Louisiana, the newly developing cotton areas of in the boot heel of Missouri, and the cotton-producing regions of Oklahoma organized local chapters of the STFU. Many of them were fully integrated unions, and they represented the first agrarian protest movement since the populists to cross the racial divide. Like the failed Farmers and Household Union of America in Phillips County, Arkansas, in 1919, they challenged planter authority. One of the cofounders of the STFU, Isaac Shaw, referred to the tragic events in Elaine at the first meeting of the union in the Sunnyside schoolhouse in rural Poinsett County, Arkansas, when he joined others in calling for an integrated union. Shaw evoked the Elaine Massacre as an example of what could happen when poor white and black farmers were divided. Burt Williams, a farmer who recalled his father had been a member of the KKK, agreed with Shaw and the matter was settled. Some historians have suggested that the STFU was a precursor to the civil rights movement of the 1950s in interracial configuration. According to George Stith, a young farmer from the Arkansas delta, the integrated union reflected the similarity of circumstances faced by landless blacks and whites. Both were being exploited by the same set of individuals, but both were also engaged in the same struggle to maintain a place in the rural South. As Jarod Roll has argued, STFU members valued the farming way of life and hoped to maintain it. Stith characterized the interracial situation aptly: Although "I didn't go over to visit your family and your family didn't come over to visit mine," he said, "there was something common there about what we did. We knew something needed to be done." The union was the answer (Whayne 1983 and 1996: 191, 197–199; Roll 2008: 2–7).

The STFU fought for survival as planters used everything in their arsenal to undermine the organization. Planter thugs attacked union meetings, harassed and beat union officials, and arrested organizers. They used their political influence with local and state officials, and although the STFU found a few receptive men in the USDA, the agency ultimately sided with planters, mostly for political reasons but also because they viewed the acceptance of the AAA program as hinging on planter cooperation. The STFU launched two successful cotton pickers' strikes in 1937 and 1938, and established the Delta Cooperative Farm in Mississippi, but the odds were stacked against them. Their array of enemies was simply too powerful, and, in fact, they were tilting against the transformation of the empire of cotton. Since the Civil War, the focus of cotton production had been slowly shifting to India and elsewhere, and soon World War II and the modernization of southern agriculture would undermine the efforts of landless farmers to remain on the soil (Grubbs 1971).

Just as southern planters had presided over the reformulation of the plantation system after the Civil War, they had managed its adaptation to modernization in the post–World War II South. The war accelerated the departure of both black and white rural people as it offered opportunities to join the military or work in the defense industry, and many of them did not return once the war was over. By that time, the trend toward mechanization was well launched, and new chemicals had been developed that further reduced the need for labor. In cotton-growing areas, for example, black labor had been necessary for certain stages of the crop that previously had to be done by hand. Weeds had to be chopped out of the crop twice during the growing season. The development of chemicals designed to destroy weeds but leave the cotton undamaged, together with giant mechanical cotton pickers, transformed the nature of plantation agriculture (Street 1957; Whayne 2011; Daniel 1990).

This was going to be a game changer. African American sharecroppers had been essential to the plantation enterprise, and planters had done everything within their power to maintain control over them and limit their mobility. But the rise of scientific agriculture rendered them superfluous, and they soon became unwanted strangers in their own land. Between 1940 and 1960, the number of sharecroppers dropped so dramatically that the 1960 agricultural census no longer included them as a separate category of farmer. A post–World War II planning commission, established in 1943, predicted the rise of scientific agriculture, the consolidation of landholdings, and the demographic revolution that would accompany it. The commission suggested no programs, however, to address the displacement of farm labor. As though to realize this self-fulfilling prophecy, the USDA offered educational programs and advice through the Farm Extension Service directed at white farm owners. The goal was to assist them in securing the latest information on scientific farming. Black farm agents, however, were left out of this loop, and found themselves increasingly marginalized and penalized for any expression of sympathy for the civil rights movement.

The Civil Rights Movement

Despite concerted white hostility, African Americans in the old Cotton Belt organized and became active in the civil rights struggle. Fannie Lou Hamer of Mississippi, undoubtedly the most famous of rural civil rights activists, organized the Student

Non Violent Coordinating Committee's (SNCC) Freedom Summer program in Mississippi. "I am sick and tired of being sick and tired," she once said, in explaining her civil rights activism. After an attempt to integrate restrooms at a bus station in Winona, Mississippi, in 1963, she was arrested, incarcerated, and beaten. The next year Hamer served as the vice chair of the Mississippi Freedom Democratic Party, which attended the Atlantic City convention protesting the seating of the all-white Democratic Party delegation. African Americans involved with SNCC in Arkansas—most of them from rural backgrounds—organized lunch counter sit-ins and voting rights drives. Arkansas and Mississippi had been targeted by SNCC for special attention, and they found other blacks, like Hamer, who were homegrown activists. However, some conservative black leaders, especially those connected to the NAACP or college administrators, opposed protest activity. Students at the University of Arkansas at Pine Bluff, for example, were expelled for their SNCC activism. But these students and other black SNCC volunteers found ready support from rural black activists, men and women of an older generation, including Carrie Dilworth of Gould, Arkansas, who had been the secretary of the local chapter of the STFU more than twenty years earlier. Dilworth allowed SNCC organizers to use a small building she owned; the building was later destroyed by fire under suspicious circumstances (Mills 2007: 56–60; Whayne 2013; Wallach and Kirk 2011; FBI 1963).

Ironically, the Civil Rights Act of 1964, which resulted in the elimination of the dual county agent system, also led to the elimination of the black farm agents entirely. Although a few found employment within the white agent's office, most were forced out. Just when black farmers needed advice the most, they had no middleman, however imperfect, to speak to their interests. White agents were not inclined to assume the responsibility for them, and black farmers were not given access to certain programs that would have helped them negotiate the onset of scientific agriculture. The discrimination was so thorough and comprehensive that a class action suit filed on behalf of black farmers led to a now famous court decision in 1999. In *Pigford v. Glickman*, a federal court ruled that between 1981 and 1996, racial discrimination within the extension program had limited the availability of loans and access to other programs for blacks. It was an important victory, both symbolically and, in fact, for those farmers who had managed to stay the course and remain on the farm. They had to establish, however, that they had once owned farms, thus it did not address the situation that confronted the landless pushed from rural areas after modernization. Although the *Pigford v. Glickman* case suggests that the civil rights movement came late to rural areas where blacks were usually isolated, the decision was not inconsequential and became even more significant after an additional decision, known as *Pigford II* in 2010, expanded the number of black farmers (still farm owners) covered under the original decision and increased the allocation to $1.25 billion (Pigford 1999; Cowan and Feder 2013; Daniel 2013; Sanders 2013; Carpenter 2012).

In the 1990s and early twenty-first century, the plantation system entered a new organizational phase. Historians like Jack Kirby had characterized the post–World War II plantation as the neoplantation, one dependent on capital rather than labor. But it was still run, principally, by local southerners. With agricultural lands rising in value in the early twenty-first century while other real estate prices were dropping, investment firms began placing their clients' funds into agricultural lands. Although insurance companies and "foreign" investors had long been investing in southern plantation lands, there is something different about the twenty-first-century "portfolio plantation," a term I use to describe the acquisition of agricultural lands by investment firms. They have few connections to the local community and operate from distant offices, placing managers on their "plantations" who are exclusively white and who hire very few African Americans. These portfolio planters are able to maximize profits by subjecting the land to greater exploitation through mechanization and the use of dangerous chemicals. Having little connection to the local communities, they have little inclination to invest in them and few concerns about the possible implications of the use of dangerous chemicals (Whayne 2011: 230–232).

Civil Rights in the Twenty-First Century

Today, only 1 percent of the rural population in the United States live on farms, and very few of that 1 percent is African American. Otherwise, rural African Americans in the twenty-first century might be characterized as occupying a world that is very similar to that of a hundred years earlier. First, poverty levels in rural areas are much higher than in urban areas, particularly in the old cotton South. In the early twentieth century, poverty was one means of maintaining a servile black labor force in a labor-intensive farming regime. Poverty in these areas in the early twenty-first century is a consequence of the rise of scientific agriculture, which reduced the number of farmhands necessary; those who remained in rural areas were left to find employment when and where they could. Those within easy reach of cities commuted to urban areas to work; some found employment in local low-wage manufacturing operations. Few African Americans secured jobs in the new Sun Belt–related industries, however, because they required educational attainments beyond the reach of the poor. Casinos and the private prison industry provided employment to some, and many others worked in low-wage domestic service or the fast-food industry (Tarmann 2015).

Although opportunities in the rural South declined for farm laborers in the second half of the twentieth century, many African Americans remained in rural areas because of an attachment to place, especially to their churches and communities. In recent decades, a back-to-the-South movement of blacks from urban areas has occurred. They return for the same reasons others remained: attachment to rural community (Stack 1996). But returning or remaining on the land requires tolerating a new environmental health hazard. In the early twentieth century, diseases like pellagra, hookworm, and malaria took a toll. In the early twenty-first century, a landscape poisoned by the heavy use of new and dangerous chemicals has resulted in a range of debilitating ailments. Although agricultural scientists and farmers had been experimenting with arsenic-based poisons since the late nineteenth century, the kinds of chemicals employed in the post–World War II period and the extent of their use have negatively affected air quality and polluted the ground water supply. Although companies like Monsanto defend their use of such chemicals on the basis that scientific agriculture feeds the world's growing population, warning that mass starvation will be the result otherwise, health officials and environmentalists observe higher rates of cancer, autism, and autoimmune and neurological diseases in rural areas (Acharya et al. 2015).

Another even more haunting point of comparison between the two eras involves the issue of disfranchisement. In the early twentieth century, southern blacks were disfranchised by a racist Democratic Party supported by a hostile white community. In the early twenty-first century, the Republican Party has employed gerrymandering to marginalize black voters. Most of this gerrymandering has taken place in cities where most of the black population now resides. They have also shortened the early voting period, which, experts argue, disproportionately affects the poor. Finally, they have passed voter ID laws to disfranchise voters. These laws are supposedly aimed at illegal immigrants but actually target black voters instead. The poor, particularly women and underage youth, find it difficult to secure the forms of identification common to middle-class America. Republican leaders justify voter

ID laws and other restrictions much like their Democratic counterparts in the late nineteenth justified literacy tests and poll taxes: to clean up the electoral process. In fact, there is little difference between the new attack on voting rights and the disfranchisement measures promoted by Democrats in the late nineteenth century. Neither the voter ID laws nor the literacy tests and poll taxes of a hundred years ago use race as the specific identifier—that would be unconstitutional—but they are meant to target African American voters as surely as gerrymandered districts are designed to disadvantage Democrats—particularly African American Democrats ("Federal Trial in North Carolina Voting Rights Case Underway" 2015; "The Big Lie Behind the Voter ID Laws" 2014; Eichelberger 2014; Lee 2012).

Just as disfranchisement has revived in the white Republican South, so too has segregation—but under de facto rather than de jure circumstances. As school integration became a reality in the last four decades of the twentieth century, white families withdrew their children from public schools, especially in heavily black areas, and placed them in private schools. Public schools in the old cotton South have thus become the province of African American students, and the funding for those schools has declined as the fortunes of those who live in those areas have deteriorated. White students are attending better funded and equipped schools while black children secure an inferior education in underfunded schools in deteriorating buildings (Lakeview 2000; Whayne Interview 2011).[16]

The racist environment rural blacks in the modern South endure is not unlike that which existed a hundred years ago. Early-twenty-first-century African Americans, like their counterparts in the old Cotton Belt in the early twentieth century, live amongst a white population that harbors a higher percentage of racist attitudes than whites in the general population. Reflecting the demographic shift accompanying the transformation of agriculture after World War II, the violence against African Americans emerges most noticeably in urban settings such as Ferguson, Missouri, and Charleston, South Carolina. Displaced black and white farmers and their families thronged into southern cities that were unprepared for the additional population. Crowded up against each other in poor neighborhoods, black and white southerners, products of a rural diaspora, collided. African Americans who were no longer isolated in rural areas but massed in black neighborhoods built new churches that became targets of white hostility during the civil rights era. The bombing of the 16th Street Baptist Church in Birmingham, Alabama, in 1963 is perhaps the most infamous of these acts of terrorism but hardly the only one.

It was in the context of the determination to maintain segregation and

disfranchisement that the hoisting of the Confederate flag over the South Carolina capitol in 1961 occurred. Although it was supposedly raised to celebrate the
hundredth anniversary of the firing on Fort Sumter, an event that signaled the
beginning of the Civil War, the flag came to symbolize the state's opposition to
civil rights and its determination to maintain the status quo in race relations, a
fact that was not lost on African Americans. Over the next several decades, the
Confederate flag grew in popularity with some white southerners. Although the flag
would come down in South Carolina after an uproar over the shooting murder of
nine black men and women at the Emanuel AMC Church in Charleston in 2015,
a series of suspicious fires of black churches erupted, many of them in rural areas,
in the weeks that followed the shooting (Gettys 2015).

During Reconstruction, arsonists targeted African American rural churches to
discourage political and economic activism, and though they decreased in the
years that followed, the racism that inspired them persisted. Once segregation and
disfranchisement had been established in the South, the fires all but died out, but
they erupted again as the civil rights era arose. In the 1960s, as the Confederate
flag waved over the South Carolina capitol, white supremacists, who understood
the role that black churches played in the fight against segregation, firebombed and
burned African American churches across the South. Another epidemic occurred
in the 1990s, a period when white supremacy flared among economically marginalized young white men in the South. Over the course of eighteen months,
sixty-six black churches went up in flames, prompting the passage of the Church
Arson Prevention Act of 1996. The eruption of similar fires after the attack in
Charleston in 2015 struck a disturbing chord within the black community (Barnes
1996; Booth 1996; Abrams 1996; Hiller 1996; "Two Black Churches Burn on
Same Night in Small Community" 1996; "Baptist Church Burns in Saline County"
1996; "Arkansas Responds to Church Fires" 1996; George 1996; Whayne 1996;
Savili 2015; Blau 2015).[17]

Some hopeful signs exist in the South for African Americans. The Great Migration seems to have reversed, and growing numbers of blacks are moving South,
most of them to the Sun Belt South (Texas, North Carolina, and Florida), where
high-tech industries are attracting African Americans who grew up in western or
northern cities (Frey 2015). Some, however, are returning to the Arkansas and
Mississippi deltas, and a few of them have settled on farms. As one commentator
reports, this new generation of black farmers "don't stop at healthy food. They're
healing trauma, instilling collective values, and changing the way their commu-

nities think about the land." Many of them engage in collective farming, grow organic vegetables, and essentially function outside the existing capitalist agricultural economy. Of the black families who never left the South, some have embraced the "food justice" movement and addressed the pervasive problem of "food insecurity" and the existence of food deserts in the midst of some of the richest and most productive land in the country (Penniman 2016; Holt-Gimenez and Wang 2016).

Conclusion

In the beginning of the twentieth century, white supremacist ideology served the interests of economic elites struggling to hold on to power. In the early twenty-first century, a different set of economic elites in a different political party are attempting to use racist language to accomplish political ends. They, however, are finding it more difficult to do as the African American population, re-enfranchised by the victories of the 1950s and 1960s, are fighting back. In the earlier era, white plantation owners were locked into the production of cotton in a global marketplace and fashioned the only system that seemed possible to them: the creation of a permanent underclass through disfranchisement, segregation, and debt peonage—another kind of slavery. In this context, racist attitudes were—and are—a legacy of slavery but also of the system implemented after Emancipation. Poor and middling white southerners were kept in check by the "bloody shirt" of the Civil War and Reconstruction, and their racist attitudes cultivated by a political party—the Democratic Party—determined to maintain white supremacy and the plantation economy. Even New South advocates who envisioned a somewhat more modern South could not fully dislodge the power of the planter class. This system remained in place until the demographic changes wrought by the New Deal, World War II, and the rise of scientific agriculture that forever changed the nature of the plantation South. The movement of black southerners to the urban South gave impetus to the civil rights revolution of the 1950s and 1960s, and a new racism emerged, one founded not on the determination to keep African Americans in rural servitude, but one based on its close associate, white supremacy. Newly enfranchised African Americans transformed the southern Democratic Party, which repudiated its racist roots and embraced the black electorate. As southern whites unable to abide this profound alteration cast about for alternatives, the Republican Party, no longer the party of Lincoln and liberty, became their refuge.

The transformation of the plantation in the post–World War II period was accomplished without significant attention to the ramifications for those who remained in the rural South. Poor blacks, who had been crucial actors in the cotton economy, became superfluous to the needs of the capital-intensive neoplantation system but remained subject to the racist ideology that had undergirded it. Once implanted in the minds and traditions of white southerners, it proved difficult to dislodge. African Americans as well as poor white rural southerners in the old Cotton Belt are no better served by the emergence of the portfolio plantation system in the early twenty-first century. Fewer owners operating ever larger holdings of agricultural land seem intent upon increasing mechanization, massive inputs of chemicals, and ever-smaller numbers of employees.

The portfolio planters grow a variety of crops, as the focus of cotton production has shifted elsewhere. The old Cotton Belt might now be referred to as the "empire of soybeans," the most consistently prominent crop grown in the region. However, in the midst of this expansion of highly intensive capitalist agriculture, alternatives have emerged in the early twenty-first century that speak to countertrends. The growing number of consumers demanding organic alternatives to corporate crops represents one area of enterprise that rural African Americans occupying the margins have embraced. The food justice movement, the efforts of organizations to address the existence of food deserts, and, most importantly, the determination of a new generation of black farmers, may herald a more hopeful future.

Acknowledgments

This chapter was originally presented at the symposium "Race and Rurality in the Global Economy," organized by Michaeline Crichlow, Ann Marie Makhulu, Patricia Northover, and Caela O'Connor. Based on the excellent feedback I received from the participants, I substantially revised the chapter. The suggestions by Juan Giusti during the editing process made the chapter much stronger, and I am grateful to him for his contribution.

Notes

1. Although the articles by Acharya et al., Frey, and Clement discuss the black vote generally, they are true in rural areas of the South as well.

2. Hahn's Pulitzer Prize–winning monograph, *A Nation under Our Feet*, persuasively sets forth the argument for black political participation from the earliest years of Emancipation to 1920.

3. The migration of African Americans westward after the Civil War has been well covered generally in the historiography but remains ripe for further research. Matkin-Rawn's excellent study provides an in-depth analysis of migration to a single state, Arkansas.

4. I accept Bandfon's depiction of the Yazoo Mississippi delta as being made up of nine counties in Mississippi: De Soto, Tunica, Coahoma, Quitman, Tallahatchie, Bolivar, Sunflower, LeFlore, and Washington; it also includes two counties in Louisiana: Sharkey and Issaquena. I drew figures from Don Holly's table 7 on page 258, but I differ with him on what constitutes a delta county. I accept a more limited view, which encompasses the major cotton-producing counties only. I use the area identified by the Arkansas Department of Finance and Administration: Clay, Greene, Mississippi, Craighead, Jackson, Poinsett, Cross, Woodruff, Prairie, Monroe, St. Francis, Lee, Phillips, Arkansas, Desha, and Chicot counties.

5. African Americans made their predicament known by letters to black newspapers in the North like the *Chicago Defender* and often to public officials in Washington, DC. They also made public their dissatisfaction by joining the Back-to-Africa movement or by their flight to the urban North. In the early twentieth century, the federal government could no longer ignore the plight that landless African Americans faced in the rural South. The United States Supreme Court, citing a statute passed in 1867 to outlaw peonage involving Hispanics in New Mexico, ruled that the debt peonage of African Americans violated the Constitution. Soon, federal prosecutors brought a number of cases to court, but it was difficult to prove peonage and nearly impossible to secure convictions. Even when perpetrators were convicted, the penalties were light and hardly dissuaded labor-hunger planters from holding their black sharecroppers in servitude. Unable to work their way out of debt, sharecroppers found it nearly impossible to acquire the capital to purchase land. By 1900, only about 2 percent of the black farmers in the old cotton plantation South were farm owners. While only 39.3 percent of the country's rural population lived on farms in 1900, the percentage was far higher for African Americans: from 80 to 90 percent.

6. A series of articles by William F. Holmes establishes that whitecapping might occur for a variety of reasons and was not always driven by race (Holmes 1993, 1969, 1980, 1973).

7. Correspondence between the US attorney in US Attorney William Whipple to the Attorney General, Jan. 20, 24, Feb. 2, 7, 21, March 16, April 18, 1905; Attorney General to Whipple, Feb. 3, 25, March 1, 1905, Justice Department, National Archives, Record Group 60.

8. The Arkansas Church Records Survey was a project of the Works Progress Administration (WPA). It was conducted by WPA workers recruited within Arkansas and usually connected to the counties they were surveying. They typically consulted longtime members of the respective churches. The records are housed in the University of Arkansas Special

Collections Division and are unique in that they are the only known such records to be preserved in their (near) entirety.

9. The cryptic reference to the division with the Woodruff County Church makes full explication impossible, but Woodruff County blacks tended to support Lightfoot. Church Records, Woodruff County, 1940, box 148, folder 35.

10. In response, his request for information in early February 1928 about the organization of black extension in other southern states, L. N. Duncan, dean of the Agriculture College at Auburn, received replies from the following. All were addressed to Duncan: Dan T. Gray, Arkansas, Feb. 17, 1928; A. P. Spence, Florida, Feb. 18, 1928; J. Phil Campbell, Georgia, Feb. 16, 1928; W. R. Perkins, Louisiana, Feb. 17, 1928; R. S. Wilson, Mississippi, Feb. 16, 1928; I. O. Schaub, North Carolina, Feb. 15, 1928; D. P. Trent, Oklahoma, Feb. 24, 1928; D. W. Watkins, South Carolina, Feb. 15, 1928; C. E. Brehm, Tennessee, Feb 16, 1928; J. R. Hutcheson, Virginia, 1928. All located in Alabama Agricultural Extension Service Papers, box 355, Special Collections and Archives, Auburn University.

11. Otis O'Neal, Special Extension Agent, to J. Phillip Campbell, director of Extension in Georgia, June 9, 1916, p. 3, General Correspondence, office of the Secretary of Agriculture, Negroes, box 1, RG 16, National Archives Two, College Park, Maryland.

12. *Osceola Times*, February 18, 1921, p. 5.

13. A statistical analysis of black churches in Mississippi County across denomination reveals that rural African American churches were rarely painted and had few adornments. Only those in the small towns of Osceola and Blytheville, supported by a small black middle class, could afford to paint their churches or fit them with bells, pianos, and so forth.

14. The Lowery lynching was covered widely and attracted national attention. The references represent a sampling of the coverage.

15. For New Deal programs in agriculture, see Pete Daniel, *Breaking the Land*; and David Hamilton, *New Day to New Deal*; for New Deal programs the South, see Kirby, *Rural Worlds Lost*; James and Namorato, eds., *The New Deal and the South*. For works specifically dealing with African Americans and the New Deal, see Sullivan, *Days of Hope*. For the controversy involving the crisis in the sharecropping and tenancy system caused by the New Deal, see Roll, *The Spirit of Rebellion*; Paul E. Mertz, *New Deal Policy*; H. L. Mitchell, *Mean Things Happening*; and Conrad, *The Forgotten Farmers*. For groundbreaking work on that conservation and modernization, see Phillips, *This Land, This Nation*; Badger, *The New Deal*; and Wright, "The New Deal and Modernization of the South."

16. For the Arkansas situation concerning school funding issues that disadvantage African Americans, see *Lakeview School District No. 25 v. Huckabee*, 340 Ark. 481 10 S.W.3d 392 (2000). For Governor Mike Beebe's perspective, see Mike Beebe interview with Jeannie Whayne, Little Rock, Arkansas, November 2, 2011, held in author's possession.

17. For the 1990s, see Barnes 1996; Booth 1996; *Northwest Arkansas Times*, August 22, 26, 1996; September 1, 1996; Abrams 1996; Hiller 1996; George 1996; Whayne, June 21, 1996. For coverage of the fires in late June and in July 2015, see Savali 2015 and Blau 2015.

References

ABC News. "Federal Trial in North Carolina Voting Rights Case Underway." July 13, 2015. Retrieved from http://abcnews.go.com/US/wireStory/federal-trial-north-carolina-voting-rights-case-begin-32413674.

Abrams, Jim. "Congress Makes Federal Case of Even Small Church Arsons." *Arkansas Democrat-Gazette*, June 19, 1996, p. 1.

Acharya, Avidit, Matthew Blackwell, and Maya Sen. 2015. "Legacy of Slavery Still Fuels Anti-Black Attitudes in the Deep South." University of Rochester. Retrieved from http://www.rochester.edu/news/show.php?id=7202.

Aiken, Charles S. 1998. *The Cotton Plantation South since the Civil War*. Baltimore and London: Johns Hopkins University Press.

Alabama Extension Service Papers. Special Collections and Archives, Auburn University.

Arkansas Church Records Survey. 1939, 1940. Works Progress Administration, Historical Records Survey, Arkansas, University of Arkansas Special Collections Division, Fayetteville, AK.

Arkansas Democrat. "Friends of Lowery Brought to Pen for Safekeeping." January 28, 1921, p. 1.

———. "Lynching of Negro May Precipitate Legislative Fight." January 27, 1921, p. 1.

———. "Slayer of Planter Taken from Train by Mob at Sardis, Miss." January 26, 1921, p. 1.

Arkansas Department of Finance and Administration. 2016. Counties of Arkansas. Retrieved from http://www.dfa.arkansas.gov/Pages/Delta.aspx.

Arkansas Gazette. "Governor Would Avert Lynching." January 25, 1921, p. 8.

———. "Will Bring Negro Back to Arkansas." January 23, 1921.

Badger, Anthony. 1989. *The New Deal: The Depression Years, 1933–1940*. London: Macmillan.

Barnes, Kenneth C. 2004. *Journey of Hope: The Back-to-Africa Movement in Arkansas in the Late 1800s*. Chapel Hill: University of North Carolina Press.

Barnes, Julian E. 1996. "'Painful Memories' of Torched Churches Yield Debatable List." *Arkansas Democrat-Gazette*, June 11, 1996.

Barry, John. 1997. *Rising Tide: The Great Mississippi Flood of 1927 and How It Changed America*. New York: Simon & Schuster.

Beck, E. M., and S. E. Tolnay. 1990. "The Killing Fields of the Deep South: The Market for Cotton and the Lynching of Blacks, 1882–1930." *American Sociological Review* 55 (4): 526–539.

Beckert, Sven. 2014. *Empire of Cotton: A Global History*. New York: Knopf.

Blackmon, Douglas A. 2008. *Slavery by Another Name: The Re-enslavement of Black People in America from the Civil War to World War II*. New York: Doubleday.

Blau, Max. "Church Burnings after Charleston: Part of a 'Long, Dark,' History that Never Stopped." *The Guardian*, July 2, 2015. Retrieved from http://www.theguardian.com/us-news/2015/jul/02/us-church-burnings-race-south-carolina.

Booth, William. "In Church Fires, a Pattern but No Conspiracy." *Washington Post*, June 19, 1996.

Brandfon, Robert L. 1967. *Cotton Kingdom of the New South: A History of the Yazoo Mississippi Delta from Reconstruction to the Twentieth Century.* Cambridge, MA: Harvard University Press.

Brundage, William Fitzhugh. 1993. *Lynching in the New South: Georgia and Virginia, 1880–1930.* Urbana: University of Illinois Press.

Carpenter, Stephen. 2012. "The USDA Discrimination Cases: Pigford, In re Black Farmers, Keepseagle, Garcia, and Love." *Drake Journal of Agricultural Law* 17 (1): 1–35. Retrieved from https://litigation-essentials.lexisnexis.com/webcd/app?action=DocumentDisplay&crawlid=1&doctype=cite&docid=17+Drake+J.+Agric.+L.+1&srctype=smi&srcid=3B15&key=eefd63069999b95348506888d76415a3.

Carrier, Lyman. 1937. "The United States Agricultural Society, 1852–1860: Its Relation to the Origin of the United States Department of Agriculture and the Land Grant Colleges." *Agricultural History* 11 (4): 278–288.

Cecelski, David, and Timothy Tyson, eds. 1998. *Democracy Betrayed: The Wilmington Race Riot of 1898 and Its Legacy.* Chapel Hill: University of North Carolina Press.

Chicago Defender. "Gasoline and Dry Leaves Used by Whites." February 5, 1921, p. 1.

Clement, Scott. "How Black Voters Could Determine the 2016 Election." *Washington Post*, June 11, 2015. Retrieved from https://www.washingtonpost.com/news/the-fix/wp/2015/06/11/how-black-voters-could-determine-the-2016-election/.

Cobb, James C., and Michael V. Namorato, eds. 1984. *The New Deal and the South.* Jackson: University Press of Mississippi.

Commercial Appeal. "Negro, Dual Slayer, Burned at Stake." February 27, 1921, p. 1.

Conrad, David Eugene. 1965. *The Forgotten Farmers: The Story of Sharecroppers in the New Deal.* Urbana: University of Illinois Press.

Cowan, Tadlock, and Jody Feder. 2013. "The Pigford Cases: USDA Settlement of Discrimination Suits by Black Farmers." Congressional Research Service. Retrieved from http://nationalaglawcenter.org/wp-content/uploads/assets/crs/RS20430.pdf.

Creech, Joe. 2006. *Righteous Indignation: Religion and the Populist Revolution.* Urbana: University of Illinois Press.

Crouch, Barry. 1992. *The Freedmen's Bureau and Black Texans.* Austin: University of Texas Press.

Danbom, David, ed. 2006. *Born in the Country: A History of Rural America.* Baltimore: Johns Hopkins University Press.

Daniel, Pete. 1972. *Shadow of Slavery: Peonage in the South, 1901–1969.* Urbana: University of Illinois Press.

———. 1977. *Deep'n as It Come: The 1927 Mississippi River Flood.* New York: Oxford University Press.

———. 1985. *Breaking the Land: The Transformation of Cotton, Tobacco, and Rice Cultures since 1880.* Urbana and Chicago: University of Illinois Press.

———. 1990. "Going Among Strangers: Southern Reactions to World War II." *Journal of American History* 77 (3): 886–911.

———. 2013. *Dispossession: Discrimination Against African American Farmers in the Age of Civil Rights.* Chapel Hill: University of North Carolina Press.

Dattel, Gene. 2009. *Cotton and Race in the Making of America: The Human Costs of Economic Power.* Chicago: Ian R. Dee.

Eichelberger, Erika. 2014. "Texas Just Won the Right to Disenfranchise 600,000 People: It's Not the First Time." *Mother Jones* (October 21, 2014) http://www.motherjones.com/print/262886. Accessed March 20, 2015.

El Paso Herald. "Negro Burned at Stake Should Think of Torture He Misses by Being in U.S. Instead of China." January 28, 1921, p. 6.

———. "Negro, Hunted by Arkansas Mob, Tells El Paso Detective of Slaying Two Men on Farm," January 19, 1921, p. 4.

Finley, Randy. 1996. *From Slavery to Uncertain Freedom: The Freedmen's Bureau in Arkansas.* Fayetteville: University of Arkansas Press.

Fite, Gilbert C. 1984. *Cotton Fields No More: Southern Agriculture, 1865–1980.* Lexington: University Press of Kentucky.

Frey, William. "Minority Turnout Determined the 2012 Election." Brookings (May 10, 2013). Retrieved from http://www.brookings.edu/research/papers/2013/05/10-election-2012-minority-voter-turnout-frey.

———. "The Black Exodus from the North—and West." Brookings (February 2, 2015). Retrieved from http://www.brookings.edu/blogs/the-avenue/posts/2015/02/02/black-exodus-north-west-frey.

George, Emmett. "Suspicious Fire Ravages Church West of Helena: Second Black Church Destroyed in Phillips County since August." *Arkansas Democrat-Gazette*, September 27, 1996.

Gettys, Travis. "SC Raised Confederate Flag in 1961 to Insult Nine Black Protesters and Took It Down to Honor Nine Slain." *Raw Story* (July 9, 2015). Retrieved from http://www.rawstory.com/2015/07/sc-raised-confederate-flag-in-1961-to-insult-nine-black-protesters-and-took-it-down-to-honor-nine-slain/.

Giesen, James C. 2011. *Boll Weevil Blues: Cotton, Myth and Power in the American South.* Chicago: University of Chicago Press.

Giggee, John M. 2008. *After Redemption: Jim Crow and the Transformation of African American Religion in the Delta, 1875–1915.* New York and London: Oxford University Press.

Goldfield, David R. 1991. *Black, White and Southern: Race Relations and Southern Culture, 1940 to the Present.* Baton Rouge: Louisiana State University Press.

Goodwyn, Lawrence. 1976. *Democratic Promise: The Populist Moment in America*. New York and London: Oxford University Press.

Graves, John William. 1990. *Town and Country: Race Relations in an Urban-Rural Context: Arkansas, 1865–1905*. Fayetteville: University of Arkansas Press.

Greene, Alison Collis. 2015. *No Depression in Heaven: The Great Depression, the New Deal, and the Transformation of Religion in the Delta*. Oxford and New York: Oxford University Press.

Gregory, James N. 2007. *The Southern Diaspora: How the Great Migrations of Black and White Southerners Transformed America*. Chapel Hill: University of North Carolina Press.

Grubbs, Donald. 1971. *Cry from the Cotton: The Southern Tenant Farmers' Union and the New Deal*. Chapel Hill: University of North Carolina Press.

Hahn, Steven. 1983. *Roots of Southern Populism: Yeoman Farmers and the Transformation of the Georgia Upcountry 1850–1890*. New York and London: Oxford University Press.

———. 2003. *A Nation under Our Feet: Black Political Struggles in the Rural South from Slavery to the Great Migration*. Cambridge, MA: Belknap Press of Harvard University Press.

Hamilton, David E. 1991. *From New Deal to New Deal: American Farm Policy from Hoover to Roosevelt, 1928–1933*. Chapel Hill: University of North Carolina Press.

Helena World. "Henry Lowery Bound to Log and Cremated." January 27, 1921, p. 1.

Hiller, Michelle. "Clues Sought in Church Ashes: Generations of Blacks Worshiped at Sites." *Arkansas Democrat-Gazette*, August 23, 1996.

Hoffschwelle, Mary S. 2006. *The Rosenwald Schools of the American South*. Gainesville and Tallahassee: University Press of Florida.

Holly, Donald. 1993. "The Plantation Heritage: Agriculture in the Arkansas Delta." In *The Arkansas Delta: Land of Paradox*, edited by Jeannie Whayne and Willard B. Gatewood. Fayetteville: University of Arkansas Press.

Holmes, William F. 1969. "Whitecapping: Agrarian Violence in Mississippi, 1902–1906." *Journal of Southern History* 35 (4): 588–611.

———. (1973). "Whitecapping in Mississippi: Agrarian Violence in the Populist Era." *Mid-America* 55 (1): 134–148.

———. (1980). "Whitecapping in Georgia: Carroll and Houston Counties, 1893." *Georgia Historical Quarterly* 64 (4): 388–404.

———. (1981). "Moonshiners and Whitecaps in Alabama, 1893." *Alabama Review* 24 (1): 31–49.

Holt-Gimenez, Eric, and Yi Wang. 2012. "Reform or Transformation? The Pivotal Role of Food Justice in the U.S. Food Movement." *Race/Ethnicity* 5 (1). Retrieved from https://foodfirst.org/publication/reform-or-transformation-the-pivotal-role-of-food-justice-in-the-us-food-movement/.

Jones-Branch, Cherrise. 2014. "Empowering Families and Communities: African American Home Demonstration Agents in Arkansas, 1913–1965." In *Race and Ethnicity in*

Arkansas: New Perspectives, edited by John A. Kirk, 85–96. Fayetteville: University of Arkansas Press.

Justice Department. 1905. United States Attorney William Whipple to Attorney General of the United States, Jan 20, 24, Feb. 2, 7, 21, March 16, April 18, 1905; Attorney General to Whipple, Feb 3, 24, March 1, 1905. National Archives, Record Group 60.

Kazin, Michael. 1995. *The Populist Persuasion: An American History*. New York: Basic Books.

Kirby, Jack Temple. 1998. *Rural Words Lost: The American South, 1920–1960*. Baton Rouge: Louisiana State University Press.

Koerselman, Gary H. 1977. "Secretary Hoover and National Farm Policy: Problems of Leadership." *Agricultural History* 51 (2): 378–395.

Kousser, Morgan. 1974. *The Shaping of Southern Politics: Suffrage Restriction and the Establishment of the One-Party South, 1880–1910*. New Haven and London: Yale University Press.

Kraut, Alan M. 2003. *Goldberger's War: The Life and work of a Public Health Crusader*. New York: Hill and Wang.

Lakeview School District No. 25 v. Huckabee, 340 Ark. 481 10 S.W.3d 392 (2000).

Lee, Suevon. "Everything You've Ever Wanted to Know About Voter ID Laws." *ProPublica* (November 5, 2012). Retrieved from http://www.propublica.org/article/everything-youve-ever-wanted-to-know-about-voter-id-laws.

Litwack, Leon F. 1979. *Been in a Storm So Long: The Aftermath of Slavery*. New York: Knopf.

Lovett, Bobby L. 2015. *America's Historically Black Colleges and Universities: A Narrative History, 1837–2009*. Macon, GA: Mercer University Press.

Maffly-Kipp, Laurie F. 2001. "The Church in the Southern Black Community." In *Documenting the American South*. Retrieved from http://www.docsouth.unc.edu/church/intro.html. Accessed May 6, 2016.

Matkin-Rawn, Story. 2013. " 'The Great Negro State of the Country': Arkansas's Reconstruction and the Other Great Migration." *Arkansas Historical Quarterly* 72 (1): 1–41.

———. (2014). " 'Send Forth More Laborers into the Vineyard': Understanding the African American Exodus to Arkansas." In *Race and Ethnicity in Arkansas: New Perspectives*, edited by John A. Kirk, 31–45. Fayetteville: University of Arkansas Press.

Mays, Benjamin E. 1960. "The Significance of the Negro Private and Church-Related College." *Journal of Negro Education* 29 (3): 245–251.

Mertz, Paul E. 1978. *New Deal Policy and Southern Rural Poverty*. Baton Rouge: Louisiana State University Press.

Mills, Kay. 2007. *This Little Light of Mine: The Life of Fannie Lou Hamer*. Lexington: University of Kentucky Press.

Minor, James T. 2008. "A Contemporary Perspective on the Role of Public HBCUs: Perspicacity from Mississippi." *Journal of Negro Education* 77 (4): 323–335.

Mitchell, H. L. 1979. *Mean Things Happening: The Life and Times of H. L. Mitchell, Co-Founder of the Southern Tenant Farmers Union*. Montclair, NJ: Allanheld, Osmun and Company Publishers.

National Association for the Advancement of Colored People. 1921. "An American Lynching: Being the Burning at Stake of Henry Lowry at Nodena, Arkansas, January 26, 1921, as Told in American Newspapers."

———. 1969. *Thirty Years of Lynching in the United States, 1889–1913*. New York: Negro Universities Press.

Nevins, Allan. 1962. *The State Universities and Democracy*. Urbana: University of Illinois Press.

New York Times. "The Big Lie Behind Voter ID Laws." October 13, 2014. Retrieved from http://www.nytimes.com/2014/10/13/opinion/the-big-lie-behind-voter-id-laws.html?_r=0.

Northwest Arkansas Times. "Arkansas Responds to Church Fires." September 1, 1996.

———. "Baptist Church Burns in Saline County." August 26, 1996.

———. "Two Black Churches Burn on Same Night in Small Community." August 22, 1996.

O'Brien, Molly Townes. 1998. "Justice John Marshall Harlan as Prophet: The Plessy Dissenter's Color-Blind Constitution." *William and Mary Bill of Rights Journal* 7 (3): 753–775. Retrieved from http://scholarhip.law.wm-edu/wmborj/fol6/iss3/5.

Osceola Times. "An Explanation," December 4, 1897, p. 4.

———. "Lowery, Negro Murderer Captured in El Paso, Texas." January 21, 1921, p. 1.

———. "Murder Most Foul." November 13, 1897, p. 1.

———. "Negro Farmers Meet." February 18, 1921, p. 5.

———. "Negro Murderer Burned at Stake." January 28, 1921, p. 1.

———. "Strung Up, According to Programme." November 20, 1897, p. 4.

———. Untitled editorial, December 18, 1897, p. 1.

Painter, Nell Irvin. 1976. *The Exodusters*. New York: W. W. North.

Penniman, Leah. "After a Century in Decline, Black Farmers are Back and On the Rise." *YES! Magazine* (May 5, 2016). Retrieved from http://www.countercurrents.org/penniman070516.htm.

Perman, Michael. 2001. *Struggle for Mastery: Disfranchisement in the South, 1888–1908*. Chapel Hill: University of North Carolina Press.

Petty, Adrienne Monteith. 2013. *Standing Their Ground: Small Farmers in North Carolina since the Civil War*. New York: Oxford University Press.

Phillips, Sarah T. 2007. *This Land, This Nation: Conservation, Rural America, and the New Deal*. New York: Cambridge University Press.

Pickens, William. 1921. "The American Congo: The Burning of Henry Lowery." *The Nation* 112 (2907) 426–428.

Pigford v. Glickman, 185 F.R.D. 82 (DC Dist. 1999).

Poddy, Ralph. *Memphis Press*. "Kill Negro by Inches." January 27, 1921, p. 1.

Postel, Charles. 2007. *The Populist Vision.* Oxford and New York: Oxford University Press.

Powell, Lawrence. 1980. *New Masters: Northern Planters during the Civil War.* New Haven, CT: Yale University Press.

Ransom, Roger L., and Richard Sutch. 1971. *One Kind of Freedom: The Economic Consequences of Emancipation.* Cambridge, UK: Cambridge University Press.

Ravage, John W. 1997. *Black Pioneers.* Salt Lake City: University of Utah Press.

Reid, Debra, and Evan Bennett. 2012. *Beyond Forty Acres and a Mule: African American Farm Owners Since Reconstruction.* Gainesville: University Press of Florida.

Richter, William L. 1991. *Overreached on All Sides: The Freedmen's Bureau Administrators in Texas, 1865–1868.* College Station: Texas A&M University Press.

Rolinson, Mary G. 2007. *The Universal Negro Improvement Association in the Rural South: 1920–1927.* Chapel Hill: University of North Carolina Press.

Roll, Jarod. 2010. *Spirit of Rebellion: Labor and Religion in the New Cotton South.* Urbana: University of Illinois Press.

Sanders, Kindaka Jamal. 2013. "Re-Assembling Osiris: Rule 23, the Black Farmers Case, and Reparations." *Penn State Law Review* 118 (2): 339–373. Retrieved from http:// www.pennstatelawreview.org/118/2/3%20-%20Sanders%20(final).pdf.

Savage, Beth L., and Carol D. Shull. 2016. *Odd Fellows Cemetery.* Oktibbeha County Mississippi Genealogy. Retrieved from http://oktibbeha.msghn.org/cemeteries/African_American_Odd_Fellows_Cemetery_Oktibbeha.shtml.

Savali, Kirsten West. "Silence Around Who Is Burning Black Churches Speaks Volumes." *The Root,* July 5, 2015. Retrieved from http://www.commondreams.org/views/2015/07/05/ silence-around-who-burning-black-churches-speaks-volumes.

Schwalm, Leslie A. 1997. " 'Sweet Dreams of Freedom': Freedwomen's Reconstruction of Life and Labor in Lowcountry South Carolina." *Journal of Women's History* 9 (1): 9–32.

Smith, Solomon K. 2000. "The Freedmen's Bureau in Shreveport: The Struggle for Control of the Red River District." *Louisiana History* 41 (4): 435–465.

Stack, Carol B. 1996. *Call to Home: African-Americans Reclaim the Rural South.* New York: Basic Books.

Stockley, Grif. 2001. *Blood in Their Eyes: The Elaine Race Massacres of 1919.* Fayetteville: University of Arkansas Press.

Street, James. 1957. *New Revolution in the Cotton Economy: Mechanization and Its Consequences.* Chapel Hill: University of North Carolina Press.

Sullivan, Patricia. 1996. *Days of Hope: Race and Democracy in the New Deal Era.* Chapel Hill: University of North Carolina Press.

The Sun (El Paso). "Fled from a Murderous Sheriff." January 19, 1921, p. 1.

Tarmann, Allison. "Fifty Years of Demographic Change in Rural America." Population Reference Bureau (January 2003). Retrieved from http://www.prb.org/Publications/ Articles/2003/FiftyYearsofDemographicChangeinRuralAmerica.aspx.

Trotter, Joe William. 2004. "African American Fraternal Organizations in American History: An Introduction." *Social Science History* 28 (3): 355–356.

USDA. 1916. Secretary of Agriculture. National Archives Two, College Park, Maryland.

Wallach, Jennifer Jensen, and John A. Kirk, eds. 2011. *Arsnick: The Student Nonviolent Coordinating Committee in Arkansas*. Fayetteville: University of Arkansas Press.

Whayne, Jeannie. 1983. Interview of George Stith, March 28, 1983. Transcript in possession of author.

———. 1992. "The Segregated Farm Program in Poinsett County, Arkansas." *Mississippi Quarterly: The Journal of Southern Culture* 45 (4): 421–438.

———. 1996. *A New Plantation South: Land, Labor, and Federal Favor in Twentieth Century Arkansas*. Charlottesville, University of Virginia Press, pp. 191, 197.

———. Letter to the editor, *Wall Street Journal*, June 21, 1996.

———. 1998. "Black Farmers and the Agricultural Cooperative Extension Service: The Alabama Experience, 1945–1965." *Agricultural History* 72 (3): 523–551.

———. 1999. "Low Villains and Wickedness in High Places: Race and Class in the Elaine Riot." *Arkansas Historical Quarterly* 58 (3): 285–313.

———. 2011. *Delta Empire: Lee Wilson and the Transformation of Agriculture in the New South*. Baton Rouge: Louisiana State University Press.

———. 2011. Interview with Governor Mike Beebe, Little Rock, Arkansas, November 2, 2011. Held in author's possession.

———. 2012. "Caging the Blind Tiger: Race, Class and Family in the Battle for Prohibition in Small Town Arkansas." *Arkansas Historical Quarterly* 71 (1): 44–60.

———. (2013). "Black Women in the Civil Rights Movement in Arkansas." In *Southern Black Women in the Modern Civil Rights Movement*, edited by Bruce A. Glasrud and Merline Pitre. College Station: Texas A&M University Press.

Whitaker, Robert. 2008. *On the Laps of Gods: The Red Summer of 1919 and the Struggle for Justice that Remade a Nation*. New York: Crown.

White, Jr., Calvin. 2012. *The Rise to Respectability: Race, Religion, and the Church of God in Christ*. Fayetteville: University of Arkansas Press.

Williamson, Joel. 1965. *After Slavery: The Negro in South Carolina during Reconstruction, 1861–1877*. Chapel Hill: University of North Carolina Press.

Woodman, Harold. 1995. *New South New Law: The Legal Foundations of Credit and Labor Relations in the Postbellum Agricultural South*. Baton Rouge and London: Louisiana State University Press.

Woodruff, Nan Elizabeth. 1985. *As Rare as Rain: Federal Relief in the Great Southern Drought of 1930–31*. Urbana: University of Illinois Press.

———. 1993. *American Congo: The African American Freedom Struggle in the Delta*. Cambridge, MA: Harvard University Press.

Woods, Randall B. 1998. *African Americans on the Western Frontier*. Niwot: University Press of Colorado.

Woodson, Carter G. 1969. *A Century of Negro Migration*. New York: Russell and Russell.

Woodward, C. Vann. 1951. *Origins of the New South, 1877–1913*. Baton Rouge: Louisiana State University Press.

Wright, Gavin. 1986. *Old South, New South: Revolutions in the Southern Economy since the Civil War*. Baton Rouge: Louisiana State University Press.

———. "The New Deal and Modernization of the South." *Federal History Online* (January 5, 2010). Retrieved from http://shfg.org/shfg/wp-content/uploads/2011/01/5-Wright-design5-_Layout-1.pdf.

CONTRIBUTORS

Daniel B. Ahlquist is an assistant professor at James Madison College at Michigan State University, where his teaching and research explore the ways in which political and economic inequalities between social actors play out through uneven relationships to the environment, technology, and capital. His current research interrogates the sociomaterial dimensions of state forest conservation and development policies, agrarian change, displacement, and changing forms of inequality and risk in upland northern Thailand.

Michaeline A. Crichlow is a professor of African and African American studies and sociology at Duke University and senior research fellow at Duke's Kenan Institute for Ethics, as well as a member of the Center of Latin American and Caribbean Studies at Duke University. She is the author with Patricia Northover of *Globalization and the Post-Creole Imagination: Notes on Fleeing the Plantation* (2009) and *Negotiating Caribbean Freedom: Peasants and the State in Development* (2005). She has recently coedited *Aimé Césaire: Negritude Revisited* (2015) with *South Atlantic Quarterly* and is currently completing a monograph on development and the politics of place in Hispaniola.

Amanda Flaim teaches at James Madison College at Michigan State University. She studies problems and paradoxes in human rights policy, including statelessness and citizenship, human trafficking, and the global expansion of rights to education and birth registration. Her current research projects explore the risk of trafficking among Cambodian and Burmese men and boys in the Thai fishing industry, and the causes and consequences of statelessness in Thailand and Nepal. She has consulted for several NGOs and United Nations agencies, including designing and leading two of the largest country-level surveys of stateless populations conducted to date. Her most recent publication can be found in the edited volume *Citizenship in Question* (2017).

James Giblin is a professor of African history at the University of Iowa. He has long experience in Tanzania. Among his publications are *A History of the Excluded: Making Family and Memory a Refuge from State in Twentieth-Century Tanzania* (2005) and (coedited with Jamie Monson) *Maji Maji: Lifting the Fog of War* (2010).

Olivia Maria Gomes da Cunha is an associate professor of Anthropology, Museu Nacional, Federal University of Rio de Janeiro. She was a postdoctoral fellow at Harvard University (1999–2000), visiting professor at New York University (2006–2007), and a John Simon Guggenheim Foundation fellow in 2002. Her research for Guggenheim resulted in a manuscript on ethnography, archives, and artifacts of knowledge in Cuba, Brazil, and the United States now under evaluation. She has published on post-Emancipation and social movements in Brazil and Cuba. Her current research is on art, creativity, and other cosmo-political transformations among the Maroon Ndyukas in Moengo, Eastern Suriname, after the late-1980s civil war.

Juan Giusti-Cordero is a professor of history at the University of Puerto Rico, Río Piedras, and director of its Caribbean Social Science Archive. His areas of interest include the social history of sugar plantation production in the Caribbean and Afro–Puerto Rican cultural history. Giusti-Cordero is coeditor of *Sugarlandia Revisited: Sugar and Colonialism in Asia and the Americas, 1800–1940* (2007) and *Sociedad y cultura contemporánea: Introducción a las ciencias sociales* (2016). He is working on a book on the history of the Afro–Puerto Rican peasant/proletarian community, Piñones (Loíza). Giusti-Cordero directed UPR's Urban Action Center (CAUCE) in the town center of Río Piedras. He has advised community groups in Piñones and Vieques on the impact of resort development and military installations.

Ray A. Kea is an emeritus professor of history, in the History Department at the University of California, Riverside. His recent publications include the following: "A Cultural and Social History of Ghana from the Seventeenth to the Nineteenth Century," in *The Gold Coast in the Age of the Trans-Atlantic Trade*, 2 vols. (2012); "Zones of Exchange and World History: Akani Captaincies on the Seventeenth Century West African Gold Coast," in *Akan Peoples in Africa and the Diaspora: A Historical Reader*, edited by Kwasi Konadu (2015); and "The Mediterranean and Africa," in *A Companion to Mediterranean History*, edited by Peregrine Horden and Sharon Kinoshita (2015).

Philip McMichael is a professor of development sociology at Cornell University. Author of the award-winning *Settlers and the Agrarian Question* (1984), *Development and Social Change: A Global Perspective* (2016, 6th edition), and *Food Regimes and Agrarian Questions* (2013, with Spanish, Portuguese, Korean, Chinese, Italian, Thai, and Bahasa translations), he has also edited *Contesting Development: Critical Struggles for Social Change* (2010). His current research is on land grabs and land rights. He has worked with FAO, UNRISD, Vía Campesina, and the International Planning Committee for Food Sovereignty, and is a member of the Civil Society Mechanism of the FAO's Committee on World Food Security.

Wazir Mohamed is an associate professor of sociology at Indiana University East in Richmond, Indiana. His most recent articles are on Guyana's social history, including "African Labor in Guyana and the Expansion of the Second Slavery," in *New Frontiers of Slavery*, edited by Dale Tomich and Rafael Marquese (2016); "Emancipation and the struggle for freedom in British Guiana in the Shadow of the Second Slavery," in *The Second Slavery: Mass Slaveries and Modernity in the Americas and in the Atlantic Basin*, edited by Javier Laviña and Michael Zeuske (2014); and "The Limits of Western Democracy," in *Social Justice, Poverty and Race: Normative and Empirical Points of View*, edited by Paul Kriese and Randall E. Osborne (2011).

Patricia Northover specializes in economic philosophy and critical development studies. She is a senior fellow in the Sir Arthur Lewis Institute of Social and Economic Studies at the University of the West Indies, Mona (SALISES, UWI) and chair of its sustainable rural and agricultural development research cluster. Northover is the author and coauthor of several articles and edited volumes on the philosophy of economics, cultural dynamics, economic growth, climate change, and Caribbean development, published in the *South Atlantic Quarterly*, *Cambridge Journal of Economics*, *Cultural Dynamics*, *Global South*, *Caribbean Dialogue*, *Small States Digest*, and *Social and Economic Studies*. She is currently completing a contracted book on *Growth Theory: A Philosophical Perspective* and a documentary on the role of sugar in modern Jamaica.

Dana E. Powell is an assistant professor of anthropology at Appalachian State University in Boone, North Carolina, where she directs the undergraduate program in Social Practice and Sustainability. Her first book, *Landscapes of Power: Politics* *of Energy in the Navajo Nation*, was published by Duke University Press in 2018. Powell has also published on territory, sovereignty, indigenous social movements, energy infrastructure, and ethnographic research in several journals, including: *Development, Journal of Political Ecology, Anthropological Quarterly*, and *Collaborative Anthropologies*, and in edited volumes such as *Indians & Energy: Exploitation and Opportunity in the American Southwest, Insurgent Encounters: Transnational Activism*, and *Ethnography.*

Gabriela Valdivia is an associate professor of geography at the University of North Carolina at Chapel Hill. Her research examines the politics of natural resource governance in Latin America, particularly the relationship between oil, citizenship, and environmental justice. She is coauthor of the book *Oil, Revolution, and Indigenous Citizenship in Ecuadorian Amazonia* (2016) with Flora Lu and Néstor Silva. She has published on environmental movements, gender and resources, resource nationalisms, and indigenous rights in the *Annals of the American Association of Geographers, Conservation & Society, Environment and Planning A, Focaal, Latin American Perspectives, Gender Place and Culture, Geoforum*, and *Political Geography*.

Jeannie Whayne is university professor of history at the University of Arkansas and author of two award-winning books, *Delta Empire: Lee Wilson and the Transformation of Agriculture in the New South* (2011) and *A New Plantation South: Land, Labor, and Federal Favor in Twentieth-Century Arkansa*s (1996). She is the editor or coauthor of nine other books, including *The Ongoing Burden of Southern History: Politics and Identity in the Twenty-First-Century South* (2012). Whayne is a distinguished lecturer with the Organization of American Historians, a fellow of the Agricultural History Society, and winner of the Arkansas Historical Association's Lifetime Achievement Award.

INDEX

Abrahams, Roger D., 203, 204, 231
accommodation: Navajo women and, 12;
rice and, 127; subsistence production
and, 144n3; tactics of, 2; in United
States' internal periphery, 13
affirmative action, 247
Afobaka dam, 102
Africa: back-to-Africa movement, 256–257,
273n5; creolization versus African
origins and identity, 203; food crops
connect Americas and, 127–128,
144n2; general underdevelopment of
contemporary, 28; global economies and
historical change in zones of rurality
of, 21–67; historiography of, 21–24;
independence in, 151; materialist
approach to history of, 24–26;
re-centering in globalizing economies,
26–29; rice coast of, 126; Universal
Negro Improvement Association and,
262. *See also* Tanzania
African Americans: agricultural bureaucracy
and black farmers, 257–260;
agricultural colleges for, 257; back-to-
Africa movement, 256–257, 273n5;
back-to-the-South movement, 268,
270–271; Black Belt, 220, 247; in
cotton production, 247, 248, 272;
decline in farm population, 267;
disenfranchisement of, 251–252,
268–269, 270, 271; Emancipation from

slavery, 249–251; fraternal organizations
of, 261; the Great Depression and,
263–265; lynching, 209, 252, 260,
262; migration to the North, 222,
256–257, 265, 269, 271; in Mississippi
Delta, 208–210, 211–213, 217–222;
modernization of capitalist agriculture
and, 13; NAACP, 252, 266; poverty
in the South, 248, 254, 267–268; race
in reconstruction of rural society in
the cotton South since the Civil War,
247–274; racial uplift philosophy, 258;
rediscovering ruralities of, 199–245;
remain in rural areas, 268; schools,
255; violence against, 252–255; voting
rights for, 249, 250–252. *See also*
black churches; civil rights movement;
segregation (Jim Crow)
Afro-Ecuadorians, 156–157, 158, 159–
161, 167, 168, 169n4
Agamben, Giorgio, 11
Agard-Jones, Vanessa, 14n2
Agiti-Ondo (Suriname), 101
agregado labor, 211
agribusiness, 247
Agricultural Adjustment Administration
(AAA), 263, 264
agricultural colleges, 257
agricultural subsidies: in New Deal, 263;
in United States for rice, 125, 133–134,
136–137, 138, 143, 144, 144n1

agriculture: agribusiness, 247; bananas, 151, 157, 158, 160, 163; bureaucracy develops, 257–260; capitalist, 13, 130–131, 272; cassava, 211, 219, 229; changing political economy of regulation and competition in, 130–132; chemicals in, 265, 268, 272; collective farming, 271; of Cottica Ndyuka, 94, 99, 102, 105–106; decline in farm population, 267–268, 272; diversification, 258; diversified, 63, 129; in Esmeraldas, Ecuador, 151; fertility rate drop in early 1900s, 255–256; free trade in, 132–133; globalization of, 130–131; global reorganization of, 247; the Great Depression and, 263–265; in Loíza, Puerto Rico, 210–211, 213–214, 219; manioc, 210, 211, 216, 219, 226, 229; mechanization of, 265, 272; in Mississippi Delta, 208–210; modernization of, 13, 264–265; Navajo Agricultural Products Industry, 186; neoplantationism, 202, 267, 272; recession of 1890s and, 255–256; scientific, 265, 267, 268, 271; soybeans, 258, 263, 272; structural adjustment policies' affect, 125, 132; swidden cultivation, 69, 73, 77–78, 81, 82, 87n4, 111; in Tabete, Ecuador, 164, 165; in Tanzania, 57–58, 63–64. *See also* agricultural subsidies; cotton; rice; sharecropping; sugar

Ahlquist, Daniel B., 8–9, 77, 82

ALCOA (Aluminum Company of America), 98–99, 118n9

Alegría, Ricardo, 236n25; ancestry of, 238n39; on Loíza Aldea, 236n26, 236n27; research in Loíza and its Santiago festivals, 218, 238n34, 239n44;

on Saint Patrick tradition in Loíza, 226; studies with Redfield, 218

aleke, 110

Alianza País, 161–162, 163, 168

Ally, Fazal, 140

Alvarez, Luis Manuel, 238n34

Amboni Estates, 59, 61

American Colonization Society (ACS), 256

American Indians: casinos, 182, 268; development and, 180; as first environmentalists, 183–184; identity of, 176–177, 178, 189; the "Indian problem," 181; policies regulating tribal membership, 178; as political subalterns, 179; "postindians," 188; racialization in land allotment to, 12, 176, 177, 179; as racial minority, 178; residing off the reservation, 176; resistance by slaves, 127; in rice cultivation in Latin America and Caribbean, 127, 128, 129, 142; settler romanticism about, 184, 191; sovereignty for, 12, 177, 179, 181, 191, 192, 193n2; terminating particular Nations, 179. *See also* Navajo Nation (Diné); reservations (American Indian)

Amin, Samir, 22, 26–27

Anderson, Folke, 151

Angelou, Maya, 233n3

anti-miscegenation policies, 262

Araghi, Farshad, 131

Arkansas: African Americans return to, 270; back-to-Africa movement in, 256–257; black churches in, 260; black farm extension agencies in, 259–260; black Odd Fellows in, 261–262; decline in voting in, 251; Delta counties of, 273n4; Farmers and Household Union of America in, 254, 264; race massacre in Phillips County in 1919, 254, 264;

Candido Sanchez, Jose, 135

Canóvanas barrio (Loíza, Puerto Rico): becomes administrative seat of municipality, 220, 234n13; church in, 238n35; Hacienda Punta and, 238n40; Hacienda San Luis in, 239n44; on map of Loíza, *214*; as Nueva Loíza, 236n26; sugar production in, 207, *221*

capitalism: in agriculture, 13, 130–131, 264–265, 272; cotton in American, 249, 254; development experiences within, 5; in Ecuadorian infrastructure development, 154; indigeneity seen as "other" of, 192; "land grabbing" by local capitalists, 145n14; in *markadugus*, 36; in Mississippi Delta, 220; modernization of capitalist agriculture, 13, 264–265; in opposition to *ujamaa* villagization, 53, 54; in plantation system, 253; portfolio plantations, 267; processes of accumulation of, 6, 7, 14, 154; resistance in Esmeraldas, Ecuador, versus subjugation to, 158; Roosevelt in saving of, 263; and rural revolution of mid-seventeenth century, 38; southern populists challenge, 251. *See also* globalization; neoliberalism

carbon sequestration, 183

Caribbean, the. *See* Latin America and the Caribbean

Caribbean Community and Common Market (CARICOM), 139, 140, 145n6, 145n12

Carney, Judith, 127–128, 144n2, 204

casinos, 182, 268

cassava, 211, 219, 229

castes, 30, 33, 252

Cattelino, Jessica, 191

Central America: Dominican Republic Central American Free Trade Act (DR-CAFTA), 126, 134, 136, 137, 143; Guatemala, 137, 138, 144; Nicaragua, 137, 138, 140, 144; rice provides jobs in, 130; subsistence crops proliferate in, 128; United States' rice exports to, 140, 143. *See also* Honduras

chaatthai, 74, 78, 82

chaokhao, 83, 86–87

chaopaa, 75, 80, 83

chemicals, agricultural, 265, 268, 272

Chicago Defender (newspaper), 256, 273n5

Chicago school, 218

Christian Aid, 126

churches, black. *See* black churches

cities: American Indians relocated to, 180; changing patterns of rural-urban continuum, 6; competing imaginaries of urban-rural spatialization, 5; economic disparity between town and country, 34; fixity of rural-urban distinctions, 166; massive movement from rural to urban areas, 131, 256–257, 269, 271; Ndyuka modalities of dwelling, 102

citizenship: in Ecuador, 10–11, 149–173; managing rurality and raciality through, 2; race and, 84, 167; racialization and unevenness of, 159; in Thailand, 71, 84–85, 86; universal, 150, 151–152, 167–168

Civil Rights Act (1964), 266

civil rights movement, 265–267; arson against black churches during, 270; black farm agents penalized for sympathizing with, 265; Southern Tenant Farmers Union seen as precursor of, 264; white hostility toward, 269

mapping: contested, 5; the foreignness of Thai hill tribes, 73–75, 80; in internal territorialization, 77; settler-mapping and counter-mapping indigenous difference, 178–181; swidden cultivation and, 78

markadugus: become fortified garrison communities, 31; defined, 22; exchange in, 26; in military aristocracies, 35–36; privileged status of, 31; and rural revolution of mid-seventeenth century, 39; way of life in, 36

market rationality, 27

Maroons, 93–124; autonomy granted to, 96, 118n5; in bauxite industry, 98–99; Catholic missionaries among, 100–102, 119n13; development transforming villages of, 95; in Esmeraldas, Ecuador, 151, 156; in Interior War, 117n3; kinship among, 95, 97, 118n6; as matrilineal, 102; relations with non-Maroons, 97, 116; transformation into rural workers, 101, 102. *See also* Ndyuka

Marsden, Terry, 3

Marshall, John, 175

Marx, Karl, 6, 14, 21, 24

Mason, Charles, 254

Massey, Doreen, 2

McMichael, Philip, 2, 131, 133

mechanization of agriculture, 265, 272

Medianía barrio (Loíza, Puerto Rico): aerial view of mouth of the Rio Grande de Loíza, *221*; alluvium at, 207; on map of Loíza, *214*; Santiago festival in, 199, 226, 229–230; as semi-urban, 204; slave population at, 211

Memoria de Melgarejo, 226–227

mercantile-capitalist global economy, 22, 24, 26, 27–28, 29

Mexico, 138

Miami rice, 134

middle classes: black church and, 274; black fraternal organizations promote values of, 261; in Ecuador's *Revolución Ciudadana*, 150; rise of emergent, 5; in Saint Patrick fiestas in Loíza, Puerto Rico, 239; voter ID laws and, 268; white farm agents from, 258

migration: of Afro–Puerto Ricans, 220; of American Indians, 177; of blacks to Mississippi Delta, 209, 212–213, 220, 248; of blacks to the North, 222, 256–257, 265; to 15 de Marzo neighborhood, 159–160; of Hondurans, 136; labor migration in Tanzania, 57; of Maroons in Suriname, 96, 104, 111, 113, 115; massive movement from rural to urban areas, 131, 256–257, 269, 271; by Mississippi Delta blacks, 210; to Tabete, Ecuador, 163; of Thai hill tribes, 73–75

Miles, Robert, 5

Millinga, Ntimanjayo, 55–56, 57

Mills, Charles, 5

Mintz, Sidney, 144n3, 236n28

Mississippi: birthplaces of recorded blues performers, *224*; civil rights movement in, 265–266; as epicenter of racial and class schism, 202; poverty in, 234n5; whitecapping in, 253. *See also* Mississippi (Yazoo-Mississippi) Delta

Mississippi (Yazoo-Mississippi) Delta: African Americans return to, 270; in antebellum period, 208; black demographic concentration and relative isolation in, 205, 217–222; black land ownership in, 208, 209, 213, 248; black migration to, 209, 212–213, 220, 248;

Mississippi (Yazoo-Mississippi) Delta
(*continued*)
black Odd Fellows in, 261; blues music
originates in, 199, 201, 222–226;
comparisons and contrasts with Loíza,
Puerto Rico, 204–205, 232; counties
of, 209, 273n4; cultivated acreage in
core counties, 1850–1900, *209*; as
cultural hot spot, 13, 202, 205; Delta
Cooperative Farm, 264; differences
in scale between Loíza, Puerto Rico,
and, 202–203, 204; drainage in, 208,
209; fertile alluvial soils of, 206, 207;
flooding in, 205–206, 223; freedom
generations in, 210; interaction with
shrinking non-plantation periphery
in, 205, 211–213; as interior basin,
205, 233n1; as internal colony, 13;
key period for cultural creation in,
202; labor regime in, 209–210; levee
construction in, 206, 209, 232; map of,
200; as microcosm of US South, 203;
as narrative historical space, 233n3;
period of expanded freedom in, 202,
208, 210; plantation expansion and
sharp transformation in labor regime
in, 205, 208–210; poverty in, 234n5;
production/consolidation of new cultural
forms in, 205, 222–226; Reconstruction
in, 13, 202, 208, 210, 226; slavery in,
201–202, 208, 210, 211–212; Universal
Negro Improvement Association in, 262;
wetland and forest ecology of, 205–207,
212; white-against-black violence in,
209
Mississippi Freedom Democratic Party, 266
modernity: backward-modern trajectory
in development, 11; creolization and
negotiations with, 203; in Ecuador,
158; Ecuador's *Revolución Ciudadana*
and engagement with, 150; historicist
modernization, 5; indigenous
modernities, 181; modernization of
agriculture, 13, 264–265; modernization
of American Black Belt, 247; New
South, 271; racialized notions of
modernization, 8. *See also* development
Moengo (Suriname), 9; ambiguity of, 111;
bauxite industry in, 98–99; Cottica
Ndyuka in, 93–94, 113; industrial
decline in, 95, 106; during Interior
War, 117n3; as Mungo, 98, 119n 10;
Ndyuka women make it a "place for
living," 94; as non-Maroon territory,
95; Pata camp near, 103; residential
units in, 103–104; Sa Yani in, 106–107;
schools in, 102; travel time to Langa
Uku, 99, 100
Mohamed, Wazir, 9–10
money, 111, 113, 115
Monsanto, 268
Moody, Tony, 51
Mooney, Patrick, 3
Moore, Donald S., 194n6
*moridugu*s: as clients or allies of *fandugu*s,
34–35; defined, 22; exchange in, 26;
in Futa Jalon imamate, 40; privileged
status of, 31; in rural revolution of mid-
seventeenth century, 38, 39; *zawiya*s
compared with, 37
Morrill Act (1862), 257
Morrill Act (1890), 257
Morris, Christopher, 212
"Mother Earth" discourses, 188–189
MPD (*Movimiento Popular Democrático;*
Popular Democratic Movement), 160,
162, 163, 165
mubashshirun, 34, 37

Polimé, T., 118n7

politics: Alianza País, 161–162, 163, 168; American Indian reservations as alternative political assemblages, 175, 192; American Indians as political subalterns, 179; biopolitics, 8, 14, 155, 176, 178; of coal, 181, 189; disenfranchisement of African Americans, 251–252; of dispossession, 6; dynamics of military aristocracies, 33; electoral, 11, 159, 161, 163, 167; exclusionary, 70; fusionist politics in American South, 251; identity, 72, 150, 152; of indigeneity, 178; indigenous political spaces, 176; MPD (*Movimiento Popular Democrático;* Popular Democratic Movement), 160, 162, 163, 165; of national belonging in Thailand, 80; Native Nations as political bodies, 176; place-based, 189, 190; political marginalization, 84; political rationality, 27; political subjects, 166; populism, 252, 254, 264; of race, 14, 167; reestablishing dominance after Askiyate, 31–32; Republican Party, 247, 248, 249, 250, 268–269, 271; sovereignty, 28; spatial, 4, 6, 180; voting rights for African Americans, 249–252; of waiting, 166. *See also* Democratic Party

poll taxes, 251, 252, 269

pollution, 268

polygamy, 112, 113

polylocality, 103, 106

populism, 252, 254, 264

Poro Society, 33

portfolio plantations, 267, 272

Portuguese Guinea (Guinea Bissau), 24–25

postcolonialism: African historiography and, 21; American Indian sovereignty

and, 12; American postcolonial, 13; development in hopeful moments of, 7; postcolonial governmentality, 2; small-scale rice cultivation and, 127; *ujamaa* villagization in Tanzania and, 47

Potter, Lesley, 129

poverty: versus dignified way of life, 153; Ecuador's *Revolución Ciudadana* and, 150, 167, 170n9; in Esmeraldas, Ecuador, 156, 158; in *fandugu* societies, 34; income supplements (*bonos*) for alleviating, 155–156; politics of waiting for dominating the poor, 166; of small-scale rice farmers, 138; structural, 156, 170n8; the Tanzanian state and, 50; Thai hill tribes and, 81; in twentieth-century American South, 13, 247–248, 254, 267–268; *zawiya*s and, 37

Powell, Dana E., 12

power: biopower, 178; colonial relations of, 125, 158; ethnic categorizing as project of, 83–84; exclusionary, 86; failures of acknowledgment as operations of, 177; in Futa Jalon imamate, 40; in institutional complexes, 22, 41; racialization and, 2, 70, 72, 142; state power in precolonial Southeast Asia, 75; topographies of rurality and topographies of, 1–2, 14. *See also* politics

Pratt, Andy, 1–2, 3–4

Preciado, Antonio, 151, 159, 170n12

Price, Richard, 94, 232

Price, Sally, 110, 112

primary system, 252

private prison industry, 268

private property, 27, 213

private schools, 269

privatization, 139, 160

protectionism: Dominican Republic Central American Free Trade Act (DR-CAFTA) eliminates tariffs, 137; in Guyana, 131; neoliberal dismantlement of, 10, 132, 135; for shielding local producers, 130; United States' agricultural subsidies, 125, 133–134, 136–137, 138, 143, 144, 144n1

Puerto Rico: African traditions in, 233n4; Irish planters in, 227–228; poverty in, 234n5; San Juan, 219, 220, 226, 227, 233n4. *See also* Loíza (Puerto Rico)

quietism, 39

Quintero Rivera, Angel, 238n34

Quito (Ecuador), 151, 154, 157, 160

race: American Indians as racial minority, 178; in biopolitics, 178; and citizenship, 84, 167; and class marginalization in globalization of rice industry, 125–148; concepts of, 3–4; versus ethnicity, 72; indigenous difference and, 177, 181; marginalization based on, 125, 129; multiraciality, 178, 179, 194n5; neoplantationist forms of racial dominance, 202; politics of, 14, 167; racial difference, 178, 192; racial triangulation of American Southwest, 184; in reconstruction of rural society in the cotton South since the Civil War, 247–274; scientific racism, 49; settler romanticism about American Indians as racism, 184; as socially significant, 193n3; spatiality of, 181; white racism in American South, 247, 252, 254, 268, 269, 271, 272. *See also* African Americans; racialization; segregation (Jim Crow)

racialization: in American Indian land allotment, 12, 176, 177, 179; of bodies, 4, 80; in the Caribbean, 125; in colonialism, 73, 142, 189; in critiques of black sovereignty, 162; defined, 72; in environmentalist discourse, 183–184; of ethnicity, 79, 80; of ethno-spatial difference, 72–73, 80, 86; genealogy of concept of, 15n8; globalization and racialized groups, 143; and historical production of contemporary land rights inequalities in upland northern Thailand, 69–91; of Navajo Nation's space, 179–180; as power-laden, 2, 70, 72; racialized division of labor, 154; racialized landscapes, 177; racialized notions of modernization, 8; racialized subaltern identities, 169n4; racialized subjects, 5; racializing governmentality, 11; rebelliousness as racialized, 151; of spaces, 4, 5, 72–73, 76, 177; of state abandonment in Ecuador, 161; in Thailand, 8–9, 81–85; in treaties, 182; in understandings of indigeneity, 190; unevenness of citizenship and, 159; working against simplistic notions of, 192

racial uplift philosophy, 258

Ray, H. C., 259

Ray, Mary, 259

recession of 1890s, 255–256

Reconstruction: arson against black churches during, 270; fear of black domination during, 252; in Mississippi Delta, 13, 202, 208, 210, 226

Redfield, Robert, 218, 220, 236n28

redistribution, 26, 27, 32, 33, 152

regionalism, open, 126

Republican Party, 247, 248, 249, 250, 268–269, 271

Sheridan, Michael, 53
Silverstein, P. A., 72
Sissako, Abderrahame, 10
sit-ins, 266
siwilai, 79, 80, 87n7
16th Street Baptist Church (Birmingham, Alabama), 269
slavery: in African historiography, 23; in cotton production, 248; Emancipation in United States, 249–251; in Futa Jalon imamate, 40, 41; Haitian revolution and, 49; legacy of, 271; in Loíza, Puerto Rico, 201, 208, 211, 213, 218, 219, 228, 229, 234n10; in *markadugu*s, 36; in Medianía barrio, Puerto Rico, 229; in mercantile-capitalist global economy, 27; in military aristocracies, 32, 33, 34; in Mississippi Delta, 201–202, 208, 210, 211–212; in precolonial Southeast Asia, 76; resistance by slaves, 127; revolt against *markadugu*s, 35; rice cultivation in Latin America and the Caribbean, 126–129; runaway slaves, 96, 97, 127, 129, 156–157, 208, 212, 215, 219; in San Juan, Puerto Rico, 227; "second slavery," 228; slave warriors, 32; in Suriname, 96, 97; trans-Atlantic trade, 28, 29, 34, 128, 190; in western/Atlantic Africa, 25, 29, 33–34, 40, 41; *zawiya*s and, 37. *See also* Maroons
Sloan, Henry, 225
Smith, Neil, 154
Smith, Paul Chaat, 184, 192, 194n4
Smith-Lever Act (1914), 257
socialism: Southern Tenant Farmers Union as socialist, 263; in Tanzania, 7, 8, 47, 54, 55
Songhai Sultanate, 23

Sourieau, Mary-Agnes, 203, 233n2
South (American): New South, 271; poverty in, 13, 247–248, 254, 267–268; race in reconstruction of rural society in since the Civil War, 247–274; South Carolina, 269, 270. *See also* Arkansas; Mississippi
South Carolina, 269, 270
Southeast Asia: discrimination against upland minority groups in, 84; group identity in, 69; precolonial, 75–77. *See also* Thailand
Southern Tenant Farmers Union (STFU), 263–264, 266
sovereignty: American Indian, 12, 177, 179, 181, 191, 192, 193n2; ethnicity and, 76; institutional complexes as sites of collective, 22; racialist critiques of black, 162; Thai state, 73, 74–75, 77, 80; in western/Atlantic Africa, 28, 38
soybeans, 258, 263, 272
space: of the blues, 231–232; colonial spaces, 11–12; competing imaginaries of urban-rural spatialization, 5; ethnic difference and, 8, 75–77, 84, 86; exclusionary politics of, 70; of flows, 28; in geocriticism, 231; in group identity in Southeast Asia, 69; hierarchizing spaces, 8; indigenous political, 176; internal territorialization and, 77; market-based flattening of social, 202; nationalization of, 80; Ndyuka modalities of dwelling, 102–104; of places, 28; racialization of, 4, 5, 72–73, 76, 80, 86, 177; Redfield on isolation, 218, 236n28; relational approach to, 219; spatiality of race, gender, and place, 181; spatial politics, 6, 180; state spaces, 86. *See also* place

violence (*continued*)
    260, 262; as political and economic tool
    against African Americans, 253–255;
    against Southern Tenant Farmers Union,
    263, 264
Vizcarrondo, Fortunato, 236n27
Vizenor, Gerald, 188
Von Freyhold, Michaela, 54–55
voter ID laws, 268, 269
voting rights, 249–252, 266

Wallace, David, 22
Wallerstein, Immanuel, 4
Wanhatti (Suriname), 97, 99, 101
Washington, Booker T., 258
Waters, Muddy, 223, 237n32
Weber, Karl, 134
Weiner, Melissa, 15n5
West, Paige, 180
Western Shoshone, 182, 194n7
Wetering, Wilhelmina van, 111, 115,
    118n8
Whayne, Jeannie, 13, 219, 251–252,
    254–255, 258–260, 262, 264–265
whitecapping, 253
white supremacy, 270, 271
Wilk, Richard, 128
Williams, Brackette, 10
Williams, Burt, 264
Williams, Raymond, 12
Wilson Industrial School (Arkansas), 255
Winant, Howard, 5, 72
Winichakul, T., 79, 80, 87n3
Wolfe, Patrick, 190
women: African American churchwomen,
    260–261; Cottica Ndyuka, 9, 93,
    94, 95, 99, 101, 102–116, 120n21,

120n27; in 15 de Marzo neighborhood,
    162–163; Home Demonstration
    program for, 260; income supplements
    (*bonos*) in Ecuador, 155–156; in Kabuku
    resettlement scheme, 61, 62; maintain
    saints' statues in Medianía barrio, 230;
    natural resources managed by American
    Indian, 180; in Navajo land tenure
    practices, 183, 188; in Navajo resistance
    to coal development, 185–192; in poor
    households in Esmeraldas, Ecuador,
    156; rural crafts associated with, 33;
    in Universal Negro Improvement
    Association, 262; voter ID laws affect,
    268; in *zawiya* organization, 37
Women's Mission Societies, 260
Wonoredjo (Suriname), 99
Woodruff, Nan, 219
Woods, Clyde, 202, 210, 219, 220, 223,
    231
World Bank, 126, 132, 143, 170n7
World Trade Organization (WTO),
    132–133, 139, 140
Wortelboer, Father, 101
Wounded Knee massacre, 177, 194n4
Wynter, Sylvia, 4, 15n8

Yaoundé Convention, 145n8
Yazoo-Mississippi Delta. *See* Mississippi
    (Yazoo-Mississippi) Delta

*zawiya*s, 37; defined, 22; exchange in,
    26; as *fandugus*, 40–41; in Futa Jalon
    imamate, 40–41; in rural revolution of
    mid-seventeenth century, 38–39, 41; as
    sites of radical transformation, 32
zunuj, 30, 31–32, 34, 38, 41

www.ingramcontent.com/pod-product-compliance
Lightning Source LLC
Chambersburg PA
CBHW030640270326
41929CB00007B/144

* 9 7 8 1 4 3 8 4 7 1 3 0 3 *